Also by Anthony Louis

....

Tarot: Plain and Simple
Horary Astrology: Plain and Simple

TAROT
BEYOND THE BASICS

About the Author

Anthony Louis (Connecticut) is a physician and psychiatrist. Astrology and tarot have been his avocations for more than thirty years. He has lectured internationally on horary astrology and has published numerous articles in magazines such as *American Astrology, The Mountain Astrologer,* and *The Horary Practitioner. Tarot Beyond the Basics* is his second tarot book with Llewellyn.

To Write to the Author

If you wish to contact the author or would like more information about this book, please write to the author in care of Llewellyn Worldwide, Ltd. and we will forward your request. The authors and publisher appreciate hearing from you and learning of your enjoyment of this book and how it has helped you. Llewellyn Worldwide, Ltd. cannot guarantee that every letter written to the author can be answered, but all will be forwarded. Please write to:

Anthony Louis
℅ Llewellyn Worldwide
2143 Wooddale Drive
Woodbury, MN 55125-2989

Please enclose a self-addressed stamped envelope for reply,
or $1.00 to cover costs. If outside the USA, enclose
an international postal reply coupon.

TAROT

BEYOND THE BASICS

Gain a Deeper Understanding
of the Meanings Behind the Cards

Anthony Louis

Llewellyn Publications
Woodbury, Minnesota

FIRST EDITION
First Printing, 2014

Book design by Bob Gaul
Cover design by Ellen Lawson
Cover images: Universal Tarot by Roberto De Angelis © Lo Scarabeo
Editing by Laura Graves
Interior art: Tarot Cards—*Classic Tarot by Barbara Moore and Eugene Smith © Llewellyn Publications*
Dame Fortune's Wheel Tarot by Paul Huson © Lo Scarabeo
Llewellyn Tarot by Anna Marie Ferguson © Llewellyn Publications
Lo Scarabeo Tarot by Mark McElroy and Anna Lazzarini © Lo Scarabeo
Robin Wood Tarot by Robin Wood © Llewellyn Publications
Universal Tarot by Roberto De Angelis © Lo Scarabeo
Astro charts and other art © Llewellyn art department

Llewellyn Publications is a registered trademark of Llewellyn Worldwide Ltd.

Library of Congress Cataloging-in-Publication Data
Louis, Anthony, b. 1945
 Tarot beyond the basics: gain a deeper understanding of the meanings behind the cards/Anthony Louis.
   pages cm.
 Includes bibliographical references.
 ISBN 978-0-7387-3944-1
 1. Tarot. I. Title.
 BF1879.T2L683 2014
 133.3'2424—dc23
                                                                2013043729

Llewellyn Publications
A Division of Llewellyn Worldwide Ltd.
2143 Wooddale Drive
Woodbury, MN 55125-2989
www.llewellyn.com

Printed in the United States of America

Acknowledgments

Sincerest thanks to Steve Lytle, Catherine Chapman, Jane Stern, and Barbara Moore, who reviewed early drafts and offered invaluable feedback. Their suggestions and insights greatly improved the presentation of ideas in this text. Paul Hughes-Barlow and Douglas Gibb were generous in answering questions about material on their websites. In addition, this book would not exist were it not for the contributions of the many authors who have written about tarot and whose names appear in the bibliography. Special mention goes to artist Pamela Colman Smith, whose spirit continues to guide us through the beautiful images she painted for Arthur Edward Waite. I am especially grateful to my family for putting up with my mumblings about esotericism and Greek philosophy for the past couple of years. Finally, my gratitude extends to all who allowed me to read their cards and whose readings appear in this book.

Contents

Introduction

Man seeks to form for himself in whatever manner is suitable for him, a simplified and
lucid image of the world, and so to overcome the world of experience by striving to
replace it to some extent by this image. This is what the painter does, and the poet,
the speculative philosopher, the natural scientist, each in his own way. [1]

ALBERT EINSTEIN

Much time has passed since *Tarot Plain and Simple* saw the light of day in 1996. I am deeply
gratified by the reception that book received from the tarot community. It was a labor of love
that chronicled my journey in learning the cards. The content was largely dictated by the cards
themselves as they appeared in countless readings and gradually revealed their shades of meaning. Since then, I have continued to use the tarot along with my other great interest, astrology,
for meditation, reflection, understanding, and enjoyment. My experience of the cards has been
similar to that of Rachel Pollack, who wrote: "When we really need to know something, the
Tarot speaks to us with absolute clarity." [2]

In 2010, perhaps in resonance with the transiting planets and my natal Virgo Sun, I felt an
urge to delve more deeply into the Western occultist symbolism that underlies both tarot and
astrology. I wanted to understand what goes on in the mind of a tarot reader during the process

....

1 Albert Einstein, "The Quotable Einstein," *Turn the Tide,* http://www.turnthetide.info/id54.htm
(accessed 7 Jan. 2012).

2 Rachel Pollack, *Tarot Wisdom: Spiritual Teachings and Deeper Meanings* (Woodbury, MN: Llewellyn
Publications, 2008), p. 139.

of divining with the cards. At that time, the planet Neptune was transiting my fifth house of creativity where it was stimulating Mars in the ninth house of higher learning, publishing, and divination. Neptune, the modern ruler of Pisces, is a mystical planet closely linked to the tarot, intuition, and to trump XII, the Hanged Man, who contemplates existence from a unique perspective as he dangles by one foot from a *tau* cross.

These two disciplines, tarot and astrology, serve to stimulate our intuition and provide fresh perspectives as we journey through life. In Jungian terms, the symbols of tarot and astrology connect us with archetypal images of the collective unconscious, the same images that pervade myths, literature, and spiritual traditions. The tarot *per se* is a product of the Renaissance. As Juliet Sharman-Burke and Liz Greene of *The Mythic Tarot* emphasize, Greek myth "seized the mind of the Renaissance and … peeps from behind the often mystifying imagery of the Tarot …"[3]

The more I study tarot and astrology, the more aware I become of how much they have in common. Whether or not tarot readers realize it, they use astrology in their practice every day. The divinatory meanings of the Waite-Smith and Crowley-Harris tarot decks derive in large measure from the Golden Dawn astrological associations. The commonalities between astrology and tarot, their historical origins and symbolic significances, are the focus of this book. A deeper understanding of their shared symbolism will take the skills of the intermediate tarot reader to a higher level.[4]

My first contact with tarot was in the 1970s. I became intrigued when an astrologer friend showed me her cards. Shortly thereafter, while browsing in a Manhattan bookstore, I came across a paperback entitled *A Complete Guide to the Tarot* by Eden Gray. This book was clear, well written, and to the point. I later learned that Rachel Pollack, a *grande dame* of tarot, also came to tarot through Eden Gray, whom she calls "the mother of modern Tarot."[5] I could not

---

3   Juliet Sharman-Burke and Liz Greene, *The New Mythic Tarot* (New York: St. Martin's Press, 2008), p. 13.

4   The Hermetic Order of the Golden Dawn was a magical order active in the UK during the late nineteenth and early twentieth centuries. Its members included such notables as the poet W. B. Yeats, occultist A. E. Waite, artist Pamela Colman Smith, and occultist Aleister Crowley. Throughout this text I have referred to it simply as the Golden Dawn.

5   Rachel Pollack, *The New Tarot Handbook* (Woodbury, MN: Llewellyn Publications, 2011), p. 2.

agree more. Many of the card meanings we use today come from Gray's writings and are not found in the tarot literature prior to the 1960s when Gray began publishing.

The tarot has a long and fascinating history. Unfortunately, many authors repeat tall tales and historical inaccuracies about the tarot's origins. To set the record straight, I will present a brief but reasonably accurate history based on current historical findings. Playing cards could not exist until paper was invented in China some two thousand years ago. Initially the Chinese used rolls of paper for writing purposes but eventually they progressed to using sheets of paper, which fostered the development of cards. Around the ninth century CE, the Chinese created card decks with four suits for playing games. Chinese playing cards subsequently spread throughout Asia and to countries along the trade routes connecting China with the Middle East.

In 1939, Leo Arie Mayer, professor of Islamic Art and Archeology at Hebrew University, discovered a twelfth-century deck of Egyptian Mamluk cards in a museum in Istanbul. The Mamluks were a diverse group of slave soldiers who won political control over several Muslim countries during the Middle Ages, and they especially enjoyed playing cards. Almost identical to modern playing cards, the Mamluk deck is made up of fifty-two cards, which include forty numbered or pip cards and twelve court cards. The court cards are called *na'ibs* and consist of a king (*malik*), his deputy (*na'ib malik*) and an under-deputy (*thani na'ib*) in each suit. The four suits are cups, dinari (coins), scimitars (swords), and polo sticks (wands). The Mamluks used their cards to play the game of deputies (*na'ibs*), which gave rise to the Spanish word *naipe* for playing card.

During the fourteenth century, the North African Arabs brought the Mamluk cards to Spain, where they became popular and eventually made their way to the rest of Europe. The Spanish converted the Mamluk court cards into Kings, Horsemen, and Pages; the Italians later added Queens. Eventually the church and secular authorities objected to the use of cards (*naipes*) for gambling. References to the game of deputies (*na'ibs*) appear in the Spanish literature as far back as 1379. One does not have to be a rocket scientist to perceive the origins of modern playing cards and the tarot in the fifty-two-card Mamluk deck of twelfth-century Egypt. Fanciful claims about the mystical origins of the tarot in ancient Egypt, however, go far beyond what the facts justify.

In the early 1400s, at the height of the Renaissance, the northern Italians became fascinated with the Mamluk-based cards from Spain. Around 1420, an Italian artist had the bright idea of adding queens (*mamma mia!*) and "trump" cards to the deck to play a game called *trionfi* (triumphs), similar to the modern game of Bridge. Eventually the game became known as *Tarocchi* in Italy and *Tarot* in France.[6] The original name, trionfi, was a reference to the triumphal marches of ancient Rome. The images for the trump cards, which were added to the Mamluk-based deck, derive from the Bible and from Pagan texts, mystical Platonism and the mythology of ancient Greece and Rome, which were in vogue at the time. The pictures on the trump cards of the trionfi deck bore no resemblance to the gods of ancient Egypt, nor did they have any connection with the Jewish Kabbalah, which was unknown in northern Italy until some sixty years after the first tarot deck was created.

Over the next few centuries (1400–1700), the trionfi deck was used primarily to play games and gamble. Occasionally the deck was used to select randomly amongst pre-written oracle texts, similar to fortune cookies, for the purpose of divination. By 1750, northern Italian cartomancers (card readers) had attributed divinatory meanings to the cards themselves. In the mid-1700s, the art of reading one's destiny in the cards became popular in France and then took the rest of Europe by storm. In his autobiography, German poet Goethe (1749–1832) mentions witnessing such a reading by a French cartomancer when he was a young man.

During the late 1700s, a series of hoaxes and absurd claims replaced the genuine history of tarot with fantastical nonsense. In Paris in 1781 (the same year that Uranus was discovered), the clergyman Antoine Court de Gébelin and the French occultist Comte de Mellet published without evidence their speculations that the tarot of Marseille contained not only the Egyptian mysteries of Isis and Thoth but also the secret mystical teachings of the twenty-two letters of the Hebrew alphabet. This conjecture was pure speculation (aka bull dung), but the gullible public and later generations of tarot readers swallowed it hook, line, and sinker. The essays by de Gébelin and de Mellet initiated a tradition of woo-woo occultism and unsubstantiated fabrication divorced from reality.

....

6   Ronald Decker, *Art and Arcana, Commentary on the Medieval Scapini Tarot* (Stamford, CT: U.S. Games Systems, 2004), p. 8.

Around 1870, another Frenchman, Jean Baptiste Pitois (aka Paul Christian, 1811–1877), continued this woo-woo trend in occultism. He coined the terms "major arcana" and "minor arcana" to refer to differing levels of presumed arcane spiritual knowledge concealed by ancient adepts in the mysterious images of the tarot—utter mumbo-jumbo! During the same period, the so-called "cipher manuscripts," yet another clever hoax in the occult literature, were "discovered" and passed on to Freemason William Lynn Wescott, who was miraculously able to decipher them in 1887. Decoding the dubious documents led directly to the dawning of the Hermetic Order of the Golden Dawn, replete with its "secret chiefs" who spoke to lesser mortals via spirit communication. By this time, European occultism had become so popular that many otherwise intelligent individuals were completely duped by the Golden Dawn ruse. This same period in history also gave rise to the saying "there's a sucker born every minute."

Out of the Golden Dawn movement grew the two most influential tarot decks of modern times: the Waite-Smith and the Crowley-Harris Thoth decks, the masterworks of artists Pamela Colman Smith (1878–1851) and Lady Frieda Harris (1877–1962), respectively. These decks are light years distant from the original tarots of northern Italy with their images from the Bible and pagan mythology. Instead, decks in the Golden Dawn tradition focus on illuminating the significance of the mystical Kabbalah in explaining the universe. Despite the fact that many profound thinkers find the Kabbalah worthy of careful contemplation, the use of this mystical tradition is by no means fundamental to tarot divination.

My goal in this book is to investigate the symbolism shared by tarot and astrology prior to the nonsense introduced by de Gébelin and de Mellet in 1781. This process will involve an examination of the symbolic roots of tarot and astrology, dating back millennia to the time of ancient Greece and Rome. The tarot has a rich iconography based on biblical teachings, pagan myths, Greek philosophy, and Neo-Platonism, which fascinated the tarot's originators in fifteenth-century Italy.

Astrology and the associated disciplines of geomancy and alchemy were part and parcel of this Renaissance worldview. Robert Place has noted the similarities between alchemical transformation and the Fool's journey through the tarot trumps. Aleister Crowley referred repeatedly to alchemical symbolism in the tarot.[7] In the nineteenth century, the Golden Dawn relied on astrological attributions and the Kabbalah to delineate the tarot suits. Ancient Egyptian gods and the Kabbalah, however, played no significant role in the creation of the original tarot.

Tarot divination is a uniquely personal endeavor, and *there are as many tarots as there are tarot readers.* The cards themselves are simply pieces of cardboard decorated with evocative images, that stimulate the imagination. The "real" tarot exists in the mind of each reader and is interlaced with his or her life history and repository of experiences, or better said, with the view of reality the reader has created from those experiences. In the pages that follow, I hope to share my own perspective on tarot and astrology, and especially on the common thread that originated in ancient Greece and continues to run through the cards.

I also wish to share my view about how I believe the tarot functions. Because of my up-bringing and life experiences, I don't place much stock in spirit guides, ascended masters, secret chiefs, ancient Egyptian gods, magical Hebrew letters, leprechauns, fairies, vampires, elemental spirits, body parts of saints, and the host of otherworldly characters and imaginary realms that purportedly play a role in tarot divination. For me the tarot is a tool that helps us tap into a natural human faculty: our intuition.

Tarot is indeed a form of divination, but the divine we commune with lies within. When doing a reading, I keep in mind the wisdom of occultist Dion Fortune, who compared divination to a weather vane that does not determine the course a ship should take but merely shows which way the wind is blowing and "how best to trim the sails."[8] When a tarot reading is spot-on, it has a magical effect. This feeling of magic reminds me of a childhood story that had a lasting impact on me. Having originally read this tale some five decades ago, I have probably misremembered the exact details, but the plot presented here is essentially correct.

Once upon a time in old Mexico, there was a farmer named Miguel who began to suffer many misfortunes. He became frantic because his crops were failing, and it was increasingly difficult for him to support his family. Though Miguel did not believe in magic, he decided to seek advice from an old woman reputed to possess magical powers. Some even said she was

....

7   The focus of this book is the connection between astrology and tarot. Alchemical symbolism is an extensive study in itself and will not be covered. Readers interested in alchemy are referred to the writings of Aleister Crowley and Robert Place for a more thorough discussion of alchemy and the tarot.

8   Dion Fortune, *Practical Occultism in Daily Life* (Northamptonshire, UK: The Aquarian Press, 1976), p. 39.

a witch. After listening to Miguel's woes, the old crone presented him with a wooden box of "magical" sand. She instructed him: "Each morning at sunrise, take a few grains of sand from a small opening on top of the box and place one grain in each corner of your fields." The old lady cautioned Miguel never to open the box until he was on his deathbed, or else the magic would disappear.

Miguel followed her instructions to the letter, and his farm began to prosper. As he walked to each corner of his farm each morning to place a grain of magical sand, he noticed tasks that had to be done to ensure a good crop. Working with his family, Miguel brought his fields back to life and obtained a good harvest year after year. Finally, with his end approaching, Miguel asked his family to bring him the box of magic sand so he could look inside. With some effort Miguel pried open the box. Within, he discovered an inscription in the handwriting of the old woman, herself now long deceased: "*Querido* Miguel, the sand in this box is just ordinary sand that can be found anywhere in Mexico. The real magic always lay within you."

ONE

Reflections on the Celtic Cross

The true tarot is symbolism; it speaks no other language and offers no other signs.
ARTHUR EDWARD WAITE, *THE PICTORIAL KEY TO THE TAROT*, 1911

In a public office building on a cold winter morning, I happened to run into Jane, a woman for whom I had done a reading a few years previously.[9] No one else was on the elevator, so Jane began to update me about how things had unfolded since I saw her last. In fact, I had recently been thinking about Jane, and events seemed to have conspired "synchronistically" to bring us in touch again. Jane said she would like another reading because things were happening in her life. We arranged to meet.

Tarot reading is a highly intuitive process that involves allowing the mind to resonate intuitively with the card's images in the context of the concerns of the querent (the person asking the question). Author Gareth Knight views the tarot as an intriguing system of images whose interpretation "requires no special clairvoyant gifts or other rare abilities, simply a knack for using

....

9 Jane is not her real name. Unless otherwise noted, in this book I have disguised or omitted personal identifying details of querents to maintain confidentiality.

the creative imagination."[10] Robert Place tells us that the Renaissance artists who created the tarot produced "a set of symbols or tools that the unconscious can use to communicate with the conscious mind."[11] Arthur Edward Waite (1857–1942), the intellectual father of the Waite-Smith deck, shared the same view. Waite believed that the tarot's images contain a "doctrine behind the veil," similar to Carl Jung's primordial images, later termed "archetypes of the collective unconscious"(1919). To quote Waite (1911):

> The Tarot embodies symbolical presentations of universal ideas, behind which lie all the implicits of the human mind, and it is in this sense that they contain secret doctrine, which is the realization, by the few, of truths imbedded in the consciousness of all, though they have not passed into express recognition by ordinary men.[12]

During a consultation, the tarot reader ponders the images on the cards in light of the client's question. In the process, the reader adopts a stance recommended by Sigmund Freud, the father of psychoanalysis. This process allows ready access to one's intuitive flashes of insight. Freud advised his disciples to listen to the free associations of the client with "evenly hovering" attention. Experienced tarot readers likewise approach a reading with no vested interest and no axe to grind, but instead allow their minds to "float" evenly above the tarot images and the client's words. As the reader listens and observes without bias, certain mental images and ideas float into consciousness. The reader then reflects these intuitions back to the querent in a gentle, nonjudgmental, respectful way.

Jane began our consultation by recounting her previous reading a couple years earlier. She vividly remembered two cards that she drew regarding her son. Jane had consulted the tarot to help clarify a decision about whether to accept a job that would involve relocating to a remote part of the world. She was especially concerned about how such a move might affect her young son. As part of the reading, Jane drew one card to represent the experience her son might have if the family stayed in the United States and a second card for her son's experience if they were to relocate abroad.

....

10   Gareth Knight, *The Magical World of the Tarot* (San Francisco: Weiser Books, 1996), p. 2.

11   Robert M. Place, *The Tarot: History, Symbolism, and Divination* (New York: Penguin Group, 2005), p. 273.

12   Arthur Edward Waite, *The Pictorial Key to the Tarot* (Secaucus, NJ: Citadel Press, 1959), p. 59.

Left to right: Stay in USA—Five of Wands *(Classic Tarot)*;
Relocate abroad—Nine of Pentacles *(Classic Tarot)*.

For remaining in the States, Jane selected the Five of Wands; for relocating abroad, the Nine of Pentacles. As my attention "hovered evenly" above the Five of Wands, I was struck by the five youths playing a game, doing the fun things that children normally do. My left brain was aware of the negative meanings attributed to this card (struggle, conflict), but my intuitive right brain was drawn to the "fun" aspects of the scene. The Nine of Pentacles struck me as a young person who was well cared for but alone and sheltered in a peaceful garden. The pet bird and snail were her only companions. Jane responded that the Nine of Pentacles captured what her son's life would be like if they relocated abroad. He would lead a sheltered existence and might miss out on the typical rough-and-tumble interactions of childhood. Seeing the two cards in juxtaposition helped Jane to clarify her thinking. She decided to remain in America so that her son could experience a more normal childhood.

For the current reading, I sensed that Jane was not ready to talk openly about her concerns. I was confident, however, that whatever was troubling her would come out in the cards. I mixed the cards thoroughly so that we could begin with a random arrangement rather than a sequence of cards left over from a previous reading. I asked Jane to shuffle the deck with the intent of obtaining an answer to her question and to stop shuffling when she felt in her gut that the time was right. I then asked her to cut the deck so we would have a point from which to begin laying the spread. We had decided to use Waite's century-old Celtic Cross arrangement.

The Celtic Cross spread is very popular. It addresses past, present, potential, and future influences in the space of only ten cards. The spread itself draws on Celtic and Christian mysticism. The use of ten cards carries the symbolism of Pythagorean number symbolism, which lies at the root of many Western occult traditions. The Celtic Cross spread is complex enough to answer difficult questions but short enough not to overwhelm the reader.

The origin of this spread was neither Celtic nor particularly related to the cross that shares its name.[13] Arthur Edward Waite first published the technique in *The Key to the Tarot,* which was included with the first Rider-Waite-Smith deck (December, 1909). In 1909, Waite simply referred to the spread as "a short process which has been used privately for many years past in England, Scotland, and Ireland."

In the 1911 version of his book, Waite named the spread an "Ancient Celtic Method of Divination." While researching the archives of the Hermetic Order of the Golden Dawn, Marcus Katz discovered a handwritten manuscript (c. 1895) penned in London by Hermetic student F. L. Gardner, who labeled the spread a "gipsy method of divination by cards." Katz concluded that the Celtic Cross was designed as an alternative to the laborious "Opening of the Key" method of the Golden Dawn and was so named because of the Celtic Revivalist interests of A. E. Waite and poet W. B. Yeats.[14]

The Celtic Cross *per se* is an old symbol, dating back at least fifteen hundred years. It consists of a circle superimposed upon a central cross. According to Irish myth, Saint Patrick used the Celtic Cross to bring together the cross of Jesus with the pagan circle representing the sun god. This theory is reminiscent of Michelangelo's depiction of Christ as Apollo in his painting of the Last Judgment. Art historians, however, argue that the Celtic Cross is a cross decorated with a victory wreath. We all have our crosses to bear, so it's nice to think we have a victory

....

13   Marcus Katz, "The Origin of the Celtic Cross," *Tarosophist International Magazine,* Vol. 1 Iss. 2
     (Spring, 2009), pp. 22–45.

14   Marcus Katz, ibid., p. 45.

wreath surrounding them. The triumphal wreath on the Six of Wands in the Waite-Smith deck may be a reference to this "gypsy method" of divination.

An alternative to the victory wreath imagery is Waite's view that the four cards surrounding the central two-card cross represent a papal blessing. In the original description of the spread, Waite, himself a Roman Catholic, followed the "sign of the cross" sequence ("from brow to breast and from shoulder to shoulder").[15] Waite placed the third card of the spread above the central two-card cross (brow), the fourth card beneath (breast), and the fifth and sixth cards on either side (shoulder to shoulder), depending on which way the significator was facing; the future being in front of him and the past, behind him. Waite's original sequence starts with a central two-card cross and makes a larger four-card papal sign of the cross around it, a kind of "double-cross," so to speak.

The cross, of course, is a fundamental Christian symbol referring to the crucifixion of Jesus. Christians believe that by dying on the cross, Jesus redeemed the human race and defeated the powers of evil and death. In the Celtic Cross spread, we can imagine the central two-card cross as the cross of Jesus and the four cards surrounding it as a depiction of the crucifixion scene: the card beneath being the ground that sustains Jesus's cross, the cards to either side being the two thieves who were crucified with him, and the card above being the placard announcing the reason for his execution.

The Six of Wands with Victory Wreath (*Classic Tarot*).

15 "Sign of the Cross," *The Catholic Encyclopedia*, http://www.newadvent.org/cathen/13785a.htm (accessed 11 Feb. 2012).

The Celtic Cross also bears a strong resemblance to the circular horoscope of Western astrology, which is connected with the myth of the resurrected Egyptian god Osiris. For the Ptolemaic Egyptians, the zodiac circle signified the cycle of the birth, death, and resurrection of the sun on its daily course through the heavens. The modern horoscope is a circle of the signs of the zodiac centered on a cross consisting of the intersection of the horizon and meridian axes at the location of birth.

Whatever the origins of the actual Celtic Cross, its namesake tarot spread consists of ten cards (or eleven, if you use a significator) placed in the following order: the first two cards, the pole and crossbeam, form the central two-card cross; the next four cards are laid like a wreath or papal blessing around the central cross; and, finally, four additional cards placed in order from bottom to top in a column resembling a totem pole to the right of the encircled cross.

Each position in the Celtic Cross is assigned a meaning, which the reader announces while laying the cards. Some readers first select a significator (often one of the court cards) to describe the querent and then lay the first card, the pole of the central cross, on top of the significator. This is a practice that I don't usually follow, largely because I like to keep things simple but also to allow all seventy-eight cards a chance to answer the client's question. This latter issue can be resolved by taking the significator card from a separate deck. A benefit of using a significator card is that the other cards may link intuitively to it and provide useful information.

In Jane's reading, we used only upright cards. I sometimes use both upright and reversed cards, but I knew from Jane's previous reading that she preferred to use only upright images.

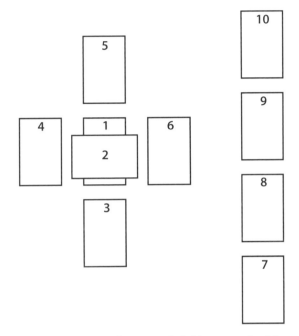

Celtic Cross layout: A central cross encircled by a wreath with a vertical
column to the right. In Waite's layout, the wreath is replaced by a papal blessing.

Card 1—The Three of Swords (Vertical Pole of the Central Two-Card Cross): What Covers You

Having reassembled Jane's shuffled and cut the deck, I placed the top card on the table and said: "This is what covers you." Had we used a significator, the first card would literally have covered the significator. According to Waite: "This card gives the influence which is affecting the person or matter of inquiry generally, the atmosphere of it in which the other currents work."[16]

Turning the first card over, I was a bit startled to see the Three of Swords. In the Waite-Smith deck, this card shows a heart pierced by three swords against a background of dark rain clouds. "Oh, my god," I thought silently, "this is serious." In my experience, the Three of

16   Arthur Edward Waite, *The Pictorial Key to the Tarot* (London: W. Rider, 1911), online in public domain at http://www.sacred-texts.com/tarot/pkt/pkt0307.htm (accessed 15 Feb. 2012).

Swords often indicates emotional pain, separation, or heartache. Not infrequently it refers to an illness requiring surgery.

Swords are sharp and incisive. They cut, sever, separate. Swords can indicate abrupt demarcations in our life. Astrologically (in the Golden Dawn system) Swords are related to the Air element, which is rational, detached, and objective. Swords are double-edged; they can help or harm. They may represent mental clarity or life-saving surgery, but can also signify strife—that

is, being cut or wounded in life's conflicts. In card 1 of this reading on the vertical pole of Jane's cross, we see three swords piercing a human heart. Who does the heart belong to? Jane? Someone else? Hearts are symbols of love and human emotions.

My attention was drawn to the number III on this card. Much of the symbolism used in tarot interpretation derives from ancient ideas about numbers, especially those of Pythagoras, whose basic tenet was that "all is number." [17] When the number three appears in a reading, a triangular situation is often implied. We speak of a "third party" or third factor being added to a dyad. Trump card III, the Empress, is a symbol of fertility and pregnancy (the triad: father—mother—baby). An upright equilateral triangle ($\triangle$) is an ancient symbol of the male genitals and the inverted triangle, the female genitalia (∇). Superimposed upon one another, these two triangles form the

The Three of Swords (*Classic Tarot*).

---

17 The Pythagoreans viewed the number one as the number of reason and the generator of dimensions; one represents a dimensionless point of pure potential. The number two was considered the first even/female number, linked to the duality of opinions and choice, and also the generator of straight lines along a single dimension. The number three was the first true male number, a generator of triangles (three points) in two dimensions or a plane (perhaps related to inner or mental/emotional space). The number four generates three dimensions and is the first number linked to outer or three-dimensional reality—like the cubic throne of the Emperor (trump IV).

In human terms, the number one refers to an individual, two to a dyadic relationship or to someone faced with two options, and three to the resultant of the combined forces of two individuals. For example, a husband (1) and a wife (2) produce a child (3) and thereby form a new entity (set of relations), a nuclear family. Alternatively, an individual (1) tries to have a dyadic relationship (2) with different partners but the end result is a love triangle (3).

Star of David, which among other things symbolizes the biblical coupling of Adam and Eve.

The Waite-Smith Three of Cups shows three women having a party. The Three of Pentacles depicts an artisan conferring with two individuals, perhaps his patrons (a triad of artisan—patrons—a work of art). The Three of Wands portrays a young man looking out to sea with the implication that he has engaged with others in a joint enterprise and is contemplating the outcome. The Three of Swords shows a heart pierced by three swords, presumably representing the grief that results from cutting away something previously important to the querent (a triad of a person—a loss, something cut from one's life, which results in grief).

Because Swords involve literal or figurative cutting, I said to Jane: "This is a reading about some kind of emotional situation that is potentially painful, possibly involving loss, cutting, or separation from something previously valued. This card can also refer to surgery, either for yourself or someone you know." Jane responded that her mother had recently undergone surgery but was doing fine postoperatively. She assured me that her mother's recovery was not troubling her. I said I was glad her mother was doing well after the operation.

Jane's prior reading was running through my mind. Was she again thinking of a job abroad? Did the Three of Swords mean she would leave behind people she cares about? At the same time, I was making a conscious effort not to jump to conclusions but rather to let the cards speak for themselves.

Card 2—The Nine of Wands (the Crossbeam of the Central Two-Card Cross): What Crosses You for Good or Bad

In the Christian tradition, card 2 literally represents the crossbar of the cross we must bear. Some readers view it as an opposing force or obstacle to be overcome. According to Waite: "It shews the nature of the obstacles in the matter. If it is a favorable card, the opposing forces will not be serious, or it may indicate that something good in itself will not be productive of good in the particular connexion." [18]

---

18 Waite, *Pictorial Key* online.

The Nine of Wands
(*Classic Tarot*).

In the *Pictorial Key to the Tarot,* the scene on the Nine of Wands is of a soldier holding a single wand with eight other wands affixed firmly to a wall behind him. In the Waite-Smith deck, the man holding the wand has a bandaged head; he has been injured in some kind of fight or battle. A typical meaning of this card is "strength in opposition." The number nine is the last of the single digits, and it refers to completions and cycles that have run their course and are now coming to an end. Cats have nine lives, after all—or do they?

After describing the Nine of Wands to Jane, I added, "It seems you've been struggling with something emotionally painful (Three of Swords), and you are calling on your inner strength to see it through to the end (Nine of Wands)." She nodded in agreement.

Card 3—The Two of Wands (Bottom of the Wreath): What Is Beneath You and Forms the Root of the Situation

Card 3 represents the ground beneath the pole of the central cross. It underlies the shaft of the two-card cross and holds it in position. In the Roman "tree cross," an actual living tree was used for crucifixion and its roots literally anchored the cross into the ground. Symbolically card 3 represents the underpinning of the matter. It may refer to unconscious attitudes, past experiences, long-standing assumptions, cherished beliefs, or events from the remote past. According to Waite: "It shews the foundation or basis of the matter, that which has already passed into actuality and which the Significator has made his own." [19]

I was puzzled by the contrast between the Two of Wands beneath Jane and the Three of Swords covering her. The Waite-Smith Two of Wands is an upbeat card representing the onset of springtime and a new cycle of growth, whereas the Three of Swords looks ominous and foreboding. How could the basis of the situation be so full of vigor and enthusiasm, as reflected in the Wands? I associated out loud to Jane about the card, saying something like:

....

19   Waite, *Pictorial Key* online.

I'm not sure how the Two of Wands forms the foundation for the heartache shown in the Three of Swords. The young man in the Two of Wands looks happy and well-off. He is standing on the parapet of a castle and looking into the distance as if asking himself, "Where do I go from here?" Everything looks serene. The "2" cards often represent choices and decisions that must be made. The two wands on the card may refer to the different options you have to choose from. As I look at the card, I'm struck by the fact that the wand the man is holding is free, whereas the other wand is clamped tightly to the wall and restricted from moving freely. Maybe you are facing two courses of action, one more restrictive than the other.

The Two of Wands
(*Classic Tarot*).

The other thing that stands out to me is the globe. It reminds me of a young person who has just completed his education and is deciding what to do about his future; where in the world to go, what course to take, whether to travel great distances, what career path to pursue, etc. I don't know if this makes sense because you are older and established, but I get the sense of someone just starting out in life and trying to discover where they want to go. Maybe it refers to going in a new direction. I wonder if you've been offered a new job that will take you far away and you can't decide what to do, but don't tell me until we look at the other cards.

When doing a reading you often notice details on the cards that did not seem important previously. Such details tend to jump out at you. Although the Two of Wands had frequently appeared in other readings, I had never before been so struck by the clamp holding one of the wands to the wall. For some reason, my intuition focused on the clamp as being especially important in understanding the Two of Wands in this particular reading.

Looking at the spread with hindsight, I now see a possible connection between the wands of the "crossing" card (Nine of Wands) and the wands of the "beneath" card (Two of Wands). As a symbol, Wands can represent the human will. Perhaps a decision rooted in the past (card 3) has resulted in the defensive embattled posture that Jane needs to assume in the crossbeam (card 2). Crowley named the Two of Wands "Dominion," implying that you must exercise your will and take charge of the direction of your life. Perhaps the basis of her situation is a decision to live more in accordance with her own desires. While doing the research for this book, I learned that in the mid-1700s, Etteilla interpreted the Two of Wands as "sorrow," another meaning consistent with Jane's reading, as we shall see.

Card 4—The Ace of Swords (Left Side of the Wreath): What Is Behind You and Is Passing Out of Existence

The Ace of Swords
(*Classic Tarot*).

Card 4 shows something in the recent past that may still be active but is passing out of existence. According to Waite, "it gives the influence that is just passed, or is now passing away."[20]

There is no firm rule about what "recent" means, but I usually regard it as something occurring within the past few months that has a connection with the concerns reflected in the central two-card cross. Whereas card 3 ("beneath") refers to pervasive and remote past influences, card 4 ("behind") identifies something more recent that bears directly on the present situation. If position 4 alludes to the Christian myth, then the issues of card 4 may be linked to entrenched attitudes or behaviors like those that prevented the "bad thief" from accepting Christ's offer of salvation.

In Jane's reading, we have the Ace of Swords in position 4. The aces correspond to the number one and represent the pure potential of a suit, the energy of the suit getting off to a fresh start. In the Ace of Swords we are dealing with pure Air, an element linked to intellect, clear thought, cool objectivity, and decision-making free of emotional encumbrances. For good or for ill, swords are used to cut and kill. Both surgeons and soldiers wound the flesh. In relationship questions, Swords refer to severing ties and making important decisions. The English word "decide" comes from the Latin *decidere*, which means "to cut off" or "to cut from" (*de-* + *caedere*). Swords are also instruments of war. With all these connotations in mind, I said to Jane:

....
20 Waite, *Pictorial Key* online.

The Ace of Swords suggests that in the recent past you've been struggling to see things clearly and make a rational decision. You may have been involved in some sort of conflict, either internally or with someone in your environment. Swords are used to cut, and the phrase "cut the crap" comes to mind. The heart being pierced by swords in card 1 gives me the feeling that you've had to cut through some emotional crap to get to the heart of a matter. But whatever you are cutting is causing pain. Maybe the Ace, being a "one" card, means you feel all alone with it. That song about one being the loneliest number comes to mind.

As I now review the spread, I notice that the upright Ace of Swords passes through a crown. Jane may be cutting away at something related to "crown" card 5, the Knight of Pentacles.

Card 5—The Knight of Pentacles (Top of the Wreath): What Crowns You and Shows a Desired, Potential, Ideal, or Best Possible Outcome

Opinions vary about the meaning of the crowning card in position 5. According to Waite, "it represents (a) the Querent's aim or ideal in the matter; (b) the best that can be achieved under the circumstances, but that which has not yet been made actual." [21] If card 3, in the "beneath" position, represents entrenched past influences and hidden or unconscious attitudes that underlie the situation, then card 5, directly "above" the querent's significator, may refer to the future, overt attitudes and beliefs, or a potential and consciously chosen resolution. Card 3, beneath the significator, is hard for the querent to see, but card 5, crowning the significator, lies in plain view. If the Christian symbolism applies, then card 5 is analogous to the inscription above the head of Christ, which proclaims the reason for his crucifixion. Whether the inscription is true or false, it is there for all to see. If the crown alludes to the crown of thorns, then the card in position 5 could signify the "weight of the crown" or the querent's burdens

The Knight of Pentacles
(*Classic Tarot*).

....
21   Waite, *Pictorial Key* online.

and responsibilities. Crowns can also signify the final step on the road to achieving monarchy and thus a desired outcome. Many tarot readers regard card 5 as a potential outcome that must be compared with the likely outcome shown by card 10.

I explained to Jane that court cards, like the Knight, can refer to actual people, personality traits, or situations and ways of handling them. If the Knight of Pentacles signified a person in her life, he would likely be young (or a man of youthful or immature stature), industrious, pragmatic, responsible, tenacious, hard-working, and a bit plodding (characteristics of the element Earth). He would devote himself to his work, sometimes at the expense of emotions and close relationships. If the card referred to her, then she might be considering adopting such traits, perhaps burying herself in her work to escape the emotional pain of the Three of Swords. If this Knight referred to a situation, it would be one that was slow to develop and involved working hard and long to reach a tangible goal.

Card 6—The Queen of Swords (Right Side of the Wreath): What Is Before You and What Is Soon to Come

The Queen of Swords
(*Classic Tarot*).

Card 6 refers to the near future and, according to Waite, "shews the influence that is coming into action and will operate in the near future."[22] As with the "recent past" card, there is no firm rule about how long a period is covered, but I usually think of it as the two or three months following the reading. If the Christian myth applies, then the card in position 6 may represent something we must pass through, like the "penitent thief," on our way to spiritual enlightenment. Following the crucifixion, the good thief allegedly joined Jesus in heaven.

The Queen of Swords appeared in position 6 of Jane's reading. This card could signify a person, personality traits, or an event of the nature of the Queen of Swords—which has been called the "widow" card. She is a perceptive, mature woman who has distanced herself from her emotions, perhaps to avoid the grief of

---

22 Waite, *Pictorial Key* online.

widowhood, loss, or some other emotional wound. She has taken refuge in her sharp intellect. If she refers to a person, the Queen can indicate the querent's mother or any mature, clear-headed woman in her life. If the Queen of Swords represents a situation, it may have to do with the severing of emotional ties, which links it thematically with the Three of Swords "covering" the querent. Jane responded that she feared becoming like the Queen of Swords. She had been keeping her feelings under wraps for some time because of what was going on in her life. She did not want to end up a cold, cruel, emotionally isolated woman.

In hindsight, the Queen of Swords may have referred to Jane's mother. Within weeks of the reading, Jane's mother died unexpectedly of complications of her recent surgery. Jane was devastated by the loss. At the time of the reading, I had not seen the Queen of Swords as implying her mother's death, but this event could have been the near-future situation indicated by card 6. The domain of the Queen of Swords includes emotional loss and bereavement. The Golden Dawn gives the Queen of Swords rulership over the region of the zodiac related to the Ten of Pentacles and the Two and Three of Swords. The Three of Swords as the covering card suggests that the querent is dealing with loss, pain, separation, and sorrow. The Three of Swords also suggests worries related to surgery. When Jane called with the news, she said that when she learned of her mother's death, she had an uncanny feeling as she suddenly recalled my asking during the reading whether she was worried about her mother's surgery.

Card 7—The Seven of Cups (Base of the Right-Hand Column): You as You Are Now

Card 7 describes the querent's state at the time of the reading. According to Waite, "the SEVENTH CARD of the operation, signifies himself—that is, the Significator [the matter or person inquired about]—whether person or thing—and shews its position or attitude in the circumstances."[23]

I explained to Jane that the Seven of Cups depicts someone in a dreamlike state, dealing with fantasies and illusions. This card often comes up when one is faced with many choices, and it refers to not seeing things clearly or deluding oneself because of wishful thinking. The card can also mean being lost in a barrage of thoughts or escaping into a world of fantasy or

....
23 Waite, *Pictorial Key* online.

intoxication. Symbolically, the number seven acts like the pause button on a TV remote; it has to do with stopping the action to ponder what to do next. I said to Jane, "Since this is the only Cups card in the spread, I think it shows you feeling confused about emotional matters and having a hard time deciding what course to take. You may be feeling confused by the options."

At this point, Jane interrupted and said, "The cards have been uncanny in describing my situation. I'm thinking about getting a divorce. What you said about the Seven of Cups really hit home. I've been in denial for years about my husband's drinking. I see

The Seven of Cups
(*Classic Tarot*).

more clearly now that he has an alcohol problem and is not there for me emotionally. He's the man you described in the Knight of Pentacles. I may need to get out of the relationship for my own sake and for our son. It's just not healthy to stay with him anymore."

I must confess that up to this point I had not been thinking about divorce in relation to the reading. I had once run into Jane and her husband at a restaurant, and they looked like a typical happily married couple. Although I read the Three of Swords as some type of painful loss or separation, I did not see it as divorce until Jane made the connection. My familiarity with Jane had clouded my ability to read all the implications in the cards. Interestingly, although I didn't know it at the time, the Golden Dawn relied on an old Arabic text, *Picatrix*, to delineate the Seven of Cups as referring to a bad marriage due to the immoderate behavior of a spouse.

Card 8—The Seven of Wands
(Second Card up in the Right-Hand Column):
Your Environment and Those Around You

Card 8 describes the state of those who surround the querent as they relate to the question. According to Waite, "the EIGHTH CARD signifies his [the querent's] house, that is, his environment and the tendencies at work therein which have an effect on the matter—for instance, his position in life, the influence of immediate friends, and so forth." [24]

The Seven of Wands
(*Classic Tarot*).

I described the Seven of Wands to Jane: a man brandishing a wand like a weapon to defend himself from six attacking wands directed at him from below. He's in a defensive posture, trying to hold his ground and stubbornly maintain his position. He's also pondering his next move. Another Seven, another pause in the action. What will be your next move after you arrive at the seventh sphere of the heavens ruled by Saturn, the outmost planet of antiquity?

"That's exactly my husband's stance," she said. "He's stubborn and won't give up the marriage easily." The tenacity of the man in the Seven of Wands is similar to that shown by the Knight of Pentacles, whom Jane has identified as her husband in this spread.

Card 9—VIII–Strength (Third Card up in the Right-Hand Column): Your Hopes and Fears

Strength
(*Classic Tarot*).

Card 9 describes the querent's hopes, wishes, and fears regarding the outcome. According to Waite, "the NINTH CARD gives his hopes or fears in the matter." [25]

As we both looked at Strength, trump VIII of the Waite-Smith deck, Jane said: "That's what I hope I can be like during this process. I'll need a lot of strength to get through this. I'm afraid I won't be able to do it." Recall that Jane is "crossed" by card 2, the Nine of Wands ("strength in opposition"). She wishes to remain strong but fears she may not be able to.

....

24 Waite, *Pictorial Key* online.

25 Waite, *Pictorial Key* online.

Card 10—Knight of Swords
(Top of the Right-Hand Column): The Likely Outcome

The Knight of Swords
(*Classic Tarot*).

Card 10 reveals the likely outcome, but it is not fixed in stone. People have free will. They can and should use the insights gleaned from the reading to adjust their life course. According to Waite, "the TENTH is what will come, the final result, the culmination which is brought about by the influences shewn by the other cards that have been turned up in the divination." [26] The outcome card must be read in the context of the other cards in the spread that lead up to it.

I again described to Jane what Knights represent in a reading. I was puzzled by this card since Jane is a middle-aged woman, and a younger man (a Knight) seemed an unlikely outcome. On the other hand, I was struck that she identified the Knight of Pentacles in position 5 as her husband, even though he is the same age as she. I thought that the youthfulness of the Knight of Pentacles referred to her husband's immaturity and excess drinking rather than his chronological age.

I said to Jane: "Since the Knight in position 5 refers to your husband, I wonder if the Knight of Swords in position 10 could refer to another man in your life." Jane responded that she was not involved with anyone else. I replied, "He doesn't have to be a lover, maybe just a friend—perhaps someone who is abrupt and a bit caustic in speech, always in a rush, wanting to get things done brusquely like the Knight of Swords."

"Oh, that would be my friend Nathan," she said. "But he's in his early fifties, though he comes across as being much younger. He's been pushing me to make a decision and get it over with. I know he really likes me. If I go ahead with a divorce, he'd probably want to get involved with me. There's even a chance we could end up together."

When she described Nathan pushing her to make a decision, the fast-paced, aggressive Knight of Swords made sense. I also noted that the Knight of Pentacles was looking rather

26 Ibid.

stationary, facing to the right while sitting in the "crown" position of the spread. The Knight of Swords in the "outcome" position was staring directly at him and seemed to be leading a charge against him.

"So maybe that's how we can understand the two Knights," I said. "The Knight of Pentacles in position 5 is your husband, and a potential outcome is for you to decide to stay with him. The Knight of Swords in position 10 could be Nathan, who is in a rush for you to cut ties with your husband so he can pursue you. Would you like to draw another card to clarify the meaning of the Knight of Swords?"

"Yes," replied Jane, and I instructed her to focus on clarifying the outcome and then randomly draw another card. She drew the Knight of Wands, yet another man in a rush to get somewhere fast with his phallic and upright wand. We both laughed when we saw the card. The tarot seemed to be hitting us over the head with its answer: pay attention to the Knights.

At the time of Jane's reading, I had forgotten that Arthur Waite considered the Knights in his deck to represent men over forty. Most modern authors disregard Waite's original intent and use Knights to represent young men (with Kings as older men). There is much confusion about Knights and Kings in the literature because of the way they were treated by the Hermetic Order of the Golden Dawn. In light of Waite's intended age range for his Knights, Jane's reading made more sense. Both her husband and her friend Nathan were men over forty.

This reading raises the intriguing question of whether the tarot reader should go with the meanings intended by the deck's creator or instead use his or her personal interpretations, regardless of the deck being consulted. James Wanless of the Voyager Tarot has a definite opinion: "When you are playing with a particular deck, use its meanings for the cards. Don't try to relate the cards to another deck."[27] In my own view the reader should follow his or her intuition about the cards in each particular reading. The cards are merely tools that awaken our intuition. In Jane's reading, the Knights were all men over forty, as detailed in Waite's original intention.

....

27 James Wanless, *Strategic Intuition for the 21st Century, Tarot for Business* (Carmel, CA: Merrill-West Publishing, 1996), p. 61.

Clarification Card—Knight of Wands:
This Clarifies the Outcome Card's Meaning

The Knight of Wands
(*Classic Tarot*).

When the outcome card is puzzling, I ask the querent to draw an additional card to clarify the meaning of the tenth card. Some readers use card 10 (or any card from the original spread) as the significator for a second Celtic Cross spread to "open up" the meaning of the card in question. In describing the Celtic Cross spread, Waite noted that a court card appearing in the tenth position means the outcome is in the hands of the person represented by the card. He then used the court card of the outcome position as the significator for a new Celtic Cross spread to determine how that court card would influence the outcome.

I don't often use this "opening up" technique because I find pondering the original ten cards plus an eleventh clarification card to be about as much as my brain can handle. For me, more is often less. On the other hand, if the clarification card is puzzling, Waite's advice to do a clarification spread is worth following. Jane and I did not have time to do an additional spread. If Jane returns for another reading, there is nothing to prevent us from doing a ten-card clarification spread to better understand the Knight of Swords, which appeared in the outcome position of her original spread. To repeat Waite's advice:

> If in any divination the Tenth Card should be a Court Card, it shews that the subject of the divination falls ultimately into the hands of a person represented by that card, and its end depends mainly on him. In this event also it is useful to take the Court Card in question as the Significator in a fresh operation, and discover what is the nature of his influence in the matter and to what issue he will bring it. [28]

....
28   Waite, *Pictorial Key* online.

In Jane's reading the Knight of Wands, as the clarification card, seemed to reinforce the meaning of the two Knights in the original spread. Jane had to decide between two men, represented by the Knights, perhaps signifying two youthful or somewhat immature men, one in a hurry to woo her (Swords and Wands) and the other in no rush to go anywhere (Pentacles). The Knight of Wands typically signifies rapid movement, departure, travel, or relocation. Will someone be departing from Jane's life? Will the outcome involve Jane moving to a new location? Will Nathan turn out to be her Knight in shining armor? Does the Knight of Swords in position 10 signify Jane cutting her husband out of her life? Or, as Waite suggests, does the outcome of Jane's concern ultimately depend on the Knight of Swords' role in her life?

Outcome

I ran into Jane several months later. Her mother had died of postsurgical complications a few weeks after the reading. She went through a period of mourning in which she put her concerns about her marriage on hold. Jane said that the Queen of Swords perfectly captured the emotional state she found herself in after her mother's passing. Her husband was quite supportive of her during her period of mourning, and she developed a different perspective on her marriage. She still was not happy with his drinking but felt less urgency to rush into a divorce. Nathan remained a good friend but nothing romantic developed between them.

In retrospect, I wonder whether the fast-paced Knight of Swords in the outcome position suggested the rapid turn of events, centered on the death of her mother, which radically altered her view of the initial question for the reading. Could the Knight of Swords have symbolized her mother's surgeon whose actions inadvertently led to her mother's untimely death? If so, Jane's marital question, as Waite indicated, literally fell into the hands of the surgeon represented by the Knight of Swords, and the outcome ultimately, though circuitously, depended on him.

On the other hand, the Golden Dawn taught that Knights don't necessarily signify a person but can mean the coming or going of a matter, as reflected in the direction the Knight is facing. The matter is often related to the minor arcana cards associated with the Knight in question (*see* appendix C). The Knight of Swords in the outcome position of Jane's reading is linked thematically to the Seven of Pentacles and to the Eight and Nine of Swords. Thus, Jane's outcome may involve pondering the return on her investment in her marriage, feeling restricted, and undergoing sleepless nights and anguish of mind. Furthermore, the Knight of Swords in Jane's reading faces the Three of Swords of the central cross and looks at the Queen of Swords in the near-future position. The Queen of Swords, who may stand for Jane's mother, looks back at the Knight. From this perspective, the Knight of Swords brings strife and sadness (Swords) to the querent (covered by the central cross) and to her mother (the Queen).

A Final Bit of Advice

Because the Celtic Cross spread can be complex in its interpretation, author Hajo Banzhaf recommends breaking it down into smaller groupings of two.[29] Readers new to the Celtic Cross spread may find Banzhaf's approach helpful. He begins with the cards in positions 4 (recent past) and 9 (hopes and fears) to get a sense of what has recently happened and where the querent fears or hopes he may be headed. Banzhaf then reads the cards in positions 1 (covering) and 2 (crossing) to determine the gist of the matter, and looks at the cards in positions 3 (unconscious factors) and 5 (conscious factors) to ascertain the situation's grounding in the past and what the querent is consciously aware of. Next he looks at cards 7 and 8 to see how the querent and those around him regard the issue. Finally, he evaluates cards 6 (near future) and 10 (likely outcome) to see how matters are likely to unfold.

My own approach varies slightly from Banzhaf's, since I regard card 5, the crowning card, as signifying a potential or ideal outcome. Thus, I read cards 5, 6, and 10 together when considering what the future may hold. I also like to read cards 4 (recent past), 1 (covering),

---

29 Hajo Banzhaf, *The Crowley Tarot* (Stamford, CT: U.S. Games Systems Publishers, 1995), p. 204.

and 6 (near future) together as a three-card Past, Present, Future spread to get a sense of the flow of events.

Each reader will eventually develop his or her own method for interpreting this popular and useful spread.

TWO

Astrology 101 for Tarot Readers

Suspiciendo despicio *(Looking upward, I see below)*[30]
TYCHO BRAHE (1546–1601)

None other than Stuart Kaplan, an expert on tarot symbolism and founder of the publishing house U.S. Games Systems, asserts: "A knowledge of astrology can greatly aid in the interpretation of the tarot, and vice versa. It was the genius of the Golden Dawn to synthesize these systems."[31] Kaplan also notes that Waite instructed artist Pamela Colman Smith (affectionately known as "Pixie") to create images for the forty pip cards that "follow very carefully the astrological significance of each suit as it is influenced by different zodiacal signs."[32]

---

30   *New World Encyclopedia,* s.v. "Brahe, Tycho," http://www.newworldencyclopedia.org/entry/Tycho_Brahe (accessed 7 Mar. 2013).

31   Stuart Kaplan, LWB for the *Hermetic Tarot* deck (Stamford, CT: U.S. Games Systems, 2006), p. 6.

32   Stuart Kaplan, *The Artwork & Times of Pamela Colman Smith* (Stamford, CT: U.S. Games Systems, 2003), p. 76.

Following Stuart Kaplan's lead, this chapter is devoted to the basics of astrology as they apply to tarot interpretation. My goal is to flesh out the astrological ideas Pixie used to create the images of the influential Waite-Smith deck. Readers unfamiliar with astrology may find the material a bit overwhelming and may wish to skim the chapter quickly now, referring back to it as they read later chapters. For those versed in astrology, actual readings are included to illustrate the combined use of astrology and tarot.

The word "astrology" comes from the Latin *astrologia,* meaning "astronomy," and the Greek *astron,* "celestial body" and *logia,* "the study of." The origins of astrology are tied to the development of the calendars needed for agriculture. Modern astrology dates back thousands of years to priestly observations of "celestial omens," correlations between heavenly phenomena and events on Earth. Such correlations ranged from what we would now call scientific—for example, "when a certain constellation appears in the sky, the Nile River will overflow its banks"—to pseudoscientific, such as "when Mars aligns with Jupiter, Babylonia will go to war."

Astrology as Divination

Both astrology and the tarot seek to fathom the will of the divine in the patterns of the natural order. Like tarot, astrology is a method of divination, but, instead of using tarot cards, astrology studies the interactions of stars and planets to decipher what the divine has to say about happenings on Earth. This principle is expressed in the famous Hermetic dictum: "As above, so below." In the thirteenth century, Italian astrologer Guido Bonatti (a contemporary of Thomas Aquinas) viewed astrology fundamentally as a method of divination (discerning the intent of the divine) and did readings for clients only after they spent sufficient time seeking divine guidance. If a client still had doubts after a period of prayer and contemplation, Bonatti would then cast a chart to divine in the symbolism of the heavens the will of the Almighty regarding the matter.

The Planets and the Signs of the Zodiac

Ancient observers noticed among the myriad stars in the night sky that certain celestial bodies appeared to wander amidst the backdrop of the fixed stars. They called these objects "planets," from the Greek *planetes*, meaning "wanderers." With the naked eye, observers were able to distinguish seven objects that appeared to move of their own volition. These wanderers included the Sun, Moon, Mercury, Venus, Mars, Jupiter, and Saturn. Each of the seven visible planets of antiquity appeared to have its own characteristics regarding color, size, periodicity, phase changes, speed, direction of motion, and so on.

The ancients also observed that recurring configurations of these wanderers correlated with events on Earth and could thus be used for prediction. They identified the wandering planets with the gods of mythology. In modern times, astrologers often view the planets as symbols of Jungian archetypes of the collective unconscious. Modern Western astrology originated in the horoscopic astrology of Hellenistic Egypt in the second and first centuries BCE and drew especially upon the myths of ancient Greece, Egypt, and Babylon. As astrology spread through the Roman Empire, the names and myths of the Roman gods supplanted those of the Greeks.

To locate the planets in the heavens, the ancient stargazers developed a coordinate system. They located each planet with reference to the path of the Sun, the major "Light" in the sky, which appeared to travel in a circle around the Earth through twelve unequal constellations of stars. The constellations of the zodiac were named after animals and mythological figures and included a thirteenth constellation, now called Ophiuchus (the "serpent bearer"), which dips into the zodiac belt between Scorpio and Sagittarius. In 1928, the International Astronomy Union set the boundaries of all eighty-eight constellations in the night sky, adding Ophiuchus to the twelve constellations of the zodiac belt.

The word *zodiac* comes from Greek and means "circle of animals." Fortunately, all the wandering planets appeared to move through the same band of constellations that encircle the Earth in the form of a "zodiac belt." Being mathematically inclined, the Hellenistic Greeks divided the 360-degree circle into twelve 30-degree segments, which they called zodiac "signs" as opposed to the "constellations" of varying widths. Astrologers named each sign after its corresponding constellation on the zodiac belt of two thousand years ago. On the basis of "as above, so below," the ancients correlated each sign with a particular part of the human body.

Further observations led the astrologers to believe that each planet "ruled" or was "exalted" in a sign where it had much "dignity." The seventeenth-century astrologer William Lilly, explaining the dignity of "exaltation," said that in some regions of the zodiac planets can "more evidently declare their effects than in others." On the contrary, a planet with little or no dignity was like a man "ready to be turned out of doors, having much ado to maintain himself in credit and reputation" or like a family "at the last gasp," … "barely able to support itself."[33] In signs where planets seemed to act weakly or badly, they were considered "debilitated," "in detriment," or "in fall." A planet in detriment occupies the sign opposite the one it rules. A planet in fall occupies the sign opposite the one where it is exalted. With regard to dignity, moving a planet to the opposite sign is similar to inverting a card in the tarot.

The accompanying figure illustrates an important historical horoscope, the *Thema Mundi,* which was used by Hellenistic astrologers to show the zodiacal positions of the seven visible planets at the beginning of time. In Hellenistic cosmology, the signs occupied by the planets in the *Thema Mundi* are the ones they naturally rule. Inspection of this figure shows that each planet lies in the middle of the 30-degree sign that it has ruled since the beginning of time. The center of this horoscope represents the position of an Egyptian observer, who is facing south toward the equator and looking up directly at Aries, the sign that marks the beginning of spring. The sign Cancer, which marks the onset of summer, is ascending on the eastern horizon. The houses of the *Thema Mundi* resemble those of a horoscope cast for the Great Pyramid of Giza at midsummer with Cancer rising and the Sun in mid-Leo.

---

33   William Lilly, *Christian Astrology (1647)* (Exeter, UK: Regulus, 1985), p. 103.

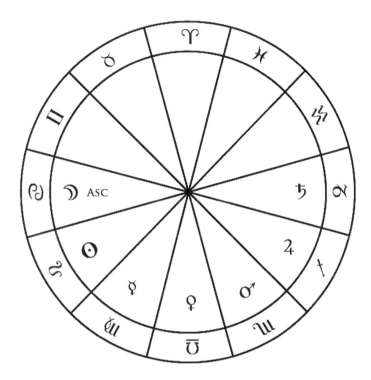

The *Thema Mundi* of Hellenistic astrology. [34]

The Seven Visible Planets

☉ Sun

The regal Sun is the heart of the solar system and the giver of light and life. The Sun governs the sign Leo ♌ and is exalted in Aries ♈. The Sun was viewed as a fatherly monarch who rules the kingdom of Leo and is an honored guest (exalted) in the kingdom of Aries, ruled by Mars. The Sun is treated like royalty when passing through Aries.

---

34   Chris Brennan, "The Thema Mundi," posted 11 Jun. 2007, *The Horoscopic Astrology Blog*, http://horoscopicastrologyblog.com/2007/06/11/the-thema-mundi/ (accessed 6 Mar. 2013), image reproduced with permission.

The Sun's day is Sunday (duh!). It is associated with daylight, vitality, power, authority, male potency, fatherhood, creation, eminence, honor, will, constancy, success, fame, heroism, kings, and government. The Sun is considered hot and dry, like the element Fire of ancient Greece.

The Golden Dawn assigned the Sun to tarot trump XIX, the Sun. This book uses the Golden Dawn system for assigning astrological symbols to tarot cards because it is so widely known and has had a considerably powerful influence on the divinatory meanings of modern tarot decks.

☽ The Moon

The inconstant Moon is the consort of the Sun and queen of the night. The Moon's appearance is constantly changing as she shifts from one phase to the next over the course of a month. In Roman mythology, the Moon was identified with Diana, the chaste hunter goddess associated with wild animals like those shown on the Moon trump of the tarot. The Moon was also linked to Hecate, the goddess of triple nature, who watched over crossroads, childbirth, dogs, the night sky, healing, and the nurturing of the young. Hecate comforted the goddess Demeter when Hades (Pluto) kidnapped her daughter Persephone and took her to the Underworld in his chariot. Hecate also became Persephone's companion in the Underworld and helped her to escape and reunite with Demeter. Jungian tarot readers often identify the Empress with Demeter, the High Priestess with Persephone, and the Moon trump with Hecate.

Our word *lunatic* comes from the Latin *luna*, meaning moon, because the insane mind is as unsteady as the ever-changing Moon. Luna rules Cancer ♋ and is exalted in Taurus ♉, the bull whose horns have the shape of a crescent Moon. The Moon signifies mothers and mothers' milk. Taurus (the cow) is a major source of milk for the human child.

The Moon's day is Monday. Luna is symbolic of periodicity, fluctuation, instability, cycles (going through phases), femininity, nurturing, food, breast milk, motherhood, families, women, domestic life, emotions, responses, instinct, habit, tides, memory, and receptivity. The Moon is considered cold and wet, like the element Water of ancient Greece. The Sun and the Moon form a fundamental complementary pair of "planets" in astrology. Other complementary pairings include Venus and Mars, and Jupiter and Saturn.

The Golden Dawn assigned the Moon to tarot trump II, the High Priestess or Female Pope, who provides spiritual "milk" to nurture the human soul.

☿ Mercury

Mercury (the Greek trickster god Hermes) is the winged messenger of the gods. Mercury rules Gemini Ⅱ and Virgo ♍. Mercury is exalted in Virgo. The English word "mercurial" is used to describe people who are volatile, fickle, swift, animated, quick-witted, or unpredictable.

Mercury's day is Wednesday. He is associated with thought, communication, storytelling, learning, education, speech, writing, literature, media, news, advertising, travel, transport, commerce, duality, cleverness, adroitness, trickery, magic, and theft. Mercury is considered cool and dry, like the element Earth of ancient Greece.

The Golden Dawn assigned quick and clever Mercury to tarot trump I, the Magician.

♀ Venus

Venus is the Roman goddess of love. Venus rules Libra ♎ and Taurus ♉. Venus is exalted in Pisces ♓. The English word "venereal" (of Venus) means "related to erotic desire or sexual intercourse," a favorite pastime of the voluptuous love goddess who sometimes followed the motto "if it feels good, do it."

Venus's day is Friday. She is associated with love, beauty, music, art, gifts, adornment, fashion, pleasure, sexual delight, indulgence, peace, harmony, charm, relationships, appeasement, sweethearts, lovemaking, and good fortune. Venus is considered wet and warm, like the element Air of ancient Greece. Venus and Mars form a complementary pair. Cupid, the god of desire and erotic love, was an offspring of the mating of Venus with the war god Mars. In early tarot decks, Cupid is seen shooting his arrows at the Lovers on trump VI.

The Golden Dawn assigned sexy Venus to tarot trump III, the Empress.

♂ Mars

The red planet Mars is the Roman god of war and bloodshed. Mars rules Aries ♈ and Scorpio ♏. Mars is exalted in Capricorn ♑. Our phrase "martial arts" comes from the Latin *martialis* (of Mars). A favorite saying of Mars is "I want what I want when I want it." The exaltation of phallic Mars in Capricorn may account for this sign's fondness for frequent sex.

Mars's day is Tuesday. He is associated with self-will, conquest, testosterone, muscular exertion, heat, fire, burning, passion, penetration, insemination, desire, drive, courage, strife, war, bloodshed, accidents, violence, competition, assertiveness, impulsivity, construction, and men in uniform. Mars is considered dry and hot, like the element Fire of ancient Greece. Classical astrology teaches that Mars expresses himself more constructively at night because the coolness of the night tempers his natural ardor and impetuousness.

The Golden Dawn assigned macho Mars to tarot trump XVI, the Tower.

♃ Jupiter

Jupiter is the king of the Roman gods. In the Greek pantheon, Jupiter was lustful Zeus, the regent of Mount Olympus, whence he could see far and wide. Jupiter rules Sagittarius ♐ and Pisces ♓. Jupiter is exalted in Cancer ♋. The Romans referred to Jupiter as Jove, which is the origin of our adjective "jovial," meaning good-humored, jolly, sanguine, and of good cheer.

Jupiter's day is Thursday. He is associated with luck, abundance, protection, expansion, excess, increase, optimism, wealth, success, aristocracy, generosity, adventure, global travel, wisdom, broadmindedness, philosophy, religious beliefs, clerics, courts, justice, the law, the professions, publishing, higher education, lust for life, and the thirst for knowledge. Jupiter is considered warm and dry, like the element Fire of ancient Greece.

The Golden Dawn assigned generous Jupiter to tarot trump X, the Wheel of Fortune.

♄ Saturn

Saturn (the Greek god Cronos) has been called Father Time, the Cosmic Teacher, the Great Taskmaster, and the Grim Reaper. Saturn rules Capricorn ♑ and Aquarius ♒ and is exalted in Libra ♎ (aka the Claws of the Scorpion). The adjective "saturnine" refers to someone who is somber, taciturn, gloomy, brooding, or bitter; it is the opposite of jovial.

Saturn's day is Saturday. As the outermost visible planet of antiquity, Saturn rules boundaries, limitation, laws, rules, regulations, tradition, stability, order, structure, delay, deprivation, burdens, death, and lessons to be learned. Lying farthest from the Sun, Saturn is the last stop on the soul's journey from Earth to heaven. Saturn is cold, strict, hard, serious, constricting, rule-bound, and inhibiting. He is considered cold and dry, like the element Earth of ancient Greece. Jupiter and Saturn form a complementary pair; Jupiter expands whereas Saturn contracts. Classical astrology taught that Saturn expresses itself more constructively during the day because the warmth of the life-giving Sun tempers Saturn's natural coldness, rigidity, and austerity.

Although in the earliest tarot decks the Hermit card displayed Saturn as Father Time carrying an hourglass, the Golden Dawn assigned Saturn to tarot trump XXI, the World, the final stop on the Fool's journey.

The Outer Planets: Uranus, Neptune, Pluto

In addition to the seven visible planets, contemporary astrologers use three "modern" or "outer" planets and numerous other celestial entities. The three outer planets—Uranus, Neptune, and Pluto—are so called because they lie outside the orbit of Saturn, which is the outer limit of the classical solar system. Astrologers have found that the movements of the three outer planets correlate with profound changes in worldly events and major shifts in one's personal life.

♅ Uranus

Often called the Awakener, Uranus was not recognized as a planet until 1781, the same year that Antoine Court de Gébelin published his essay that created excitement about the tarot throughout the popular culture of the time. The discovery of Uranus shattered the structure of classical astrology, whose theoretical foundation rested on the existence of seven visible planets, no more and no less. Strictly speaking, Uranus is just barely visible to the naked eye but the ancients were unable to see it, blinded as they were by traditional astrological theory, which allowed only seven visible planets. Believing was seeing.

Uranus is linked to the types of insights provided by the mathematical symbolism of astrology, and many astrologers have Uranus prominent in their birth charts. Contemporary astrologers believe Uranus rules Aquarius ♒ (Saturn is the classical ruler). Uranus is associated with shocking events, novelty, disruption, unconventionality, upheaval, divorce, the unexpected, revolution, anarchy, rebellion, accidents, earthquakes, innovation, sudden insights, bursts of light, inventions, electricity, modern technology, liberation, breaking free, and abstract systems of thought. Uranus shatters the structures Saturn has built.

Modern occultists associate the maverick Uranus with tarot trump 0, the Fool.

♆ Neptune

Neptune, named after Roman god of the sea, was discovered in 1846, perhaps heralding the 1848 revolutions in Europe. Neptune (or Poseidon, the Greek god of earthquakes and the sea) has a special link with the intuitive insights based upon the archetypal images of the tarot. In the birth charts of tarot readers, Neptune tends to figure prominently, often in aspect to the Moon, which is also related to intuition and psychic awareness.

Contemporary astrologers give Neptune rulership over Pisces ♓ (Jupiter is the classical ruler). Ralph Waldo Emerson was clearly in tune with Neptune when he wrote in 1836:

> Standing on the bare ground,—my head bathed by the blithe air and uplifted into infinite space,—all mean egotism vanishes. I become a transparent eye-ball; I am nothing; I see all; the currents of the Universal Being circulate through me; I am part or particle of God.[35]

Neptune is associated with illusion, mystery, mysticism, dreams, symbolism, imagination, the unconscious, intuition, poetry, music, film, transcendence, universality, idealism, spirituality, merging, fogginess, escapism, sacrifice, intoxication, deception, scandal, and the dissolution or blurring of boundaries. Neptune erodes and dissolves the structures built by Saturn. The discovery of Neptune occurred in the same year that Marx and Engels published their utopian view of society in the *Communist Manifesto*.

Modern occultists associate Neptune with tarot trump XII, the Hanged Man, who is suspended by his foot (the part of the body ruled by Pisces).

♇ Pluto

Pluto, named after the Roman god of the underworld, was discovered in 1930. Contemporary astrologers give Pluto rulership of Scorpio ♏ (Mars is the classical ruler). Pluto (the Greek god Hades) is associated with divination because it symbolizes the revelation of secret or occult knowledge. Astronomers have reclassified Pluto as a dwarf planet; nonetheless, astrologers continue to regard Pluto as immensely powerful in a horoscope. Conan O'Brien was speaking of a Plutonian experience when he told the 2011 Dartmouth graduating class: "There are few things more liberating in this life than having your worst fear realized."[36]

....

35 Ralph Waldo Emerson, "Nature" (1836), http://oregonstate.edu/instruct/phl302/texts/emerson /nature-contents.html (accessed 5 Mar. 2012).

36 Conan O'Brien, "Dartmouth College Commencement Address," Dartmouth College, http://www .dartmouth.edu/~commence/news/speeches/2011/obrien-speech.html (accessed 17 June 2012).

Pluto has become associated with atomic power, metamorphosis, transformation, regeneration, volcanic eruption, sweeping change, deep emotion, psychoanalysis, research, in-depth understanding, uncovering that which lies hidden beneath the surface, detective work, irresistible force, life-changing events, wakeup calls, the occult, the underworld, the wealth provided by natural resources, death, rebirth, and regeneration. Pluto completely uproots and radically transforms the structures built by Saturn.

Modern occultists associate Pluto with tarot trump XX, Judgment.

The Outer Planets in the Life of Tiger Woods

To illustrate the impact of the outer planets, let's consider an example from the life of Tiger Woods. His birth data is 10:50 p.m., 30 December 1975, Long Beach, California. On November 25, 2009, *The National Enquirer* reported that the golf pro was having an extramarital affair with a New York City nightclub manager. A couple days later Tiger had a dramatic car accident which focused media attention on his marital problems. On August 23, 2010, Tiger Woods and Elin Nordegren finalized their divorce. Such life-altering events almost always involve transits of the outer planets to the birth chart.

The accompanying table lists *all* the major hard aspects of Uranus (the planet of upheaval and divorce), Neptune (dissolution and deception), and Pluto (radical change and transformation) to Woods's birth chart during the five-year period 2008–2013. Hard aspects are based on division of the circle by 4, the number of manifestation. The major hard aspects include the conjunction (two planets at the same point on the zodiac circle), the square (two planets $90°$ apart) and the opposition (two planets $180°$ apart). Because the transiting outer planets move so slowly, their interactions with the birth chart correlate with events that are experienced for months either side of the date they become exact. Most astrologers do not believe planets "cause" events but rather that important correlations occur between changing planetary patterns and life events on Earth. Correlation is not causation.

Hard Outer-Planet Aspects to the Natal Chart of Tiger Woods, 2008–2013		
Aspect	Date(s)	Typical Meanings & Tarot Associations
Transiting Uranus square (90°) natal Mars	Feb. 18, 2008	Feeling tense and frustrated. Needing to find an outlet for pent-up sexual and aggressive impulses. (The *Fool* confronts the *Tower*.)
Transiting Uranus square (90°) natal Moon	May 31, 2008 July 23, 2008 Mar. 8, 2009	Disruptions in domestic life. Wanting to break free of emotional constraints. (The *Fool* confronts the *High Priestess*.)
Transiting Uranus square (90°) Midheaven axis	April 5, 2009 Oct. 5, 2009 Jan. 25, 2010	Tension and stress in professional life that may affect home and family. Sudden changes, accidents, or disruptions affecting career or domestic life. (The *Fool* confronts the *Devil*.)
	Nov. 25, 2009	*News breaks about extramarital affair.*
Transiting Uranus oppose (180°) Ascendant (i.e., conjunct the Descendant or cusp of the marriage House)	April 14, 2009 Sep. 22, 2009 Feb. 5, 2010	"Your relationship with your partner now becomes the target for disruptions and change, particularly if there have been problems which have been pushed underground in the past."* A classic "divorce aspect." (The *Fool* enters the house analogous to Libra, the sign of *Justice*.)
	Aug. 23 2010	*Divorce finalized.*
Transiting Neptune square (90°) Venus	May 6, 2010 Jun. 26, 2010 Feb. 20, 2011 Dec. 16, 2011	Secret love affairs. Confusion, illusion or deception in love. Dissolution of an intimate partnership. Scandal. (The *Hanged Man* confronts the *Empress*.)
Transiting Pluto conjunct (0°) natal Sun	Feb. 21, 2012 May 31, 2012 Dec. 21, 2012	Radical change, life-changing events, profound personal transformation. Life is never the same afterward. (*Judgment* in the light of the *Sun*.)

* Interpretation of transiting Uranus oppose Ascendant, Solar Fire Gold, v 7.3.1 (Stepney, South Australia: Esoteric Technologies, 2010).

Tropical Astrology: The Four Seasons and the Zodiac

I recall from my teenage years the stir caused in the United States by the 1961 publication of Henry Miller's *Tropic of Cancer* and the subsequent obscenity trial that challenged this country's laws on pornography. The astronomical Tropic of Cancer is not as sexy as the novel. Instead, it refers to the Northern Tropic, that is, the northernmost circle of latitude (approximately 23° 26' 21" N) at which the Sun appears directly overhead during its annual cycle.

Each year the Sun reaches the Tropic of Cancer on the day of the June solstice, the beginning of summer in the northern hemisphere and the onset of winter south of the equator. In geography, the tropics and equinoxes indicate the start of the four seasons. The equinoxes occur twice per year on the first day of autumn (September 23) and spring (March 21) when the number of hours of daylight equals the length of the night (hence, *equi-nox*). At the moment of the equinox, the tilt of the Earth's axis is inclined neither away from nor toward the Sun.

In ancient times, astrologers had to choose where to start the zodiac. There were two options. In the West, astrologers chose to begin the zodiac at 0° Aries, which they assigned to the spring equinox (March 21). Thus, Western astrologers defined the zodiac by the Earth's seasons, and the Western zodiac is called the "tropical" or season-based zodiac. In contrast, Hindu or Vedic astrologers, who also start the zodiac at 0° Aries, assigned the start of the zodiac to the beginning of the constellation of stars known as Aries. Thus, Western astrologers use a tropical (season-based or Sun-based) zodiac whereas Indian astrologers use a sidereal (star-based) zodiac determined by the constellations. Because the Earth wobbles slowly on its axis (the precession of the equinoxes), the two zodiacs have drifted apart since Ptolemy wrote about it in the second century CE. In fact, the two zodiacs coincide only once in every 26,000 years! Currently in the West, the zodiac begins at 0° Aries on March 21 but it begins on April 15 in the sidereal system of India. Both the tropical and the sidereal zodiacs divide the circle into twelve equal segments called "signs," which are mathematical constructs named after the constellations in the sky.

By definition, a zodiacal sign is one-twelfth of the zodiac circle. There are important philosophical reasons why astrologers divide the 360° circle by twelve. Essentially there are four fundamental energies called elements (Fire, Water, Air, and Earth) that can express themselves in three distinct ways (cardinal, fixed, and mutable). These twelve possible manifestations of energy (4 x 3 = 12) are called the signs of the zodiac. Debunkers of astrology lack this basic understanding of astrology as a mathematical model that posits twelve equal, 30-degree signs, regardless of the number of constellations on the zodiac belt. The astrological signs merely get their names from the constellations. Every so often a story appears in the media claiming that scientists have discovered a thirteenth sign, which is tantamount to saying that scientific research has recently discovered that thirteen items make a dozen. Poppycock!

The Twelve Signs of the Zodiac

To recap, Western astrologers opted to begin the zodiac at the onset of spring, the vernal equinox, which occurs around March 21 each year north of the equator. The tropical zodiac is based on which season the Earth is experiencing. Each season is allotted ninety degrees of the full circle. Spring begins at 0° Aries, summer at 0° Cancer, autumn at 0° Libra, and winter at 0° Capricorn. The four signs that begin the seasons are called the *cardinal signs* (from the Latin *cardo,* meaning "pivot" or "hinge") because the seasons of the year hinge on them.

Keywords & Associations for the Modalities and Tarot Pip Cards	
Modality	Keywords & Associations
Cardinal (Pips 2, 3, 4)	Leads, initiates, instigates, incites, commands, plans, pioneers, rouses, forges ahead, likes to take action and run the show
Fixed (Pips 5, 6, 7)	Stable, steady, persevering, dependable, established, stubborn, entrenched, enduring, slow to change, works persistently to bring plans to full realization
Mutable (Pips 8, 9, 10)	Transitioning, flexible, restless, adaptable, communicative, mobile, thrives on change, likes to prepare for ending and moving on

Being keen observers, the ancient astrologers noticed that people tended to display certain character traits according to the season in which they were born. For example, children born in late summer (at the time of the harvest) grew up to be hard-working, meticulous, and perfectionist adults. Instead of calling these kids "late summer babies," astrologers used the shorthand that the Sun in Virgo is critical and detail-oriented, and so on. Virgo is the last zodiac sign of summer, that is, the last thirty-degree segment of the summer quadrant initiated by 0° Cancer. Key properties of the sun signs are summarized in the accompanying table.

Keywords for the Signs of the Zodiac			
Sun Sign	Properties	Sun Sign across the Wheel	Properties
Aries (+)	*Cardinal Fire.* Ardent, self-seeking, impulsive, assertive, pioneering.	**Libra (+)**	*Cardinal Air.* Balanced, sociable, indecisive, relationship-oriented.
Taurus (-)	*Fixed Earth.* Reliable, steady, practical, fond of luxury, reluctant to change.	**Scorpio (-)**	*Fixed Water.* Intense, private, determined, penetrating, secretive.
Gemini (+)	*Mutable Air.* Versatile, chatty, communicative, mobile, scattered.	**Sagittarius (+)**	*Mutable Fire.* Frank, freedom-loving, tolerant, adventurous, philosophical.
Cancer (-)	*Cardinal Water.* Protective, domestic, shy, nurturing, security-conscious.	**Capricorn (-)**	*Cardinal Earth.* Ambitious, reserved, practical, hard-working, status-oriented.
Leo (+)	*Fixed Fire.* Proud, fun-loving, creative, enthusiastic, dramatic, bossy.	**Aquarius (+)**	*Fixed Air.* Detached, modern, inventive, outgoing, unique, eccentric.
Virgo (-)	*Mutable Earth.* Meticulous, critical, analytical, modest, discerning, service-oriented.	**Pisces (-)**	*Mutable Water.* Sensitive, artistic, intuitive, poetic, dreamy, escapist, gullible.

Just as the year is divided into four seasons, the zodiac wheel is divided into four quadrants measured counterclockwise starting at 0° Aries at the very left on the eastern horizon. In the horoscope, the horizon is represented by a horizontal line that divides the circle into equal hemispheres above and below. The direction east is located to the left because astrologers faced southward toward the equator when they studied the night sky. In short, the horoscope is a map of the heavens with due south placed at the top of the map.

Each season has a beginning, middle, and an end—each of which corresponds to the three zodiac signs that make up the quadrant. The accompanying diagram of a square horoscope lists the zodiac signs that comprise the four quadrants and the four seasons:

Quadrants, Directions, Seasons, Signs, and Houses of the Natural Horoscope	
SOUTH ↑	**Midheaven**
4th Quadrant	3rd Quadrant
(Winter)	*(Autumn)*
10. ♑ **Capricorn**	9. ♐ Sagittarius
11. ♒ Aquarius	8. ♏ Scorpio
12. ♓ Pisces	7. ♎ **Libra**
Ascendant	**WEST →**
← EAST	**Descendant**
1st Quadrant	2nd Quadrant
(Spring)	*(Summer)*
1. ♈ **Aries**	6. ♍ Virgo
2. ♉ Taurus	5. ♌ Leo
3. ♊ Gemini	4. ♋ **Cancer**
Imum Coeli	↓ **NORTH**

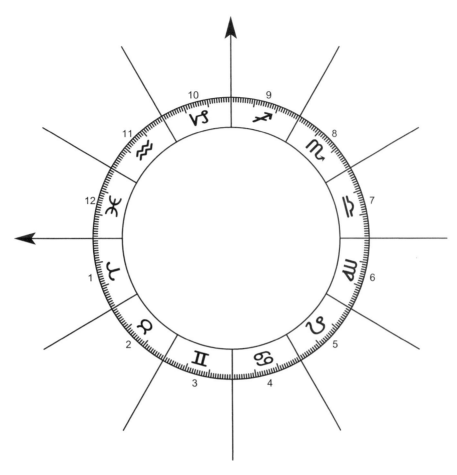

The natural Aries-rising zodiac.

The Qualities: Cardinal, Fixed, Mutable

Astrologers saw as symbolic the fact that each season is divided into three parts: a beginning, a middle, and an end. The signs that initiate seasons are called *cardinal* because the entry into the season hinges on them. The signs in the middle of the season are called *fixed* because the season is in full force at its middle. Finally, the signs at the end of a season are called *mutable* because they cover the period when a season is breaking down so that the next season can break through.

By analogy, people born with their Sun in cardinal signs are enterprising and like to initiate new ventures. Those with their Sun in fixed signs tend to be somewhat stubborn, dedicated, firm in their opinions, slow to change, and set in their ways. People born with their Sun in mutable signs tend to be adaptable, clever, quick to learn, mercurial, and able to act as "go-betweens" and cope with transition. In the nineteenth century, the Golden Dawn used these distinctions to delineate the tarot pip cards numbered 2 through 10. The Golden Dawn regarded the pips numbered 2, 3, and 4 of each suit to be of a cardinal or initiatory nature; the pips numbered 5, 6, and 7 to be fixed and more entrenched; and the pip cards numbered 8, 9, and 10 to be mutable or transitional, giving way to a new cycle.

Zodiac Signs and the Four Elements

In addition to assigning the qualities of cardinal, fixed, or mutable to each sign, the ancient astrologers also allotted them one of the four elements of Greek philosophy in the order Fire, Earth, Air, Water. The first sign Aries was a Fire sign; the second sign Taurus, an Earth sign; the third sign Gemini, an Air sign; and the fourth sign Cancer, a Water sign. This pattern was repeated around the wheel. Key symbolic features of each element included:

- Fire is ambitious, enlivening, enthusiastic, active, expansive, adventurous, competitive, outgoing, enterprising, energetic, and future-oriented. (The blossoming Wands of the tarot are associated with Fire. The Queen of Wands acts as midwife to the onset of spring.)

- Water is emotional, sensitive, artistic, flowing, empathetic, nurturing, caring, and oriented toward the past. (The receptive Cups of the tarot are associated with Water. The Queen of Cups acts as midwife to the start of summer.)

- Air is communicative, mental, social, associative, inventive, and relationship-oriented. (The piercing Swords of the tarot are associated with Air. The Queen of Swords acts as midwife to the beginning of autumn.)

- Earth is grounded, practical, tangible, diligent, reliable, detail-oriented, health-conscious, orderly, and industrious. (The serviceable Coins/Disks/Pentacles of the tarot are associated with Earth. The Queen of Pentacles acts as midwife to the onset of winter.)

As mentioned, the philosophical concepts of three qualities and four elements form the theoretical basis for the twelve signs of the zodiac. The twelve signs are archetypes or ways of being in the universe. Because the material universe can be explained in terms of the four elements, and each element can behave in one of three modes (cardinal, fixed, mutable), there are only twelve distinct archetypal ways of being in the world. Having decided on exactly twelve archetypal ways of being represented by the signs, the ancient astrologers named each of the twelve signs after one of the constellations along the zodiac belt. The Golden Dawn would later assign the tarot pip cards to the signs of the zodiac as shown in the table.

The Twelve Signs as Manifestations of the Three Qualities and the Four Elements				
	Fire Triplicity:	Water Triplicity:	Air Triplicity:	Earth Triplicity:
Cardinal: *(Pips 2, 3, 4)*	Aries	Cancer	Libra	Capricorn
Fixed: *(Pips 5, 6, 7)*	Leo	Scorpio	Aquarius	Taurus
Mutable: *(Pips 8, 9, 10)*	Sagittarius	Pisces	Gemini	Virgo

The 24-Hour Day Reflected in the Horoscope

The Earth rotates on its axis once every twenty-four hours and revolves around the sun once a year. The sun's annual cycle is related to the four seasons and the twelve signs of the zodiac. The daily cycle of the sun, due to the rotation of the Earth, accounts for the cycle of day and night, which is represented in the horoscope as the twelve astrological houses.

The twelve houses symbolize twelve distinct areas of life. The cusp of the first house is called the Ascendant because it is the degree of the zodiac ascending or rising on the eastern horizon at the time of birth. It is also called the rising sign. The Ascendant carries the symbolism of sunrise, birth, and coming into being; as such, it is the most important point in the horoscope. Next in importance is the Midheaven, the point on the zodiac circle that the Sun occupies at midday. The Midheaven is the highest, most visible, and prominent point in the horoscope. Symbolically it signifies our personal high noon: career, worldly status, reputation, and public standing. At the Ascendant we come into the world, and at the Midheaven we make our mark on it.

The twelve houses are analogous to the twelve signs of the zodiac and share some of their symbolism. Astrological houses and the zodiacal signs, however, are distinct concepts; they cannot be equated as some modern astrologers erroneously try to do. The renowned astrologer Dane Rudhyar stressed that zodiacal signs are twelve modes of life energy, whereas astrological houses are sections of space that represent twelve fields of experience. The meanings of the houses derive from centuries of observations of the horoscopes of people, nations, and worldly events. Unlike the thirty-degree signs, the twelve houses are not of equal size because of the "obliquity of the ecliptic," the fact that the Earth's axis is tilted about 23.4° with respect to the zodiac circle. The horoscope is a two-dimensional map of the heavens; when three-dimensional space is projected onto a two-dimensional surface, the houses appear to be uneven in width.

The houses come in pairs. Drawing on the symbolism of night and day, the ancients considered the nighttime hemisphere below the horizon to be personal and subjective, and the daytime hemisphere above the horizon to be public and objective. Each hemisphere contains six houses. Houses that oppose each other across the wheel are complementary pairs. The seventeenth-century astrologer Morin de Villefranche taught that each astrological house participates "accidentally" in the symbolism of the house opposite; that is, each house has its own essential nature and also partakes of the meaning of the house directly opposite.

Meanings of the Twelve Houses

The first house represents one's body, life, physical appearance, vitality, basic motivation, and sense of identity. The opposite seventh house signifies one's spouse or partner but also open enemies, opponents, wars, lawsuits, and thieves. The first and seventh houses represent the duality of self and other. Lying opposite the first house, planets in the seventh can stressfully affect the native's health and vitality. In mundane astrology (the astrology of world events), the first house symbolizes the nation, its populace, and its image in the world. The opposite seventh house stands for treaties, contracts, lawsuits, agreements, foreign relations, allies, opponents, wars, and disputes.

The second house signifies income, money, resources, supports, values, and belongings (moveable goods). The opposite eighth house represents death, the goods of the dead, legacies, the partner's money, joint finances, shared resources, danger, fear, anguish of mind, taboos, the occult, and esoteric interests. In mundane astrology, the second house stands for banks, financial institutions, the money market, and the nation's wealth. The opposite eighth house symbolizes taxes, probate, inheritances, borrowed money, international finance, and multinational corporations.

The third house signifies siblings, kin, modes of communication, news, gossip, the sharing of ideas, learning, reading, writing, early education, neighborhood matters, transport, and local travel. The opposite ninth house (of the Sun god, who daily transports the Sun across the sky in his chariot) represents long journeys, higher education, knowledge, philosophy, the law, religion, the clergy, expanded horizons, dreams, prophecy, divination, the dissemination of ideas, in-laws, and foreign affairs. In mundane astrology, the third house stands for schools, education, media, transport, roads, bridges, and the postal service. The opposite ninth house signifies foreign nations and peoples, higher education, publishing, the church, ecclesiastical affairs, the law, the justice system, and foreign travel.

The fourth house refers to home, father, family, progenitors, homeland, ancestry, heredity, early environment, real estate, things hidden in the earth, buried treasure, the end of matters, and the grave. The opposite tenth house signifies authority figures, mother, career, office, achievements, professional ambitions, social status, reputation, honors, and public standing. In mundane astrology, the fourth house represents the land, the housing industry, agriculture, farming, mines, natural resources (in the ground), the weather, and the political party opposing the ruling party. The opposite tenth house signifies the ruling political party, the government, judges, the chief executive, and the prestige and honor of the nation.

The fifth house signifies children, pleasures, recreation, hobbies, games, gambling, sexual delights, pregnancy, love affairs, and creative self-expression. The opposite eleventh house signifies friends, alliances, groups of like-minded persons, social activities, confidence, praise, trust, hopes, wishes, and humanitarian concerns. In mundane astrology, the fifth house represents the entertainment industry, amusements, recreation, leisure activities, the arts, theatre, fashion, sports, children, speculation, casinos, the stock market, and colonies of the nation. The opposite eleventh house shows resources and supporters of the government or whoever is in command.

Finally, the sixth house refers to illness, ailments, duties, service, routine tasks, the workplace, daily toil, subordinates, servants, caretaking, pets, small animals, detailed work, apprenticeship, and the organization and storage of information. The complementary twelfth house represents confinement, seclusion, exile, prison, hospitals, infirmaries, charitable work, secret enemies, clandestine affairs, false friends, suffering, sorrows, illness, limitations, scandal, self-undoing, large animals, and spirituality. In mundane astrology, the sixth house signifies medical services, the army, navy, police force, civil service, animal control, trade unions, the food industry, sanitation, public health, service organizations, and the working classes. The twelfth house represents large institutions, hospitals, captives, slaves, witches, prisons, asylums, places of detention or confinement, monasteries, spiritual retreats, charities, secret organizations, sedition, terrorists, and hidden enemies.

Horoscope Tarot Spreads

Tarot readers often lay out one or more cards per house around a horoscope wheel and interpret the cards in the context of the house where they fall. It is also possible to represent one's birth chart using the Golden Dawn assignments of tarot cards to signs and planets in one's nativity. The birth chart can be read as a horoscope spread, utilizing the houses into which the cards for each sign and planet fall. Astrologers can also use this method to read what the tarot has to say about the year ahead in their annual solar return.

For example, Tiger Woods, whose romantic escapades are a matter of public record, has Mercury (the Magician) in Capricorn (the Devil) in his fifth house of love and romance. A possible reading of this combination is that such a person might act like a cunning trickster (Mercury the Magician) in a devilish pursuit (Capricorn the Devil) of sexual delight (fifth house). In Woods's chart, Mercury occupies the Sun decan of Capricorn, which is linked to the Four of Pentacles, a card of covetousness and the wish to have as much as one can get. The Sun, ruler of this decan, is a quintessential symbol of male potency. [37]

Keywords for Houses	
1. Self, body, life, vitality, personality, character, appearance, personal initiative	7. Marriage, divorce, close partnerships, consultants, open enemies, disputes, war, lawsuits, thieves
2. Valuables, income, goods, assets, possessions, money, wealth, resources	8. Resources of partners, death, loss, the dead, legacies, surgery, the occult, fear, anguish of mind, transformation
3. Siblings, kin, news, communication, messages, writing, short trips, learning, education, local environment	9. Higher education, journeys, foreign lands, prophecy, dreams, publishing, philosophy, religion, clergy, in-laws
4. Home, family, fathers, real estate, roots, foundation, tradition, the end of matters, the grave	10. Career, profession, achievements, public standing, honors, reputation, dignity, authority, judges, mothers
5. Fun, romance, pleasure, lovemaking, children, pregnancy, creative self-expression, gambling, vacations	11. Resources related to career, friends, social groups, hopes, praise, trust, fidelity, optimism, fulfillment of wishes
6. Daily routine, service, caretaking, toil, labor, disease, ailments, subordinates, tenants, pets, small animals	12. Self-undoing, sacrifice, confinement, seclusion, exile, secret enemies, sorrow, defects, charity, large animals

The Thirty-Six Decans

A knowledge of decans is essential to understanding the Golden Dawn system of tarot interpretation. The word *decan* (pronounced like "deck-an") derives from the Latin *decanus*, meaning the chief of a group of ten. A decan results from dividing a zodiac sign into three equal 10-degree

....

37   Tiger Woods's natal chart can be seen at "Sex Addict?," *Anthony Louis Astrology and Tarot* blog, http://tonylouis.wordpress.com/2013/03/31/sex-addict/ (accessed 31 Mar. 2013).

segments. In ancient Greece, the number ten was sacred. It was natural for Hellenistic astrologers to divide the 360° circle into 36 decans (360° = 36 x 10°). When it came to distributing the seven visible planets among the 36 decans, each planet was given five decans (5 x 7 = 35) and one got an extra decan (35 + 1 = 36). The planet chosen to receive the extra decan was Mars who, because of his heat, was given the last decan of winter and the first decan of spring.

In the thinking of the occultists, the transition from winter to spring at the beginning of Aries required an extra boost of the fiery energy of Mars. This symbolism is reflected in the Waite-Smith Two of Wands by the crossing of two plant stems, one bearing white lilies on either end and the other with red roses on each end. Pisces is a cold Water sign that marks the end of winter. Mars ruling the last decan of Pisces serves to melt the white snow (the color of lilies and virginity) and prepare the way for the blossoming of the flowers in spring (the red roses, red being the color of Mars and a symbol of passion and the defloration of the virgin).

The Golden Dawn followed the Chaldean method of assigning the thirty-six decans to the seven known planets, starting with Mars in the first decan of Aries and proceeding in the descending order of the planets' speed of motion. Specifically, the Chaldean order is: (1) Saturn, (2) Jupiter, (3) Mars, (4) the Sun, (5) Venus, (6) Mercury, and finally (7) the Moon. As we shall see, these assignments are incorporated into the delineation of the tarot, specifically in the traditional meanings of the pip cards numbered two through ten.

The ancient Greek astrologers were influenced by Pythagorean number symbolism and most likely were aware that the cross formed by the horizon and meridian axes of the horoscope was flanked by the decan rulers in Chaldean order. The two adjacent Mars decans in the east mark the spring equinox at the Ascendant of the natural Aries-rising horoscope. The adjacent Sun and Venus decans at the bottom flank the summer solstice at the *Imum Coeli* (IC). The adjacent Moon and Mercury decans in the west mark the fall equinox at the descendant. Finally, the adjacent Saturn and Jupiter decans at the top straddle the winter solstice at the Midheaven.

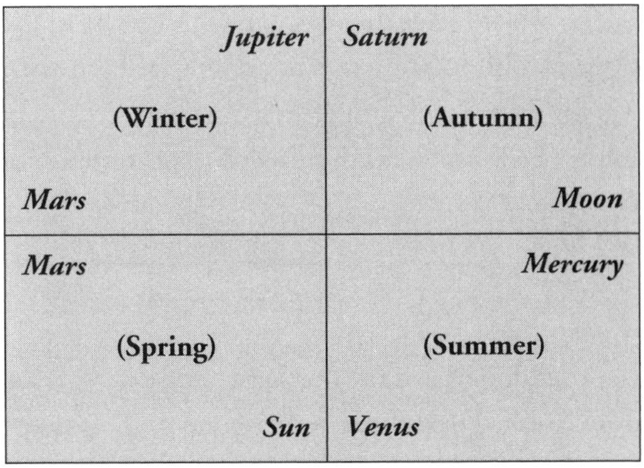

Jupiter **Saturn**	
(Winter) **(Autumn)**	
Mars *Moon*	
Mars *Mercury*	
(Spring) **(Summer)**	
Sun *Venus*	

The central axis or cross that divides the year into four seasons,
flanked by the planetary decan rulers in Chaldean order.

The Four Seasons, the Thirty-Six Decans, and the Tarot

Let's look the meanings attributed to some tarot cards today. As mentioned, nineteenth-century occultists, particularly the Order of the Golden Dawn, relied on astrology to assign meanings to the cards. In the early twentieth century, Waite instructed illustrator Pamela Colman Smith to use her knowledge of astrology to illustrate the pip cards. As you read the following, you may wish to lay out the pip cards being discussed in the pattern of the central horizon/meridian cross in the accompanying diagram. And if you have ever wondered why the Ten of Swords has such a negative reputation in the tarot, you are about to find out.

Spring (0° Aries)
Ten of Cups–Two of Wands
Mars/Pisces–Mars/Aries

The beginning of the cycle of seasons occurs at the spring equinox (around March 21 in the northern hemisphere). It is flanked by two decans: Mars/Pisces and Mars/Aries. The Golden Dawn assigned these decans to the Ten of Cups and the Two of Wands, respectively. At the vernal equinox, day and night are equal in duration, that is, the amounts of light and darkness are in perfect balance. The Waite-Smith Ten of Cups corresponds to the final days of winter just before the spring equinox. It depicts a scene of family harmony beneath a rainbow. The subsequent Two of Wands (the start of spring) shows a young man trying to decide how to engage in the fresh energy of springtime with its many opportunities for new life.

Summer (0° Cancer)
Ten of Swords–Two of Cups
Sun/Gemini–Venus/Cancer

The summer solstice (around June 21 in the northern hemisphere) is flanked by two decans: Sun/Gemini and Venus/Cancer. These decans correspond to the Ten of Swords and the Two of Cups, respectively. At the summer solstice, the Sun appears to stop and change direction from traveling northward to heading south. The summer solstice is the longest day of the year; it has the most sunlight and the smallest amount of darkness.

Leading up to the summer solstice is the Sun decan of Gemini, which is assigned to the Ten of Swords (the ending of spring). The Waite-Smith Ten of Swords shows a dead man with ten swords in his back. Crowley labels this card "Ruin." How could the life-affirming Sun in the mental sign Gemini have such an ominous significance? The answer lies in the astrological symbolism of the summer solstice, the fourth-house cusp, and the opposition of the third to the ninth house of the sun god. In its passage through Gemini, the Sun travels opposite the ninth house (of the sun god) of the natural Aries-rising horoscope. In astrology, opposition indicates stress, disharmony, and conflict. In Gemini, the Sun is weakened by opposing a house where it is treated like a god. As Lincoln observed, "A house divided against itself cannot stand."

Furthermore, on its annual path, the Sun slows down in Gemini and makes a complete stop (symbolic of death) when it reaches the end of Gemini at the summer solstice. The end of Gemini/beginning of Cancer also corresponds to the midnight point of the natural zodiac, that is, the point of maximum darkness in the Sun's daily course around the Earth. The symbolism is again of death. At midnight, the Sun is at its weakest point of the day, the point furthest from high noon where the Sun is at its most powerful. In the natural Aries-rising horoscope, the cusp of the fourth house corresponds to the change from Gemini to Cancer and signifies final endings. At midnight, the Sun has reached rock bottom, its darkest night of the soul. The only way to go from here is upward.

Autumn (0° Libra)
Ten of Pentacles–Two of Swords
Mercury/Virgo–Moon/Libra

The fall equinox (around September 23) is flanked by two decans: Mercury/Virgo and Moon/Libra. These decans correspond to the Ten of Pentacles and the Two of Swords, respectively. At the fall equinox, day and night are equal in duration. There is a perfect balance between light and darkness. The Waite-Smith Ten of Pentacles (the end of summer), which leads up to the fall equinox, depicts a scene of family prosperity, harmony, and contentment. Often this card is taken to mean an inheritance, that is, an equitable distribution of family wealth just as the hours of day and night are equally divided at the equinox. The Two of Swords (the start of autumn), which follows the Ten of Pentacles, depicts a woman carefully pondering equally weighted choices. Etteilla viewed the Two of Swords as a card of friendship, which involves balancing your own needs against those of someone you care about.

Winter (0° Capricorn)
Ten of Wands–Two of Pentacles
Saturn/Sagittarius–Jupiter/Capricorn

The winter solstice (around December 21) is flanked by two decans: Saturn/Sagittarius and Jupiter/Capricorn. These decans correspond to the Ten of Wands and the Two of Pentacles, respectively. The Waite-Smith Ten of Wands (the end of autumn) shows a man burdened with a heavy load. The Sun comes to a complete stop at the end of Sagittarius/beginning of Capricorn. The beginning of winter (0° Capricorn) is the shortest day of the year, with the least sunlight and the greatest amount of darkness. Randy Capricorn is assigned to the Devil trump; the devil, as we all know, is the Prince of Darkness.

Because Saturn rules the last decan of Sagittarius, the Sun in this decan must act in concert with Saturn, whose nature is to weigh down and inhibit. The Ten of Wands thus depicts the fiery ambition of the Sun being weighted down by Saturn. The Ten of Wands, however, is not as negative as the Ten of Swords. Having assumed the heavy load of Saturn in the last decan of Sagittarius, the Sun next moves into the first decan of Capricorn, which is associated with Jupiter and the start of winter. Jupiter represents expansion and abundance, and Capricorn is a sign of responsibilities. Thus, the Jupiter decan of Capricorn (the Two of Pentacles) carries the meaning of juggling a host of duties and responsibilities.

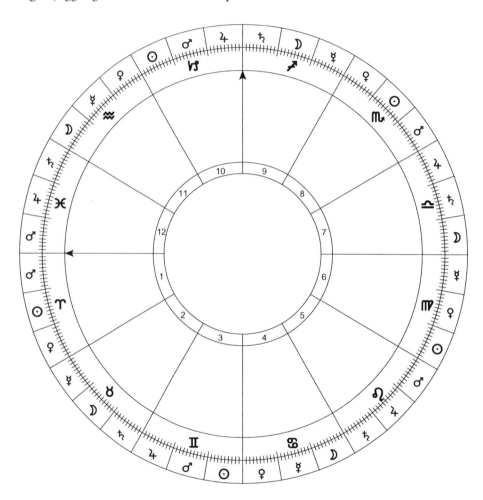

The Chaldean rulers of the thirty-six decans used by the Golden Dawn.

Aleister Crowley and the Thirty-Six Decans

Aleister Crowley (1875–1947), the intellectual creator of the Thoth deck, served as a ghostwriter for the famous New York astrologer Evangeline Adams, who popularized astrology in the United States in the early decades of the twentieth century. Although different systems of correlation exist, Crowley's teachings, based on the Golden Dawn correspondences, have played an important role in my own development as an astrologer and tarot reader. Astrological correlations can add a valuable dimension to tarot reading. Especially useful are the associations between the pip cards numbered two through ten and the thirty-six decans:

- Pips 2, 3, and 4 are assigned in order to the three decans of the cardinal signs (Aries, Cancer, Libra, Capricorn), which symbolize creation, initiation, and action.

- Pips 5, 6, and 7 are assigned in order to the three decans of the fixed signs (Taurus, Leo, Scorpio, Aquarius), which symbolize purpose, consolidation, and stabilization.

- Pips 8, 9, and 10 are assigned in order to the three decans of the mutable signs (Gemini, Virgo, Sagittarius, Pisces), which symbolize adaptation, transition, and letting go.

These relationships are summarized in the accompanying tables.

Pip	WANDS (hot & dry)			Thoth deck
#	**Sign**	**Decan**	**Ruler**	**Name**
2	Aries	1st	Mars	Dominion
3	Aries	2nd	Sun	Virtue
4	Aries	3rd	Venus	Completion
5	Leo	1st	Saturn	Strife
6	Leo	2nd	Jupiter	Victory
7	Leo	3rd	Mars	Valour
8	Sagittarius	1st	Mercury	Swiftness
9	Sagittarius	2nd	Moon	Strength
10	Sagittarius	3rd	Saturn	Oppression

The Decans of the Hot Masculine Phallic Suits (Fire and Air) ctd.

Pip	SWORDS (wet & hot)			Thoth deck
#	**Sign**	**Decan**	**Ruler**	**Name**
2	Libra	1st	Moon	Peace
3	Libra	2nd	Saturn	Sorrow
4	Libra	3rd	Jupiter	Truce
5	Aquarius	1st	Venus	Defeat
6	Aquarius	2nd	Mercury	Science
7	Aquarius	3rd	Moon	Futility
8	Gemini	1st	Jupiter	Interference
9	Gemini	2nd	Mars	Cruelty
10	Gemini	3rd	Sun	Ruin

The Decans of the Cold Feminine Receptive Suits (Water and Earth)

Pip	CUPS (cold & wet)			Thoth deck
#	Sign	Decan	Ruler	Name
2	Cancer	1st	Venus	Love
3	Cancer	2nd	Mercury	Abundance
4	Cancer	3rd	Moon	Luxury
5	Scorpio	1st	Mars	Disappointment
6	Scorpio	2nd	Sun	Pleasure
7	Scorpio	3rd	Venus	Debauch
8	Pisces	1st	Saturn	Indolence
9	Pisces	2nd	Jupiter	Happiness
10	Pisces	3rd	Mars	Satiety

The Decans of the Cold Feminine Receptive Suits (Water and Earth) ctd.

Pip	PENTACLES (dry & cold)			Thoth deck
#	Sign	Decan	Ruler	Name
2	Capricorn	1st	Jupiter	Change
3	Capricorn	2nd	Mars	Work
4	Capricorn	3rd	Sun	Power
5	Taurus	1st	Mercury	Worry
6	Taurus	2nd	Moon	Success
7	Taurus	3rd	Saturn	Failure
8	Virgo	1st	Sun	Prudence
9	Virgo	2nd	Venus	Gain
10	Virgo	3rd	Mercury	Wealth

The Use of Decans in a Spread about Marital Problems

I received an email from a man I'll call Dimitri, who asked for a reading about his marriage. He offered little background information except to say that things were going badly and he was worried about divorce. I did a Celtic Cross spread using the Lo Scarabeo Tarot, their flagship deck that combines three major traditions—Marseille, Waite-Smith, and Crowley-Harris. I noted the time I read his email to be able to cast a horary chart and correlate the astrology with the tarot. Horary astrology is an ancient method of answering questions based on the horoscope for the "birth" of the question in the astrologer's mind. In Dimitri's case, I first did the Celtic Cross spread and studied the horary chart. The order is reversed in the following.

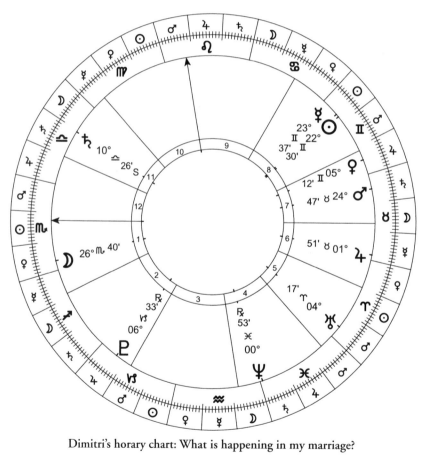

Dimitri's horary chart: What is happening in my marriage?

The Ascendant of Dimitri's horary chart lies in the middle decan of Scorpio. The Ascendant signifies the querent, so Dimitri is represented by Scorpio and its ruler Mars. The Sun governs the middle decan of Scorpio, which Crowley links to the Six of Cups ("Pleasure"). This card makes sense because Dimitri is worried that the pleasure has gone out of his marriage. Modern readers view the Six of Cups as representing nostalgia for the past, also an apt meaning given his concerns.

Dimitri's Ascendant-ruler Mars occupies the third decan of Taurus in the seventh house of marriage. This last decan of Taurus is ruled by Saturn, the planet of harsh reality, which is connected with the Seven of Pentacles ("Failure," according to Crowley). Dimitri is worried about the possible failure of his marriage and the poor "return on his investment" (another meaning of the Seven of Pentacles) in the relationship.

Dimitri's wife is symbolized by the seventh-house cusp (Descendant) in Taurus, ruled by Venus. The seventh-house cusp lies in the second decan of Taurus ("Success"), implying that his wife has the upper hand. Both Mars (Dimitri) and Venus (his wife) occupy Dimitri's seventh house of marriage, but Venus is moving away from Mars, about to leave the seventh house. Symbolically, Dimitri's wife is thinking about leaving the marriage. Venus (his wife) lies in the first decan of Gemini, which is ruled by Jupiter and associated with the Eight of Swords ("Interference"). The symbolism suggests that his wife feels trapped in the marriage and wants to get out.

Venus (his wife) is headed toward a union with the Sun, which rules the tenth house with Leo on its cusp. In horary astrology, the tenth house symbolizes the final ending of the seventh-house marriage (the tenth is the fourth house of endings from the fourth). Again, the chart suggests that his wife (Venus) is thinking of ending the marriage (the Sun).

This interpretation is reinforced by the fact that the Sun occupies and rules the third decan of Gemini, which is associated with the Ten of Sword ("Ruin"), another card of endings. At the end of Gemini, the Sun (representing the end of the marriage) lies at the lowest point of the natural Aries-rising horoscope, so symbolically their marriage has hit bottom. Finally, the cusp of the tenth house, which symbolizes the end of the marriage, lies in the third decan of Leo, ruled by Mars (Dimitri) and associated with the Seven of Wands ("Valour"). Typically the Seven of Wands represents quarreling, opposition, a defensive stance, and victory only in small matters. The fact that Mars (Dimitri) rules the decan occupied by the tenth-house cusp (the end of the marriage) suggests that Dimitri's own behavior will play a major role in the outcome.

Now let's look at the Celtic Cross spread for the same question, which I cast using only upright cards:

1. This covers you: The Magician, trump I

2. This crosses you: Three of Swords

3. This is beneath you: Nine of Swords

4. This is behind you: King of Swords

5. This crowns you: The Emperor, trump IV

6. This lies ahead of you: Two of Wands

7. This represents you in the situation: Page of Pentacles

8. This represents those around you: Eight of Pentacles

9. This is your hopes and fears: Nine of Pentacles

10. This is the likely outcome: The Lovers, trump VI

Not knowing the specifics of his situation, I responded to Dimitri as follows:

This is a generally favorable spread. You have the resources you need to overcome the situation (the Magician). Most likely you are dealing with a lawyer and facing a legal situation (King of Swords), which has caused you much heartache (Three of Swords). The Three of Swords crosses you and suggests separation, sadness, tears, and sometimes a need for surgery. You have experienced stress and anxiety in your marriage for a long time (Nine of Swords). This is the foundation of your question. You may have acted in an insensitive way toward your spouse, and she may now be dealing with an attorney (King of Swords). Your conscious goal is to reestablish yourself in a powerful position (the Emperor) and again become king of your castle. A partnership (Two of Wands) may lie in the near future. This could be a sexual relationship or possibly a business partnership. If it is sexual, it would be important to keep contraception in mind because the Emperor often signifies fatherhood, and the Two of Wands refers to new life that emerges at the start of spring. You may also need to make a decision about what path to take and how you want to live your life in the future (Two of Wands).

You are feeling a need to start over financially (Page of Pentacles). Those around you are advising you to act prudently and proceed step-by-step to get your financial affairs in order (Eight of Pentacles); you will need to work diligently to get back on your feet. You fear that you will have to pay a large alimony, which will make it more difficult for you to achieve your own financial independence (Nine of Pentacles). In the end, you are likely to find a new love, which will restore your happiness (the Lovers), and you may need to choose between reconciliation with your wife and a new love relationship. There are no Cups in the spread but there are many Swords and Pentacles, placing an emphasis on conflict, legalities, and money issues rather than love and intimate relationships.

Dimitri responded that my comments were on target. He provided further details. For a long time, his wife had been complaining that he was not attentive enough, spent too much time on his own leisure interests, and did not provide well for her and the children. Dimitri told her she should not try to change him but should accept him as he is. She responded by consulting a lawyer and asking Dimitri to move out. When a family member unexpectedly needed surgery, Dimitri hoped there would be a thaw in their relationship, but it was short-lived, and he would be facing divorce proceedings in the coming month.

I responded by reviewing the horary chart in terms of the tarot reading. His wife appeared to be moving away from him emotionally, but reconciliation was still possible if he was willing to make the changes she wanted. The Lovers in the outcome position looked favorable. I felt that ultimately he would find emotional satisfaction either with his wife or in a new relationship. Dimitri answered that he and his wife were both very stubborn and neither was likely to modify their positions any time soon. Given their fixed attitudes, divorce seemed likely. The horary Ascendant, signifying Dimitri, lying in the fixed sign Scorpio, and the Descendant (his wife) in the fixed sign Taurus, mirrored their mutual obstinacy, which eventually did lead to divorce.

Using Tarot to Delineate the Ascendant

Let's consider the horoscope of a man born on September 10, 1968, with 18° Capricorn rising and Saturn at 24° Aries. The Ascendant is the most important point in the horoscope, as it represents one's life force and basic motivations. We expect this man to show traits associated with Capricorn and its ruler Saturn, the planet of patience, concentration, hard work, duty, and responsibility. Capricorn rising suggests someone who is practical, ambitious, just, reserved, and conscientious. It often indicates an "emotional and introspective type, a love of music or other forms of art being a common characteristic." [38]

The Ascendant falls in the middle (Mars) decan of Capricorn, which is associated with the Three of Pentacles. Mars is the assertive god of war. This man had spent part of his career in the military and had a fondness for implements of war. The Three of Pentacles suggests someone who is hard-working and proud of his accomplishments.

The Four of Wands:
the Venus decan of Aries
(Universal Tarot).

To further delineate the Ascendant, we consider the placement of the Ascendant-ruler Saturn, which falls in the third decan of Aries. Saturn signifies lessons to be learned and Aries represents assertion and self-reliance. We expect him to have to learn how to assert himself confidently in his life. Because Saturn lies in a decan ruled by Venus, we also expect him to be fond of music and art (ruled by Venus), but these fun activities may cause some consternation because of stern Saturn's influence.

The Golden Dawn assigned the Four of Wands to the Venus decan of Aries, which is occupied by Saturn in his chart. Crowley called the Four of Wands "Completion," and Waite associated this card with a haven of refuge, a country harvest-home, prosperity, harmony, and perfected work. The Four of Wands also refers to stability, rites of passage, social success, marriage, and a happy home. With Saturn as the Ascendant ruler, this man will need to work hard to achieve the promises of the Four of Wands. All this activity takes place in his third house of sib-

---

38   Charles E. O. Carter, *The Principles of Astrology* (London: Quest Books, 1963), p. 77.

lings, kin, education, communication, writing, teaching, transport, and local travel. No doubt these third-house matters play a major role in his life. When I presented this delineation to the person in question, he readily identified with the Four of Wands and thought that the comments accurately described him.

Using the Tarot with a Horary Chart

On Memorial Day of 2011 (Monday, May 30, at 12:10 p.m. EDT), my wife asked me to help her locate her sandals. They were nowhere to be found, and she had looked in all the usual places. As we were discussing the missing sandals, it occurred to her to ask a horary question. In the past, I had been able to find missing items for her using this ancient technique.

The chart indicated that within ten hours she would find the sandals in a location related to the ninth house. This puzzled me because the ninth house has to do with higher education, religion, travel, and the dissemination of ideas; she normally would have placed the sandals in the bedroom closet. I suggested she look in her study, which has travel books and a computer connected to the Internet, all ninth-house associations. No sandals there.

I looked again at the chart and noticed Mercury, the signifier of her sandals, in the Earth sign Taurus. Earth suggests a ground floor location, but her study was upstairs. We looked around the ground floor of our house, and still no sandals. I suggested that we stop looking because the chart indicated that within ten hours she would find them anyway. Around 8 p.m. my wife was in our sunroom, which has a wall of windows and two walls of sliding glass doors. She happened to spot the sandals in a basket we use for the dog's toys. Someone (not me, of course) must have been tidying up and put them there.

The ancients called the ninth "the house of the Sun god." The cusp of the second house, which signifies the missing item, lies in the third decan of Virgo, associated with the tarot Ten of Pentacles. This card traditionally means material gain (she would get her sandals back) and shows a family enjoying a sunny day with their two dogs prominently displayed in the foreground—duh!

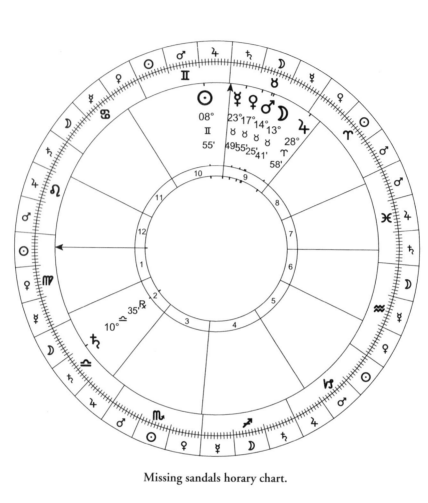

Missing sandals horary chart.

For the astrologically inclined, let me review further details of the horary technique. The Ascendant represents the querent, in this case, my wife. Virgo rises, so my wife is ruled by Mercury. The missing sandals are signified by the second house of possessions, whose cusp is also in Virgo. Thus, the same planet Mercury simultaneously rules both the sandals and my wife, suggesting that she will find them. The cusp of the second house lies in the Mercury decan of Virgo, associated with the Ten of Pentacles.

Mercury (the sandals) resides in the ninth house and in the Saturn decan of Taurus. Its location in an Earth sign suggests the ground floor. Had I envisioned the ninth as the domain of the Sun god, my wife would have found her sandals sooner. Why the delay? Mercury occupies the Saturn decan of Taurus, and Saturn implies delays. The Saturn decan of Taurus is linked to the Seven of Pentacles, which shows a farmer pausing to look at his crop. It is called "Success Unfulfilled" by the Golden Dawn. Why ten hours? In horary astrology, the Moon co-rules the querent. In this chart, the Moon (my wife) in Taurus is distant from Mercury (the sandals) by ten degrees, symbolizing the number of hours that will transpire before the outcome.

If we create a two-card spread using the cards associated with the second house and its ruler, representing the missing item, we get the Ten of Pentacles followed by the Seven of Pentacles. The Ten of Pentacles suggests a sunny location where a family might gather with its dogs and the Seven of Pentacles, a period of patient waiting for the outcome.

Missing sandals two-card spread, left to right:
Ten and Seven of Pentacles *(Universal Tarot).*

How Pixie Chose Images for Her Cards

As mentioned earlier, Waite instructed Pamela ("Pixie") Colman Smith to use her knowledge of astrology to illustrate the cards of each suit. Let me conclude this chapter with a hypothesis on how Pixie did it. Both Waite and Smith were well versed in the celestial art and the teachings of the Golden Dawn. Waite rearranged the major arcana to place Justice as number

XI, exactly in the center of the twenty-one numbered trumps, because he associated Justice with Libra, the sign of balance, which marks the start of autumn at the midpoint of the sun's annual cycle. In older decks, the unnumbered Fool stood outside of the trump cards as an observer. In those decks, Justice was number VIII, not XI. Waite reordered the traditional sequence of the major arcana to make his deck consistent with astrological symbolism.

Except for the Sola Busca tarot of 1491, traditional decks prior to Waite-Smith did not illustrate the pip cards; they looked more like modern playing cards. Pixie studied the Sola Busca deck and selected images to fit with astrological symbolism. The best example of this occurs with the Three of Swords, which is almost identical in both decks. Images that did not correspond astrologically had to be created anew, using the following principles.

In his 1911 text *The Pictorial Key to the Tarot,* Waite used the sequence of the four seasons (spring, summer, autumn, winter) to order the suits of his tarot. The year begins with Aries at the start of spring. Thus, Waite's minor arcana begins with the fiery suit of budding Wands associated with creation, enterprise, and the spark of life. Spring gives way to summer in the sign Cancer. Next in order comes the watery suit of Cups, linked to the world of emotions, joy, and nurturing. Summer yields to autumn at midyear with the Air sign Libra; hence, Cups are followed by Swords, symbolizing intellect, worry, strife, and affliction. Finally, winter arrives with the Earth sign Capricorn, representing tangible reality, worldly ambition, and manifestation on an earthly plane. This developmental sequence terminates in Pisces, the final zodiac sign of winter. The cycle begins anew in Aries with the start of the following springtime.

Not only did Pixie have in mind the symbolism of the four seasons but she also took into account the nature of the zodiac sign and decan associated each pip when she painted her cards. We will elaborate this theme in more detail in the chapter on number symbolism. Suffice it to say here that Pixie used the meanings of the astrological modalities (cardinal, fixed, mutable) in combination with the symbolism of the four seasons, the three decans (beginning, middle, end), and the nature of each tarot suit to stimulate her artistic imagination.

A useful metaphor for the sequence of modalities (and the parallel symbolism of the three decans: first—middle—last) comes from gardening. In the cardinal or first phase, we plant the seeds and clear the weeds to ensure that the seeds have optimal growing conditions. In the fixed or middle phase, we cultivate the garden so the plants can reach full bloom. In the mutable or final phase, we harvest our crops and allow what remains to wither, die, and return nutrients to the soil for the next generation.

In an analogous way, pips 2, 3, and 4 of each suit relate to planting seeds and clearing weeds; decans 2, 3, and 4 are the beginning, middle, and end stages of the initiatory phase of a new season. Pips 5, 6, and 7 relate to cultivating the garden so that what was planted will endure and fully develop; decans 5, 6, and 7 are the beginning, middle, and end stages of a season now established and in full bloom. Finally, pips 8, 9, and 10 relate to harvesting our crops and allowing old plants to wither and die so the next generation can flourish; decans 8, 9, and 10 are the beginning, middle, and end stages of the terminal phase of a season that is fading away to make room for the next season of the year.

As an illustrative example, let's select a card at random from the Waite-Smith deck, say, the Six of Cups, which Etteilla delineates simply as "the past" and Waite describes as "children in an old garden, their cups filled with flowers … a card of the past and of memories, looking back, as for example on childhood; happiness, enjoyment, but coming rather from the past."[39] In Pixie's mind, six refers to the middle or second decan of a fixed sign, which has to do with the desire to consolidate and make enduring. The Sun, which rules this decan, is linked to children and happiness through its connection with Leo and the fifth house. The watery Cups allude to emotions, relationships, and pleasant experiences. The fixed Water sign Scorpio is noted for clinging to past emotions. From such associations, Pixie's imagination generated an image to portray the idea "to make enduring pleasant feelings clung to from the past."

I hope by now the reader is convinced of the tremendous role played by astrology in assigning meanings to cards in the Waite-Smith tradition. In the next chapter, we will look at tarot reversals.

The Six of Cups: Middle decan of the fixed sign Scorpio, ruled by the Sun *(Universal Tarot).*

....

39 Waite, *Pictorial Key* (1959), p. 214.

THREE

The Topsy-Turvy World of Tarot Reversals

Reading Tarot cards is really very easy. All you have to
do is look at the cards and say what you see![40]
WILMA CARROLL, *THE 2-HOUR TAROT TUTOR*

Even experienced tarot readers are puzzled by cards that appear upside-down in a spread. Some readers simply turn all the cards upright, as I did with Jane's reading in chapter one. Robert Place, an advocate of this method, explains: "It is not necessary to confuse the reading with upside-down images."[41] In contrast, Mary Greer has written an entire book devoted exclusively to the many ways to interpret reversed cards.[42] Etteilla found that reversed cards were in common use by Parisian cartomancers in 1753. My own preference has been to allow the cards to fall as they may, and I have never found any hard and fast rule about how to interpret inverted cards. Given the confusion that reversals can engender, turning all the cards upright

40 Wilma Carroll, *The 2-Hour Tarot Tutor* (New York: Berkeley Books, 2004), p. 8.

41 Place, *The Tarot: History, Symbolism*, p. 274.

42 Mary Greer, *The Complete Book of Tarot Reversals* (Woodbury, MN: Llewellyn, 2002).

has great appeal. Nonetheless, many cards, even in their upright position, contain inverted images. It is worthwhile, then, to probe the meaning of reversals in general.

The significance of an inverted card (or of reversed images on an upright card) depends on the particular spread, the position of the flipped card, its modification by surrounding cards, the question posed by the querent, and the intuition of the reader. It is overly simplistic to think that a reversed card simply means the opposite or negation of its upright position, though that is sometimes the case. In common English parlance, the term "reversal" can signify a setback, delay, period of adversity, or a diversion away from one's goal. On the contrary, science fiction movies routinely employ a "reversal of polarity" to save the Earth from utter destruction. Thank God for reversals! Without them, the human race might fail to survive an attack by aliens.

The use of reversals to represent complementary or polar opposites has a long history. The alchemical symbols for Fire and Water are an upright and an inverted equilateral triangle—$\triangle$ and ∇—respectively. The ancient Greeks considered the element Fire masculine, and its symbol was patterned after the male genitalia—an upright phallus rising above two testicles. The inverted image signified Water, a feminine element whose symbol was modeled after the female escutcheon. [43] Historically, dairy herdsmen have used the pubic hair of cattle as a divination tool to foretell the capacity of a cow to give milk on the basis of the shape of the cow's escutcheon. Perhaps amidst the next generation of tarot decks, the Dairy Cow Escutcheon Tarot will make its debut.

A phenomenon in astrology can aid our understanding of tarot reversals. Millennia ago, astrologers viewed the Earth as the center of the universe with the Sun, the Moon, and the planets in orbit around it. We currently theorize that the planets, including Earth, revolve around the Sun. From an Earth-centric viewpoint, the planets appear occasionally to stop and move backward with respect to the Earth. This apparent reversal of direction, called "retrograde motion," is analogous to the inversion of a tarot card and has special interpretive significance.

For example, when fast-moving Mercury (the messenger of the gods) appears to stop and reverse direction in the heavens, miscommunications and misunderstandings capture our awareness. Many astrologers find that people with retrograde planets in their birth charts are inhib-

43 J. C. Segen, *The Dictionary of Modern Medicine* (London: Taylor & Francis, 1992), p. 199: "The patch of pubic hair; the normal female escutcheon is a triangle pointing downward, sharply cut off at the level of the pubic symphysis; the male escutcheon is diamond-shaped with both downward and upward angles."

ited in the outward expression of the energies symbolized by the planets traveling in reverse. Astrologers have also observed that retrograde planets relate to inner psychological characteristics of a person rather than the outer manifestation of the planets in mundane reality. By analogy, a tarot reversal may refer to one's inner life rather than behavior in the outer world.

Just as astrologers regard retrograde planets as symbols of the inhibition of expression of a planet's energy, tarot readers often view inverted cards as signifying blockages in the flow of a card's energy. For example, Philippe Camoin interprets reversed cards as problems in need of resolution. He advises students to draw a "solution card" and place it upright above or below the "problem card." The solution card "indicates the direction to take, what needs to be done to clear the blockage of the 'problem card': it is the card that heals the reversed card."[44]

Camoin also recommends noting which direction the figures on the card are facing and what or whom they are looking at. He is following the lead of the Golden Dawn, which recommends paying careful attention to the direction in which the querent's significator is facing. Whatever lies ahead of the significator is entering the querent's life, and what lies behind belongs to the querent's past.

Donald Tyson is another author whose interpretations make use of reversals and the directionality of figures. Like many tarot readers, Tyson believes that "a card always has the same identity" although its inversion may weaken, obstruct or hinder the action of the card.[45] With regard to court cards, Tyson finds that if the figures on the cards face each other, they are in communication or agreement; but if they face in opposite directions, the people they signify may disagree or be concerned with different issues. If they are facing each other with one upright and other inverted, the individuals represented may be engaged in an argument.[46] And so on.

Teresa Michelson notes that the tarot literature views inverted cards in many ways. For instance, a reversed card can indicate issues that are in some way problematic, extreme, unresolved, blocked, imbalanced, hidden, deceptive, repressed, unhelpful, internalized, unlikely to occur, or better to avoid. Like Camoin, Michelson advocates reading reversed cards as

....

44   Philippe Camoin, "The Law of the Solution Card," http://en.camoin.com/tarot/Law-Solution-Card.html (accessed 11 Apr. 2011).

45   Donald Tyson, *1*2*3 Tarot* (Woodbury, MN: Llewellyn Publications, 2004), p. 7.

46   Tyson, 1*2*3 Tarot, pp. 21–22.

obstacles to overcome and points out that the inverted card actually suggests a solution. For example, a reversed Magician trump suggests that the querent is not adequately tapping into his or her own skills to manage a situation. To avoid confusion, Michelson advises us to state in advance to ourselves and to the querent how we will be interpreting reversed cards in a spread. She believes that "reversed cards can actually mean anything you want them to mean, as long as you specifically define their meaning before you conduct the reading." [47]

Paul Fenton-Smith has a novel approach to reversals. [48] He believes that an inverted card implies a need to return to the previous card of the suit to learn a developmental lesson that has not yet been mastered, much like repeating a grade at school. Like many tarot readers, Fenton-Smith views the pip cards of each suit as a series of lessons to be learned in sequence from one through ten. Rather than viewing a card in isolation, he always considers the card of the same suit that came before it and the one that comes after it. What did the situation depicted on the card evolve from and where is it heading?

Fenton-Smith argues, for example, that if the Ten of Wands is reversed, the querent needs to revisit the lesson of the Nine of Wands in order to move forward. The reversed Ten of Wands might indicate feeling overburdened by responsibilities. By returning to the lesson of the Nine, the querent is able to reassess his priorities and shoulder his burden more effectively. Likewise, if the ace of a suit is reversed, Fenton's advice is to return to the lesson of the ten of that suit. The lessons of the major arcana are also learned in sequential order. Thus, a reversed Moon card, which may indicate troublesome emotions emerging from the unconscious, advises the querent to return to the upright Star "to enjoy the lighter, less threatening aspect of your mind." [49]

In a workshop at the 2011 Readers Studio in New York, James Wells emphasized that the core meaning of a card remains unchanged regardless of its orientation. [50] Wells noted that the inversion of a card may alter the person's experience of the energy of the card. In his view, upright cards represent the essence of the card in a way that is objective, overt, clear, public, conscious, external, accessible, straightforward, and evident. Reversed cards, in contrast, indicate

47 Teresa C. Michelson, *The Complete Tarot Reader* (Woodbury, MN: Llewellyn Publications, 2005) p. 178.

48 Paul Fenton-Smith, *Tarot Masterclass* (Crows Nest, NSW, Australia: Allen & Unwin, 2007), p. 14.

49 Fenton-Smith, *Tarot Masterclass,* p. 223.

50 James Wells, workshop "The Minor Arcana," *2011 Readers Studio* Workshop (New York, 30 Apr. 2011).

the same core meaning of the card but in a manner that is more subjective, covert, private, internal, unconscious, indirect, inaccessible, vague, behind the scenes, or out of awareness.

Applying these ideas to our astrological analogy, we might say that upright cards resemble planets in plain view (near the Midheaven or the high-noon point) of the chart, reflecting our worldly status for all to see. Reversed cards are more like planets in the twelfth house of hidden affairs or planets below the horizon, obscured by the darkness of night. In planetary symbolism, upright cards resemble the Sun and Mars, which are clear, well-defined, evident, and direct, whereas inverted cards are more like the Moon or Neptune, whose effects are powerful but often amorphous, foggy, ill-defined, and unconscious.

While writing this chapter, I had a "eureka moment" during a bathroom break when I realized that we experience reversals daily in the way we hang our toilet paper. Whether a roll of paper is hung so that the first sheet emerges from the top or the bottom is often a matter of controversy. Entire marriages have probably ended in divorce over irreconcilable differences on this issue, and spouses tend to rub each other's noses in it. The purpose and meaning of the toilet paper does not change whether the primary sheet is drawn from the top or the bottom of the roll, but the attitudes and feelings of the end users (no pun intended) run the gamut.

The definitive source of information about this topic is the *Toilet Paper Encyclopedia*.[51] A survey by the makers of the Cottonelle brand of toilet paper found that a whopping 72 percent of users prefer their toilet paper to come over the top, whereas a paltry 28 percent believe retrieving hygienic sheets from the bottom of the roll is morally superior. The ratio of "tops" to "bottoms" in the general population is 5 to 2, at least with regard to preferences for hanging toilet paper. In the end, both toilet paper and tarot cards have the same core function whether upright or reversed, but the user's experience can be vastly different, depending on the orientation of the roll or the card.

Before leaving the topic of reversals, I would like to emphasize that the final outcome depends on how skillfully the querent uses the card's basic meaning. In the following passage, the reader can substitute the words "tarot card" wherever there is a mention of bathroom tissue:

....
51 *The Toilet Paper Encyclopedia,* "toilet paper statistics,"s.vv. http://encyclopedia.toiletpaperworld.com /surveys-stories/toilet-paper-statistics (accessed 1 May 2012).

Toilet paper has a natural curve, a *way of being* that lends itself to certain orientations on the toilet paper spool. If handled with skill and knowledge, it can provide an abundance of both sanitation *and* comfort, quilted together in each square of pillowy ply. If handled with clumsy ignorance, or worse, *carelessness*, it will beset the user with pain, filth, and frustration. [52]

Scatology aside, a study of the tarot cards with reversed images in their upright positions may provide further clues about what reversals mean. In the Waite-Smith deck, some of the trump cards that contain reversed images include the Hanged Man (trump XII), the Devil (trump XV) and the Tower (trump XVI). Among the pip cards, the Swords often display swords being held either upright or reversed. Readers who use different decks may wish to study the cards containing reversals in their deck of their choice.

The Hanged Man is suspended upside-down by his foot from a high *tau* cross. He looks comfortable and serene, as if enjoying the new perspective offered by his reversed position. He is viewing the world with a new orientation and appears gratified by the result. The term "inversion" is sometimes used as a euphemism for homosexuality because it involves a reversal of the usual sexual orientation associated with one's gender at birth. The core desire for sexual union with another person remains unchanged, but the object of the desire changes. In a broader sense, a reversed court card could refer to any type of role reversal. For example, the Empress reversed in a reading for an unemployed husband might represent his role as a stay-at-home dad and a wish to return to the workplace

In early tarot decks, the Hanged Man was called the "Traitor" and lacked the airy-fairy halo of the Waite-Smith deck. Gertrude Moakley made a compelling argument that the prototype for the Hanged Man was Muzio Attendolo Sforza (1369–1424), who opposed the pope and was subsequently humiliated via "shame paintings," which depicted him hanging upside-down by one foot. [53] The vindictive Holy Father ordered paintings of the disloyal "traitor" to be posted on the gates and bridges of Rome.

....

52 "Essential Life Lesson #1: Over is Right, Under is Wrong," *Current Configuration*, http://currentconfig .com/2005/02/22/essential-life-lesson-1-over-is-right-under-is-wrong/ (accessed 4 May 2012).

53 Ronald Decker, *The Esoteric Tarot*, (Wheaton, IL: Quest Books, 2013), p. 109.

Some historians believe the impetus for the Hanged Man was Judas Iscariot who, for thirty pieces of silver, betrayed Jesus with a kiss.[54] According to the Gospel of Matthew (27:5), a guilt-ridden Judas returned the money and hanged himself. An alternate account in the Acts of the Apostles (1:18) has Judas using the silver to buy a field into which he fell headfirst, causing his bowels to gush out. In keeping with the modern symbolism of the Hanged Man, Gnostic Christian texts praise Judas for being the catalyst for Christ's crucifixion, the end result of which was the salvation of humanity. The Gnostic view would consider Judas, as the Hanged Man, a traitor who fulfilled a higher spiritual purpose at great personal expense.

The Hanged Man
(Universal Tarot).

No doubt the Hanged Man can represent a reversal or a "betrayal" of an accepted view. A couple of "Hanged Man" moments spring to mind from my early days in psychiatry in which I was totally taken by surprise. While working in a hospital emergency room, I once interviewed a woman brought in by the police. She had been found wandering the streets, hallucinating and talking nonsense. During our interview, she told me that God had been talking to her and she was simply responding to what God was saying. I asked her what he was saying to her. She became irate and rebuked me, "What makes you think God is a man?" Despite her psychotic state, her keen insight and ability to embrace an alternate worldview forced me to confront my own blind acceptance of the cultural stereotype of a male deity.

Another "Hanged Man" moment occurred when I began working with a "chronic" patient in a psychiatric clinic. He had been treated by other trainees over many years, and every July he had to start anew with a beginning psychiatrist. In our first interview, I asked him how he felt about stopping with his previous doctor and starting with me. He responded: "It's a real pain, doc; every year I have to train a new group of student psychiatrists." His comments offered me a perspective on switching doctors that I would never otherwise have appreciated.

....

54   The name Iscariot may derive from the Latin *sicarius* meaning "dagger-man," a term used to describe a group of Jewish assassins around 40 CE who carried concealed daggers to drive the Romans out of Judea by stabbing them in the back. The Romans considered these Jewish assassins to be traitors, but the Jews revered them as saints. The themes of the Hanged Man card are clearly present in this story.

The Devil
(Universal Tarot).

In the Waite-Smith Devil card (trump XV), the pentagram on his forehead is upside-down. Among other things, pentagrams symbolize the five senses and the human form with its head and four limbs. The humans on the Devil card, having reversed their moral compass, are now slaves to their five senses. In bondage to their material desires, they are heading in a wrong direction. The scene on the Devil card is the antithesis of the image on the Lovers card (trump VI) in which an angel hovers above two young lovers, perhaps symbolizing Adam and Eve.

Both the Devil and the Lovers trumps relate to making choices and joining with someone or something we love. Numerologists note that the number of the Devil trump, XV, reduces to VI (1 + 5 = 6), revealing an underlying numerological connection to the Lovers (VI). In a sense, the Devil is the Lovers trump turned upside-down. The basic drives are the same but the drives are being put to different uses, which lead to different outcomes. Perhaps when we see a card reversed, we should ask ourselves how and to what end we are using the basic energies of the card. What choices are we making about the issues reflected in the card? Are we headed in the right direction?

In the Waite-Smith Tower card (XVI), two people fall head-first from a height after a cataclysmic event. Their ordinary world has been turned upside down, yet this shock enables them to clear away what no longer serves them so they can make a new beginning. The theme is reminiscent of the biblical passage: "Unless a grain of wheat falls into the earth and dies, it remains alone; but if it dies, it bears much fruit."[55]

The Tower
(Universal Tarot).

....

55 John 12:24 (New American Standard Bible).

The message of the Tower is similar to that of the Hanged Man—a new perspective is needed so that we can get on with our life. Clinging to old views does not lead us to what we truly desire. In the Hanged Man, we seek a new way of viewing reality, whereas in the Tower card a new awareness may be thrust upon us. The basic message is a need to look at things differently or suffer the consequences.

These three Waite-Smith trumps with reversed images suggest that when we see an inverted card, we should ask questions such as: Do I need a new way of looking at this situation? What assumptions am I making and are they valid? Am I stuck in a rut or confined by some conventional view? Am I blindly accepting a cultural stereotype? What can I become aware of if I assume a different posture or attitude? Can I reframe the matter in a way that allows me to get on with my life? To what use am I putting the energies of the card? What choices am I making? Do these choices foster or hinder my progress? Am I looking in the right places? Am I going in the right direction? Is something causing a delay in my fulfillment of the promise of the card?

As I weigh this list of questions against the backdrop of how to hang toilet paper, it occurs to me that tarot reversals have to do with how to live a good life. Many authors believe the major arcana are patterned after the old morality plays that served to teach the Fool lessons about behaving with virtue to reach salvation. The four suits of the tarot are often paired with the four cardinal virtues: fortitude (Wands), temperance (Cups), justice (Swords), and prudence (Pentacles). When a card of one of the suit is inverted, we may be inadequately displaying the corresponding virtue. Inverted Wands may be too cowardly for their own good; inverted Cups, too self-indulgent; inverted Swords, too cruel or unfair; and inverted Pentacles, too greedy or imprudent.

Author Gareth Knight has another useful approach to tarot reversals. He teaches his students to meditate on the images in the cards so that they can "build flexible personal images around each archetype."[56] Knight believes that inverted cards modify the normal expression of "the complex of forces that naturally channel through each card."[57] Understanding the nature of the modification depends on the context of the question and the intuition of the reader.

....

56 Knight, *Magical World*, p. 29.

57 Ibid., p. 81.

A one-card reading I did back in 1999 illustrates these principles. On July 16, 1999, John Kennedy, Jr., together with his wife and sister-in-law, were reported missing after taking off in a Piper airplane from a New Jersey airport. The group failed to arrive at its destination on Martha's Vineyard, and a search was begun. Upon hearing the news of the disappearance, I took out my Robin Wood tarot deck and asked what had happened to John Kennedy. I drew the Eight of Wands, *reversed,* and the image of a plane crashing into the ocean immediately came to mind.

The **Eight of Wands reversed** (*Robin Wood Tarot*).

The Waite-Smith Eight of Wands shows eight rods flying rapidly through the air. The Thoth deck labels this card "Swiftness" and associates it with the winged god Mercury who rules the first decan of Sagittarius (incidentally, Kennedy's natal Sun is located in this decan). In the reversed position, the eight rods are still flying rapidly through the air but in the wrong direction! The outcome was alarmingly clear. On July 21, the three bodies were discovered off Martha's Vineyard where the plane had crashed into the Atlantic. The National Transportation Safety Board ruled the cause of the crash to be pilot error, namely, the failure to maintain control of the airplane during a nighttime descent over water as a result of spatial disorientation. Kennedy was not certified to fly a plane by "instruments only." Wands are phallic symbols representative of the element Fire. Upright, Wands signify boldness, daring, and enthusiasm; reversed, they can indicate choices based on an overestimation of one's masculine prowess.

The writings of Aleister Crowley and Israel Regardie suggest that the Golden Dawn occultists did not alter the meaning of a card on the basis of being upright or reversed. The direction in which the figure on the card was facing, however, was of utmost importance. Regarding tarot reversals, Israel Regardie wrote:

In the laying out of the Cards, if any are inverted they must remain so and must not be turned around, as that would alter the direction in which they would be looking. *A card has the same meaning and forces whether right or inverted*... [italics mine].[58]

The Golden Dawn utilized the direction the figure on the card was facing and incorporated that view into the interpretation, especially with reference to the querent's significator.[59] For example, a King looking toward the significator meant that a person or event was about to enter the life of the querent. On the contrary, a King looking away from the significator indicated someone or some situation was leaving the querent behind.

Left to right: The Ace of Swords upright and reversed *(Universal Tarot).*

58 Israel Regardie, *The Golden Dawn* (Woodbury, MN: Llewellyn Publications, 1989), p. 568.
59 According to Paul Huson (*Mystical Origins of the Tarot,* Rochester, VT: Destiny Books, 2004, p. 68), Mathers simply copied Etteilla's divinatory meanings and applied Etteilla's negative interpretations to inverted tarot cards.

In describing the Golden Dawn's Ace of Swords, Regardie comments that reversing the sword *per se* changes its meaning from a heavenly force (an upright blade pointed toward the heavens) to an equally powerful but diabolical one (a blade pointing downward toward the underworld). To be clear, Regardie is referring to an inversion of the *image* of the sword on the card rather than a reversal of the card itself: "Raised upward, it invokes the Divine Crown of Spiritual Brightness. But reversed it is the invocation of demonic force and becomes a fearfully evil symbol…"[60] Regardie's equation of *upright* with *heavenly*, and *reversed* with *diabolical*, may be a source of the practice of giving a negative meaning to a card that has been inverted.

The Seven of Swords
(Universal Tarot).

In the upright Waite-Smith Seven of Swords (inspired by the 1491 Sola Busca deck), all the swords appear "reversed" (pointing downward). Nancy Shavick interprets the Seven of Swords as doing your own thing and establishing "your own beliefs, thoughts, morality, general philosophy, and preferred life-style."[61] In Colman Smith's drawing, a man tiptoes away from a camp. He is the only character in the entire Waite-Smith deck to carry swords by their blades in his bare hands, certainly not the proper or "upright" way to transport a cache of swords. In a matter of time, the sharp blades will slice open his hands, and his effort will not endure. This is the artist's way of depicting the Golden Dawn meaning of "unstable effort" for this card. In a reading I once did for a man, the Seven of Swords came up when his heart went into atrial fibrillation and could only make an unstable effort to pump blood.

60 Regardie, *The Golden Dawn*, p. 543.

61 Nancy Shavick, *Traveling the Royal Road: Mastering the Tarot* (New York: Berkley Books, 1992), pp. 68–69.

Swords are associated with the element Air, which symbolizes one's thoughts, communication, philosophy, beliefs, and plans. Upright swords can represent ideas that are publicly shared. Reversed swords, in contrast, can symbolize personal or private thoughts about how to live one's life. Shavick concurs with Gail Fairfield's view that upright swords signify "ways in which you manifest your philosophy in obvious, public forms" whereas reversed swords symbolize the "personal philosophical ideas and ideals [that] lie beneath the opinions you publicly express."[62]

Tarot readers thus need to consider not only the orientation of the cards but also whether the images on the cards appear upright or reversed. Inverting a card may convert a public image into a private one, and vice versa. An upright sword can represent a shared view of a matter, while an inverted sword can signify private beliefs at variance with the norms of society. Similarly, an upright sword might represent what someone tells you to your face whereas an inverted sword might signify what they say behind your back.

Unlike Regardie and the Golden Dawn, many authors give distinct meanings to reversed cards. In his classic 1911 text, Arthur Edward Waite provided separate meanings for upright and reversed cards. Etteilla (Jean-Baptiste Alliette, 1738–1791), one of the first to popularize the tarot, also gave distinct meanings to inverted cards. Etteilla claimed to have learned tarot card reading from an Italian cartomancer in the mid-1700s, which makes sense since the tarot appears to have originated in northern Italy. His first book—*Etteilla, or How to Entertain Yourself with a Deck of Cards* (1770)—contained instructions for using regular playing cards for divination.[63] Etteilla included meanings for each playing card, both upright and inverted. He also introduced the use of a special card, which he called an *Etteilla*, to be used as a significator. One of his teachers, a card reader from Piedmont, Italy, apparently introduced him to the tarot in 1757; in his 1785 text, Etteilla extended his method of card reading to the tarot deck. Modern tarot decks in the Golden Dawn and Waite-Smith traditions have largely abandoned Etteilla's divinatory meanings, but author Paul Huson has produced an attractive deck, The Dame's Fortune Wheel Tarot, based on Etteilla's interpretations from 1785.

....

62 Gail Fairfield, *Choice Centered Tarot* (Smithville, IN: Ramp Creek Publishing, 1984), p. 42.

63 The original title in French is *Etteilla, ou manière de se récréer avec un jeu de cartes.*

Having reviewed a bit of the history of tarot reversals, let's turn our attention to some readings that illustrate reversals.

Kevin's Celtic Cross Spreads with Reversals

Kevin, an American living in Japan, consulted me about a spread regarding finding a job. During his career, Kevin had spent time in Japan, where he met and married a Japanese woman. They settled in America and started a family. Kevin worked as an IT professional until he got laid off in the economic slump of 2009. After nine months of searching for new employment in the States, Kevin and his wife decided to relocate with their children to Japan where his wife had a promise of employment.

Unable to speak Japanese, Kevin stayed home and took care of the children. Nonetheless, he wanted to support his family and eventually heard of an opening for an English teacher. He was nervous about applying because he was not trained as a teacher, but he decided to give it a try and asked the tarot what to expect. Kevin cast a Celtic Cross spread, which contained three reversals:

1. This covers you: Knight of Swords

2. This crosses you: Three of Cups

3. This is beneath you: Two of Wands

4. This is behind you: Eight of Wands

5. This crowns you: Judgment

6. This is ahead of you: The Devil (reversed)

7. This represents you in this situation: The Empress (reversed)

8. This is those around you—your environment: The Magician

9. This is your hopes and fears: Queen of Pentacles (reversed)

10. This is the likely outcome: Two of Cups

Kevin was puzzled by the layout and asked my opinion. He explained: "My biggest concern is not ever having taught before. Will my lack of those teaching skills hinder my progress here?"

It was late evening when his email arrived but I didn't want to leave Kevin hanging, so I sent a quick reply:

Just a few initial impressions: The Knight of Swords covering you and the Eight of Wands in the recent-past position suggest that you are feeling rushed. The Two of Wands beneath you suggests that you are looking to the future and planning how you want to proceed. The Judgment trump above you suggests a new beginning as a potential or optimal outcome. The Two of Cups in the likely outcome position is positive and suggests emotional fulfillment. The Queen of Pentacles *reversed*, I think, is your anxiety about teaching. Pentacles have to do with learning and study. Queens are good teachers. You may be worried that you won't do the job as well as a professional teacher. The Queen may even be a teacher that you had in the past and would like to emulate. This is in the hopes and fears position.

I'm not sure what to make of the Devil *reversed* in the near-future position. The Devil usually has to do with material desires and temptations. The Empress in position 7 signifies you at the time of the reading. The Empress and the Queen of Pentacles have a lot in common. They are both fertile, productive women. The Magician represents those around you. It's a nice card and suggests that people in your environment have the skills and know-how to help you get what you want. The Three of Cups crossing you is some kind of challenge. Maybe you will have to give up some good times with your family to be able to teach. Maybe the pay won't be what you would like and life will have less of a festive tone.

Kevin responded:

The spread now makes more sense: The Knight of Swords may indicate the manager who will interview me. Judgment could mean being accepted by this manager. The Three of Cups crossing may suggest that I will lose a lot of free time and the enjoyment of spending so much time with my kids? Or maybe it's less pay or fewer hours than I would like?

The Eight of Wands may suggest that I feel rushed to find a job as the money is running out. I would have loved to get back into IT, as the money is so much better, but not being able to speak and read Japanese is a huge obstacle here. Teaching for me represents the best way of getting out into the community, making friends, and interacting with the Japanese. I am excited to learn about their culture and language.

The reversed Devil for me is very clear. It indicates a release from bondage. I feel imprisoned here. Day to day I'm virtually housebound; I have very little interaction with people except for going to the gym and the grocery store. If I can teach, I will have much more interaction with the community.

Both the reversed Empress and Queen of Pentacles could show my doubtful state of mind and worries. The Two of Cups could mean a contract, a business deal, or mutual respect (perhaps with the Knight of Swords?).

Three adjacent cards, left to right: The Devil, the Empress, and the Queen of Pentacles, all reversed *(Universal Tarot)*.

Kevin and I continued to correspond as his situation progressed. He learned that he had to pass a rigorous grammar exam to qualify for the job—a test that we thought might be represented by the Devil card. The devil is in the details, after all. Because Kevin had put on some weight, he needed to buy some new clothes for the interview. Perhaps this was indicated by the Devil trump with its oversized naked demon and characters in need of clothing.

Finally, the day of the interview came. Kevin found the grammar test grueling; he was sure he failed. He also learned that the job required at least four months of teaching experience, but he had none. Still, Kevin was quite dismayed when he learned that he did not get the job. In his email he wrote:

> There were two interviewers in the room. They conferred with each other every step of the way. So this answers the final Two of Cups (card 10) in my mind. The decision was between them.

In retrospect, the Two of Cups (the Lord of Love) was puzzling as the outcome card in a spread about a job interview. Because neither of us had a clear sense of what it meant, it would have been wise to follow Waite's advice and "open up" the Two of Cups by using it as a significator for a new Celtic Cross spread. Because the Two of Cups has such a positive meaning for one's emotional life, it seemed that, whether or not he got the job, the outcome would involve a growth experience that would bring Kevin and his wife closer together. When Kevin wrote to the interviewers to ask for feedback, they responded with encouraging and helpful advice about how to find employment in Japan.

About a week after being rejected for the job, Kevin wrote that he had now done a follow-up Celtic Cross spread in which he asked the tarot to "give [him] career advice." Essentially Kevin "opened up" the Two of Cups (card 10) of his original spread. The accompanying table lists the cards in his original and clarification spreads.

Kevin's Celtic Cross Spreads about Finding a Job			
Position	Meaning	Original Spread	Clarifying Spread
0	Significator card	None chosen	Two of Cups (implied)
1	This covers you	Knight of Swords	Four of Wands, reversed
2	This crosses you	Three of Cups	Queen of Pentacles
3	This is beneath you	Two of Wands	Six of Swords
4	This is behind you	Eight of Wands	Six of Cups, reversed
5	This crowns you	Judgment	Ace of Swords
6	This is ahead of you	The Devil, reversed	Seven of Swords, reversed
7	This represents you	The Empress, reversed	Four of Cups, reversed
8	This is those around you	The Magician	Five of Pentacles
9	This is your hopes & fears	Queen of Pentacles, reversed	The Tower
10	This is the likely outcome	Two of Cups	The Fool

As a result of our discussions, Kevin was feeling more confident about his ability to read the Celtic Cross. He offered the following interpretation:

OK, so this reading is a pretty good one. It really seemed to capture the situation to a T. I reasoned that it is showing delayed but impending success (Four of Wands) and the need to manage meager finances (Queen of Pentacles and Five of Pentacles). The sneak-thief reversed (Seven of Swords) may suggest the need to get creative to solve my difficulties, hence the need for training and volunteering. The Tower scares me. Drastic change? More bad luck? The Fool and the Ace of Swords would indicate to me the start of a new enterprise or job, and great adventure. Oh yes and the Four of Cups seems to indicate the end of discontent, coming out of my shell, and new ideas, new people, and new experiences.

After pondering his experience in the job interview in light of both tarot spreads, Kevin decided to pursue training and become a certified teacher. This is an example of an excellent use of the tarot. Kevin asked a pressing question and used his intuition to relate the cards to his personal life. In doing so, he was able to see his situation in a new light, clarify his thinking, take responsibility for his life, and make an important decision about how to go forward.

Kevin volunteered to teach English at his daughter's kindergarten and pursued contacts in his local community with people who might be able to guide him toward gaining teaching experience. The Two of Cups (the Lord of Love) in position 10 of the original spread now made more sense. The outcome of the job interview was not that he would be offered a job (as both of us were hoping) but that he would volunteer his services as a teacher out of the goodness of his heart. The second spread, which clarified the Two of Cups, advised him to become like the Fool and embark on the new adventure of learning how to teach.

The Subset of Reversed Cards in Catherine's Reading

If the cards have been thoroughly mixed and randomly inverted, roughly 50 percent of them will appear upside-down in a spread. If only a small number of cards turn out to be reversed, they will stand out from the upright cards. In such a case, the tarot may be asking us to pay special attention to the few cards that have assumed postures so distinct from the rest. It is as if the inverted cards are forming a vocal minority (or better said, a "visual minority") that demands our attention. Perhaps reading this noticeable subset of cards as a separate spread will yield important information. Consider the following example.

In their book *Beyond the Celtic Cross*, Paul Hughes-Barlow and Catherine Chapman discuss a reading in which three of the ten cards in the Celtic Cross spread are inverted:

- Card 1: The Heart of the Matter—The Eight of Cups, reversed

- Card 4: The Recent Past—The Three of Swords, reversed

- Card 10: The Likely Outcome—The Knight of Wands, reversed

The querent is Catherine (who coauthored the book). She had asked, "Will I meet the man of my dreams?"

I have omitted the seven upright cards of the Celtic Cross spread to focus exclusively on the three cards that are highlighted by being reversed.

The Eight of Cups reversed *(Universal Tarot).*

Card 1

The Eight of Cups reversed "covers" her. The Waite-Smith Eight of Cups shows someone walking away from an unsatisfying situation in search of something better to satisfy her needs. A simplistic interpretation of the reversal would be that she ought not withdraw from the situation but rather should stay with it. My gut feeling about the reversal of this card, however, is that she has already moved on and is unsure about what to do next, or is questioning what will happen as a result.

Card 4

The reversed Three of Swords (a heart pierced by three swords) occupies the recent-past position, suggesting that she has already experienced emotional pain, perhaps due to a loss or breakup and is trying to get over it (a possible meaning of the reversal). I have found it useful to consider the astrological attributions of the Golden Dawn and Crowley's Thoth deck. Though this process can be a bit tedious, it often produces deeper insights into a situation, so bear with me as I go through some astrological details.

Crowley labels the Three of Swords "Sorrow" and links it to the planet Saturn, which rules the second decan of Libra (the sign of partnerships, ruled by Venus, the goddess of love). Saturn, as a symbol, has both "light" and "shadow" aspects.

The Three of Swords reversed *(Universal Tarot).*

It can mean hardship and loss but also seriousness and responsibility. Perhaps the Three of Swords (Saturn in Libra), reversed, refers to getting serious (Saturn) about matters of the heart (Libra). In Regardie's view, the individual swords on the reversed Three of Swords card all have their blades pointing upward and thus possess a "heavenly" rather than a "diabolical" significance.

With regard to the covering card in position 1, Crowley calls the Eight of Cups "Indolence" and associates it with the Saturn decan of Pisces (roughly the last ten days of winter). Saturn slows things down; Pisces is the emotional Water sign that ends the zodiac cycle. Catherine may feel stuck, as if immersed in stagnant water, a metaphor for her emotional state. The querent is suffering from a double dose of Saturn in the reversed cards of this spread, as the leaden planet appears in the cards of positions 1 and 4.

Indolence (the Eight of Cups) suggests inactivity and inertia; there is something she needs to overcome so she can get moving again. Saturn is a planet of restriction, delay, and deprivation. Pisces is associated with dreams, visions, fantasies, and illusions. The reversed Eight of Cups may mean that she needs to overcome her inertia and step out of the world of illusion to find the man of her dreams. It also raises the question of whether that man might simply be a Piscean fantasy. Undoing her indolence and getting unstuck from illusion are the means of escape from this winter of her discontent.

Card 10

The outcome card is the fiery Knight of Wands reversed. Catherine is looking for a man of the nature of Fire—vigorous, enthusiastic, creative, intelligent, and spirited—a chivalric Knight in shining armor. His reversal poses several questions. Will there be a delay in her meeting this Knight? Is Catherine pursuing a dream instead of a reality? Does she need to adopt a more realistic view of who she wants to be with if she wishes to find him? Is she looking right at him, perhaps unaware that he is the man she

The Knight of Wands reversed *(Universal Tarot).*

has been seeking all along? Does she need to "reverse her polarity" and view him in a different light to be able to see who he really is?

Crowley associates the Knight of Wands with the fiery part of Fire and assigns it to the last decan of Scorpio and the first two decans of Sagittarius. Catherine's fiery Knight may be a person with his natal Sun or Ascendant in one of these signs, particularly the span from 20 degrees Scorpio to 20 degrees Sagittarius, or he may be someone with the characteristics of these signs (emotionally intense, ardent, adventurous, philosophical, broad-minded, living at a distance, of foreign background, etc.).

The Waite-Smith Knight of Wands is a dashing young man in search of adventure on his galloping steed. His Sagittarian motto could easily come from *Star Trek,* "to explore strange new worlds, to seek out new life and new civilizations, to boldly go where no man has gone before." The peripatetic Knight of Wands often implies swift movement, travel and even a change of residence. Could the reversal of this Knight in Catherine's reading mean she will need to endure a stressful move to find him? Reversals can mean hardship, delay, or extra effort to reach one's goals.

Although I regard Knights as youthful adult men, Arthur Waite, designer of this deck, identifies Knights as men older than forty. If we follow Waite's lead, the man of her dreams could be someone older, possibly of fair complexion with yellow or auburn hair and blue eyes.[64] Modern authors tend to ignore Waite's age attributions (Kings as men under forty, and Knights older than forty years old) and instead view Knights as adult men who are younger than Kings. Could the reversal of this Knight be saying something about his age? Should we reverse Waite's age attribution and regard him as a man under forty? Could he be of a different age than the man she is imagining?

If card 10 indicates the timing of the outcome, the Knight of Wands highlights the period from November 13 through December 12 in the tropical zodiac preferred by Western astrologers.[65] If the reversal of card 10 refers to timing, it could be telling us to use the sidereal zodiac, which begins at the start of the *constellation* Aries. This was the preferred method of MacGregor Mathers of the Golden Dawn.

....

64   Waite, *Pictorial Key* (1959), p. 299.

65   These dates are based on the tropical zodiac. The Golden Dawn, however, used the sidereal zodiac, which gives the dates for the Knight of Wands as December 6 through January 5. *See* appendix C.

In the sidereal zodiac, Catherine would have to wait until the period from December 6 to January 5 to meet her man, or perhaps her Knight of Wands was born during that period. Another possibility is that the inverted card in the outcome position points to a time directly across the zodiac wheel. The Knight of Wands, reversed, may refer to its zodiacal complement, the Knight of Swords, who rules the period from May 11 to June 10 in the tropical zodiac.

We might also say that the inversion of the Knight of Wands as an outcome card could mean that events will not manifest as she expects. The upside-down Knight could refer to someone she knows in another capacity but whose relationship to her will "turn" into something different, namely, the romance that she desires when he "flips" for her. The Waite-Smith Knight of Wands is riding his horse toward the querent, which means that in the inverted position he is riding away from her. How will they meet if he is speeding in the opposite direction? Will she have to go after him? And if she does pursue him, where will he lead her?

If the Knight of Wands refers to a person involved in the outcome, there may be clues about him in the pip cards associated with the decans covered by this Knight in the Golden Dawn system (*see* appendix C):

- Third decan of Scorpio—Seven of Cups—Venus in Scorpio—"Debauch"

- First decan of Sagittarius—Eight of Wands—Mercury in Sagittarius—"Swiftness"

- Second decan of Sagittarius—Nine of Wands—Moon in Sagittarius—"Strength"

Which, if any, of these three cards is significant? Perhaps they all are. I find court cards in the outcome position difficult to interpret and usually ask the querent to draw a clarification card. Waite recommended doing an entirely new Celtic Cross spread using the court card as significator to clarify its role in the outcome. In this case, Catherine drew trump XIV Temperance, upright, as her clarification card: a harmonious blending of opposites. A good omen for a relationship!

Temperance
(Universal Tarot).

Temperance is linked to Sagittarius, a Fire sign ruled by Jupiter, spanning the period from November 23 to December 21 of each year. Again we have a reference to Sagittarius. Will her Knight be born under Sagittarius or have a personality like the man-horse archer of the zodiac? The Temperance trump also suggests a need for patience, moderation, and inner balance. The English word "temperance" comes from the Latin *temperare* meaning "to mingle in due proportion."

On the Waite-Smith card, the archangel Michael is pouring water from one chalice to another. He has one foot in water and the other foot on earth and wears a solar disc (a Fire symbol) on his forehead. Presumably the angel is blending diverse elements into a harmonious amalgam as part of his mission to guide souls on their path to spiritual enlightenment. This path is seen on the lower left of the card leading from the pond to the mountaintop where the sun is beaming.

Temperance is a positive card linked with Sagittarius whose ruler, Jupiter, is called the Greater Benefic. Because Temperance is a major arcana card, most readers regard it as highly significant. The reversed Knight of Wands as the outcome card, in combination with Temperance as its clarifying card, suggests that Catherine may indeed find the Sagittarian man of her dreams, someone with whom she can blend harmoniously (Temperance), but only after a period of patient waiting (Temperance combined with the inverted Knight of Wands).

Reversals and Astrology

Let me further elaborate my ideas about reversals and the astrological associations of the tarot cards. This material can be a bit detailed; if astrology is not your cup of tea, feel free to skip this section. By way of review, the horoscope is divided into twelve houses, six below the horizon and six above. Each house is paired symbolically with its opposite house directly across the wheel. Thus, the first house represents the self and the opposite seventh house signifies one's intimate partner or complementary other. The second house refers to one's money and income and the complementary eighth house (across the wheel) stands for the money of others. This pattern continues around the wheel in such a way that each house below the horizon "looks at" its complementary house above the horizon, and vice versa.

What does the pairing of the zodiacal houses have to do with tarot reversals? Occultists, especially the Order of the Golden Dawn, have linked each tarot card to a planet or a position on the zodiac circle. Thus, each card "looks at" a complementary card directly across the horoscope wheel. A detailed account of this idea of the complementarity of opposing signs and houses can be found in my 1991 book on horary astrology. [66]

Upright cards on one side of the wheel appear to be upside-down with respect to their complementary cards that lie opposite. Wands look at Swords of the same number (for pip cards) or rank (for court cards), and vice versa. Cup cards look at Pentacles of the same number or rank, and vice versa. The major arcana, which are associated with the twelve zodiacal signs, look at the trump card linked to the opposite zodiac sign. The trump cards that are paired with planets are an exception in that the World (Saturn) looks at not one but two other trump cards: the Sun (associated with the sun) and the High Priestess (associated with the moon).

The accompanying tables illustrate the complementary sets formed by the trump cards associated with the zodiacal signs and planets by the Golden Dawn. Readers who use alternative systems to correlate astrology with the tarot will need to work out their own sets of correspondences. The Golden Dawn attributions are widely accepted—and in my experience give good results in practice.

....
66   Anthony Louis, *Horary Astrology Plain and Simple: The History and Practice of Astro-Divination* (St. Paul, MN: Llewellyn Publications, 1991).

Complementary Major Arcana Viewing Each Other Across the Zodiac	
Major Arcana & Zodiac Sign ←	→ Major Arcana & Zodiac Sign
The Emperor–Aries	Justice–Libra
The Hierophant–Taurus	Death–Scorpio
The Lovers–Gemini	Temperance–Sagittarius
The Chariot–Cancer	The Devil–Capricorn
Strength–Leo	The Star–Aquarius
The Hermit–Virgo	The Moon–Pisces

Planetary Pairings of Major Arcana by Sign Rulerships	
Trump–(Planet & signs ruled):	Looks at:
The Sun–(Sun, ruler of Leo)	The World–(Saturn, ruler of Aquarius)
The High Priestess–(Moon, ruler of Cancer)	The World–(Saturn, ruler of Capricorn)
The Magician–(Mercury, ruler of Gemini & Virgo)	The Wheel of Fortune–(Jupiter, ruler of Sagittarius & Pisces)
The Empress–(Venus, ruler of Taurus & Libra)	The Tower–(Mars, ruler of Scorpio & Aries)
The Tower–(Mars, ruler of Aries & Scorpio)	The Empress–(Venus, ruler of Libra & Taurus)
The Wheel of Fortune–(Jupiter, ruler of Sagittarius & Pisces)	The Magician–(Mercury, ruler of Gemini & Virgo)
The World–(Saturn, ruler of Capricorn & Aquarius)	The High Priestess & The Sun–(Moon, ruler of Cancer and Sun, ruler of Leo)

If my hunch is correct, reversed cards refer us to their complementary partners across the zodiac, perhaps as a way to resolve the upset implied by the original reversal. If we apply Camoin's idea that reversals indicate problems to be solved, then a reversed card's complement across the wheel may hold a key to the solution. In Catherine's spread we see:

Catherine's "covering" card, the reversed Eight of Cups ("Indolence"), is linked to the Saturn decan of Pisces. Its complement across the wheel, the Eight of Pentacles, is called "Prudence" in the Thoth deck and refers to the Sun decan of Virgo. The Eight of Pentacles suggests the diligent use of one's creative skills in one's daily work. The gloom of Saturn in the Eight of Cups is turned upside-down and connects us with the light of the Sun in the Eight of Pentacles.

In the recent-past position, the reversed Three of Swords ("Sorrow," the Saturn decan of Libra) looks across the wheel at the Three of Wands, which the Thoth deck names "Virtue" and links to the Sun decan of Aries. The Three of Wands refers to an enterprising project in collaboration with others. Again, the gloom of Saturn (Three of Swords) is reversed and points toward the brightness of the Sun (Three of Wands). If she wants to deal with the heaviness of these reversed cards of the original spread, she may need to apply the lessons of their upright complementary cards (Eight of Pentacles, Three of Wands) across the wheel.

The Knight of Wands reversed, in the outcome position, refers us to his zodiacal complement, the Knight of Swords, which rules the first decan of Gemini and the two decans immediately adjacent to it (from 20 degrees Taurus to 20 degrees Gemini). Gemini loves to write and communicate. The Knight of Swords is often a man of haste, acerbic wit, and clever intellect. Perhaps such a man will be important in the outcome.

The clarification card, Temperance (associated with Sagittarius), though not reversed, is linked to its complementary trump across the wheel, the Lovers (associated with Gemini). Sagittarius has to do with higher learning, publishing, prophecy, and affairs at a distance. Its complementary sign Gemini is connected with communications, writing, study, and transport. In the modern world, these complementary signs can refer to the Internet, which allows us to communicate at a distance. One outcome of Catherine's question was to write a book with Paul Hughes-Barlow via e-mails over the Internet. The themes of writing, publishing, learning, teaching, and distant communication were all present in her outcome.

To avoid stealing Catherine's thunder, I refer the reader to *Beyond the Celtic Cross* for the remainder of the story. It is a book worth reading for a deeper understanding of the use of Golden Dawn techniques such as card counting and elemental dignities for interpreting the cards.

Tarot Reversals and the Heartless Queen of Hearts

The Queen of Cups reversed *(Universal Tarot).*

Let me conclude this chapter with an "aha!" moment I experienced when a Google search about the tarot and playing cards made reference to Lewis Carroll's Queen of Hearts. The reader will recall that the Queen of Hearts from *Alice in Wonderland* (1865), a member of the royalty of a pack of playing cards, behaved anything but like a queen with a heart. "The Queen had only one way of settling all difficulties, great or small. 'Off with his head!' she said, without even looking round." [67] No doubt this Queen of Hearts must be "reversed" in the deck she governs. As one would expect, the Queen of Hearts is ruled by her emotions. The love symbolized by "hearts" is inverted and manifests as wrath and vindictiveness. Fortunately, the Queen's demands to execute anyone who displeases her are rarely carried out. When his wife is not looking, the "upright" King of Hearts remains true to his nature and pardons those whom the Queen has condemned to death.

---

67   Lewis Carrol, *Alice in Wonderland,* http://www.gutenberg.org/files/11/11-h/11-h.htm#link2HCH0008, chapter VIII, (accessed 3 Sep 2012).

FOUR

The Role of Intuition in Divination

Write down the thoughts of the moment. Those that come
unsought for are commonly the most valuable. [68]
SIR FRANCIS BACON (1561–1626)

Intuition is such an important topic in tarot divination that this entire chapter is devoted to it. As Francis Bacon suggests, thoughts that come unbidden during a reading are often the most telling. Author Richard Roberts was so impressed by the significance of intuition that he advised his readers to throw away their interpretation books. [69] Please don't throw away this book, however.

One has to wonder why "unsought for thoughts" during a reading are so revealing. Whence do these unbidden ideas arise? Modern authors usually attribute the origin of such thoughts to empathy, intuition, and the subconscious mind. The traditional view, which spans several millennia, holds that such flashes of insight are gifts from a higher power such as angelic beings,

....

68   Francis Bacon, *Quotations Book*, http://quotationsbook.com/quote/32163/ (accessed 13 Jun. 2012).
69   Richard Roberts, *The Original Tarot & You* (Berwick, ME: Ibis Press, 2005), p. 108.

spirits of deceased ancestors, or the gods themselves. Even Aleister Crowley, the "wickedest man in the world," recited the Golden Dawn invocation prior to each tarot divination:

> I invoke thee, IAO, that thou wilt send HRU, the great Angel that is set over the operation of this secret Wisdom, to lay his hand invisibly upon these consecrated cards of art, that thereby we may obtain true knowledge of hidden things to the glory of thine ineffable name. [70]

May HRU also watch over the writing of this book. Amen.

The 9/11 Phenomenon

On Tuesday, September 11, 2001, New York City suffered a devastating attack that destroyed the World Trade Center. Many tarot enthusiasts saw an uncanny resemblance to the image in tarot trump XVI, the Tower. Exactly one year later on Wednesday, September 11, 2002, many New Yorkers played "911" in the daily lottery. As luck would have it, selecting "911" produced a winning number on the first anniversary of the attack. According to lottery officials, a total of 5,631 people played "911" that day. Instead of winning a million dollar jackpot, each lucky player took home only $500—still not bad for a one dollar investment.

Some critics, believing that anything science can't explain must *de facto* be mere coincidence, were quick to point out that the odds of such an occurrence were one in 500 and concluded that the incident was mere chance. [71] Individuals not blinded by the prejudices of modern science wondered whether some type of collective consciousness, world spirit or psychokinetic effect might have been at play. Is it possible that large numbers of people sharing the same intention at the same moment in time can affect material reality? Could the community of tarot readers, for instance, by using the same divinatory interpretation of a card determine its meaning at a particular point in history?

....

70   James Wasserman, *Instructions for Aleister Crowley's Thoth Tarot Deck* (Stamford, CT: U.S. Games Systems, 1978), pp. 7–8.

71   John Allen Paulos, "The 9-11 Lottery Coincidence,"ABC News, http://abcnews.go.com/Technology /WhosCounting/story?id=97845&page=1 (accessed 5 Jan. 2012).

Whatever your take on the New York lottery number on the first anniversary of 9/11, such meaningful coincidences form the basis of divination. Priests in ancient China used to read the cracks in heated tortoise shells and oxen bones to prognosticate for the emperor. This method of divination was codified into the Chinese classic, the *I Ching*. Generations of ancient Babylonian priests recorded the positions of the stars on slabs of clay (the Mul-Apin tablets) and noted regular correspondences between the positions of heavenly bodies and events on Earth. Observations of such celestial "coincidences" with mundane events became the basis for astrology. Carl Jung coined the term "synchronicities" to refer to events that appear to have meaningful connections but no apparent causal link and no scientific explanation. With the rise of modern science, the collective worldview has shifted to scientific materialism, and the truths of the occult disciplines are regarded as mere products of chance.

Not everyone is as narrow-minded as the dogmatists who reject esoteric disciplines on the basis of their circular reasoning: anything science can't explain must be coincidence because science can't explain it. A notable exception is Wolfgang Pauli (1900–1958), who won a Nobel Prize in physics for his contributions to quantum mechanics. Pauli even has a psychokinetic effect named after him, the so-called Pauli effect named after his alleged ability to disrupt experimental equipment merely by being in the vicinity. (My wife seems to have a similar effect on our home computer.) Pauli was aware of his reputation and appeared delighted whenever the effect manifested. He was also noted for his investigations into parapsychology and his collaboration with Carl Jung on the concept of synchronicity.

To the best of my knowledge, Pauli did not study the tarot, but there are some tarot readers who believe that psychokinesis is involved in the ordering of the cards to match the concerns of the querent. Pauli did, however, collaborate with Jung on a paper about "confirmation bias," the idea that humans seek out and embrace information that confirms their preconceptions while they avoid and reject data that runs counter to their beliefs. Five centuries ago, Sir Francis Bacon called attention to confirmation bias when he wrote: "The general root of superstition [is that] men observe when things hit, and not when they miss, and commit to memory the one, and pass over the other."[72] Besides its role in superstition, confirmation bias is seen in the arguments of skeptics who begin with the belief that "there is nothing to astrology" or that "tarot

....

72   "Sir Francis Bacon," *Today in Science History,* http://www.todayinsci.com/B/Bacon_Francis/Bacon Francis-Quotations.htm (accessed 15 Nov. 2011).

can't possibly work" and then search for studies to support their claims while rejecting evidence to the contrary.

Littlewood's "Miracle a Month" Law

Cambridge University professor J. E. Littlewood has attempted to discredit the idea of synchronicity by cleverly redefining the term "miracle" and then arguing that miracles, and presumably synchronistic events, can be explained on the basis of chance alone.[73] According to Littlewood's smart-ass logic, a miracle is an event of special significance that occurs at a rate of one in a million. Assuming that people experience one new event every second of their waking life, the good professor calculates that on average we can expect to experience a miracle once every thirty-five days, or about ten times a year. Hence "miracles" are commonplace occurrences, entirely predictable by the laws of probability, and the universe is devoid of meaningful coincidence. We must thank Professor Littlewood for his nifty exercise in confirmation bias.

Remembering Forward

Anyone who practices divination would do well to ponder the writings of Lewis Carroll, who offers us a "Hanged Man" view of reality. Carl Jung, in discussing the idea of synchronicity, was especially fascinated by *Through the Looking Glass,* in which the White Queen says to Alice: "It's a poor sort of memory that only works backwards."[74] The Queen was insisting that memory can work both forward and backward. Alice found the Queen's words disconcerting and protested that she could not remember things before they happen. Apparently Alice had never learned to read an astrological chart or a tarot spread, which would have allowed her to "remember forward."

Tarot and Intuition—the Devil Is in the Details

In my view, the tarot is a tool that enables us to tap into our intuition. As such, tarot cards are similar to any other tool used for divination such as the planets of astrology, the hexagrams of the *I Ching*, the figures of geomantic divination, tortoise shells, runes, playing cards, the Bible

....

73   John E. Littlewood, *Littlewood's Miscellany* (Cambridge, UK: Cambridge University Press, 1986).

74   Lewis Carroll, *Through the Looking Glass,* http://www.gutenberg.org/files/12/12-h/12-h.htm #link2HCH0005 chapter V, (accessed 3 Sep. 2012).

passages of bibliomancy, and so on. As tarot readers, we use the cards intuitively to trigger associations derived from our life history, the metaphorical meanings of our native language and culture, our own study and theoretical understanding of the cards, and our personal as well as the collective unconscious. The advice of my psychotherapy mentor applies equally well to tarot: "Learn as much as you can about the various schools of psychotherapy, but when you sit down with your patient, take off your theoretical spectacles and simply listen attentively to what the patient tells you."

Humpty Dumpty and the Tarot

The following passage by Lewis Carroll, in which Humpty Dumpty and Alice discuss birthdays, is relevant to our understanding of the tarot. As the scene begins, Humpty has just asked Alice how many days of the year do *not* correspond to her birthday. Alice replies that there are 364 such days, but Humpty looks doubtful. Alice does the arithmetic on her memo pad and hands it to Humpty, who takes the notebook and looks at it upside-down. The dialogue continues:

Humpty Dumpty took the book and looked at it carefully. "That seems to be done right—" he began.

"You're holding it upside down!" Alice interrupted.

"To be sure I was!" Humpty Dumpty said gaily as she turned it round for him. "I thought it looked a little queer. As I was saying, that **seems** to be done right—though I haven't time to look it over thoroughly just now—and that shows that there are three hundred and sixty-four days when you might get un-birthday presents—"

"Certainly," said Alice.

"And only **one** for birthday presents, you know. There's glory for you!"

"I don't know what you mean by 'glory'," Alice said.

Humpty Dumpty smiled contemptuously. "Of course you don't—till I tell you. I meant 'there's a nice knock-down argument for you!'"

"But 'glory' doesn't mean 'a nice knock-down argument'," Alice objected.

"When *I* use a word," Humpty Dumpty said, in rather a scornful tone, "it means just what I choose it to mean—neither more nor less."

"The question is," said Alice, "whether you *can* make words mean so many different things."

"The question is," said Humpty Dumpty, "which is to be master—that's all." [75]

Reading without Theoretical Spectacles

Two "Humpty Dumpty moments" during tarot readings come to mind. Both readings took place within several weeks of each other and are presented here in the order in which they occurred. My hope is that pondering what went on in these readings will give us further insight into what the tarot is and how it functions.

William's Reading

A young man, whom I will call William, asked for a reading about romance. The majority of questions asked of the tarot seem to be about love, money, or health. William, a college student, told me he was gay and had recently experienced a painful breakup that left him feeling quite lonely. He was hoping to start a new relationship and felt attracted to a fellow student, Derek. William wanted to know whether it was advisable to pursue the relationship.

In the course of the consultation, William revealed that he knew little about Derek and asked whether the cards could tell him something about his potential beau. William's request prompted a brief discussion of tarot ethics and the oft-repeated idea that you should not ask anything about someone who is not there and has not given permission. [76] In my view, the wording of this precept is misleading; it is too absolute and does not pierce to the ethical heart of the issue.

Tarot readings almost always deal with how other people relate to us and influence our lives. For example, card 8 of the Celtic Cross spread *always* asks about the people in the querent's surroundings, yet readers do not regard it as unethical to read the card in position 8 of the Celtic Cross. [77] If it were unethical for tarot readers to ask about "someone who is not there

....

75   Lewis Carroll, *Through the Looking Glass* http://www.gutenberg.org/files/12/12-h/12-h.htm Chapter VI (accessed 3 Sep. 2012).

76   Pollack, *Tarot Wisdom,* p. 439.

77   Rachel Pollack (*Tarot Wisdom*, p. 450) reads card 8 of the Celtic Cross as "others" … "the impact of other people on the situation" … "the influence of another person" …

and has not given permission," then the Celtic Cross spread would have to be abolished from the repertoire of tarot spreads.

In reality, tarot readings consist of our *subjective* interpretations of the cards. The tarot is not a nanny-cam, and card readings carry no weight as evidence in a court of law. The ethical issue lies in the intent of the reader, in how the reader and querent intend to use the information. Does the querent wish to "spy" on an unsuspecting victim, or is the intention rather to gather impressions from the cards that will help the querent make a wise decision without harm to the person inquired about? With this principle in mind, I asked William to draw two cards to clarify what he might need to know about Derek to help him make a wise decision.

William selected the Eight of Pentacles and the Five of Wands from the Llewellyn Tarot by Anna-Marie Ferguson. I commented that the young man in the Eight of Pentacles appeared diligent and hard-working, which suggested that Derek was most likely a serious and dedicated student. William confirmed that Derek came from a poor family and was working hard to complete his college degree to escape poverty. In fact, Derek was so busy with his studies that William was worried he might not be available for romance.

Left to right: Eight of Pentacles, Five of Wands *(Llewellyn Tarot).*

The next card, the Five of Wands, depicts five young men engaged in some kind of game or competition. I asked William whether Derek played sports (the answer was no) and added that based on this card, Derek appeared to be an active, energetic, and competitive person. As I looked at the Five of Wands, the young man on the left side of Ferguson's drawing, with his rod erect, stood out prominently in my field of vision. Knowing that William was seeking a romantic relationship with Derek, I intuitively saw the image as a young man engaging sexually with his peers (not a standard interpretation of this card, though Wands certainly symbolize the phallus), and I asked William whether Derek was known to date many other men. William said his college friends had warned him that in fact Derek had a reputation for sleeping around. One of William's worries was that his last relationship had ended badly because of his partner's infidelity. He was looking for a new and faithful boyfriend, not a one-night stand.

The next "insight" took me by surprise. As William was telling his story, I continued to look at the two cards he had selected about what he needed to know about Derek. Suddenly the two cards merged in my mind with the single thought "a young man hard at work, having sex with multiple partners." This idea seemed to well up from my subconscious. Recalling that Derek was struggling with money for tuition, I asked whether it was possible that Derek might be selling himself for sex. William said he had heard rumors to that effect and hoped they were not true.

Ace of Wands sideways with top of wand
pointing to the right *(Universal Tarot).*

An aside: not long after William's reading, a friend asked my opinion about the Ace of Wands falling perfectly *sideways* out of the deck while her querent, a young male college student, was shuffling the cards. With the phallic significance of Wands fresh in mind, I responded, "Looks like something he might do in the privacy of his dorm room." My friend chuckled and said she had not thought of it that way.

To return to William's reading, he next asked whether Derek would be faithful if they got involved. To answer the question, I had William draw another card. He selected Ferguson's Seven of Swords, a card that Crowley links to the Moon decan of Aquarius and calls "Futility." The Golden Dawn labels this card "Unstable Effort." The inconstant watery Moon is out of its element in detached Aquarius, an Air sign; emotional matters do not fare well here. In many decks, the man on the Seven of Swords looks rather sneaky, and some authors link this card to a secret love affair.

The Seven of Swords
(Llewellyn Tarot).

In Ferguson's drawing, an older man is walking toward the left of the card, burdened by five swords in a sack on his back (like the bundle in the Ten of Wands). One sword lies on the ground in front of his feet. A small boy trails behind the man and drags the seventh sword by its hilt; the youngster looks rather lost and bewildered. William, who was himself a student of the tarot, commented: "Isn't that a card of theft and betrayal? That answers my question, then."

William used the impressions he gleaned from the cards to make an important decision. He wanted to avoid betrayal in love and concluded that involvement with Derek might well prove unwise. William had no intention of repeating to anyone what he deduced from the cards nor did he want to harm Derek in any way. Although we had inquired about Derek in this reading without Derek's knowledge or consent, I believe we did it in an ethical manner.

A Reading about a Reluctant Author

This second reading is a four-card spread that I "invented" on the spot to answer a specific set of questions. When trying to address a particular issue, it is often helpful to divide the concern into a list of specific questions and draw a card to answer each of them. At the time of this spread, I was writing an article and wanted to quote a passage by an author I did not know personally. Fortunately, I was able to get the author's email from a mutual acquaintance. My colleague cautioned me that this author might be reluctant to give a stranger permission to quote his work. Nonetheless, I sent an email to explain my intention and request permission. In the process, I drew four cards from the Lo Scarabeo Universal Tarot deck to answer the specific questions:

1. What past influences underlie the author's reluctance to give permission?

2. What are the present influences?

3. What specifically is the author worried about?

4. How should I best conduct myself in this matter?

The cards I selected and my interpretations are as follows:

(1) **The Ace of Pentacles:** The publication I wanted to quote from had been very successful.

(2) **The Queen of Wands:** this author was proud of what he had written and, as ruler of his domain, wanted to remain in control. The black cat standing in front of the Queen stood out to me intuitively as being important in this particular reading. I began to think about black cats and their meanings in our culture. Maybe this author was afraid to let a black cat cross his path (this is not a standard meaning of this card). Could he fear that sharing his work would bring him bad luck?

Left to right: Ace of Pentacles upright, Queen of Wands upright,
Seven of Swords reversed, Nine of Pentacles upright *(Universal Tarot)*.

(3) **The Seven of Swords, reversed:** This reading took place several weeks after the above reading about William and Derek, and the Seven of Swords was fresh in my mind. I thought of William's fear of being betrayed and wondered whether the author had similar worries about me. William had called the Seven of Swords "a card of theft and betrayal." Did the author view my request as potentially sneaky or underhanded? Did he think I would try to rob something of his that didn't belong to me? Would he conclude that my intentions were "heavenly" (upward-pointing swords) or "diabolical" (downward-pointing swords)?

(4) **The Nine of Pentacles:** My first thoughts went to the astrological attribution of the Nine of Pentacles to the second decan of Virgo, the location of my natal Sun. Perhaps I was being advised to simply be myself and let my own Sun shine. In other words, I didn't need to do anything special to get permission. The woman in the Nine of Pentacles stands in a lush and beautiful garden. Whether this author would say yes or no, there were other authors whose work I might cite in my article.

The outcome was that I heard from the author and we had a pleasant exchange of ideas. He agreed to give permission to quote him and explained his initial reluctance. A couple of years earlier, a similar request had come from another author. They exchanged emails and he thought a relationship of trust had developed, but then the other author published a scathing attack on his work. He felt betrayed and "once burned, twice shy." It occurs to me now that the black cat on the Queen of Wands is the color of something charred and may symbolize the author feeling "burned" by the underhanded behavior of his erstwhile literary "friend."

In reflecting on these two readings, we see that there is indeed a reliance on the general meanings of the cards as derived from occult theories and the experiences of the tarot community. In an individual reading, however, the interaction with the querent is paramount. The reader must tie together the general meanings of the cards with the specific concerns of the querent, who is in dynamic interaction with the tarot reader at that moment.

In addition, the intuitive flashes of insight that come unbidden are often the most valuable. The most significant clues may lie in the "unimportant" details of the cards: things you have seen a thousand times but never perceived in this way before. How often have we seen Wands next to Pentacles in a spread without thinking of a male prostitute? How often has the black cat of the Queen of Wands made us think that she is worried about bad luck crossing her path or being burned by a friend? No theoretical link between the cards and the planets, the Kabbalah, the *I Ching*, geomancy, etc., will provide these glimpses into the querent's concerns. Only intuition in the context of the moment can offer such insights.

During the process, tarot readers must take off their theoretical spectacles and listen attentively to what the querent and the cards are telling them. The standard textbook meanings may be of little use in this movement from general to specific. In the words of Raven Willowmagic: "When you throw the cards, take a look at the spread. What are you drawn to, where do your eyes want to go? Trust this. Often it is the most important thing, or the root of the reading."[78]

Tarot's Dirty Little Secret

Humpty Dumpty's comments about "words" apply equally well to the tarot. Consider the following interaction between Alice and Madame Dumpty (Humpty's wife) during a tarot reading:

"I don't know what you mean by the Seven of Swords," Alice said.

Madame Dumpty smiled contemptuously. "Of course you don't—till I tell you."

"When *I* read a card," Madame Dumpty said, in rather a scornful tone, "it means just what I choose it to mean—neither more nor less."

....

78   Raven Willowmagic, *Tarot Tips of the Trade: Tying It All Together* (self-published, 2010), Kindle edition.

"The question is," said Alice, "whether you *can* make the cards mean so many different things."

"The question is," said Madame Dumpty, "which is to be master—that's all."

If truth be told, the tarot is simply a pack of cards painted with interesting images. These scenes depict aspects of the human condition with a rich historical and cultural significance. In any given spread, the meanings of the tarot images are the creative constructions of the minds of the reader and the querent, reflecting jointly on the cards. There is no "right answer" about what a particular card means in a specific reading. To be sure, there is a flow from general to specific, but at its core, interpreting the tarot is a dynamic process that involves searching for meaningful coincidences (synchronicities) between the images on the cards and the concerns of the querent. In this sense, tarot reading is part of our perennial search for meaning, eloquently articulated by Victor Frankl in his book *Man's Search for Meaning*. As Frankl put it, "What matters, therefore, is not the meaning of life in general, but rather the specific meaning of a person's life at a given moment."[79]

the universe wished to drive home Frankl's point about the "specific meaning of a ʻe at a given moment," at the time I happened to be reading two books by different ho each were commenting on the Seven of Swords. Janina Renée told a story about of Swords appearing in her personal readings on days when she goes to the library up "walking out the door with a load of books in my arms," much like the man on the ith card with his arms full of swords.[80] In contrast, Marcus Katz and Tali Goodwin the "flip title," or reversed meaning, of the Seven of Swords is: "A Man Borrowing Books from a Library."[81]

Both authors are right, of course. Katz and Goodwin suggest that the upright Seven of Swords means the opposite of borrowing books from a library; in contrast, the upright card precedes a productive trip to the library for Janina Renée. What's sauce for the goose may not be sauce for the gander. "When **I** read a card," Madame Dumpty said, in rather a scornful tone,

....
79   Viktor E. Frankl, *Man's Search for Meaning* (New York: Washington Square Press, 1963), p. 171.
80   Janina Renée, *Tarot for a New Generation* (Woodbury, MN: Llewellyn Publications, 2003), p. 38.
81   Marcus Katz and Tali Goodwin, *Tarot Flip* (Keswick, Cumbria, UK: Forge Press, 2010), p. 19.

"it means just what I choose it to mean—neither more nor less." Or perhaps a core meaning of the Seven of Swords (whether upright or flipped) has something to do with borrowing for personal use something that does not really belong to us.

A Humpty Dumpty Moment in the Tarot Literature

In his classic text, *Tarot & You*, Richard Roberts presents transcripts of readings he did for clients between 1970 and 1971. His is the only book I know of that presents in such detail the verbatim interchange that occurs between reader and client. Although Roberts is well acquainted with the standard meanings of the cards, he repeatedly stresses the need to "take off your theoretical spectacles" (my words), attend to the images on the cards, associate to the details that most activate your intuition, and pay attention to impressions that well up from the unconscious at the time of the reading.

Roberts warns readers not to feel bound by the interpretations in textbooks. His volume is replete with examples in which small details on a card, as distinct from the card's textbook meanings, hold the key to understanding the concerns of the querent. He customarily reads the cards without knowing the specific concerns of the inquirer and allows the cards to lead him to it.

Left to right: Death next to the Six of Pentacles with five reversed cards *(Universal Tarot)*.
In the original spread, the seven cards are all laid out in the same row.

In November 1970, Roberts did a "Three Sevens" spread for a man in his late fifties. This spread consists of three rows (past, present, and future) of seven cards, laid in order from right to left. In this reading, the first five cards of the middle row (the present) all fell upside-down. Roberts took these five inverted cards to mean that the querent was feeling worried about the recent setbacks. The final two cards of the middle row (the two on the left) were Death and the Six of Pentacles, both upright. The weighing scale on the Six of Pentacles seemed to form a bridge between the five reversed cards and Death (the leftmost card). Thus, the cards in the middle row, symbolizing the querent's present circumstances, began with setbacks (reversed cards) and ended with Death, with the Six of Pentacles acting as a bridge between them.

The Six of Pentacles typically suggests benevolent giving, but Roberts's intuition led him to a nontraditional interpretation. He concluded that the querent must be worried about a health matter (the five inverted cards) that could potentially result in death (trump XIII). Let's try to decipher the workings of Robert's mind, in which he intuitively combines astrology with tarot.

Roberts was using the Aquarian Tarot, a Waite-Smith clone, in which the Six of Pentacles shows a man looking at two pentacles on a table before him. Prominent beneath these two pentacles is the name SIX OF PENTACLES in capital letters. Roberts' eyes were immediately drawn to two details on the Six of Pentacles: the weighing scale and the word "Six." His intuition associated the "Six" on the card with the astrological sixth house of illness.

My hunch is that, in addition, Roberts had unconsciously registered that the Six of Pentacles occupied position 13 of this spread, the number of the Death trump. The bottom row contained seven cards and the middle row began with five reversed cards (7 + 5 = 12); hence, the Six of Pentacles appeared in position 13. His intuition was accurate because the querent admitted he was facing heart surgery and was worried about dying. In commenting on his insights, Roberts said: "It's really funny the way I'll get the same card in two different readings, and each time my consciousness will focus on whatever there is in the card that holds a clue."[82]

----

82 Roberts, *The Original Tarot*, p. 131.

In contrast to Roberts's intuitive interpretation, most textbooks relate the Six of Pentacles to the Moon's exaltation in Taurus, suggesting good health, generosity, harmony in the workplace, material success, and so on. Author Michele Morgan, however, advises readers to "hold off on the traditional meanings of the cards until your intuition has had a chance to comment."[83] By following his intuition, Roberts read the Six of Pentacles in this spread as health problems that could result in death. Quite a contrast! "The question is," said Alice, "whether you **can** make the cards mean so many different things." In fact, good tarot readers are able to make the cards mean so many different things because of their personal familiarity with each card after years of experience and their intuitions at the time of the reading.

Tarot Sarcasm

Not only can tarot cards potentially represent the opposite of their accepted meanings, but at times the tarot even seems to employ sarcasm. For example, one day my wife phoned to say that a restaurant near her office was offering for take-out one of my favorite dishes, stuffed peppers. Because this establishment generally has excellent food, she planned to bring some peppers home for dinner. I was pleasantly surprised but skeptical because in my experience, good stuffed peppers are extremely hard to find.[84]

I happened to have a tarot deck at the office and for the fun of it drew a single card while pondering the question, "Will I enjoy the stuffed peppers tonight?" What to my wondering eyes should appear but the Three of Swords with all three swords pointing diabolically downward! Not exactly Santa Claus. What could this card have to do with stuffed peppers? Would I be disappointed with their quality? Would I need a sword to cut into them? Would the peppers make me sick, cause indigestion or even the need for surgery? The image on the Waite-Smith card shows three swords piercing a bright red heart suspended amidst rain and storm clouds. Would the peppers be colored red like the heart? I concluded that the tarot was most likely saying I would be somehow disappointed. The Three of Swords looks quite dramatic, as if to imply I would end up heartbroken. Etteilla delineates this card as "separation."

---

83   Michele Morgan, *A Magical Course in Tarot* (Berkeley, CA: Conari Press, 2002), p. 39.

84   My favorite stuffed pepper recipe is from Michele Scicolone, *The Italian Slow Cooker* (New York: Houghton Mifflin Harcourt, 2010), p. 136.

At the end of the day, I drove home anticipating delicious red stuffed peppers for dinner. Shortly thereafter my wife arrived and informed me that when she went to buy the take-out, the attendant told her there was a mistake on the menu and no stuffed peppers were available. Rats! As the card had warned me, I felt disappointed although not exactly heartbroken. The Three of Swords, after all, does indicate separation from something or someone you love. I did feel, however, that the tarot was having a laugh at my expense. Ask a stupid question, get a stupid answer. There I was suffering separation anxiety from my beloved stuffed peppers, and red ones at that. And to make matters worse, I was the victim of tarot sarcasm!

The Three of Swords
(Classic Tarot).

Dion Fortune and the Intuitive School of Tarot Reading

As I ponder the readings in this chapter, I realize that my own approach, like that of Richard Roberts, belongs in large measure to the intuitive school. While acknowledging the generally accepted meanings of the cards, the intuitive reader pays most attention to the specific details and interrelationships among the cards as they relate to the concerns of the querent at the time of the reading. A major proponent of the intuitive method was the British occultist Dion Fortune (aka Violet Mary Firth Evans, 1890–1946). Her advice on learning the tarot can be found in a handful of invaluable paragraphs of *Practical Occultism in Daily Life*, first published in 1935.[85]

In Fortune's view, tarot reading is not an intellectual exercise based on memorizing the meanings of cards. Instead, she recommends starting with a deck that attracts you and proceeding to learn the basic meanings given by the designer or the deck. The suggested keywords form a scaffold upon which you can get "in touch with the forces behind the cards" to build your own set of meanings.[86] Regarding the deck that you choose, Robert Place advises

....

85   Fortune, *Practical Occultism*, pp. 40–42.
86   Ibid.

readers to "become familiar with the unique qualities of the deck and always interpret the cards based on the pictures that are presented by the designer." [87]

The next and most important step is to spend considerable time becoming familiar with the cards on a gut level. Fortune advises students to carry the cards with them, handle the cards frequently, sleep with them under the pillow, and ponder whenever possible the meaning of the images in light of the deck's instruction booklet to get in touch with the significance of the cards. Details on each card merely act as reminders of the underlying meaning, which you need to discover and register on a deep feeling level. Only after you have gathered your own personal associations and can perceive significance in each card are you ready to use the deck for divination.

Why Does the Tarot Give Wrong Answers?

Authors have differing views about why the tarot occasionally gives an inaccurate response. One possibility is that the answer does indeed lie in the cards but for some reason we are not able to perceive it. Perhaps our minds are clouded by some hope or expectation so that we can't read the cards objectively. Maybe some emotional state is hampering our intuition. Most tarot readers have had the experience of the cards primarily reflecting the emotional state of a distraught querent. For example, I once did a Celtic Cross reading for an unemployed man who asked about finding a job. Six of the ten cards of the spread were Cups, and the other cards had more to do with personal relationships than with business and enterprise. Although he asked overtly about a job, he had recently ended a relationship and his mind was primarily focused on finding a new love interest rather than work.

Another reason for a poor tarot reading is that we may have not shuffled the deck adequately. Many authors regard the shuffling process as a reverential, almost prayerful experience. The querent must relax and clear his or her mind and then shuffle with the intent that the cards will end up in a meaningful arrangement that will answer the question. The mixing is to stop when the querent's intuition signals that the amount of shuffling has been sufficient to produce a valid divination. The querent will know intuitively when the time is right. The

....

87 Place, *The Tarot: History, Symbolism,* p. 277.

sincerity of intent is crucial because intent generates meaning. Shuffling without sincerity of intent merely produces a random arrangement devoid of meaning. Garbage in, garbage out.

This discussion reminds me of a book I read years ago about the nature of scientific evidence. The author was commenting about how people who believe in ghosts are the very ones who claim to see them whereas nonbelievers never report ghost sightings. The scientific stance is that the viewers' beliefs distort their perceptions so that they misperceive what they see as ghosts, which as every scientist knows *a priori,* simply don't exist. The author then asks a provocative question: what if the universe is structured in such a way that a belief in ghosts is a necessary precondition for being able to see them? To rephrase the question in terms of the tarot: what if a tarot divination is valid only if the querent shuffles the deck with the sincere intent to receive a valid answer from the cards?

Considerations before Judgment

Unlike many authors, Dion Fortune recommends performing a divination three times, taking careful notes in the process. If certain cards or card suits recur in each of the three divinations, then the reading most likely conveys a valid message. If the three divinations have little in common and appear unconnected thematically, then the tarot is probably not providing a meaningful answer and the divination should be abandoned.

Dion Fortune's method resembles the "considerations before judgment" of horary astrology. These considerations help the astrologer to determine whether the querent is sincere and whether the horoscope will provide a meaningful response. A similar screening process exists in astrological geomancy. If the geomantic figures *rubeus* or *cauda draconis* appear in the first house of the divination, the chart should be discarded as invalid. Why should the tarot be exempt from similar considerations before judgment?

Dion Fortune's advice to perform three consecutive divinations to test the validity of a particular spread is evident in a card reading described by the German poet Johann Wolfgang von Goethe (1749–1832). Goethe was familiar with esoteric topics and even begins his autobiography with a mention of his natal horoscope. As a young man of twenty, Goethe took dance lessons from a French instructor who had two daughters close to his age, the elder of whom had a crush on him. One day the younger daughter invited a "woman who tells fortunes from the cards" (most likely a French cartomancer) to do a reading about her prospects for love. The younger girl was pleased to learn from the cards that an absent boyfriend still cared for her. Her older sister, however, was distraught when the cards revealed that she was in love with someone [obviously Goethe] who would not requite her love because his heart belonged to another. Observing the older sister's distress, the reader cast a second spread for clarification. Goethe describes the cards that appeared in the spread; my comments appear in brackets:

> The fair one [the card signifying the girl with a crush on Goethe] stood, not only more lonely, but surrounded with many sorrows [cards signifying sadness]. Her lover [the card signifying her beloved] had moved somewhat farther, and the intervening figures nearer. The old woman wished to try it a third time, in hopes of a better prospect; but the beautiful girl could restrain herself no longer,—she broke out into uncontrollable weeping, her lovely bosom heaved violently, she turned round, and rushed out of the room. [88]

In this case, the second divination confirmed the original reading and gave further information. The girl's distress over never having Goethe as her lover made a third reading impossible. Her reaction is a warning to future generations of card readers to use empathy and tact when interpreting the cards. Presumably none of us would want our clients to break into uncontrollable weeping and run from the room as a result of our readings.

Despite Dion Fortune's advice to confirm a reading's validity, there is a widely held belief within the tarot community that, unlike people, the cards never lie. If the tarot's message appears confusing or inaccurate, the fault lies in the reader and not the cards! To my mind, this view is similar to the Pope's claim of infallibility. Didn't an infallible pope condemn Galileo for his observations that contradicted the biblical view of the solar system? With due respect for the nuns who taught me, I simply can't accept the notion of infallibility in any field, be it religion, science, politics, or tarot.

Not long ago on the tarot website of Douglas Gibb, I came across a reading his friend did for a woman who was worried about her husband's health. [89] Gibb does not mention which

88 Goethe, *Autobiography, Truth and Fiction Relating to My Life*, Gottingen Edition, trans. by John Oxenford, Project Gutenberg, EBook #5733, 2004, http://www.gutenberg.org/ebooks/5733 (accessed 15 Nov 2012).

89 Douglas Gibb, "Three Techniques for Reading Health Questions," March 12, 2010, *Tarot Eon*, http://taroteon .com/tips-and-techniques/three-techniques-for-reading-health-questions/ (accessed 5 May 2011).

deck his friend used, but the outcome card was the Empress, and other cards included the Star and the Sun. Given such positive major arcana cards, Gibb's friend predicted a full recovery. To his friend's chagrin, the woman's husband died. Oops! How to account for this apparently wrong answer? After pondering the matter, Gibb and his friend concluded that the Empress signified a woman of means, whose wealth was dependent on the inheritance left by her deceased husband.

The majority of tarot readers appear to hold the view that the tarot always gives a valid answer but our ability to understand the cards may be lacking. Teresa Michelson advises tarot readers to "trust that the universe, or your guides, or your subconscious will choose the right cards even if your conscious mind has no idea what they mean."[90] Michelson's advice is generally sound, but is it always valid? Although Gibb and his friend may be correct in their retrospective analysis of the meaning of the Empress, is it possible that this particular divination simply gave a wrong answer?

The Empress
(Universal Tarot).

Perhaps it is heresy, but I believe that the tarot does not always tell the truth. Fortunately I am not alone in this view, so I'll have a partner when I burn at the stake. Author Janina Renée notes that tarot readings are sometimes inaccurate. She advises readers to view the tarot "as a tool to be used in combination with your own intuition and common sense, in helping you to analyze all your possibilities."[91] Gareth Knight goes so far as to say that the "Spirit of the Tarot" sometimes *deliberately* misleads us to foster our growth and teach us lessons for our own good.[92] A crafty little devil, that tarot!

....

90   Michelson, *Complete Tarot Reader*, p. 150.

91   Renée, *New Generation*, p. 37.

92   Knight, *Magical World of the Tarot*, pp. 17–18.

As mentioned, Dion Fortune did not believe that the cards invariably provide a valid answer. She recommended verifying each divination with two additional readings. Aleister Crowley takes a similar stance in his performance of the "first operation" of the Golden Dawn's "Opening of the Key" reading. [93] Like Richard Roberts, Crowley avoids asking the querent the subject of the consultation. He chooses a significator card to represent the querent, thoroughly shuffles the deck, and cuts it into four stacks representing the letters of God's name, *Yod—Heh—Vau—Heh*. [94]

Crowley Cut the Deck into Four Stacks (Listed with Associations)			
(4) *Heh* (Earth, Disks, Princesses/Pages) Wealth, health, steady effort, material goods	(3) *Vau* (Air, Swords, Princes/Kings) Strife, scandal, loss, conflict, affliction	(2) *Heh* (Water, Cups, Queens) Love, marriage, fun, feelings, relationships	(1) *Yod* (Fire, Wands, Knights) Career, ambition, new life, valor, enterprise

The first or *Yod* stack (Fire, Wands) on the far right represents works, career, business, and enterprise. The adjoining *Heh* stack (Water, Cups; not to be confused with a haystack) stands for love, marriage, romance, feelings, and pleasure. The *Vau* stack (Air, Swords) relates to trouble, loss, scandal, and conflict. The final *Heh* stack (Earth, Disks) on the far left signifies money, property, practical efforts, resources, and material well-being.

Crowley locates the pile containing the querent's significator and states what the question *should* be about, according to the meaning of the stack where the significator appears. If the querent does not agree, Crowley terminates the reading. To quote him verbatim: after identifying which stack contains the significator "tell the Querent what he has come for: *if wrong, abandon the divination*" [95] (italics mine). If correct, use the methods of card-counting and card-pairing

....

93   Special thanks to Steve Little for calling to my attention Crowley's advice on when to abandon a reading in Aleister Crowley, *The Book of Thoth* (San Francisco: Weiser Books, 2008), p. 250.

94   Unlike English, Hebrew is written from right to left. The pack is first cut into two piles with the top half of the deck placed to the left of the bottom half. Then each of those piles is cut in a similar manner with the top pile placed immediately to the left of the bottom pile. The result is four stacks that are designated *Yod—Heh—Vau—Heh*, from right to left (in the order of written Hebrew).

95   Crowley, *The Book of Thoth*, p. 250.

to create a "story" from the cards in the pile containing the significator. [96, 97] "But the main lines ought to be laid down firmly, with correctness, *or the divination should be abandoned*" (italics mine). [98]

When such "considerations before judgment" appear in horary astrology, it usually means that the querent is not asking the question that is most pressing or that the inquirer should ask again after the situation has developed further. We might speculate in the case of Gibb's friend that the querent was aware on a gut level of the terminal nature of her husband's illness. She may have been imagining what her life would be like as a wealthy widow (the Empress) but too embarrassed to ask the question directly.

Not knowing which deck Gibb's friend used puts us at a disadvantage. Any card can be depicted in various ways. Depending on the artist, the Empress of one deck may look radically different from the Empress of another and thus trigger our intuition in a different way. A detail on a card from one deck may simply be absent on the same card painted by another artist. For instance, in some early decks (like the Visconti-Sforza) the shield of the Empress portrays an imperial eagle, which also happens to be a Christian symbol for the resurrection of Christ. Most likely the artist intended the Empress' eagle as a symbol of Roman heraldry, but the eagle may still carry an association with the death of Christ in the culture of the epoch.

In astrology, the eagle is one of the animals associated with Scorpio, the zodiacal sign of death (the other symbols being the scorpion and the phoenix rising from its ashes, representing the resurrection). If the black eagle of the Empress card were to catch one's intuitive eye, one might think of a woman alone after the ascension of her husband to heaven. The color black of the Empress' eagle is also associated in our culture with Scorpio and death.

....

96 *Card-counting* involves spreading the pack that contains the significator, face upward, and then counting cards in the direction the significator faces, always including the initial card in the count. The numerical equivalent of each card is as follows: Pages = 7, non-Page court cards = 4, Aces = 11, pip cards = their own number, elemental trumps = 3, planetary trumps = 9, and zodiacal trumps = 12. The reader makes up a story from the cards that are related by counting in this way. If the main lines of the story are not "laid down firmly, with correctness," then "the divination should be abandoned."—Crowley, *The Book of Thoth*, p. 251.

97 *Card-pairing* involves pairing the cards on either side of the significator, then the next two cards out, and so on to the ends of the row of cards. The reader makes up a story from the successive pairs of cards to fill in the details of the story invented from the card-counting method.

98 Crowley, *The Book of Thoth*, p. 251.

The Ten of Cups
(Universal Tarot).

Gibb's case is similar to one reported by Ly de Angeles. Early in the HIV epidemic, she did many readings for men who were suffering from AIDS with little prospect of recovery. The "outcome card" of these readings was frequently the Ten of Cups, which is typically a happy card. How could the Ten of Cups also be a harbinger of death?

Waite viewed the Ten of Cups as a card of contentment and of repose of the heart. Colman Smith painted this card with ten cups floating in a rainbow to symbolize the happy ending of an emotional matter. Crowley notes that the rainbow symbolizes a stage of alchemical transformation that follows upon putrefaction, implying that one must pass through a process of decay to reach the rainbow.[99] In mythology, the goddess Iris carried the souls of deceased women along a rainbow to their final resting place. In modern times, the rainbow has become a symbol of gay pride. Ly de Angeles concluded that the Ten of Cups could mean "a final resting or release—but only when there has been long-term illness or pain..."[100] First putrefaction, then the rainbow.

The Golden Dawn associates the Ten of Cups with the planet Mars (ruler of Scorpio, the sign associated with putrefaction) and Pisces, or more specifically with the Mars decan of Pisces. This final decan of Pisces represents the end of a complete cycle of the zodiac before it renews itself at 0° Aries—an apt symbol for death on an earthy plane and rebirth in heaven. Along these lines, in a prescient comment in their 1918 text on medical astrology, Max and Augusta Heindel observed that "when Mars is afflicted in Pisces the indulgence of clandestine intercourse will bring trouble into the life."[101] Here Mars as a phallic symbol suggests sexual activity, and Pisces as the twelfth sign analogous to the twelfth house refers to clandestine affairs. Crowley calls the

99   Crowley, *The Book of Thoth*, p. 103.

100   Ly de Angeles, *Tarot, Theory & Practice* (Woodbury, MN: Llewellyn Publications, 2007), pp. 27–28 and p. 135.

101   Max and Augusta Heindel, *The Message of the Stars* (Rosicrucian Fellowship, 1918), p. 327, online at http://books .google.com/books?id=vDRDAAAAIAAJ&ots=0S9ZfNOZab&dq=heindel%20message%20of%20the%20stars &pg=PA327#v=onepage&q=clandestine%20intercourse&f=false

Ten of Cups "Satiety," related to the pursuit of pleasure and its consequences and adds, "Having got everything that one wanted, one did not want it after all; now one must pay."[102]

Different Decks Can Produce Different Readings

As we saw above, the choice of a deck can alter the reading because of the symbols included on or omitted from the cards. The following example illustrates this point. I work in a psychiatric clinic in an inner city neighborhood. Once while dealing with two severely alcoholic patients who were wreaking havoc in the community, we asked for a consultation from the office of the commissioner. Curious about how the meeting might go, I did a quick three-card reading: the Moon, the Ace of Wands, and the Six of Wands.

The cards were drawn from the Lo Scarabeo Tarot by Mark McElroy and Anna Lazzarini. The Moon trump in this deck is unique in that, while following the traditional Waite-Smith imagery, the artist added an image of an overturned cup and a coin encrusted with the figure of a crustacean. The Moon card's link to Pisces and alcohol intoxication is emphasized by the overturned cup. The cost of the excessive drinking to the community is reflected in the coin.

Left to right: The Moon, Ace of Wands, Six of Wands *(Lo Scarabeo Tarot)*.

....

102 Crowley, *The Book of Thoth*, p. 187.

These details would have been missing had I used a different deck. The Ace of Wands and the Six of Wands suggested that the conference would produce a new idea leading to a successful outcome, and such was the case.

Tarot at the Opera

As mentioned, when a small detail on a card provides a key insight during a reading, I am often struck by the fact that the same detail would have been missing had a different deck been used. The interpretation of the same card may vary from deck to deck, depending on the artist's choice of images. Let me give another humble example.

On April 9, 2011, I went to see Rossini's opera *Le Comte Ory*, live in HD from the Metropolitan Opera in New York. It was not an opera that I knew and I'm not a particular fan of Rossini, but I knew I'd enjoy the Peruvian lead tenor, Juan Diego Flórez. At the time, I was working with Crowley's Thoth deck and decided to do a three-card reading for the question "What will my experience of this opera be like?" My intent was to learn more about the Thoth cards by comparing my experience of the opera with the imagery on the cards. (The Classic Tarot is substituted below.)

Tarot at the Opera, left to right: The Lovers,
Two of Pentacles, and the Queen of Cups *(Classic Tarot)*.

I took out my Thoth deck, shuffled it meditatively, cut the deck, and drew three cards: The Lovers, the Two of Disks, and the Queen of Cups. I assumed the Lovers had to do with the plot because a typical opera storyline centers on a lovers' triangle. *Le Comte Ory* is about a lecherous count who disguises himself as a nun to gain entrance to a castle full of young women whose husbands are away at the Crusades. The Waite-Smith Lovers trump is perfect for this situation. The young woman is lost in thought about her absent husband, perhaps praying to her guardian angel to keep him safe, while the lustful count is staring at her naked body. I drew a blank on the Two of Disks except to think that it had to do with juggling responsibilities and the ups and downs of life. I took the Queen of Cups to mean having a good time emotionally. I would enjoy the opera.

What was the outcome? Shortly before the 1 p.m. starting time, the HD broadcast hostess Renée Fleming announced that Juan Diego Flórez was still on his way to the Met and would arrive on time for the performance. He had been up all night because his wife was giving birth to their first child, who was born at 12:25 p.m. (just thirty-five minutes before the start of the opera!). At intermission, Juan Diego added that he and his wife had opted for a natural childbirth in a birthing pool at their Manhattan apartment. This reminded me of the waters behind the figure on the Waite-Smith Two of Pentacles. Juan Diego expressed his love for his wife, his family, his new son Leandro, and the people of his home country, Peru.

My three Thoth tarot cards came to mind. Here was Juan Diego (trump VI, the Lovers), who had left behind his beloved wife with the newborn child while he went out to fulfill his commitment at the Met (juggling responsibilities, the Two of Disks). The Thoth Queen of Cups shows a woman standing at the edge of a pool with a storklike bird at her feet. What better image for a woman about to deliver a baby in a birthing pool! I can think of no other deck in which the Queen of Cups so precisely depicts what transpired in the life of singer Juan Diego Flórez or my experience at the Met that day. I hadn't paid much attention to the bird at the pool on the Thoth Queen of Cups until Juan Diego's baby was born. Thank you, Juan, for an unforgettable performance and a memorable lesson in tarot symbolism!

A Reading without Words

The following reading took place almost entirely without words. When my son was in high school, an exchange student from Spain stayed with our family for a couple of weeks. His English was limited, and I could speak little Spanish at the time. The student was able to communicate, however, that he'd heard a rumor that his girlfriend back home might have started seeing another boy while he was away. He noticed my Robin Wood tarot deck and asked for a reading. I had him draw three cards for a "Past, Present, Future" spread, which turned out to be: the Lovers, Eight of Cups, Five of Cups.

I did my best to explain the meanings of the cards in broken Spanish. The young man motioned for me to stop and indicated that he understood what the cards were saying simply by looking at them. The sequence of images was sufficient to trigger his intuition and provide him with an answer. His suspicions were confirmed. He realized that his girlfriend in Spain had moved on to another relationship and left him feeling forlorn. The pictures were worth a thousand words.

A reading without words: Past, present, future—The Lovers,
the Eight of Cups, and the Five of Cups *(Robin Wood Tarot).*

Other Schools of Tarot Reading

I don't mean to imply that Dion Fortune's intuitive approach is the only way to read the cards, though it is my personal preference. There are many approaches to tarot divination, and a preferred method of reading has mostly to do with the personality, interests and mood of the reader. I am indebted to Michael McLaughlin for the following scheme of dividing the approaches to tarot into seven schools: intuitive, historical, systems-based, traditional, psychological-archetypal, personal-interpretive, and integrative. [103]

Putting the Schools to the Test

Let's look at another example from Douglas Gibb's website to see how each of the schools functions. In this case we will consider how various methods of interpretation might deal with a specific card: the Seven of Pentacles. Gibb mentions that a friend made the suggestion, "Next time you see the 7 of Disks in a Tarot reading, try using this interpretation: *this is about someone at work you find attractive.*" [104]

Gibb was using the Crowley-Harris Thoth Seven of Disks, which depicts seven disks set against a gloomy leaden background of dying vegetation (the Classic Tarot is substituted here). Crowley named this card "Failure." How would each of McLaughlin's seven schools come to view the Seven of Disks as "finding someone at work attractive?" To answer this question, let us invent a hypothetical querent and tarot reader, who will offer a reading based on the principles of each school.

Our imaginary inquirer is an attractive young Jewish woman who works for an established firm. She requests a consultation with our hypothetical male reader a week after attending the wedding of a friend. She is wearing no rings on her fingers, from which he surmises that she may

The Seven of Pentacles
(Classic Tarot).

---

103   Sean "Michael" McLaughlin, "Introduction to the Schools of Tarot Interpretation" TarotMichael, YouTube, http://www.youtube.com/watch?v=7k11D7RwWPI (accessed 11 Jun. 2012).

104   Douglas Gibb, "Quick Tip: Interpreting the Seven of Disks," September 21, 2010, *Tarot Eon*, http://taroteon .com/tarot-lexicon/quick-tip-interpreting-the-7-of-disks/ (accessed 10 May 2011).

be single. He asks her to thoroughly shuffle the deck while they are speaking and instructs her to follow her gut and select a card at random to start the reading. She draws the Seven of Disks/Coins/Pentacles. How would a hypothetical reader from each school approach the interpretation?

1. *Intuitive School*: Looking at the Thoth Seven of Disks, the intuitive reader comments on the heavy dark tones in the card and on the meaning of disks as they relate to finances and work. The young woman agrees that something at work is weighing on her mind. The reader is struck by the number seven and recalls that the woman is Jewish. Images of a Jewish wedding with the bride circling seven times around the groom and the Jewish tradition of seven days of wedding celebration flash through the reader's mind. His intuition also shifts to the astrological seventh house of marriage. He then asks the young woman: "Is this about someone at work you find attractive?"

2. *Historical School:* The historical reader uses the Marseille-pattern deck of Nicholas Conver, which depicts seven disks arranged vertically in four rows. The second row from the top has only one disk. All the other rows have two. He is aware that historical sources relate this card to money, work, and finances, as well as to the third decan of Taurus, ruled by Saturn. Being a good historian, he recalls Agrippa's description of this decan as a man holding a serpent and an arrow in his hands, symbolizing both profit and misery. His intuition links the phallic serpent and the arrow (perhaps Cupid's arrow) with male sexuality. He recalls Etteilla's attribution of this decan to money and riches and also to whiteness, silverware, and the moon, all feminine symbols related to marriage. It dawns on him that the disks depicted on the card are laid out like the geomantic figure *rubeus* (related to Mars, Scorpio, and sexuality). He also realizes that the inverted card has the form of the geomantic figure *albus*, which refers to whiteness and the domestic sign Cancer, ruled by the silvery moon. Putting together his historical associations about the color white, domesticity, slithering serpents, Cupid's arrows, and the workplace, he asks*:* "Is this about someone at work you find attractive?"

Albus ("White," the Moon).　　　　　　Rubeus ("Red," Mars).

3. *Systems-based School:* The systems-based reader goes through a process similar to that of the historical reader. He immediately seizes upon the geomantic pattern of *rubeus* (Mars, Scorpio, sexuality) and links it to Saturn (career, commitment, seriousness) because the Golden Dawn assigns this card to the Saturn decan of Taurus (fertility) and to the number seven (the astrological seventh house of marriage). Pondering his various associations to the card, the reader asks: "Is this about someone at work you find attractive?"

4. *Traditional Waite-Smith School:* This reader uses the Seven of Pentacles from the Waite-Smith deck with its pensive young man staring at a bush instead of harvesting the pentacles thereon. The young man's hands are resting on his upright rod (pun intended), and a single pentacle (a womb symbol) lies on the ground beneath his crotch. The reader recalls Waite's 1911 words about the card: "A young man, leaning on his staff, looks intently at seven pentacles attached to a clump of greenery on his right; one would say that these were his treasures and that his heart was there." Struck by the erotic tone of Waite's description of the youth holding his erect rod while gazing intently at his heart's desire in a clump of greenery on a verdant bush, the reader asks: "Is this about someone at work you find attractive?"

5. *Psychological-Archetypal School:* The reader continues to meditate on the card after the querent has left the consulting room. He has already discussed with the querent her attraction for someone in the workplace, but he has a sense that there is a more profound meaning in the cards. He ponders how the planet Saturn has manifested in his own life. He wonders in what way he has behaved like ponderous Saturn toward his own family, including his parents, his children, and his wife. As a result of this meditation, he has a deeper sense of the archetypal significance of Saturn as it relates to the Seven of Disks. He can draw on his new understanding the next time this card appears in a reading.

6. *Personal Interpretation School:* The reader uses the Waite-Smith deck and asks the querent to say what *she* sees in the card. The young woman responds that she sees a farmer who is taking a break from his work to ponder something. The reader asks whether this situation resonates with some aspect of her life, perhaps related to her own work life. The young woman smiles coyly and says: "Yes, there is someone at the office I find attractive and I think about him all the time, even when I should be doing my job."

7. *Integrationist School:* The integrationist reader borrows from all of the above and comes to the same conclusion.

The Blind Men and the Tarot

Making sense of the tarot is reminiscent of the Indian fable about the blind men and the elephant, retold in a poem by John Godfrey Saxe (1816–1887), in which six wise men go to "see" an elephant, though all of them are blind. The first man falls against the elephant's side and concludes, "It's very much like a wall." The second man feels a tusk and claims, "It's very much like a spear." The third man runs into the elephant's trunk and shouts, "It's very much like a snake!" The fourth man bumps into the elephant's knee and declares that it's very much like a tree. The fifth man grabs the elephant's ear and exclaims that it's very much like a fan. The sixth man yanks the elephant's tail and shouts, "It's very much like a rope!" The poet continues:

And so these men of Indostan disputed loud and long, each in his own opinion exceeding stiff and strong, though each was partly in the right, and all were in the wrong! MORAL. So oft in theologic wars, the disputants, I ween, rail on in utter ignorance of what each other mean, *and prate about an Elephant not one of them has seen!*[105]

Are tarot readers any different?

---

105 John Godfrey Saxe, *The Blind Men and the Elephant*, 1873, http://www.noogenesis.com/pineapple/blind_men_elephant.html (accessed 10 May 2012).

FIVE

Number Symbolism and the Tarot

> Number is the ruler of forms and ideas, and the cause of gods and daemons. There is geometry in the humming of the strings; there is music in the spacing of the spheres.
>
> PYTHAGORAS

Numbers are an essential feature of the tarot, and understanding their symbolism will greatly enhance our ability to read the cards. A standard tarot deck consists of seventy-eight cards with pictures, names, and numbers on them. The deck can be used to play games like *les tarots* (France) or *tarrochi* (Italy) and can also be used for divination. The numbers, which arrange the cards in numerical order, have a symbolic significance dating back at least to the time of Pythagoras. The symbolic properties of numbers offer important insights into the principles that underlie both astrology and tarot.

Before turning to the numbers, let us briefly consider the pictures on the Waite-Smith cards. These metaphorical images speak directly to the intuitive "right-brain" portion of our minds. The Waite-Smith cards depict scenes of ordinary life (especially the minor arcana) as well as what Carl Jung calls "archetypal images" (the major arcana), like those found in mythology, literature, great art, and world religions.

Some of the modern tarot images, particularly those on the twenty-two trump cards, allude to esoteric systems like Freemasonry, Kabbalah, and alchemy, especially as elaborated by the Hermetic Order of the Golden Dawn. Certain tarot readers find these systems to be valuable spiritual practices, but in my view the tarot is a discipline unto itself and such extraneous systems are not essential to reading the cards. Undoubtedly the Kabbalah and related beliefs form part of the womb from which the modern tarot emerged, but the baby is now born and has developed a life of its own. This is not to deny, however, that an appreciation of the history of the tarot's development can aid us in appreciating the traditional meanings of the cards.

The Kabbalah and the Tarot

Although I have read about the Kabbalah over the years, this occult discipline has never caught my fancy. Perhaps my lack of enthusiasm has to do with a distrust of organized religion and those who purport to speak on God's behalf, as if one could really know what she is thinking. In addition, the correlation with a manmade alphabet that happens to contain twenty-two letters does not carry much weight when compared with correspondences to natural phenomena. Even tarot enthusiasts who write about the supposed connections between Kabbalah and the tarot must honestly acknowledge that "to do so is to pointedly disagree with some very great Jewish scholars, who state that no such relationship exists." [106]

Nonetheless, the mystical aspects of Rabbinic Judaism have gotten much press in the tarot literature, and there is no question that in recent centuries the Kabbalah has played a role in assigning meanings to the cards. Aleister Crowley, for example, states unequivocally that the tarot is "a deliberate attempt to represent, in pictorial form, the doctrines of the Qabalah." [107] To my mind, Crowley was barking up the wrong tree; my dog is familiar with the same tree and uses it for other purposes. I can't imagine God muttering to herself during the Big Bang, in a language consisting of words formed from a twenty-two-letter, manmade alphabet, while engaged in creating the universe with its wondrous stars, galaxies, atoms, subatomic particles, and the miracle of DNA.

---

106 Robert Wang, *The Qabalistic Tarot* (San Francisco: Weiser Books, 1987), p. xv.
107 Crowley, *The Book of Thoth*, p. 10.

The alleged connection between tarot and Kabbalah is based on the coincidence of certain key numbers in each system. There are twenty-two letters in the current Hebrew alphabet, and there are twenty-two cards in the major arcana—oh my! Kabbalists link the ten pip cards of the tarot with the ten emanations, called *Sephirah*, comprising the Kabbalistic Tree of Life. The four worlds created by God allegedly correspond to the four suits of the tarot. And what's more, the Hebrew name for God has four letters: *Yod—Heh—Vau—Heh*.[108] Holy tetragrammaton, Batman! On the basis of such coincidences, occultists of the nineteenth century, particularly Eliphas Lévi, invented the wild and wooly notion that the tarot is an expression of the mysticism of the Kabbalah. There is no historical basis for such a claim. As Robert Place explains:

> …Tarot is not inherently Kabbalistic. Its connection with the Kabbalah is primarily the invention of the 19th century French occultist, Eliphas Levi, who included this theory in his bombastic but obscure doctrine of "High Magic." Many occultists have taken Levi's unsupported claims as the "gospel truth" …[109]

Robert Place's reference to "gospel truth" reminds us that the tarot trumps were created during the Renaissance by northern Italian artists who were steeped in the mythology of the Bible. The choice of twenty-two trumps is just as likely to be related to the twenty-two chapters of the Book of Revelation, the final installment of the New Testament. In fact, the World trump depicting the New Jerusalem in older tarot decks is numbered XXI, the number of the chapter in Revelations that mentions the coming of the Holy City at the end of time: "And I, John, saw the holy city, new Jerusalem, coming down from God out of heaven, prepared as a bride adorned for her husband" (Revelation 21:2).[110]

In his books and lectures, Robert Place explains how the tarot originally came to him in dreams and visions. Never once did a Hebrew letter appear in his dreams. Place is not the first or the only scholar to question the value of the assigning of Hebrew letters within the

....

108   The Hebrew consonants *Yod*, *He*, *Vau*, and *He* are rendered in English as JHVH, JHWH, YHWH, or YHVH.

109   Robert Michael Place, "History," The Tarot School, http://www.tarotschool.com/ArticleHistory.html (accessed 12 Nov. 2012).

110   Revelation 21:2 (King James Bible).

Kabbalah. The noted English occultist John Dee (1527–c. 1608) devoted his life to discovering the universal language of creation and to understanding the divine forms ("pure verities") that underlie material reality. Having studied the Kabbalah extensively, the venerable Dee made a distinction between the "true" Kabbalah, "which was born to us by the law of creation," and the "vulgar" Kabbalah, "which rests on well-known letters that can be written by man" [the Hebrew alphabet].[111]

Historian Philip Beitchman, an expert in the role of the Kabbalah during the Renaissance, dismisses the notion that in the beginning God spoke Hebrew. Beitchman notes that "Hebrew was not the language the Jews brought to Canaan but the one they adopted there."[112] Furthermore, the ancient Hebrew language most likely had twenty-three letters, having lost a letter over time to become modern Hebrew, which has only twenty-two![113] Does it seem likely that at the time of the Creation God spoke an ancient language with a twenty-three-letter alphabet, a language that was not even spoken by the Jews until they reached Canaan? These logical inconsistencies suggest that the attribution of the twenty-two tarot trumps to the letters of the Hebrew alphabet is sheer nonsense, a flight into fancy much like the untenable belief that the tarot is the ancient Egyptian Book of Thoth.

The Ten Sephirot

Even though the alleged parallel between the tarot and the "vulgar" Kabbalah flies in the face of historical fact (the Kabbalah was unknown in Italy when the first tarot decks were created), it is useful for students of tarot to know something about the meanings of the ten Sephirot. Occultists like Crowley, Waite, and the Golden Dawn used such associations to assign meanings to the cards. The term *Sephirah* ("number" in Hebrew; plural, sephirot) refers to ten numerations, which Jewish mystics took to mean "any of the 10 emanations, or powers, by which God the Creator was said to become manifest."[114] This concept, an offshoot of the Pythagorean belief

....

111 John Dee, quoted in Philip Beitchman, *Alchemy of the Word: Cabala of the Renaissance* (Albany, NY: State University of New York Press, 1998), p. 243.

112 Beitchman, ibid., p. 243.

113 Jeff A. Benner, "Letters Missing from the Hebrew Alphabet," Ancient Hebrew Research Center, http://www.ancient-hebrew.org/4_missing.html (accessed 15 Jun. 2012).

114 *Encyclopedia Britannica*, s. v. "sefira," http://www.britannica.com/EBchecked/topic/532613/sefira (accessed 5 Aug. 2012).

that "all is number," was mentioned in the *Sepher Yetzira*, or "Book of Creation," which spoke of ten ideal numbers. The individual Sephirah are generally interpreted as:

1. Kether—Supreme crown, divine will to create, the Christian God the Father

2. Chokhmah—Wisdom

3. Binah—Intelligence, understanding, contemplation

4. Chesed—Loving kindness, compassion, grace, mercy

5. Geburah—Might, power, severity, harshness, retribution, punishment, awe of God

6. Tiphareth—Beauty, symmetry, balance, the Christian God the Son

7. Netzah—Eternity, victory, perpetuity, endurance

8. Hod—Majesty, splendor, glory, surrender, sincerity

9. Yesod—Foundation, vessel to bring action, the Christian Holy Spirit

10. Malkuth—Kingship, the realm of matter; "Malkuth gives tangible form to the other emanations" [115]

There is an orderly progression of creation in this model. It begins with divine will in the number one of Kether (similar in meaning to the element Fire, the suit of Wands, and the tarot's four aces) and ends in the tangible reality of the number ten in Malkuth (linked in meaning to the element Earth, the suit of Pentacles, and the four Pages of the tarot). If you are puzzled by the meaning of a card in the Golden Dawn tradition, a glance at this list and the number on the card may provide a clue as to why the originator of the deck chose a particular interpretation.

115   *Wikipedia*, s.v. "Malkuth" http://en.wikipedia.org/wiki/Malchut (accessed 5 Aug. 2012).

Paul Marteau and the Golden Dawn Attributions

In 1930, the French card historian Paul Marteau printed a restoration of an old Marseille deck ("Le Tarot de Marseille de Paul Marteau"), now referred to as the Grimaud edition of the Marseille tarot, which had been manufactured by his grand-uncle Baptiste-Paul Grimaud (1817–1899). In 1949, Marteau published a book in which he proposed interpreting the Marseille cards by combining the meaning of the card's number with the symbolism of its suit.[116] This idea originated with the Golden Dawn, which had connected the sequence of numbers one through ten with the Tree of Life and the element of each suit.

Marteau's method was highly influential in attributing meanings to the tarot in the twentieth century. The genius of his approach lay in articulating a developmental sequence for each suit in which the pip cards, in numerical order, told a story about the unfolding of a human situation typical of the suit's element (e.g., Wands, enterprise; Cups, love; Swords, strife; Pentacles, material concerns). Because Marteau's ideas had such a powerful effect, I will summarize his meanings below:

- 1: unity and a starting point of development that unfolds sequentially in the nine numbers that follow.

- 2: a symbol of passivity and polarity, elements of gestation which constitute the material of further development.

- 3: an introduction of activity into passivity (2 + 1 = 3), which provides direction to the gestation of 2.

- 4: a product of 2 x 2, crystallization and transition, 4 being intermediate between 3 and 5. Relative stability, order, security, and consolidation.

- 5: a transition (4 + 1), the passage from one plane to another, 4 being completion and 1 being the addition of a new beginning to the completion of 4). A sense of multiplicity, diffusion, and radiation.

- 6: a harmonious balance or equilibrium (3 + 3 = 2 x 3), latent power or potential that can be called upon later.

---

116 Paul Marteau, *Le Tarot de Marseille* (Paris, France: Arts et Métiers Graphiques, 1949).

- 7: the force and subsequent action latent in the potential of 6 (7 = 6 + 1), which can be used to reach a successful conclusion or synthesis.

- 8: eight (4 + 4) combines the cross and the quadrate, the material plane and the interior life of divine existence, into a solid equilibrium that is not abstract like the equilibrium of 6. Like infinity, 8 is a perfect number, complete unto itself.

- 9: the orientation of the abstract toward the concrete. The number 9 adds unity to the perfection of 8—that is, new action and the start of another cycle, the penetration of force into matter.

- 10: the single digits, 1 through 9, generated from the potential of 1, are now condensed by the combination of 1 with 0 into the number 10, a number of reason and tranquility. In 9, the abstract makes contact with the physical; in 10, it maintains this balance or equilibrium with the physical (10 = 2 x 5 = 5 + 5).

If we compare Marteau's abstruse ideas (1949) with the earlier teachings of the Golden Dawn, we see a remarkable similarity. Each zodiac sign consists of three decans: a first or "initiatory" decan, a middle or "stabilizing" decan, and a final or "transitional" decan. The symbolism of the sequence of decans (initiate—stabilize—move on) combined with the symbolism of the numbers from one to ten generates in large measure the Golden Dawn meanings for the pip cards.

- 1: (Kether) The force of Spirit acting on and through an element. This initial spark of pure elemental energy will undergo development and maturation as it moves toward the 10 of the suit. In Kether, the energy is pure potential and has not yet manifested (like an idea in the mind of God).

- 2: (Chokmah) The initiation and fecundation of a thing. [117] The element of the suit appears in its original harmonious condition and first tangible form, not yet affected by outside factors. The pip twos are associated with the initial decan of the "initiating" or cardinal signs of the zodiac and exhibit a double dose of the desire to manifest something new.

- 3: (Binah) Action launched and realized, for good or evil. The action characteristic of the element has commenced and manifests in a form of initial completion. The pip threes are associated with the "stabilizing" middle decan of the "initiating" or cardinal signs and signify an initial consolidation of what was started in the twos.

- 4: (Chesed) Realization, making a matter fixed and settled. The energy now solidifies and manifests in established reality. The pip fours are associated with the final decan of the "initiating" or cardinal signs, which will soon transition to the fixed signs of the zodiac and represent a desire to let go of what was begun in the twos and threes to move on to something more enduring.

- 5: (Geburah) Obstacles, opposition, conflict, and strife. The energy now runs into trials and obstacles in its development. The pip fives are associated with the initial decan of the "stabilizing" or fixed signs. A conflict develops between the fixity of the sign (the desire to maintain the status quo) and the initiatory nature of the first decan (the desire to start something new).

- 6: (Tiphareth) Accomplishment and the carrying out of a matter. The energy of the suit has reached the "stabilizing" middle decan of a "consolidating" or fixed sign, which results in a double dose of fixity and the desire to maintain what has been achieved thus far. Harmony has been restored after the tension of the fives, and the element can now express itself at its practical best.

---

117 The Golden Dawn uses the term "fecundation," which means to impregnate, make fruitful, or fertilize.

- 7: (Netzach) A force transcending the material plane; a result dependent on the action taken. Having reached its peak of stability in the sixes, the energy next enters the "transitional" final decan of a "stabilizing" or fixed sign. It now prepares to advance to an "adaptable" mutable sign. In this final decan of the fixed sign, a desire to maintain the status quo (fixity) conflicts with the need to let go.

- 8: (Hod) Solitary or time-limited success. The energy enters the initial decan of a "transitional" or mutable sign, signifying the beginning of the ending of the manifestation of the element. The energy cannot remain long in this initial phase of letting go; rather it seeks a way to move forward toward the culmination of its expression.

- 9: (Yesod) Firmly based fundamental force; executive power. The energy enters the "consolidating" middle decan of a "transitional" or mutable sign. It has established deep roots during its development and thus can express itself powerfully, but it must now prepare to enter the last stage of its existence.

- 10: (Malkuth) Culminated or completed force; a matter fully determined. The energy has reached the final "transitional" decan of a "transitional" or mutable sign; this is the terminal stage of the end game. It has arrived at the culmination of its development and completed a full cycle of existence, much as the spring starts anew at the end of winter.

At first glance, the ideas of Marteau and the Golden Dawn may seem abstract and highfalutin, but in practice they can be quite helpful. An instructive exercise is to lay out each suit in numerical order and to use the number meanings to create a story about someone who displays the qualities of the suit. For example, let's take the suit of Pentacles and invent a brief story about the earthy Page. Here goes:

Once upon a time there was a dutiful, hard-working teenager (Page of Pentacles). One day he was offered his first job (Ace of Pentacles). He worked hard at more than one job (Two of Pentacles) and became quite skillful (Three of Pentacles). He carefully saved his money (Four of Pentacles) but then the Great Recession hit and depleted his resources (Five of Pentacles). His experience of financial hardship taught him the value of money and he became more generous toward others (Six of Pentacles).

And so on. The reader is welcome to finish the story.

How Many Lives Hath a Cat?

Symbols can change in meaning over time. Their significance depends on the prevailing symbolic winds of the culture in which they appear. Collective consciousness, and perhaps also the collective unconscious, evolve in step with the human race. One example occurs with the swastika, a symbol of ancient India and classical antiquity to denote good fortune. The word itself comes from the Sanskrit *svastika* meaning "lucky object." Try telling that to Jewish people. The Nazis converted the ancient swastika, originally a symbol of good fortune, into one of hatred, bigotry, and, in the words of the poet, "man's inhumanity to man."[118]

A less weighty example can be found in the expression that cats have nine lives. Once while practicing Spanish with a South American friend, I happened to use the expression that a cat has nine lives. "What are you talking about?" corrected my friend, "A cat has only seven lives." As often happens in discussions with people from foreign countries, I realized we were standing at the precipice of a cultural divide.

To my surprise, I learned that in the Spanish-speaking world, cats have only seven lives—*los gatos tienen siete vidas.* Spanish-born cats concerned about their longevity regard England or the United States as *the* place to be.[119] Why the discrepancy? I suspect the answer lies in differences in the symbolic significance of seven and nine in the two cultures. In like manner, the cultural assumptions of tarot readers influence what they see in the cards.

....

118   Robert Burns, "Man Was Made to Mourn: A Dirge" http://www.robertburns.org/works/55.shtml (accessed 3 Sep. 2012).

119   Rumor has it that cats form part of the human diet in certain areas of Australia, Cameroon, China, Ghana, Peru, and Switzerland, so those regions are best avoided by our feline friends.

The Exemplary and Marvelous Sacred Number Seven

The number seven has long been considered to have magical, spiritual and mystical properties. The philosopher Philo of Alexandria (c. 15 BCE–c. 50 CE) viewed seven as an "exemplary and marvelous" number because "it neither begets nor is begotten." [120] Say what? Philo was referring to the fact that seven is neither the product of other single digits, nor can you divide seven into any other single digit. Impressive!

The number seven's symbolism is part and parcel of human history, natural science, culture, and religion. God supposedly created the world in seven days. In the cosmology of various major religions, including Judaism, Islam, and Hinduism, the throne of God is located at or above the seventh heaven. Once you move beyond the seventh heaven, you come face to face with the deity. Thus, seven carries a sense of having reached an important threshold or limit and being on the verge of something greater. In *Genesis,* God rested on the seventh day after creating woman on the sixth.

Other examples of seven's importance abound. There are seven notes of the musical scale; seven colors of the rainbow; seven visible planets; seven levels of heaven; seven days of the week; seven chakras; seven deadly sins; seven sorrows of the Virgin Mary; seven metals of alchemy; seven Seals of the Apocalypse, and the list goes on. Historically, occultists often made correspondences among these diverse groups of seven. Timothy Bright in *A Treatise of Melancholie* (1586) discusses the "seven ages of man" and makes the following associations:

> … the seven planets, whereof our infancy is compared to the Moon, in which we seem only to live and grow, as plants; the second age to Mercury, wherein we are taught and instructed; our third age to Venus, the days of love, desire and vanity; the fourth to the Sun, the strong flourishing and beautiful age of man's life; the fifth to Mars, in which we seek honour and victory, and in which our thoughts travel to ambitious ends; the sixth age is ascribed to Jupiter, in which we begin to take account of our times, judge of ourselves and grow to the perfection of our understanding; the last, and seventh, to Saturn, wherein our days are sad and overcast, and in which we find, by dear and

....
120 A. G. Mackey and H. L. Haywood, *Encyclopedia of Masonry, Part 2* (Whitefish, MT: Kessinger Publishing, 2003), p. 931.

lamentable experience and by the loss which can never be repaired, that of all our vain passions and affection past the sorrow only abides. [121]

With regard to astrology and tarot, the most important group of seven consists of the seven visible planets (wanderers in the sky against a backdrop of fixed stars), in Chaldean order: Saturn, Jupiter, Mars, Sun, Venus, Mercury, and the Moon. These seven planets formed the basis of astrological theory until the discovery of Uranus in 1781. The seven visible planets gave us the seven days of the week, which would not have come into existence without them.

To return to our Spanish cat, in the Hispanic world, the idea of cats having seven lives is probably related to linking each cat-life with one of the classical visible planets. Once the cat passes the seventh sphere, which is the realm of Saturn, the final planet that marks the boundary of our solar system, then the next step is the afterlife. Beyond the sphere of Saturn lies the vault of heaven where fixed stars and the souls of dead cats reside. Arriving at the number seven puts one at a threshold beyond which bigger and better things, like the godhead and eternal life (or an endless supply of mice), are waiting.

What advice would our Spanish cat, who is allotted only one life for each of the seven planets, give to the tarot reader who draws a seven card? The feline might say (or meow): "Take your time and think carefully about what you're doing. This may be your last chance to get it right." (A rough translation of the Spanish cat's actual words is: "*Tómese su tiempo y piense cuidadosamente acerca de lo que está haciendo. Esta puede ser su última oportunidad para hacerlo bien.*") I leave it to the reader to reflect on trump VII, the Chariot, and on the pip cards numbered seven to decide whether the cat's advice is worth heeding.

Why do cats gain two additional lives in the English-speaking world? My hunch is that it has to do with the number symbolism of Great Britain versus that of Spain. The reason may lie in the sacredness of the number nine in Celtic mythology, only traces of which survived the invasion by the Romans and the conversion of Europe to Christianity. Druid tradition held nine

....

121   Timothy Bright, *A Treatise of Melancholie* (1586), quoted at *Internet Shakespeare Editions*, http://internet-shakespeare.uvic.ca/Library/SLT/ideas/the%20universe/spheres.html#7ages (accessed 4 Sep. 2012).

trees to be sacred. An ancient poem begins with, "I was made from the Nine-fold elements,"[122] highlighting the importance of the number nine in Celtic religion. An Irish legend tells us that ocean waves come in nines; in every series of nine waves, the ninth wave—the largest—is called "Cliodna's wave" in honor of the Irish goddess of that name. The Celtic reverence for the number nine and for cycles of nine is the likely basis for the belief in the English-speaking world that cats have nine lives.

The symbolic traditions surrounding the numbers seven and nine appear to have made their way into modern interpretations of the tarot. The seven and nine cards often reflect a pause in a journey and the need to reflect before moving on.

The Tetractys of the Phythagoreans

The tetractys is a mystical symbol found in the teachings of the Pythagoreans. It consists of ten points arranged symmetrically in an equilateral triangle of four rows. The Pythagoreans believed ten to be a perfect number because the sum of the first four whole numbers adds up to ten (1 + 2 + 3 + 4 = 10), and four is the number of three-dimensional reality. The ideas embodied in the tetractys are ingrained in Western occultism and have found their way into the modern tarot with its ten pip cards and four court cards in each of the four suits. The tetractys has also influenced astrology with its four elements, four humors, four seasons, four cardinal points, and so on. The ancient numerology of the tetractys influenced the Kabbalah with its four letters of the name of God (*Yod—Heh—Vau—Heh*) and ten spheres of emanation of the Tree of Life, all of which influenced the development of the modern tarot. To quote Crowley: "It seems probable that the Qabalists who invented the Tree of Life were inspired by the Pythagoreans."[123]

....

122 Taliesin, Chief Bard of the Britons, *Nine Elements* (c. 600 CE) in the Cad Goddeu, trans. by Caitlin Matthews, http://www.celticcallings.com/resources/celtic_traditions/0_celtic_traditions.htm (accessed 20 Aug. 2012).

123 Crowley, *The Book of Thoth*, p. 31.

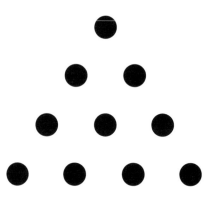

The Tetractys of Pythagoras.

Some tarot readers use the tetractys as the template for a spread. In one version of the spread, the top row with its single point represents the core issue; the second row with its two points signifies the influence of the cosmos and the reaction of the cosmos to the actions of the querent; the third row with its three points stands for the Hindu triad of Creator, Sustainer, and Destroyer (or "Past, Present, Future") as they relate to the querent's decision; and the final row with its four points shows how the four elements—Earth, Water, Air, and Fire—affect the querent's concern. Earth relates to money, health, diligence, and material realities; Water, to love, relationships, healing and emotions; Air to thoughts, strategies, strife, and conflict; and Fire to creativity, ambition, spirit, enterprise, and will.

The tetractys can be viewed as a set of three triangles, each one stacked upon the other. The first triangle is made up of three dots, the second of six dots, and the third of ten. Hence the numbers three, six, and ten can be considered triangular numbers. If we add additional rows to the tetractys, we obtain a sequence of triangular numbers, many of which have significance for the tarot. The accompanying table arranges the triangular numbers according to the number of rows in the stacked triangles.

Triangular Numbers	
Number of Rows in the Triangle	Number of Dots in the Triangle
1	1 (a single point)
2	3 (1 + 2): the first triangular number
3	6 (1 + 2 + 3)
4 (1 x 4: the tetractys)	*10 (1 + 2 + 3 + 4: the number of pip cards in each suit)*
5	15 (1 + 2 + 3 + 4 + 5)
6	21 (1 + 2 + 3 + 4 + 5 + 6): the total number of trump cards; the Fool is not numbered and is not part of the sequence of trumps in early decks
7	28 (1 + 2 + 3 + 4 + 5 + 6 +7): the number of lunar mansions in Chinese and Western astrology
8 (2 x 4: double the original tetractys)	*36 (1 + 2 + 3 + 4 + 5 + 6 +7 + 8): the number of decans in the horoscope, Petit Lenormand cards, and possible combinations of throwing two dice*
9	45 (1 + 2 + 3 + 4 + 5 + 6 +7 + 8 + 9)
10	55 (1 + 2 + 3 + 4 + 5 + 6 +7 + 8 + 9 + 10)
11	66 (1 + 2 + 3 + 4 + 5 + 6 +7 + 8 + 9 + 10 + 11)
12 (3 x 4: triple the original tetractys)	*78 (1 + 2 + 3 + 4 + 5 + 6 +7 + 8 + 9 + 10 + 11 + 12): the total number of cards in a tarot deck*

According to the Pythagoreans, "all is number," and numerical relationships reveal the structure of the universe. Pythagoras, observing the various lengths of strings on musical instruments, deduced that musical tones bear whole-number relationships to one another, which is the basis of our experience of harmony and disharmony. Astrologers, drawing an analogy between Pythagorean ideas about harmony and the angles formed among planets in the heavens, developed the notion of harmonious and stressful angles (aspects) between planets and signs of the zodiac.

Following is an example of a type of pattern that fascinated the Pythagoreans. If you add a series of consecutive odd numbers, beginning with the number one, the sum is the same as the product of the quantity of odd numbers that were added together. Say what? For example, adding the first seven odd numbers produces the same result as multiplying seven by seven (1 + 2 + 3 + 4 + 5 + 6 + 7 equals 7 x 7, or 49). The interest of the Pythagoreans in such mathematical relationships and in the abstract properties of numbers themselves represents the birth of modern mathematics in Western culture. Numbers were no longer used merely for counting but became abstract ideas, like Plato's forms, to be studied in their own right. According to Brumbaugh, "It is hard for us today, familiar as we are with pure mathematical abstraction and with the mental act of generalisation, to appreciate the originality of this Pythagorean contribution."[124]

The Individual Numbers of the Tetractys

The Pythagoreans attributed certain properties to the ten digits that comprise the tetractys. Some of these properties were alluded to in the chapter on the Celtic Cross. Below is a detailed discussion of the whole numbers one through ten, found on the pip cards of the tarot. We will consider not only the Pythagorean attributions but also the ideas of other esoteric traditions, among them the writings of sixteenth-century occultist Henry Cornelius Agrippa (1486–1535).

You may wish to lay out the four pip cards that share the same number to see how the symbolism is portrayed in the pips of your deck. The number associations are helpful when your mind goes blank while looking at the image on a card. As with any symbolic system, the associations that most resonate with you are the most valuable for constructing your own meanings of the cards. Feel free to discard any that seem irrelevant. Quite likely you will discover new connections of your own.

The Number One (Monad)

A single point is an abstract mathematical concept. It has no dimension of its own. When combined with points distinct from itself, however, it has the power to create new dimensions. The number one is the monad, a symbol of perfect unity and pure potential.

....

124   Robert S. Brumbaugh, *The Philosophers of Greece* (Albany, NY: State University of New York Press, 1982), p. 33.

Philosophers and theologians have linked the number one to *logos,* meaning "word," the rational principle of the cosmos and the creative word of God. The Gospel of Saint John states: "In the beginning was the Word, and the Word was with God, and the Word was God … Through him all things were made; without him nothing was made that has been made."[125] In the tarot, the Aces are numbered one and represent the pure potential of each suit; they are the "roots" of the four elements. Anatomically, this number is associated with the male sexual organ—the numeral 1 is phallic in shape.

In Crowley's system, the Knights correspond to the Hebrew letter, Yod, the first letter of the name of the Hebrew deity. Crowley depicted his Thoth knights as riding powerful steeds, symbolic of the potent phallus of the father-god who created the universe. The action of the Knights is swift, violent, and transient like an orgasm; Knights represent the "most sublime, original, active part of the Energy of the Element."[126] In Crowley's mind, the Big Bang was a divine orgasm.

Numerologists associate the number one with pure potential, unity, oneness, creation, initial manifestation, new growth, conception, assertive action, innovation, new opportunity, originality, will, initiative, ambition, leadership, self-assertion, individuality, perfection, and new beginnings.[127] Its Sephirah is Kether, the Supreme Crown or God the Father.

The tarot pips numbered one (the Aces) relate to creation, root-force, beginning, new life, the urge to generate, and the fresh expression of issues related to the suit. Typical keywords for the Aces in the Waite-Smith tradition include:

- *Ace of Wands*: creation, invention, the start of an enterprise, power, money, fortune, inheritance

- *Ace of Cups*: joy, contentment, abode, nourishment, abundance, fertility

- *Ace of Swords*: triumph, conquest, crowning, great force, the excessive degree in everything

- *Ace of Pentacles:* wealth, prosperity, comfortable material conditions, contentment, felicity, ecstasy, speedy intelligence, gold

125   John I: 1–3 (New International Version).
126   Crowley, *The Book of Thoth*, p. 149.
127   Thomas Saunders, *The Authentic Tarot* (London: Watkins Publishing, 2007), pp. 29–47.

The Number Two (Duad)

When you connect two distinct points, you form a straight line that connects two entities that in many ways are the same but also complementary. Duality is born; conflict and cooperation are now possible. In a natal horoscope, the first house represents the individual, and the opposite seventh house signifies his or her mate. Because two points form a line, the number two is considered the generator of one-dimensional space. Two is the "duad," the symbol of polarization and diversity. The intersection of two paths is a "crossroads," the same term we use for decision points in our lives. In the Book of Genesis, God created day and night, separating primal unity into duality. Chinese philosophy refers to this duality as yin and yang. Two is the first feminine number: the vagina with its two labia or liplike structures that cover the vaginal opening. The Pythagoreans considered even numbers feminine and odd numbers masculine.

Even though Pythagoras allowed the women of his cult to function on an equal footing with men, he is quoted as saying: "There exists a good principle which created order, light and man, and an evil principle which created chaos, darkness, and woman." Pythagoras was not a misogynist, however! He probably had in mind the number one as the rational creative principle and two as the principle of diversity and polarity. Because one is all good, the existence of the number two requires evil or strife to exist. The logic goes: one is all good, two is not one, therefore two is not all good; hence two must be partly bad.

In Crowley's system, the Queens correspond to the Hebrew letter *Heh*, the second letter of the name of the biblical deity. The Thoth Queens are complements of the phallic primary Knights and represent the "second stage in the process of creation."[128] Queens receive, ferment, and transmit the original energy of the Knight. Crowley regards the "2" pips of each suit as the harmonious expression of the element associated with the suit.

Numerologists associate two with polarity, duality, choice, comparison, decision-making, crossroads, planning, symmetry, balancing, diversity, opinion, dialogue, complementary opposites, antithesis, contrast, equilibrium, diplomacy, peace, tact, composure, cooperation, partnership, friendship, reticence, receptivity, being at a crossroads in one's life, and the awareness of and effort to understand others. The Sephirah of two is Chokmah, Wisdom.

....
128   Crowley, *The Book of Thoth*, p. 150.

The tarot pips numbered 2 relate to themes of duality, gestation, balance, crossroads, reconciling opposites, and awareness of the other. In the Golden Dawn system, the number two refers to the first decan of the cardinal signs: the initiation and fecundation of a new season of one's life. Typical keywords for the "2" cards in the Waite-Smith tradition include:

- *Two of Wands*: a lord overlooking his dominion and alternately contemplating a globe, the sadness of Alexander amidst the grandeur of this world's wealth

- *Two of Cups*: love, passion, friendship, union, affinity, concord, sympathy, the interrelation of the sexes

- *Two of Swords*: conformity, equipoise, courage, friendship, concord, tenderness, affection, intimacy, a tense harmony

- *Two of Pentacles:* dancing, gaiety, recreation, news, written messages, obstacles, agitation, troubles, embroilment

The Number Three (Triad)

Three distinct points generate a triangular figure in two-dimensional space. The triangle is the first possible geometrical shape. The upper three points of the tetractys form a triangle identical in shape to the tetractys proper. The third point adds a new dimension, completing what was begun by the first two points, which made possible the straight line. Notice how each time we add a distinct point, we add a new dimension. Modern string theory of theoretical physics posits the existence of perhaps eleven dimensions to explain physical reality. In the Pythagorean system, twelve distinct points would be needed to generate eleven-dimensional space.

Pythagoreans regarded three as the first true odd number, the result of combining one (the monad) with two (the duad). The number three is also the first true masculine number. Witness the male genitalia, consisting of a phallus and two testicles (1 + 2 = 3). Three is the first triangular number. In Jane's reading from chapter one, we considered how three is the first quantity to make triangular relationships possible. In English, the term "third party" refers to a person or entity, not involved in an interaction but called upon as a consultant to help resolve a matter. The philosopher Hegel made famous the triad: thesis—antithesis—synthesis.

In the tarot, whenever a "3" card appears, the reader might wonder whether the querent is dealing with a triangular situation, such as a love triangle or a family issue (father, mother, child). The Empress (trump III) is often depicted as pregnant. The Three of Swords can indicate emotional pain due to a triangular relationship (e.g., one partner cheating on another). The Three of Swords can also refer to the need for surgery. Here the patient has a triangular relationship with his or her own body: the triangle becomes that of patient, surgeon, and dysfunctional body part that needs to be cut away.

The fifth-century Neo-Platonist Proclus argued that reality has a triadic structure: the One, the Intellect, and the Soul. This basic threefold structure, and the idea that the intelligible world emanates from the One, had a major influence on the development of tarot. Many authors divide the twenty-one major arcana into three sets of seven, corresponding to the triune nature of reality and the soul's journey toward enlightenment. The importance of the trinity or "threeness" is seen in the popularity of three-card spreads to answer a variety of questions. In astrology, the basic energy of each element can be expressed in one of three basic modalities. Zodiac signs consist of three decans representing a beginning, middle, and end.

The triple spiral (or triskele) is an ancient symbol found in many cultures and appears to have an archetypal significance. Triple spirals are found at Celtic and pre-Celtic sites like the entrance stone to the tomb at Newgrange in Ireland. Christians adopted the triskele as a symbol of the three-in-one nature of the deity: Father, Son, and Holy Ghost. Christianity is not the only religion to espouse a triune godhead. This idea appears in the myths of various cultures, and Carl Jung classified the tripartite god as one of the archetypes. The Hindu Trinity, for example, consists of Brahma the Creator, Vishnu the Preserver, and Shiva the Destroyer, similar in nature to the three modalities of astrology: cardinal, fixed, and mutable.

Moon goddesses of antiquity are often depicted as having three aspects, after the phases of the moon: maiden, mother, crone. Sculptors portray the Greek goddess Hecate as three women joined at their backs. The Roman name for Hecate was Trivia. She was the goddess of witchcraft, graveyards, and three-way crossroads. The modern word "trivia" derives from the Latin *tri,* meaning "three," and *via,* meaning "road." In Roman times "trivial" information was posted at three-way intersections to help travelers find their way. Such "tri-vial" information was specific to a particular three-road junction and had no value at other locations.

In astrology, the zodiac signs that are distanced one-third of the way around the wheel from each other share the same elemental nature and are in harmony. Each season of the year is divided into three signs that mark the beginning, middle, and end of the season. Four seasons multiplied by three zodiac signs gives the twelve signs of the zodiac. Thus, the number three has an association with the ending of one season and the transition to the next. When a "3" card appears, one might wonder whether the querent is transitioning from one phase of life to another, i.e., is metaphorically undergoing a change of season in his or her life.

In Crowley's system, the Thoth Princes (Waite's Kings) correspond to the Hebrew letter *Vau*, the third letter of the name of the biblical deity. The Thoth Prince is the son of the Queen and Knight, their "active issue," "intellectual image," and manifestation of their union, whose action is "more enduring" as he sets forth to "carry out the combined energy of his parents."[129]

The iris, a three-petal flower that appears in many tarot decks, is named after the Greek goddess of the rainbow. The goddess Iris used rainbows to travel to Earth with messages from Juno and to transport souls of deceased women to the Elysian Fields where they could find eternal peace. The rainbow consists of seven colors, one for each of the classical planets of astrology.

Numerologists associate the number three with imagination, creativity, first fruits, versatility, trios, triangles, talent, artistic ability, creating something in consultation with others, planning, strategizing, achievement, self-expression, growth, expansion, sociability, fun, gaiety, friendship, family (the triad of father-mother-child), and networking. The Sephirah of three is Binah, Understanding.

The tarot pips numbered 3 center on themes of networking, joint creations, and the vicissitudes of triadic relationships. In the Golden Dawn system, the number three refers to the middle decan of the cardinal signs: the characteristic activity of the new season begins to manifest in one's life. Typical keywords for the "3" cards in the Waite-Smith tradition include:

- *Three of Wands*: established strength, enterprise, effort, trade, commerce, discovery, ships carrying your goods at sea, cooperation in business, help from a powerful ally, the end of troubles

- *Three of Cups*: celebration among friends, perfection, merriment, plenty, a happy ending, fulfillment, solace, healing

....
129 Crowley, *The Book of Thoth*, p. 150.

- *Three of Swords*: absence, delay, removal, division, rupture, dispersion, stormy weather for the emotions

- *Three of Pentacles:* a skilled artisan, a master craftsman, reward for work well done, skilled labor, mastery of one's craft, working in earnest, renown, glory, nobility

The Number Four (Tetrad)

The early Greek philosophers believed that reality was comprised of four elements: Fire, Water, Air, and Earth. Every time we walk through a rectangular doorway we subliminally experience the sense of structure that "four-ness" affords our lives. The Pythagoreans regarded the number four as the number of manifestation and material reality because four contains within itself all the principles of the tetractys (1, 2, 3, and 4) and is the generator of three-dimensional space. Four distinct points generate a three-dimensional solid, such as the tetrahedron—a geometric figure with four vertices and four faces. The ancients associated the tetrahedron with the element Fire, perhaps because of its phallic resemblance. The alchemical symbol for Fire, an equilateral triangle, is one face of the tetrahedron. Tarot trump IV, the Emperor, is linked to the masculine power of the Fire sign Aries. Crowley tells us that the number four "expresses the Rule of Law."[130]

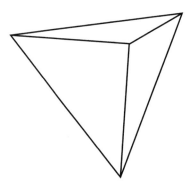

Phallic, fiery tetrahedron generated by four points.

....

130 Crowley, *The Book of Thoth*, p. 179.

In his dialogue *The Republic*, the Greek philosopher Plato (427–347 BCE) identified four essential virtues: Temperance (moderation, self-control), Fortitude (strength, courage), Prudence, and Justice. All four virtues appear in the modern tarot. Christian writers (e.g., Saint Ambrose, Augustine of Hippo, and Thomas Aquinas) called these the four *cardinal virtues* (from the Latin *cardo* meaning "hinge") because moral life hinges on them. In astrology, the term "cardinal" is used to describe the cardinal signs (Aries, Cancer, Libra and Capricorn) because the four seasons hinge on them. In addition to the cardinal virtues, Christian writers identified three "theological" virtues from the writings of Saint Paul: "And now abideth faith, hope, charity, these three; but the greatest of these is charity."[131] Four cardinal virtues plus three theological virtues add up to the sacred number seven.

In Crowley's system, the four Princesses (Waite's Pages) correspond to the Hebrew letter *Heh*, the fourth and final letter of the earthy part of the name of the biblical deity. Earth is the fourth element in the order of the seasons and the four letters of the tetragrammaton. Thoth Princesses represent "the ultimate issue of the original Energy in its completion, its crystallization, its materialization" … "the Silence into which all things return … at the same time permanent and nonexistent."[132] The four Pages/Princesses rule the four quarters of heaven around the North Pole and constitute the four "thrones" or seats of power of the four Aces, representing the root-force of the four elements that manifest in the material universe.

Modern genetics emphasizes the significance of the number four as a fundamental building block of biological organisms. The structure of DNA, which transmits the genetic information in living cells, consists of two chains of nucleotides twisted into a double helix. The two helices are joined by hydrogen bonds between complementary bases: adenine binds to thymine, and cytosine binds to guanine. Just four bases and their sequencing along the two helices of DNA carry all the information needed to construct a human being!

Astrology posits that all of reality can be symbolically represented within the twelve signs of the zodiac. Such is the case because reality is made up of four fundamental Elements—Fire, Water, Air, and Earth—that can manifest in one of three possible modalities—cardinal, fixed, and mutable. Four elements times three modalities results in the twelve signs of the zodiac.

....
131   Corinthians 1:13 (King James Bible).
132   Crowley, *The Book of Thoth*, p. 150.

In Pythagorean terms, twelve points determine an eleven-dimensional space. Recall that three points are needed to form a triangle in two-dimensional space. The number of determining points exceeds the number of dimensions by one. If we regard each sign of the zodiac as a distinct determining point of the universe, the astrological model is consistent with modern string theory, which posits eleven dimensions (ten of space and one of time). To the naked eye, and to common sense, the universe consists of only four dimensions: three of space and one of time. Theoretical physics has extended the number of dimensions from four to eleven, as implied by the mathematical structure of the zodiac with its twelve distinct signs around the wheel.

Numerologists associate the number four with matter, structure, consolidation, stability, security, hardening, manifestation, establishment, endurance, order, power, law, protection, stillness, safety, diligence, work, business, discipline, crystallization, and the laying of solid foundations. Arithmetic is based on four fundamental operations: addition, subtraction, multiplication, and division. There are four ranks among the court cards of the tarot: page, knight, queen, and king. The sephirah of four is Chesed, Loving Kindness.

The tarot pips numbered 4 center on the theme of creating a secure and enduring base from which to proceed. In the Golden Dawn system, the number four refers to the final decan of the cardinal signs: the initial phase of the new season is now established and gives way to the full manifestation of the season in the fixed sign of the element. Typical keywords for the "4" cards in the Waite-Smith tradition include:

- *Four of Wands*: country life, haven of refuge, domestic harvest-home, repose, harmony, concord, prosperity, peace, felicity, beauty, increase

- *Four of Cups*: discontent with one's environment, weariness, disgust, aversion, imaginary vexations, inability to find consolation, blended pleasure

- *Four of Swords*: an attitude of prayer, vigilance, retreat, solitude, exile, hermit's repose, a tomb or coffin

- *Four of Pentacles:* holding on tight, the security of possessions, gift, legacy, inheritance

The Pivotal Number Five (Pentad)

Because the fifth point of the tetractys lies exactly in the center of the triangle and because five occupies the midpoint of the nine single digits, the Pythagoreans associated this number with balance and justice. On philosophical grounds, the ancient Greeks did not consider zero a number. How could a symbol for no-thing represent some-thing? The central position of five in the set of nine digits resembles a pivot. The importance of this symmetry can be visualized by writing the sequence in Arabic numerals: 1 2 3 4 5 6 7 8 9. Because 5 lies in the middle, it also conveys a sense of instability as a "tipping point" between the first four and the last four single digits.

Another way to visualize the pivotal nature of the number five is to picture a bell curve with the number five at its midpoint. The pentacles on the stained glass of the Waite-Smith Five of Pentacles resemble a normal distribution curve. The man on crutches wears a bell around his neck, a method of warning people that a leper was approaching. A bell is also figures in the medieval tale of belling the cat; a group of mice decide it is a good idea to place a bell around the cat's neck but none of the mice is willing to volunteer to do it.

Left to right: Five of Pentacles *(Universal Tarot)*,
Scales of Justice above the single digits.

If we accept the Pythagorean notion that each additional digit adds a new dimension and that a minimum of four points generates a three-dimensional structure, then the number five adds the notion of motion as a fourth dimension. In other words, five distinct points make possible the generation of three-dimensional solids that can move in time. Mathematics was originally a science of measurement, and the measurement of motion requires a concept of the passage of time. From the Pythagorean perspective, the number four is static and five is the first number to make motion possible. With the introduction of motion come the inevitable changes that take place over time. Thus, five fundamentally suggests change and instability as portrayed in the related tarot pips.

Mathematicians have long been fascinated by the symmetry of the five Platonic solids (the tetrahedron, cube, octahedron, dodecahedron, and icosahedron, which have four, six, eight, twelve, and twenty faces respectively). Five appears to be a pivotal number in the construction of the universe; there are five, and only five, solids in which all the faces are congruent regular polygons with the same number of faces meeting at each vertex. Kepler discovered his laws of planetary motion in a failed attempt to relate the orbits of the planets to Plato's five solids.

During the Spanish Civil War (1936–1939), the Nationalist general Emilio Mola Vidal coined the term "fifth column" to refer to his militant supporters within Madrid who were trying to undermine the loyalist government while the general's four columns of forces marched on the capital city. Ernest Hemingway borrowed Mola Vidals' term "fifth column" for the title of a play. Since then, "fifth column" has come to mean any subversive clandestine group that tries to disrupt and undermine a nation's solidarity (which in Pythagorean terms would be symbolized by the number four).

Pentagrams, or five-pointed stars, were important religious symbols for both the Babylonians and the Pythagoreans of ancient Greece, who connected them with the goddess of health. The five points of a pentagram symbolize the human form. The Renaissance occultist Agrippa viewed the pentagram as a magical symbol whose five points represented the five elements of Neo-Platonism. In the 1800s, Eliphas Lévi replaced the coins of the early tarot decks with pentacles, modeled after the pentagram. In Lévi's view, the inverted pentacle was a sign of evil that attracts sinister influences because it represents the triumph of base desires over spiritual ideals.

Five is also the number of petals of the wild rose, which appears in many cards of the tarot. In Christianity, the red rose came to symbolize the five wounds and the blood of Christ. The ancient Greeks and Romans associated the rose with Venus, goddess of love. Christian writers changed this association to the Virgin Mary. The Romans painted roses on ceilings of their banquet rooms to warn that anything spoken beneath the rose should be kept secret or *sub rosa*. The god Eros/Cupid, son of Venus/Aphrodite, gave a rose to Harpocrates, the god of silence, to ensure that the sexual escapades of his mother would be kept secret.

In the Christian iconography of the Renaissance, the number five alluded to the five wounds of Christ and his travail and suffering on the cross. Nails were used to fasten each hand and foot of Jesus to the cross, and a Roman soldier thrust a lance into Christ's side to make sure he was dead. The term "Passion of Christ" derives from the Greek word *pasch,* meaning "to suffer." The Waite-Smith Ace of Cups shows five streams of life-giving water flowing from the chalice of the Catholic Mass, in which wine symbolizes the sacrificial blood of Christ. The water pouring on the earth in the Waite-Smith Star trump splits into five small streams, symbolizing the hope that the suffering of Christ brought to humankind.

Jerusalem Cross symbolizing the five wounds of Christ.

The Jerusalem Cross, or Crusader's Cross, with its large central cross surrounded by four smaller crosses, commemorates Christ's suffering. This pattern of a central figure adorned by smaller ones in the four corners can be found throughout Christian art. In early tarot decks, trump XXI, the Universe, depicts a central risen Christ surrounded by the four evangelists, as represented by the astrological symbols of the fixed signs of the zodiac. A sixteenth-century woodcut by Sigmund Grimm, strongly reminiscent of the World trump, shows the large central bleeding heart of Jesus with his nail-pierced hands and feet occupying the four corners.

Numerologists associate the number five with crisis, challenge, instability, restlessness, struggle, turning points, tension, the human senses, uncertainty, risk, unpredictability, impatience, travel, freedom, adventure, the passage of time, the urge for change, versatility, curiosity, sensuality, sexual charisma (the red rose, the affairs of Eros and Aphrodite), and the dislike of restriction. The Sephirah of five is Geburah: Severity, Might, Harshness, Punishment, and Retribution.

The tarot pips numbered 5 draw on the Pythagorean idea of change through motion and the Christian theme of travail, symbolized by the five wounds of Christ. In the Golden Dawn system, the number five refers to the first decan of the fixed signs: the initial phase of full manifestation of the season with an inherent tension between stability and change, leading to conflict and strife. Typical keywords for the "5" cards in the Waite-Smith tradition include:

- *Five of Wands*: sport or strife, mimic warfare, sham fight, strenuous competition, the struggle of the search after riches and fortune, the battle of life

- *Five of Cups*: a card of loss with something remaining, inheriting less than expected, a marriage with bitterness and frustration

- *Five of Swords*: disdain, dejection, dishonor, loss, degradation, seeking mastery over others, taking possession of the field

- *Five of Pentacles:* material trouble, hardship, destitution

The Number Six (Hexad)

A Platonic solid formed by six points is the eight-faced octahedron, traditionally associated with the element Air. The faces of the octahedron consist of upright and reversed equilateral triangles, one above the other, uniting the alchemical symbols for Fire (active, male) and Water (receptive, female) into a single coherent form, which is symbolic of marriage. The Waite-Smith pip sixes all depict this union of opposites of the octahedron as an active upright male positioned above or higher than a passive receptive figure.

The Pythagoreans associated the number six with marriage because it is the product of the first true feminine and masculine numbers: 2 x 3 = 6. Multiplication is employed because marriage brings forth children, and is more than the sum of its parts. The cube is a solid structure with six faces and thus analogous to marriage, which is a solid social structure providing the foundation for raising a family.

The lily blossom has two sets of three petals for a total of six. Lilies are symbols of purity, chastity, peace, virtue, and divine generosity. Not even Solomon in all his glory was arrayed like the lilies of the field, which neither toil nor spin. In Christian art, lilies refer to the virgin birth of Jesus. In ancient Egypt, lilies symbolized fertility.

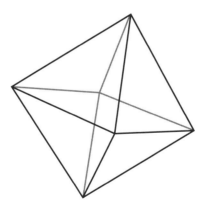

Platonic Octahedron with six vertices and eight faces.

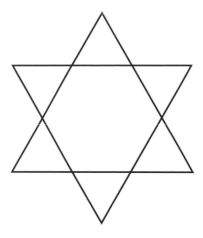

Six-pointed Star of David.

The six-pointed Star of David is an important symbol in Judaism. King David displayed the star on the round metal shield he carried into battle. The king attributed his many victories to God's power and protection, which were symbolized by the star. David's star became associated with victory, unity, hope, success, honor, balance, generosity, and good deeds. These meanings are also found in the pip sixes of the tarot. In addition, the overlapping triangles of the Star of David symbolize the intermingling or interpenetration of God (upward-pointing triangle) and humanity (downward-pointing triangle).

Because God created woman to be Adam's companion on the sixth day or creation, the interlaced triangles are also taken to symbolize the loving interpenetration of man and woman, who are equal but opposite in orientation. Interestingly, the tarot Lovers trump is numbered VI in most decks. Furthermore, each 6 pip of the Waite-Smith deck portrays behavior that falls along the feminine, nurturing spectrum. The Six of Wands depicts someone being praised for doing a good job; the Six of Cups, someone cherishing fond memories from the past; the Six of Swords, someone helping others escape from difficult circumstances; and the Six of Pentacles, someone giving financial aid to those less fortunate.

Numerologists associate the number six with harmony, cooperation, generosity, empathy, kindness, balance, dependability, service, sharing, responsibility, compassion, domesticity, smooth sailing, and the desire for peace and tranquility (not rocking the boat). The

Sephirah of six is Tiphareth: Beauty, Balance, and Harmony (associated with Jesus, the Son in the middle of the Christian Trinity).

The tarot pips numbered 6 center on the themes of compassion, sharing, bounty, happiness, skill, honor, accomplishment and strength in union with others. In the Golden Dawn system, the number six refers to the middle decan of the fixed signs: the consolidating phase of the full expression of the season with a strong desire for enduring stability. Typical keywords for the 6 cards in the Waite-Smith tradition include:

- *Six of Wands*: triumph, victory, honor, recognition, receiving laurels, great news, expectation crowned with desire

- *Six of Cups*: the past, memories, looking back, nostalgia, childhood happiness and enjoyments, things that have vanished

- *Six of Swords*: journey by water, smooth sailing, moving to a distant shore, envoy

- *Six of Pentacles:* distribution of wealth, goodness of heart, generosity, helping those in need, testimonies of one's success, gifts, presents, gratification, prosperity

The Number Seven (Heptad)

Seven has long been considered a sacred number. In the Old Testament God created the universe in seven days. It took God six days to fashion all of reality and he reserved the seventh day for rest, reflection, and evaluation of what he had done. The biblical deity created the Earth with seven continents and seven seas. He also created the seven visible planets after which man fashioned the seven-day week. Saturn is the outermost of the seven visible planets, and marks the outer limit of the classical solar system. Whenever a seven appears in the tarot, we are likely to confront some type of threshold or boundary that limits or defines the space we live in, and which requires us to take the time to reflect and assess what we have been accomplishing.

Each biblical plague in Egypt lasted seven days. The academic sabbatical occurs every seven years, and the Waite-Smith Seven of Pentacles depicts a farmer taking a sabbatical of sorts. God created seven levels of heaven; hence the expression "to be in seventh heaven." The Kabbalah regards seven as symbolic of wholeness and completion. In Judaism, when a close relative dies, the family sits *shiva* (the Hebrew word for "seven") for seven days. In a Jewish wedding, the bride circles the groom seven times under the wedding canopy (called a *chuppah*, much like the structure on the Waite-Smith Four of Wands.) The human head has seven orifices through which we admit the outside world: two eyes, two ears, two nostrils, and one mouth. Hence, the number seven may have something to do with contemplating the world around us and deciding what to take into ourselves.

Numerologists associate seven with self-awareness, objectivity, wisdom, mystery, secrecy, solitary action, withdrawal, introspection, reflection, contemplation, meditation, psychic insight, detachment, analysis, ingenuity, self-examination, careful assessment, challenge, knowledge, and intellectual pursuits. The twenty-one numbered major arcana consist of three sets of seven. The Sephirah of seven is Netzah: Eternity, Victory, and Endurance.

The tarot pips numbered 7 relate to pausing at a threshold that marks where we will go next with our lives; the result depends on the action taken. In the Golden Dawn system, the number seven refers to the last decan of the fixed signs; that is, the end of the full expression of the season and the need to let go of the equilibrium of the number six and cross the threshold to enter the final stage of existence. Typical keywords for the "7" cards in the Waite-Smith tradition include:

- *Seven of Wands*: valor, a position of advantage, discussion, strife, negotiations, barter, trade wars, competition, success

- *Seven of Cups*: imagination, sentiment, fantasy, images of reflection or contemplation, insubstantial attainments

- *Seven of Swords*: design, attempt, wish, hope, confidence, a plan that may fail, quarrelling, annoyance

- *Seven of Pentacles:* "For where your treasure is, there your heart will be also" (King James Bible, 1769); money, business, barter, innocence, ingenuity

The Number Eight (Octad)

The number four is associated with manifestation and tangible reality. Eight is twice four; thus eight is doubly implicated in the material world ($8 = 2 \times 4 = 2 \times 2 \times 2 = 2 + 2 + 2 + 2$). The tetrahedron with its four vertices is the Platonic solid associated with four, and the cube with its eight vertices is the figure related to the number eight. Cubes are formed by connecting eight discrete points. In his dialogue *Timaeus,* Plato assigned the cube to the element Earth. In this tradition, the regal thrones depicted on many tarot cards, which are symbolic of worldly power, are often cubical in shape.

The lotus blossom, which figures prominently in the Crowley-Harris Thoth Tarot, is one of the eight auspicious symbols of Buddhism. The lotus, which floats above the muddy waters of attachment and desire, is a symbol of purity of body, mind, and speech. It is also a symbol of death and resurrection. An ancient Egyptian myth tells of the lotus giving birth to the sun god Atum, based on the observation that the lotus closes at night to sink beneath the water and reemerges out of the mud to bloom again the next day.

In Hinduism, Ashta Lakshmi (Sanskrit for "eight Lakshmis") is a group of eight goddesses representing the powers of Shri-Lakshmi (the Hindu goddess of wealth) and presiding over the eight sources of wealth. The Star of Lakshmi consists of two rectangles at 45-degree angles superimposed upon one another. Lakshmi's symbol appears at the center of the tarot coins in the eighteenth-century Tarot Classic deck published by AGMuller.

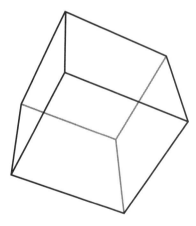

Platonic Cube of eight vertices and six faces (Hexahedron).

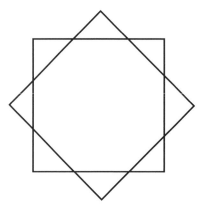

Eight-pointed Star of Lakshmi, signifying the eight sources of wealth.

Numerologists associate the number eight with wealth, mastery, maturity, worldly involvement, material success, leadership, organization, movement, power, self-discipline, efficiency, authority, tangible results, executive ability, and the desire for worldly status. The Sephirah of eight is Hod: Majesty, Splendor, and Glory.

The tarot pips numbered eight center on the themes of arriving at a mature level of development and preparing to move on, which is characterized by solitary or temporary success. In the Golden Dawn system, the number eight refers to the first decan of the mutable signs, that is, the earliest stage of the final expression of the season as it begins to wind down. Typical keywords for the "8" cards in the Waite-Smith tradition include:

- *Eight of Wands*: motion, flight, activity, swiftness, haste, immediacy, being on the verge of something, things being on the move, rapid developments, great hope, fast progress, the arrows of love

- *Eight of Cups*: the decline of a matter, dejection, leaving an undertaking behind, deserting the cups of one's felicity, putting things in perspective, reducing mountains to molehills

- *Eight of Swords*: temporary bondage or limitation, feeling bound and blindfolded, bad news, conflict, illness, chagrin, censure, disquiet

- *Eight of Pentacles:* work, employment, commission, artistry, skill in a craft or in business, preparation, ingenuity, exhibiting one's work or talents

The Number Nine (Ennead)

Nine is the last of the single-digit numbers in our base-ten number system; thus, it represents the end of a cycle. Once we pass nine, we either start a new cycle at one or move on to the double-digit numbers beginning with ten. The number nine carries with it a sense of achievement, completion, intensity, and fullness (9 = 3 x 3 = 3 + 3 + 3). Ten— 9 + 1—suggests excess or being overly full. In our discussion of the nine lives of an English-speaking cat, we saw the importance of nine in Celtic myth.

Men have a total of nine bodily openings, two of which serve to expel substances: the anus and the urethra. Women have an additional opening, the vagina, for a total of ten. The vaginal orifice has a dual role; it is a conduit through which things can either enter or leave the body. Perhaps this male-female difference has to do with the symbolic meaning of nine and ten among the pip cards. Both these numbers can signify the end of a cycle: nine being the culmination of a masculine cycle, and ten the ending of a feminine one. God created woman because Adam felt incomplete.

Numerologists associate the number nine with mental and spiritual achievements, abundance, idealism, compassion, tolerance, altruism, spirituality, inspiration, completion of the cycle of single digits, the end of one cycle and preparation for a new one. The Sephirah of nine is Yesod: Foundation, Vessel to bring action, the Christian Holy Spirit.

The pips numbered nine center on themes of achieving a firm basis and a high level of achievement, mastery or intensity in matters related to the suit. In the Waite-Smith deck, the nine cards depict the energy of the suit pushed to its limit. The Nine of Wands shows the result of unchecked ambition and love of challenge; the Nine of Swords, the outcome of excessive worry and affliction; the Nine of Pentacles, the solitariness and wealth that results from steady effort to achieve material well-being; and the Nine of Cups, the intense pleasure and satiety that results from having all your wishes granted.

In the Golden Dawn system, the number nine refers to the middle decan of the mutable signs, that is, the consolidation and fullness of the final expression of the season—its last hurrah. The element of the suit is now firmly rooted and able to express itself powerfully, for good or evil. Typical keywords for the "9" cards in the Waite-Smith tradition include:

- *Nine of Wands*: strength in opposition, courage in adversity, boldness, preparedness, expectant waiting, delay, suspension, adjournment

- *Nine of Cups*: feasting, abundance, a secure future, physical well-being, satisfaction, contentment, victory, success, advantage

- *Nine of Swords*: sorrow, lamentation, disappointment, despair, desolation, failure, miscarriage, delay, deception, death

- *Nine of Pentacles:* material well-being, success, plenty in all things, prudence, safety, accomplishment, discernment

The Number Ten (Decad)—△

For the Pythagoreans, ten was the perfect number. In ancient Greece, there were two systems for representing numbers. The system used in inscriptions and laws since the fifth century BCE "represents basic numbers by the first letter of the denoting word." [133] For example, pi stands for the Greek number *penta* (five), and *delta* represents the Greek number *deka* (ten). A separate representational system used the letters of the Greek alphabet to signify numbers. For example, delta is the fourth letter of the Greek alphabet, whose symbol is a triangle in the shape of the tetractys (1 + 2 + 3 + 4 = 10). The delta symbol is also the alchemical signifier of Fire. It is no surprise that the phallic symbol delta is also associated with leadership and dominion. Consider the shape of the pyramids of Egypt, erected to honor the pharaohs, or the Washington Monument, erected to honor the father of the United States.

When we reach ten, the sequence of the nine single digits has ended and thus ten is "one too many." Numerologists associate the number ten with abundance, fullness, excess, completion, fulfillment, reaching a limit, and being at the end of the line so that the only options

....

133   Michael Lahanas, "Greek Numbers," http://www.mlahanas.de/Greeks/Counting.htm
      (accessed 9 Jun. 2012).

remaining are transition and a new beginning. One might say of ten that "the buck stops here" and responsibility does not pass beyond this point. The Sephirah of ten is Malkuth, Kingship.

The tarot pips numbered ten relate to themes of excess, abundance, culmination, completion, fulfillment, and responsibility. In the Golden Dawn system, the number ten refers to the last decan of the mutable signs, that is, the end stage of the final expression of the season, which must pass out of existence so that a new season can begin. Matters of the element have been fully determined and can undergo no further development. From this point on, they can only fade from existence. Typical keywords for the 10 cards in the Waite-Smith tradition include:

- *Ten of Wands*: the oppression of fortune, gain, or success.

- *Ten of Cups*: contentment, repose of the heart, perfection of human love and friendship, whatever is in the querent's best interests.

- *Ten of Swords*: a painful ending, affliction, tears, sadness, desolation.

- *Ten of Pentacles:* gain, riches, family matters, archives, the family abode.

A Triangle of Seventy-Eight Dots

Have you ever wondered why the tarot now has seventy-eight cards? The earliest known tarocchi deck dates back to the year 1441 and contains eighty-six rather than seventy-eight cards. At some point in the early history of tarot, eight trump cards were discarded, leaving the seventy-eight-card deck we use today. How and why this change occurred is lost to history. It seems likely to me that the eventual adoption of only seventy-eight cards was based on numerological principles, because for the first few centuries of its existence the tarot was only an enjoyable game of cards.

Given the importance of triangular numbers to the Pythagoreans and the fundamental role of the number twelve in human culture (twelve signs of the zodiac, twelve tribes of Israel, twelve apostles of Christ, and so on), I constructed a triangle of twelve rows—three times the number of rows in the tetractys—and found that it had exactly seventy-eight dots, the number of cards in the tarot.[134] The sum of the dots in each row of the triangle ($1 + 2 + 3 + 4 + 5 + 6 + 7 + 8 + 9 + 10 + 11 + 12$) turns out to be seventy-eight.

....

134 I first lectured publicly on this idea in 1998 at the Astrological Society of Connecticut, http://www.myasc .org/tapesbyspeaker.htm

A triangle of twelve rows and seventy-eight dots; a "Tripled" Tetractys.

The Tetractys, the Decans, and the Tarot

It seems significant that the four-row tetractys, when "tripled" to form a triangle of twelve rows, produces seventy-eight points—the number of cards in the modern tarot. Pythagoras also observed that whole number ratios underlie musical harmony. When we double the length of string on a musical instrument, it produces a sound in harmony with the original string. To extend this musical analogy, by constructing a triangle of twelve rows, we have created a structure that resonates harmoniously with the original tetractys but is two "octaves" removed.

What if we were to construct a triangle only one "octave" removed from the tetractys by simply doubling the number of rows from four to eight? This new triangle of eight rows would have a total of thirty-six dots (1 + 2 + 3 + 4 + 5 + 6 + 7 + 8 = 36). Those versed in astrology will recognize thirty-six as the number of decans in the zodiac wheel (twelve signs with three decans in each). Again we are left wondering whether the structure of the tarot resonates in a fundamental way with the tetractys and its first two "octaves." To summarize:

- The tetractys of Pythagoras is a triangle of four rows made up of a total of ten dots, ten being the perfect number as well as the *number of pip cards in each suit* of the tarot.

- "Doubling" the tetractys produces a triangle of eight rows with a total of thirty-six dots: the total *number of decans in the zodiac.*

- "Tripling" the tetractys generates a triangle of twelve rows with a total of seventy-eight dots: the total *number of cards in the modern tarot deck.*

The Thirty-Six Decans and the Three Modalities of Astrology

By way of review, the horoscope is divided into four quadrants, representing the four seasons of the year. Each season has a beginning, a middle, and an end. Symbolically, this tripartite division is the basis for the three modalities of astrology: cardinal, fixed, and mutable. Cardinal signs initiate the season, fixed signs represent the season in full bloom, and mutable signs signal the transition from one season to the next. According to the Golden Dawn, the aces are the unmanifested pure potential of each season or suit; the remaining pip cards, numbers two through ten, are distributed among the three astrological modalities:

- Pips 2, 3, 4: *cardinal modality*—starting, initiating, pioneering, coming into being, creating something fresh and new, the early stages of creation

- Pips 5, 6, 7: *fixed modality*—stabilizing, consolidating, establishing, laying down structure, managing, enduring, sustaining, coming into full bloom

- Pips 8, 9, 10: *mutable modality*—transitioning, adapting, loosening structure, giving way, fading, letting go, moving on, dying, ending the old to make way for the new

These associations between the thirty-six decans and the tarot pip cards underlie many of the modern meanings used in interpretation with decks in the Waite-Smith tradition. The Golden Dawn approach to the decans is detailed in Corrine Kenner's text, *Tarot and Astrology* (Llewellyn, 2011).

The Fool and the Invention of Zero [135]

Tarot readers will be interested in the number zero because, in many decks, zero is the number of the Fool card. But is zero really a number? A deeper understanding of zero will help us appreciate its symbolism in the tarot. Noticing that 0 has the shape of an egg, Crowley placed a Cosmic Egg on his Thoth Hermit trump. In pre-Greek mythology, the Cosmic Egg was hatched because the birdlike Mother of Creation rubbed the North Wind between her hands, turning him into a giant phallic snake that impregnated her and fathered a giant egg. [136] (Crowley loved odd sexual practices.) The serpent then encircled the egg seven times, seven being a sacred number linked to the seven planets of antiquity. Incubated by the snake, the Cosmic Egg split open, releasing the solar system and all life on Earth. [137]

Borrowing a phrase from Wallace Stevens's *The Snow Man,* Robert Kaplan calls zero "the nothing that is." [138] Kaplan writes, "Zero began its career as two wedges pressed in a wet lump of clay." [139] About five thousand years ago, the Sumerians used an empty space to indicate the value of a position within a written number. Around 400 BCE they began to use two wedges to represent the empty place in their positional number system. Today we employ zero in the

....

135 See Charles Seife's *Zero: The Biography of a Dangerous Idea* (New York: Penguin, 2000) and Robert Kaplan's *The Nothing That Is: A Natural History of Zero* (New York: Oxford University Press, 2000).

136 The Hebrew letter *Yod* on Crowley's Hermit card means "hand," perhaps alluding to her "hand-ling" of the North Wind.

137 Robert Graves, *The Greek Myths* (London: Penguin Books, 1992), pp. 170–171.

138 Wallace Stevens, *The Snow Man* (1921), http://www.writing.upenn.edu/~afilreis/88/stevens-snowman.html (accessed 5 May 2012).

139 Kaplan, *The Nothing That Is*, p. 6.

same way. Our use of zero allows us to understand the difference in value between 92 and 902. In contrast, the Romans had no position holder and found it difficult to perform even the simplest arithmetic. Kaplan suggests trying to add 43 + 24 using Roman numerals: XLIII + XXIV = ? Oh my god!

For the Sumerians, zero was not a true number. It served merely as a punctuation mark, a way of indicating an empty position within a written number. The ancient Greeks also used zero as a placeholder, but instead of two wedges they used a small circle to indicate the zero place, perhaps because it looks like an empty hole. The Greeks had a hard time conceiving of zero as a number because numbers, they believed, were abstractions from *things* in the real world. Thus, 1 referred to one-thing, 2 to two-things, and so on. How could a number, which implies *some*-thing, refer to *no*-thing? For the Greeks, zero simply stood for nothingness. To conceive of zero as a number implied to the Greeks, and later to medieval philosophers, that existence could come from nonexistence—a profound religious and philosophical question related to the Neo-Platonic beliefs that underlie the tarot trumps. Robert Place has extensively discussed Neo-Platonism and the tarot in his book, *Tarot—History, Symbolism, and Divination.*

By 650 CE, the mathematicians of India began to use zero as a number, not merely as a holder for an empty space. This use of zero, along with the Hindu numerals, was adopted by the Arabs who, like bees pollinating flowers, eventually transported it to Europe where the Hindu digits were erroneously called Arabic numerals. The use of zero as a number rather than a placeholder caused tremendous philosophical and theological debate. Zero stands uniquely apart from all other numbers. When added to or subtracted from any number, it leaves the number unchanged. Multiplication by zero always produces zero. Division by zero is impossible and leads to a breakdown of the laws of physics. The closer we get to dividing by zero, the more rapidly we approach infinity.

Number Symbolism and Card Counting

No discussion of number symbolism would be complete without a mention of the Golden Dawn method of card counting. The Golden Dawn advanced this idea in its "Opening of the Key" method. A review of this technique would take us too far afield from the main theme of the book. For those who are interested, I recommend Douglas Gibb's presentation at *www .taroteon.com*. [140] The idea behind card counting is that any tarot card can be linked thematically to another card in a layout according to the numerical value the card is assigned. Cards can be counted either forward or backward from the starting card, which is always regarded as number one in the sequence. The Golden Dawn assigned numerical values to the cards as follows:

- Aces = 5

- Non-ace pip cards = the number on the card

- Pages = 7

- Knights, Queens, and Kings = 4

- Major Arcana associated with zodiacal signs = 12

- Major Arcana associated with the planets = 9

- Major Arcana associated with an element (the Fool, Hanged Man, or Judgment) = 3

To illustrate, recall Jane's Celtic Cross reading in chapter one. Suppose we wanted more information about the Knight of Pentacles in the "crown" position. Knights are counted as four. Hence, in the Golden Dawn system, counting from this Knight as the first card in the sequence, the second card is the "future" position of the Celtic Cross, the third card is the querent as she is now, and the fourth card is in the "environment" position or card 8 of the Celtic Cross, which happens to be the Seven of Wands. Card counting tells us that the Knight of Pentacles, who represents her husband, is the man assuming a defensive posture in

....

140   Douglas Gibb, "How to Read with the Opening of the Key and Still Keep Your Sanity," June 1, 2011, *Tarot Eon,* http://taroteon.com/tarot-tutorial/how-to-read-with-the-opening-of-the-key-and-still-keep -your-sanity/ (accessed 15 Nov. 2011).

card 8 of the spread. Counting backward from the Knight of Pentacles takes us to card 2, the "crossing" card—the Nine of Wands—which also depicts a man taking a defensive stance.

Our brief discussion of card counting brings this chapter on number symbolism to a close. Perhaps the most important lesson about numbers is summarized in a poster that Einstein kept on his office wall at Princeton University: *Not everything that counts can be counted, and not everything that can be counted counts.* Good advice for nerds of all ages!

SIX

The Four Elements

The Temperament of Man is hot and dry, and
that of the Woman is cold and moist. [141]
Dr. Marin Cureau de la Chambre, France, 1665

Modern divinatory meanings in astrology and tarot are greatly indebted to the theory of four elements of Greek philosophy. Occultists have long associated tarot cards with the classical elements—Fire, Water, Air, and Earth—and have used the underlying qualities of the elements to suggest affinity or antipathy among the cards. The Golden Dawn, so influential in the development of modern tarot interpretations, explained the interaction of the tarot cards as follows:

- Wands (Fire) are antagonistic toward Cups (Water), and vice versa.
  (Water extinguishes fire.)

- Swords (Air) are antagonistic toward Pentacles (Earth), and vice versa.
  (Picture a sword shattering earthenware pottery, or King Arthur finding a sword stuck in a stone.)

- Cards are strongly reinforced when next to cards of the same element.

....

141   Marin Cureau de la Chambre (French physician), *The Art of How to Know Men,* trans. John Davies (London: Thomas Dring Publishers, 1665), p. 12.

- Cards are weakened when next to cards of the antipathetic element.

- Wands (Fire) are supported by adjacent Swords (Air) or Pentacles (Earth).

- Swords (Air) are supported by adjacent Wands (Fire) or Cups (Water)

- Cups (Water) are supported by adjacent Swords (Air) or Pentacles (Earth).

- Pentacles (Earth) are supported by adjacent Wands (Fire) or Cups (Water).

To understand this system of the Golden Dawn, we need to study the four elements and their primary qualities. This topic can be complex, but it is worth the effort because these ideas underlie much of the symbolism of both astrology and tarot. Understanding the four elements will give the reader a fundamental understanding of tarot symbolism that cannot be achieved by any other means. Don't worry if philosophy is not your cup of tea. I will explain things as simply as possible, though you may need to read certain sections more than once. No pain, no gain. Or perhaps a better refrain would be: "Where there's smoke, there's fire." The alchemical symbols of the elements are as follows:

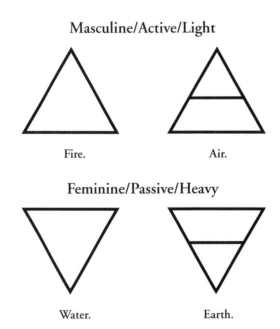

Masculine/Active/Light

Fire.   Air.

Feminine/Passive/Heavy

Water.   Earth.

The symbols for the masculine/active/light phallic elements, Fire and Air, point upward. In contrast, the symbols for the feminine/passive/heavy receptive elements, Water and Earth, point downward. The resemblance in shape to human genitalia is no coincidence. Ronald Decker notes that Italian card players called the Cups and Coins the "round suits" and the Batons and Swords the "long suits." [142] Tarot interpreters would later regard Wands/Batons (Fire) and Swords (Air) as phallic symbols, and Cups (Water) and Coins/Pentacles (Earth) as womb symbols. As the authors of *Tarot for Relationships* explain, "the male penis is seen as active, hard, and penetrating, while the female vagina is seen as passive, soft, and yielding, and the female womb as receptive and nurturing." [143]

Another way to view the four elements is to compare them to the classic figure of yin and yang of Chinese philosophy. Yin is considered the female, passive, receptive principle of nature; it is related to shade, cold, nighttime, and the moon. In the tarot, the even-numbered cards are considered yin. Yang is the male, active, assertive principle of nature; it is related to light, heat, daytime, and the sun. In the tarot, the odd-numbered cards are considered yang.

The ancient philosophers often based their ideas on analogies with nature, especially the form and function of the human body. Men were considered fiery (hot and dry) and were portrayed in Renaissance art as tanned and trim, with muscular torsos because the lightness of Fire (heat rises) causes male flesh to distribute itself preferentially in the muscles of the upper regions of the body. Women, on the other hand, were considered watery (cold and wet) and were portrayed in art with pale skin, rounded features, large hips, and bountiful buttocks because the heaviness of Water, a cold element, causes female flesh, to settle preferentially in the lower parts of the body (cold sinks, water flows downward).

Fire refers to radiant energy, like the light emanating from the sun and the stars. Ovid in his *Metamorphoses* mentions that Fire is the lightest and highest element. Its symbol is an upright equilateral triangle. Each element has a particular directionality. Being light and hot by nature, Fire and Air tend to rise above the surface of the earth. On the other hand, Water and Earth,

....

142   Ronald Decker, *Art and Arcana*, p. 73.

143   Jocelyn Almond and Keith Seddon, *Tarot for Relationships* (Northamptonshire, UK: The Aquarian Press, 1990), p. 12.

being heavy and cold, tend to sink below the surface of the earth, and their triangular symbols point downward.

"Hot" Fire and Air expand upward and outward or, as Aristotle says, move centrifugally toward the outer limit. "Cold" Water and Earth contract downward and inward or, as Aristotle says, move centripetally toward the center. Earth, being the "heaviest" and slowest-moving element, can be found beneath the bodies of water that it sustains. From lightest to heaviest, according to Aristotle the elements run in order as follows: Fire, Air, Water and Earth. [144] Schwickert and Weiss make the following analogy between modern ideas about states of matter and ancient concepts of the four elements:

- Fire—radiant energy

- Air—gaseous state

- Water—liquid state

- Earth—solid state [145]

The idea of four elements is attributed to the Greek philosopher Empedocles of Sicily (c. 492–c. 432 BCE) who explained the world in terms of four "roots of all things." His writings contain many botanical metaphors, and historians believe Empedocles may have been a healer familiar with the curative properties of plants. Later philosophers renamed Empedocles's four "roots" the four "elements" and used them to explain the natural world. The Greek word for "element," *stoicheia*, is the same word used for the various letters in the Greek alphabet. Empedocles pictured the elements or roots as building blocks of matter much as the letters of the alphabet form the words of a language. Everything that exists in the material world is considered a combination of the four elements.

According to Empedocles, in the beginning there existed two primal and opposing forces in the universe: Love and Strife. These primal forces acted on the four elements, causing them to interact and form the material universe. Love (*philia* in Greek) seeks harmonious union and is

....

144 G. E. R. Lloyd, *Aristotle: The Growth and Structure of his Thought* (Cambridge, UK: Cambridge University Press, 1968), chapters 7–8.

145 Friedrich Schwickert and Adolf Weiss, *Cornerstones of Astrology* (Dallas: Sangreal Foundation, 1972), p. 7.

associated with the Greek love goddess Aphrodite, or the Roman Venus. Strife (*neikos* in Greek) seeks differentiation and is associated with the Greek war-god Ares, or the Roman god Mars.

Love brings together. Strife pushes apart. Psychoanalysts will see a parallel between Empedocles's notions of Love and Strife and Freud's ideas about libido and thanatos, the death instinct. Physicists will recognize Empedocles's description of the action of Love in the natural world in Newton's theories about the force of gravity. Modern cosmologists will see a parallel between Empedocles's Strife and the dark energy still pushing the universe apart so many years after the Big Bang.

In Empedocles's theory, the cosmos begins as a divine harmonious sphere in which Love has homogeneously fused together the four eternal elements into a state of loving unity— something akin to homogenized milk. This perfect blending of the four elements into a loving homogeneous sphere renders the existence of matter impossible. All that exists in the beginning is an immaterial sphere of homogeneous "oneness" of the elements which are united by Love (a kind of hippie utopia from the 1960s). This loving Oneness has the as-yet-unmanifested potential to develop into material reality.

Along comes Strife, the nemesis of Love. Strife is the odd one out, relegated to the outer limits of the cosmos. Gradually Strife bores his way into the primal loving sphere and cleaved the One into many—a philosophical Big Bang. In our milk analogy, Strife caused the cream to separate from the homogenized milk. Love favors oneness and unity, but Strife fosters separation and differentiation.

In the tarot, the even-numbered cards come under the influence of Love and often depict scenes of harmony, giving, union, contemplation, or repose. The odd-numbered cards, lacking the balance of loving evenness, are minions of Strife and often depict tension, attack, challenge, defense, and separation. Under the influence of Strife, the eternal elements precipitate out from the primal sphere, like cream rising to the top of the milk. The four elements then combine with one another in various proportions, and the world of discrete matter takes form.

Under the ongoing pressure of Strife, material reality will eventually come to an end. Strife ultimately causes the elements to separate into their pure forms. Empedocles calls this new state, under the total domination of Strife, the whirl. In this whirl of Strife, the four elements have completely separated from one another into four distinct groups, each homogenously comprised of a single element. The world of matter as we know it ceases to exist. But then along comes Love, who reasserts herself against the whirl of Strife. Love's embrace causes the elements to combine again, forming a new universe of material reality as the disparate elements unite in various proportions. Under the continuing influence of Love, the elements eventually reunite into the primal sphere of loving Oneness. The material universe again ceases to exist until Strife upsets the balance and the endless cycle begins anew.

We can view Empedocles's theory of Love and Strife from the viewpoint of the lemniscate (the infinity symbol, a figure 8 turned on its side). The lemniscate—a popular symbol in many tarot decks—is a special case of the Cassini oval. In 1680, the Italian astronomer Giovanni Cassini studied all the curves that could be formed in a plane by a set of points distributed such that the product of the distances of any point on the curve from two fixed points (or foci) remained constant. For the mathematically challenged, you take any point on the curve, measure the distance from that point to the two central foci, multiply those two distances together, and the product is always the same number. This particular Cassini oval plays a prominent role in the Waite-Smith and Crowley-Harris decks. It may not be obvious, but there is a connection between the lemniscate and Empedocles's creation myth (Love, Strife, the four elements, and the cosmic cycle). Understanding this connection can give us a greater appreciation of this symbol on cards like the Waite-Smith Magician, Strength, and Two of Pentacles.

Empedocles's Loving sphere and Strife-generated whirl correspond to the central point where the loops of the lemniscate intersect—the midpoint of the sideways figure eight. At this midpoint, the material world cannot exist. If we assign Strife to the right-hand loop of the lemniscate and Love to the left, then the right-hand side represents the world of matter as we know it, brought into existence by Strife's increasing influence on the Loving sphere.

Infinity Symbol (Lemniscate).

As we proceed around the loop of Strife, we eventually return to the central point, which under the influence of Strife now consists of four pure elemental groups of the whirl where matter as we know it cannot exist. Love reenters the picture and these elemental groups begin to combine again, producing a new material world on the left, a kind of parallel universe. As we travel around the loop of Love on the left, we eventually return to the central point, which now has the form of a homogenous sphere of Oneness, and the cycle starts over.

Empedocles's account of the origin of the universe resembles the modern theory of the Big Bang, in which there was a great initial explosion that created an expanding universe filled with matter and antimatter. These particles and antiparticles were originally together at a unified central point of homogeneous nothingness. For some reason (perhaps the influence of Strife), the laws of physics dictated an imbalance in the amounts of matter and antimatter in the universe. For every billion particles of antimatter there were a billion and one particles of matter (Love and Strife were not evenly matched). As these particles of opposite polarities proceeded to annihilate one other and return to their primal state of blended oneness (under the unifying power of Love), the remaining particles of matter combined to form the world as we know it.

After pondering Empedocles's theories, Aristotle (384–322 BCE) offered his own view on how material reality comes into being and goes out of existence.[146] He began with the idea that the material world consists of objects that we can perceive, especially with our sense of touch. If we can touch something, we know it exists. Through touch we become aware of certain qualities of an object, qualities that fall into complementary pairs such as hot or cold, wet or dry, hard or soft, rough or smooth, viscous or brittle, and so on. These qualities also describe Empedocles's four "immutable" elements because all matter consists of combinations of the eternal four elements. Aristotle believed, however, that Empedocles's elements are not immutable because they can morph into one another. Thus, the four elements must be composed of something even more basic, namely qualities that truly are immutable.

Aristotle argued that the various tangible qualities can be grouped into two broad categories: those that are *active* or have the power to act, versus those that are *passive* or *receptive* and susceptible to being acted upon. In making this distinction, Aristotle had in mind the duality of male and female, that is, the active erect phallus versus the passive receptive vagina. He regarded

....
146 Aristotle, *De Generatione et Corruptione,* trans. C. J. F. Williams (Oxford, UK: Oxford, 1982).

four qualities in particular as being essential because all other tangible qualities can be derived from them. The four distinguishing qualities fall into the polarities: *hot* versus *cold,* and *wet (*or *moist)* versus *dry.* It is important to keep in mind that Aristotle is talking about philosophical principles rather what we mean commonly when describing things as hot, cold, wet, and dry.

Having narrowed the essential qualities down to four, Aristotle states that the two qualities of the first pair, "hot versus cold," are *active* and have the power to *act by associating.* In contrast, the two qualities of the second pair, "dry versus wet," are *passive* and involve *being acted upon,* that is, being susceptible or conforming.

Aristotle's main idea about heat and cold is that they are active principles that associate things. Heat and cold differ, however, in the kind of things that they bring together. Citing various examples from nature, Aristotle notes that the heat of fire actively "associates things of the same kind" in a process of purification that burns away the dross. Cold, on the other hand, joins together and actively "associates things of different kinds." Consider for example the modern alcoholic beverage, the frozen daiquiri, which brings together disparate ingredients into a slushy, semifrozen mix. Or better yet, think of a child who licks a shiny flagpole on a freezing winter's day only to find his tongue securely united with the icy pole.

The quality of wetness (fluidity) is found in air and water because these elements flow and assume the shape of their containers. Something "wet" is fluid and malleable, adaptable in shape, plastic, conforming, easily molded, and not determined by a boundary of its own. Something "dry" is passive in the sense that its shape must conform to its essential nature and inherent definition. Dry things tend to be inflexible, rigid, shriveled, hard, distinct, resistant to change, and not easily molded. In Aristotle's words, "dry" is that which is "readily determinable by its own limit, but not readily adaptable in shape." [147] In other words, "dry" things are self-determined or self-defined. Aristotle had in mind Plato's ideal forms (archetypes) to which objects in the natural world conform.

Having concluded that all tangible qualities can be derived from four essential ones, Aristotle argues that these four qualities cannot be further subdivided. Thus, they constitute the four most fundamental qualities of the universe:

....

147 Aristotle, *De Generatione et Corruptione.*

It is clear, then, that all the other differences [in tangible qualities] reduce to the first four, but that these admit of no further reduction. For the hot is not essentially moist or dry, nor the moist essentially hot or cold: nor are the cold and the dry derivative forms, either of one another or of the hot and the moist. Hence these must be four. [148]

Aristotle's view is rather amazing. He maintains that *all* properties of physical matter can be described in terms of just four essential ones: hot, cold, wet, and dry. Let's take a closer look. Remember that we are describing philosophical principles and not the commonplace meanings of these four words:

- *Heat* is the life force, the dynamic principle that animates living things. According to Aristotle, the element most emblematic of heat is Fire. Heat rises, enlivens, expands, energizes, propels, radiates, excites, impassions, leads, mobilizes, feels passion, looks to the future, moves outward, and keeps on going. An exploding supernova illustrates the dynamic, expansive, radiant nature of heat. A fan of *Star Trek* might say that heat is a centrifugal force, pushing upward and outward "to boldly go where no man has gone before." A dog "in heat" demonstrates certain properties of heat, as does the advertising icon the Energizer Bunny. Heat purifies and actively brings together things of the same kind by burning the chaff from the wheat, so to speak. In the ancient theory of bodily humors, "hot" men were adept at actively promoting their singleminded point of view. Heat produces leaders who actively influence others.

- *Cold*, being the opposite of heat, inhibits animation, moves downward and inward, and saps vital energy. According to Aristotle, the element most emblematic of cold is Water. The action of cold is to slow, calm, center, contract, congeal, adhere, unite, concentrate, move inward, deliberate, condense, devitalize, retract, crystallize, shrink, depress, plod, drain, sink, and deaden. Unlike heat, cold is a centripetal force that pulls

148 Ibid.

downward and inward, like gravity. A black hole, in which all matter, even light, is pulled in toward the center exemplifies this property of cold.

Volcanic eruptions demonstrate the contrast between hot and cold. During a volcanic eruption, hot lava is propelled upward and outward; but as cooling takes place the lava flows downward until it congeals and turns into solid rock. We call people who are unfeeling "cold-hearted" and those who commit heinous crimes without remorse "cold-blooded." Cold actively brings together things of different kinds into a chilled mass of disparate entities, somewhat like a frozen asteroid in outer space. In human terms, cold seeks to join people into one big (happy or dysfunctional) family. In the ancient theory of body humors, "cold" women are inwardly focused and gifted at pulling people together and getting them to cooperate by uniting disparate points of view.

• *Wet* is the principle of fluidity, elasticity, flexibility, plasticity, moistness, softening, yielding, surrendering, merging, dissolving, conformity, fusion, and malleability. According to Aristotle, Air is the element most emblematic of wetness (fluidity). Initially I was puzzled that he considered Air to be wetter (more fluid) than Water until I realized that we commonly refer to the "flow" of thoughts and the "stream" of consciousness. The Air signs in astrology are mental and communicative.

"Wet" people play softball rather than hardball. Wetness earns water its reputation as a universal solvent. Wet things, like air and water, do not determine their own shape but passively conform to an external limit. Because of their blurred boundaries, wet things are not clearly defined. Wetness accounts for our capacity for whimsy. We say politicians are "all wet" when they lack backbone and bend to the will of moneyed lobbyists. Dryness, in contrast, has a backbone that is rigid and unyielding.

Wetness goes with the flow and does not determine its own shape. "Wet" human bodies tend to be rounded and soft because of the abundance of fatty tissue overlying the muscles beneath the skin.

In the ancient theory of bodily humors, women (considered "cold and wet") had rounded bodies and soft features. Excessive wetness produces people who are passive and submissive; they morph easily, have poor boundaries, and tend to merge with others. Have you ever spilled water (wet) on a dry page of text written with a fountain pen?

- *Dry* is the principle of rigidity, self-definition, clear form, inflexibility, inelasticity, tension, desiccation, dominion, sharp boundaries, precision and vehement energetic activity. According to Aristotle, the element most emblematic of dryness is Earth. Dry people play hardball rather than softball. Something dry has a precisely defined form or boundary that conforms to its inherent nature. Dryness reduces things to their most essential form and they may become brittle or crisp in the process; there is little or no padding. Mathematics lectures are often irremediably "dry." Excessive dryness produces a state that is shrunken, rigid, distinct, and breakable, like a dry bone. Have you ever seen an Egyptian mummy in a museum? With extreme dryness, things may simply crumble: "Dust thou art, and unto dust shalt thou return." [149]

Dryness has sharply defined limits, vehemently resists change, and does not go with the flow. What you see is what you get. If pressure is applied, dry things tend to snap. Like Polonius in Shakespeare's *Hamlet*, dryness says, "This above all: to thine own self be true." Unlike wetness, which regards separation as an illusion, dryness adheres to an inner ideal or limit, an inherent form that distinguishes it as unique and different from others. Dry human bodies tensely maintain their inherent form; they have sharply defined features and a "ripped" appearance because of the tension in the muscles and the scarcity of body fat. In the ancient theory of bodily humors, men were considered "hot and dry" and were depicted in art with chiseled muscles put to dynamic action.

....
149   Genesis 3:19 (King James Bible).

The Four Qualities and the Elements		
FIRE △ *(hot* > dry) **	**HOT** (energizes, activates; unites "like" things)	*AIR* △ *(wet* > hot)
DRY (tensely self-determined form)	↑ (bonding) ← (conforming) → ↓	**WET** (fluidly other-determined form)
EARTH ▽ *(dry* > cold)	**COLD** (chills, sinks, slows; unites "unlike" things)	*WATER* ▽ *(cold* > wet)

** In this text, I have used the mathematical symbol ">" for "is greater than" and "<" for "is less than."

**The vertical axis is active and bonding or affiliating;
the horizontal axis is passive and adapting or conforming.**

Aristotle's four qualities lie along two dimensions—one, active and associative; the other, passive and conforming. The qualities of hot and cold are opposites that lie along the active dimension of bonding, affiliating, or joining together. "Hot" purifies and joins together things of the same kind whereas "cold" combines and amalgamates things of different kinds. On the other hand, the qualities of dry and wet are opposites that lie along a passive dimension of conforming or adapting to some inner or outer structure. The shape of a "dry" object conforms to its inherent essential nature and is thus self-determined. In contrast, something "wet" conforms to the shape of its container and is determined by something outside itself.

Keywords for the Four Primary Qualities of the Elements		
Essential Quality	Keywords	Body Type
Hot	Expansive, moving upward and outward, arousing, radiant, enlivening, energizing, vital, passionate, future-oriented, impulsive, active, speeding up, enterprising, "in heat"; bonds together things of the same kind in pure form	Full-bodied, muscular; warm and rosy skin
Dry	Tense, vehement, unyielding, exaggerated, precise, sharply defined, hard, inflexible, bossy, self-defined, dominating; resists change, has a rigid structure, reduces things to their essentials, is self-determined by its own inherent form	Sharply defined; chiseled, "ripped" or tense musculature; coarse and dark skin
Cold	Contractive, moving downward and inward, centered, calm, settled, deliberate, heavy, concentrating, plodding, slowing, pessimistic, contemplative, fearful; tends toward inactivity, brings together things of different kinds	Thin; cool, dull, and marblelike skin
Wet	Fluid, yielding, obliging, softening, pacific, surrendering, merging, loosening, soft, flexible, adaptable, lacks its own form, impressionable, kind; goes with the flow, lacks backbone, passively conforms to the shape of its vessel	Rounded body, soft features; muscles not well-defined; warm, moist, and pale skin

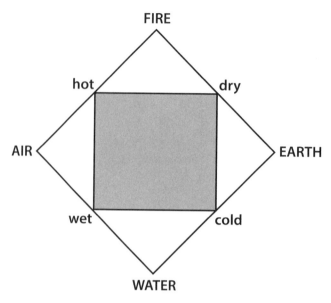

Properties of the Four Elements according to Aristotle.

Ten Essential Principles of Creation

In summary, in the beginning there was a dimensionless point of Loving Oneness that contained within it the potential to create the material universe. Strife acted on this primordial Oneness, to produce a "big bang" that set in motion the process of combination of the four elements to create matter as we know it. Aristotle believed that the four eternal elements (Fire, Water, Air, and Earth) have their own "subatomic" structure, namely, the four primary qualities (hot, cold, wet, dry). Thus, ten essential principles underlie all of creation: Love, Strife, the four elements, and the four qualities. The Pythagoreans regarded "10" as fundamental to all of creation, as did the Kabbalists who borrowed this idea from Pythagoras to explain their ten steps of creation. I believe it was Crowley who made a connection between the fundamental nature of the number ten $(1 + 2 + 3 + 4 = 10)$, the twelve signs of the zodiac (3 modalities x 4 elements = 12), and the twenty-two trumps of the tarot $(10 + 12 = 22)$.

An Elemental Algebra for Tarot Readers

Aristotle noted that the four essential qualities are not evenly distributed among the elements. In fact, a different quality predominates in each of the four elements. If we use the letters H for *hot*, C for *cold*, W for *wet*, and D for *dry*, we can create a kind of "algebra" to indicate in an easy way the predominance of qualities of each element. This system of notation is a general guide and is not intended to be mathematically precise. In other words, our proposed algebra of the elements is more "wet" than "dry."

- *Fire* is primarily *hot* and secondarily *dry*. Fire = HH D.

- *Air* is primarily *wet* and secondarily *hot*. Air = WW H.
  (Here *wet* refers to the fluidity of Air or Water.)

- *Water* is primarily *cold* and secondarily *wet*. Water = CC W.

- *Earth* is primarily *dry* and secondarily *cold*. Earth = DD C.

This system of notation allows us quickly to see the inner composition of each element and to determine what would happen if we were to combine two elements. Heat (H) counterbalances cold (C), and wetness (W) counterbalances dryness (D). The element Fire (HH D) is the opposite of Water (CC W), and the element Air (WW H) is the opposite of Earth (DD C).

In Aristotle's view, the elements can be converted into one another by making changes in the qualities that compose them. Two elements with a primary quality in common can easily be converted into one another. Two elements with no primary quality in common require considerable effort and a two-stage process to convert one into another. Occultists absorbed Aristotle's distinction into the concept of "dignity." Thus, two tarot cards that share a primary quality (e.g., Wands with Pentacles or with Swords, or Cups with Pentacles or with Swords) are said to dignify one another. Two cards that have no primary quality in common (e.g., Wands with Cups, or Swords with Pentacles) weaken one another.

In the occult worldview, when Fire (HH D) joins with Water (CC W), they *appear to* cancel each other out and *seem to* return to primordial nothingness (HH counterbalances CC, and D counterbalances W)—something akin to matter annihilating antimatter. In the world of Empedocles, however, the elements cannot annihilate one another. Fire and Water, being eternal, continue to exist; but if the amount of each element is perfectly matched by its polar opposite, the net result of their interaction will be a return to the perfect loving Oneness of the primal Sphere, which manifests as a kind of paralysis of action in the mundane world. [150]

One can compare the combining of antagonistic elements to the state of the U.S. Congress when equal proportions of Democrats and Republicans are in power. The two political parties continue to exist but pull in opposite directions so that nothing gets done. A state of paralysis pervades the Senate and House of Representatives. This analogy is not perfect because even when the two parties are unevenly distributed, nothing seems to get done.

In any case, when Earth (DD C) joins with Air (WW H), they also appear to negate one another because DD counterbalances WW, and C counterbalances H. As in the case of Fire and Water, the elements Earth and Air continue to exist; but if they are in a perfectly balanced state, the action of one counterbalances that of the other, resulting in paralysis.

In the real world the elements are never perfectly matched and their elemental qualities are not able to cancel each other out. Generally there is a predominance of certain qualities over others. If something strongly Fire mixes with something moderately Water, then heat and dryness have an edge over cold and wetness, and the net result is mildly fiery. For example, the tarot Queens are associated with Water, but the Queen of Cups, a member of a feminine Water suit, is decidedly more "Watery" than the Queen of Wands, who belongs to a masculine Fire suit.

In summary:

- Fire when mixed with Water can create paralysis because these two elements have nothing in common. Water extinguishes fire. Wands surrounded by Cups are constrained and ill-dignified, and vice versa.

- Earth when mixed with Air can create paralysis because these two elements have nothing in common. Earth mixed with air produces life-threatening smog. Ever been to Los Angeles? Pentacles surrounded by Swords are constrained and ill-dignified, and vice versa.

....

150 Aristotle believed that the four elements can be converted into one another by making changes in the qualities that compose them.

- All other combinations of elements (and of their corresponding tarot suits) have at least one elemental quality in common. Cards that share elemental qualities support or "dignify" one another. Beware, however, that an excess of a given element can indicate an imbalance and thus a potential problem. Too much heat, for example, can indicate impulsiveness, excessive haste, excessive optimism, and so on.

Qualities of the Four Elements							
++ Primary + Secondary	Hot: H	Cold: C	Wet: W	Dry: D	Directionality or Heaviness	Alchemical Symbol	Gender
Fire (HH D)	++			+	↑ ↑	△	Active, Masculine
Air (WW H)	+		++		↑	△	Active, Masculine
Water (CC W)		++	+		↓	▽	Passive, Feminine
Earth (DD C)		+		++	↓ ↓	▽	Passive, Feminine

In ancient Greek medicine, the four essential qualities gave rise to the notion of the four bodily humors described by Hippocrates. In a fascinating book entitled *Hot Dry Men, Cold Wet Women: The Theory of Humors in Western European Art 1575–1700,* art historian Zirka Filipczak shows how the idea of four temperaments influenced the manner in which the human form was depicted in Renaissance art. As one reviewer comments, "Explanations of sexual difference that were current then sound very strange now," yet these are the views that underlie the symbolism of astrology and tarot as we practice them today.[151]

....

151 Robin Davey, review of *Hot Dry Men, Cold Wet Women: The Theory of Humors in Western European Art 1575-1700,* by Zirka Z. Filipczak (New York: American Federation of Arts, 1997), at http://www.amazon.com/Hot-Dry-Men-Cold-Women/dp/1885444060/ref=cm_cr-mr-title (accessed 19 Jun. 2011).

The idea of temperaments, based on the four elements and four bodily humors, influenced Western medicine (and astrology) for roughly two thousand years and held sway from ancient Greece until the advent of modern medicine in the nineteenth century. Over the centuries, the division of personality into four basic types has undergone many revisions, most notably in recent years in the theories of Carl Jung and the related Myers-Briggs profile, which divides humanity into sixteen personality types closely resembling the sixteen court cards of the tarot.

The main proponent of the theory of humoral temperaments was Galen (c. 129–c. 216 CE), a prominent Roman physician of Greek ethnicity. Galen associated the bodily humors with the essential qualities of Aristotle and the four "roots" of Empedocles. The ideal temperament consisted of a balanced mixture of all four qualities. A predominance of a particular humor led to a specific temperament with psychological as well as physical ramifications. When we study the sixteen court cards of the tarot in the next chapter, we will see how each court card represents a different mixture of primary qualities and thus displays different temperaments. Dr. Stephen Montgomery believes the idea of four temperaments dates back thousands of years. [152] He cites the book of Ezekiel of the Old Testament, which describes an apparition of four faces of humankind:

> As for the likeness of their faces, they four had the face of a man, and the face of a lion, on the right side: and they four had the face of an ox on the left side; they four also had the face of an eagle. (Ezekiel 1:10, King James Bible)

This passage is echoed in the New Testament's Book of Revelation:

> And the first beast was like a lion, and the second beast like a calf, and the third beast had a face as a man, and the fourth beast was like a flying eagle. (Revelation 4:7, King James Bible)

---

152 Stephen Montgomery, *People Patterns: A Modern Guide to the Four Temperaments* (Del Mar, CA: Archer Publications, 2002).

Astrologers view the four faces mentioned in Ezekiel as representing the four fixed signs of the zodiac: Leo the Lion, Taurus the Bull, Aquarius the Water Bearer, and Scorpio the Scorpion/Eagle. These are the same symbols that appear in the four corners of tarot trump XXI, the World or Universe of many tarot decks.

Fiction writers use ideas about temperament to create characters. In the *Star Trek* series, for example, Captain Kirk was an exuberant Fire type; Mr. Spock, an analytical Air type; Doctor McCoy, a nurturing Water type; and Chief Engineer Scotty, a pragmatic Earth type. The watery doctor often kept fiery Kirk's wild enthusiasm in check. The engineer's nuts-and-bolts approach to problem solving often conflicted with the precise theoretical logic of Mr. Spock.

The Golden Dawn looked to the elemental qualities to determine how the tarot cards interact with one another. As mentioned above, cards of the same element greatly strengthen one another whereas cards of opposite elements (Fire versus Water, Earth versus Air) cancel out or neutralize each other's influence. All other card combinations are considered friendly.

A more subtle picture emerges when we consider the sixteen (4 x 4) possible ways of combining the four elements with one another. Two cards, A and B, can be: (1) kindred spirits—having an identical makeup because they share the same primary and secondary qualities; (2) B can be a close friend of A because the primary quality of A matches the secondary quality of B; (3) B can be a friendly acquaintance of A because the secondary quality of A matches the primary quality of B; and (4) A and B can have nothing in common, that is, no qualities in common. To summarize in obsessive detail for the nerdy among us, myself included:

1. When one tarot card is paired with another of the same element (suit), the two cards greatly reinforce one another because they have an identical makeup. Example: Steve and Jim both love heavy metal music and like jazz to a lesser extent. Their interests are identical and they thoroughly enjoy each other's company.

2. When the primary quality of card A matches the secondary quality of card B, then A thoroughly enjoys B's company and benefits by it. Card A feels it has found a good friend in B because they both share A's primary interest. Through its primary quality, Fire gets along well with Air, Water with Earth, Air with Water, and Earth with Fire. Example: Steve is crazy

about heavy metal music but enjoys jazz to some extent. Jim is crazy about jazz but enjoys heavy metal to a lesser degree. Steve is happiest when he and Jim attend a heavy metal concert, but Steve is willing to accompany Jim to a jazz concert though it's not Steve's first choice, and vice versa. This same example applies to the next point (#3).

3. When the secondary quality of card A matches the primary quality of card B, then card B has a primary connection with A and benefits greatly by the relationship. B considers A to be a good friend. Because card A has only a secondary connection with B, however, A regards B as a friendly acquaintance rather than a close friend. Fire connects through its secondary quality to Earth; Water to Air; Air to Fire; and Earth to Water.

4. When two cards have no primary qualities in common, they possess opposite traits and don't support one another. They pursue divergent interests and effectively neutralize each other, which can lead to a state of paralysis when they spend time together. Having contrasting qualities, they could even become enemies. Fire is the opposite of Water, and Earth is the opposite of Air. Example: Jim loves extreme sports and heavy metal concerts. Mary loves sitting at home to read a good book and listening to opera. What are the chances that Mary and Jim will have a successful date?

Applying these ideas to the tarot suits:

• Wands share heat (liveliness, vitality, movement, expansiveness) with Swords. Wands share dryness (vehemence, unyieldingness) with Pentacles. Wands and Cups have contrary qualities and counterbalance each other's actions.

• Cups share cold (concentration, deliberation, cohesion, inner-directedness) with Pentacles. Cups share wetness (flexibility, fluidity) with Swords. Cups and Wands have contrary qualities and counterbalance each other's actions.

- Swords share wetness (flexibility, fluidity, blurriness, softness) with Cups. Swords share heat (liveliness, vitality, expansiveness) with Wands. Swords and Pentacles have contrary qualities and counterbalance each other's actions.

- Pentacles share dryness (vehemence, tension, unyieldingness, clear definition, hardness) with Wands. Pentacles share cold (concentration, deliberation, inner-directedness) with Cups. Pentacles and Swords have contrary qualities and counterbalance each other's actions.

Elemental Affinities among the Tarot Cards (read across)				
Suit:	Kindred Spirit (Birds of a Feather)	Close Friend	Friendly Acquaintance	Nothing in Common, Potential Enemies
Wands (Fire) → HH D	Wands (Fire) HH D	Swords (Air) WW H	Disks (Earth) DD C	Cups (Water) CC W
Cups (Water) → CC W	Cups (Water) CC W	Disks (Earth) DD C	Swords (Air) WW H	Wands (Fire) HH D
Swords (Air) → WW H	Swords (Air) WW H	Cups (Water) CC W	Wands (Fire) HH D	Disks (Earth) DD C
Disks (Earth) → DD C	Disks (Earth) DD C	Wands (Fire) HH D	Cups (Water) CC W	Swords (Air) WW H

A Tarot Reading Using Our Elemental Algebra

Let's look at an example to bring these philosophical ideas to life. Recall the reading done by Kevin in Japan regarding his search for a teaching job. Kevin finally decided to do volunteer work to gain experience in the classroom. Because he was anxious about his first day as a volunteer at school, we did a three-card reading to ask how the day would go. The cards that appeared were:

Four of Wands—The Star—Five of Wands

The Four of Wands seemed to mean that his first day as a volunteer was an important and harmonious milestone in his life. The Star in the middle is a card of hope, suggesting that his dream is in the process of manifesting. The Five of Wands on the right suggests Kevin spending a spirited time with a group of youngsters. Kevin was delighted with the reading and said it was right on target. He added that he had been invited recently to join a karate class, which he felt was also indicated by the Five of Wands.

Let's consider an elemental overview of these three cards. Wands are an active masculine suit associated with Fire, whose qualities are hot and dry. In the Golden Dawn system, the Star trump is an active masculine Air card (Aquarius), whose qualities are wet and hot. The fact that all three cards in the spread are active and masculine suggests that Kevin is taking charge and making things happen in his life. Had the cards belonged to the passive feminine suits, he might have been more laid back and less willing to assert himself on his first day in the classroom. Now let's look at the specific elemental qualities in the spread:

Four of Wands (HH D)—The Star (WW H)—Five of Wands (HH D)

How will Kevin's first day at school go? In terms of the combined elemental qualities of the three cards, his day will be five parts hot, two parts dry, two parts wet, and not the least bit cold: HHHHH DD WW. Applying our keywords to these qualities, we can say that Kevin's day will be predominantly *hot* (dynamic, animated, enthusiastic, energizing), somewhat *dry* (tense, conforming to an inner ideal, true to his inner self), somewhat *wet* (fluid, flexible, going with the flow), and not at all *cold* (inhibiting, slowing, depressing, lacking animation). The dryness (DD) and the wetness (WW) are in perfect balance, allowing heat (HHHHH) to predominate.

Fire and Air, being active masculine suits, are friendly toward each other; hence, the enthusiastic Wands that flank the central airy Star support Kevin in realizing his hopes. Although he was a bit tense, Kevin reported that he did go with the flow in the classroom and enjoyed an animated and expansive day as a school volunteer.

The Elemental Properties of the Planets

The following section is included for tarot readers who are particularly interested in astrology. In the second century CE, Ptolemy wrote that the planets possess natural powers to heat or cool, and to dry or moisten. These powers depended on the planet's proximity to the hot dry Sun and the wet cold Moon.[153] In Chaldean order, Ptolemy viewed the planets as follows:

- Saturn produces coldness and dryness because it is the outermost planet, farthest from the Sun's heat and the Earth's moist vapors. Excessive cold and dryness are inimical to life; hence Saturn is a malefic planet.

- Jupiter, in an intermediate position between cold Saturn and hot Mars, has a temperate influence, that is, he warms and moistens. As a temperate planet, Jupiter is benefic because warmth and moisture promote life.

- Mars chiefly produces dryness but is also fiercely hot. Excessive heat and dryness are inimical to life; hence Mars is malefic.

- The Sun is the source of vital heat and produces moderate dryness. Like Mercury, the life-giving Sun is able to partake of all four essential qualities. Ptolemy regarded the Sun and Mercury as being of common influence, meaning that they can produce either good or evil depending on the nature of the planet they ally with.

- Venus is warm and moist because of her proximity to the hot dry Sun and the wet cold Moon. Being temperate (moderately hot and moist), Venus promotes life and is thus benefic.

- Mercury can either dry or moisten. Lying intermediate between the wet cold Moon and the dry hot Sun, Mercury can swing either way, depending on its speed (rapidity excites Mercury) and proximity to the celestial lights. Being of such common influence, Mercury is considered androgynous.

---

153 Robert S. Westman, *The Copernican Question: Prognostication, Skepticism, and Celestial Order* (Berkeley, CA: University of California Press, 2011), pp. 52–57.

- The Moon primarily produces moisture. Though naturally cold (having no heat of her own), the humid Moon can generate warmth by reflecting the light of the Sun. When the Moon is producing moisture and warmth, she acts like a benefic.

- The Earth is a font of moist exhalations.

Over the centuries, various authors modified Ptolemy's theories. For example, in the seventeenth century, French astrologer Morin de Villefranche studied the existing literature and assigned numerical proportions to the elemental qualities of each planet. Morin concluded:

- The hottest planets are the Sun and Mars (the Sun being twice as hot as Mars).

- The warm (temperate, not excessively hot) planets are Venus and Jupiter.

- The coldest planets are the Moon and Saturn (the Moon being almost 1.5 times as cold as Saturn).

- The wettest planets are the Moon and Venus (the Moon being 1.5 times as cold as Venus).

- The driest planets are Saturn and Mars (equally dry).

- The moderately dry planets are Jupiter and Mercury.

- Mercury is cool (not excessively cold) and moderately dry.

The properties of the elements can be applied to the signs of the zodiac and help us to understand how the planets fare in each of the signs according to how well their elements mix with each other. The Fire signs (Aries, Leo, Sagittarius) are hot and dry. The Air signs (Gemini, Libra, Aquarius) are wet and hot. The Earth signs (Taurus, Virgo, Capricorn) are dry and cold. Finally, the Water signs (Cancer, Scorpio, Pisces) are cold and wet.

Let's apply these ideas to a couple of the pip cards in the Golden Dawn system: the Ten of Cups and the Two of Wands. The Golden Dawn links each of these cards to a decan of the zodiac ruled by Mars. The Ten of Cups is associated with the final decan of the zodiac, the Mars decan of

Pisces. The Two of Wands is connected with the first decan of the zodiac, the Mars decan of Aries. Below is a schematic analysis of the planet and decan associated with each of these cards.

Ten of Cups:

Mars is primarily dry and secondarily hot (DD H). Pisces, a Water sign, is primarily cold and secondarily wet (CC W). The predominant effect of this combination is coldness and dryness (CC DD W H), which is characteristic of Earth, an element associated with matters related to family, health, security, stability, and material comfort.

Two of Wands:

Mars is primarily dry and secondarily hot (DD H). Aries, a Fire sign, is primarily hot and secondarily dry (HH D). The net effect of this combination is a mixture of heat and dryness (HHH DDD), which is characteristic of Fire, an element that is expansive, outwardly directed, future-oriented, and enterprising. The strong dryness of Mars emphasizes the features of self-assertion and dominion, which are associated with this card.

Another Reading Using Elemental Dignities

A woman asked for a reading because she was worried about her daughter's upcoming surgery. She happened to be an experienced tarot reader but was having trouble being objective in reading the cards about her daughter's health. I did a three-card reading to answer her question, "What will be the outcome of my daughter's surgery?" The following cards appeared:

Two of Swords—Three of Wands—Judgment

The Two of Swords perfectly captured this woman's state. She was worried about her child's upcoming surgery, but she could not decide what the tarot was telling her because she was too emotionally involved in the outcome. The Three of Wands has to do with planning for the future. In this case, the three people involved in the planning were the woman, her daughter, and the surgeon. The sequence of cards suggested that she was feeling "blindfolded," like the woman on the Two of Swords, and could not clearly perceive the outcome in her tarot readings about this matter.

The outcome card was trump XX, Judgment, which in health questions usually means renewal and restoration to a better life. Modern occultists relate Judgment to the planet Pluto, lord of the underworld and a symbol of deep transformation. In astrology, Pluto rules Scorpio, a sign connected with surgery and healing, but also with death. Given the ambiguity of XX–Judgment, I drew a clarification card, which turned out to be the Six of Wands, a card of victory. The ambiguity of the Judgment trump probably reflected the mother's worries about the outcome of the surgery. The six on the Six of Wands reminded me of the sixth house in astrology, which refers to illness. I felt confident in this case that the Judgment trump could be interpreted as "victory" in health matters, that is, a successful outcome.

For further confirmation, I looked at the elemental dignities of the cards:

Two of Swords—Three of Wands—XX Judgment—Six of Wands

Air (WW H)—Fire (HH D)—Fire (HH D)—Fire (HH D)

All four cards of the spread share heat (H) and are thus compatible and support one another. Heat is the quality most closely associated with life-giving energy. The Golden Dawn links Judgment to Fire. The Judgment trump lies between two fiery Wands cards, which greatly strengthen it. The compatibility of all four cards and the fortification of trump XX in the outcome position further confirmed that her daughter's surgery would be successful.

An Important Caveat

This chapter has been devoted to the contribution of the four elements to the divinatory meanings of the cards. We must not forget, however, the crucial role played by the images by which we identify the four suits: Wands, Cups, Swords, and Pentacles. Fire is assigned to Wands, which were originally polo sticks in the Mamluk deck. Competing teams on horseback made use of these sticks to play the lively, high-energy game of polo. The tarot's fiery Knights are now portrayed on horseback, and the tarot Wands are generally depicted as budding with new life. Cups were bowl-shaped containers or chalices, implements for drinking and sharing good times with others. In medieval times, Cups also had a special significance as containers for the communion wine of the Catholic Mass. Swords were weapons of war used for piercing, severing, settling conflict, and exacting justice. Pentacles were originally coins (dinars) employed to exchange goods, amass wealth, and meet life's material needs.

SEVEN

The Elemental Personalities of the Court Cards

The meeting of two personalities is like the contact of two chemical substances; if there is any reaction, both are transformed.[154]
CARL JUNG

There is no consensus about how to interpret the court cards. With experience, each reader must develop a personal meaning for each of the sixteen "people" cards. Tarot readers generally agree that court cards, especially the kings and queens, can represent people of differing ages and genders. Court cards can also be read as different types of situations, life experiences, lifestyles, societal roles, available energies, personality traits, messages, opinions, viewpoints, zodiac signs, or times of the year. In addition, the themes reflected in the three pip cards associated with each non-Page court card often have relevance in the reading (*see* appendix C).

....
154   Carl Jung, "Quotations by author: Carl Jung (1875–1961)," *The Quotations Page*, http://www.quotations
-page.com/quotes/Carl_Jung/ (accessed 5 Dec. 2011).

By considering the nature and predominance of elemental qualities in each of the court cards, we can get a sense of the personality of each card. The descriptions in this chapter are meant to be evocative of the Golden Dawn attributions used in the Waite-Smith deck. Readers are invited to fill in the details based on their own experience with the cards.

Elements and Qualities of the Court Cards [H = Hot, C = Cold, W = Wet, D = Dry]				
Element/Suit → Part ↓	Fire (HH D)– Wands (active masculine)	Water (CC W)– Cups (passive feminine)	Air (WW H)– Swords (active masculine)	Earth (DD C)– Pentacles (passive feminine)
Earthy (DD C)– Pages/Princesses	Princess/Page of Wands (DDD HH C)	Princess/Page of Cups (CCC DD W)	Princess/Page of Swords (WW DD H C)	Princess/Page of Pentacles (DDDD CC)
Fiery (HH D)– Knights	Knight of Wands (HHHH DD)	Knight of Cups (CC HH D W)	Knight of Swords (HHH WW D)	Knight of Pentacles (DDD HH C)
Watery (CC W)– Queens	Queen of Wands (HH CC D W)	Queen of Cups (CCCC WW)	Queen of Swords (WWW CC H)	Queen of Pentacles (CCC DD W)
Airy (WW H)– Kings/Princes	King/Prince of Wands (HHH WW D)	King/Prince of Cups (WWW CC H)	King/Prince of Swords (WWWW HH)	King/Prince of Pentacles (DD WW H C)

A popular book proclaims that men are from Mars and women are from Venus. In Chinese philosophy, Mars is of yang energy (active, dynamic, warm, confident, and extroverted) and Venus exemplifies yin (reactive, reflective, cool, cautious, and introverted). For completeness, in the following summary of traits related to the qualities of the four elements, I have included the relevant astrological associations:

- "Hot" is yang, outer-directed, active, dynamic, ardent, energetic, expansive, action-oriented, quick to react, high-spirited, optimistic, penetrating, passionate, enthusiastic, impetuous, enlivening, exciting, quickening, future-oriented, and on the move. "Hot" is associated with the brightness and warmth of sunlight. Heat energizes, expands, rises, activates, excites, moves, disperses, and circulates. Its action is centrifugal, moving away from a center. In astrology, "hot" planets include the Sun and Mars. Jupiter and Venus are moderately hot, that is, temperate or warm. Ptolemy characterized *summer* as hot, becoming dry. The quality of hotness combined with dryness is considered stereotypical of masculine behavior. Wands and Swords, both phallic symbols, are the "hot" suits of the tarot.

- "Cold" is yin, inner-directed, slow to react, cool, calm, dark, self-oriented, sedate, pensive, reserved, withdrawn, reclusive, methodical, practical, pragmatic, inert, inactive, energy-conserving, consolidating, dispassionate, contracting, plodding, depressive, cautious, heavy, and serious. "Cold" is associated with the coolness and darkness of night with its absence of sunlight. "Cold" chills, freezes, congeals, slows down, calms, sedates, reduces, contracts, blocks, hardens, and decreases the energy level. Its action is centripetal, moving toward a center. In astrology, the "cold" planets are the Moon and Saturn. Mercury is considered cool (not excessively cold). Venus is variously described as either cool or warm. Ptolemy characterized *winter* as cold, becoming wet. The quality of coldness combined with wetness is considered stereotypical of feminine behavior. Cups and Pentacles, symbols of the vagina and the womb, are the "cold" suits of the tarot.

- "Dry" is yang, hard, stiff, taut, tense, brittle, rigid, sharply outlined, self-defined, unyielding, distinct, separate, precise, clear-cut, objective, impatient, inflexible, self-determined, abrupt, resistant to change, and vehemently energetic. Dryness tends to act rapidly, get to the point, and remain true to an inner ideal. The process of drying causes friction and causes things to tighten and shrink down to their bare essentials. In astrology, the "dry" planets are the Sun, Mars, and Saturn. The planets Jupiter and Mercury are moderately dry. Ptolemy characterized *autumn* as dry, becoming cold. Wands and Pentacles are the "dry" suits of the tarot.

- "Wet" is yin, fluid, yielding, subjective, whimsical, ill-defined, flexible, receptive, patient, relationship-oriented, empathetic, gradual, imprecise, and hard to pin down. Wetness loosens and meanders; it does not have sharp boundaries and is ready to adapt and go with the flow. Water is the universal solvent. "Wet" softens, lubricates, loosens, makes flexible, and blurs boundaries. In astrology, the "wet" planets are the Moon and Venus (the two feminine planets). Ptolemy characterized *spring* as wet, becoming hot. Cups and Swords are the "wet" suits of the tarot.

Elemental Attributions of the Court Cards

Crowley and the Golden Dawn viewed the court cards as follows:

- The Pages/Princesses comprise the *earthy* part (dry and cool, of melancholic temperament) of their respective suits. Being cool and dry, pages may be as curious as Mercury and as dutiful as Saturn. The element Earth represents consolidation and manifestation in tangible form. Earthy people tend to be dependable, practical, and diligent but may be uncomfortable expressing emotions. The Earth signs are Taurus, Virgo, and Capricorn. Rather than link the Pages to the zodiac circle, the Golden Dawn assigned each page to a quadrant of the heavens around the North Pole. The four Pages symbolize the four elements and serve to ground the four Aces, which represent the force of Spirit acting in each element. As Corrine Kenner puts it, "Not only do they embody the elements of fire, earth, air, and water, but they also serve as the earthly 'thrones'—the seat of power of the four Aces." [155]

- The Queens comprise the *watery* part (cool and moist, of phlegmatic temperament) of their respective suits. Being cold and wet, the Queens are stereotypically feminine and behave like the nurturing Moon and the love goddess Venus. Water symbolizes receptivity, poetic imagination, emotional support, and maternal care. Watery people tend to be empathic, obliging, affectionate, and fond of nurturing others. The Water signs are Cancer, Scorpio, and Pisces. The Golden Dawn assigned the Queens to the last decan of mutable signs and the first two decans of cardinal signs, and to the pip cards associated with those decans. The Queens oversee the birth and early development of a new season and also the final stage of the season that is passing away. The Queens pass the baton to the Kings, who oversee the full realization of the season.

- The Knights comprise the *fiery* part (hot and dry, of choleric temperament) of their respective suits. Being hot and dry, the Knights are stereotypically masculine and have much in common with passionate Mars and the life-giving Sun. Fire represents the initial spark of life. Fiery people tend to be self-willed, ambitious, fond of challenge and ready to sow their wild oats. Fire seeks to expand its horizons through travel and adventure. The Fire signs are Aries, Leo, and Sagittarius. Ever wonder why the tarot's knights are depicted as powerful men thrusting forward on horseback, much like the man-horse Sagittarius? The Golden Dawn assigned the knights to the last decan of fixed signs and the first two decans of mutable signs, and to the pip cards associated with those decans. The Knights govern the period just

---

155 Corrine Kenner, *Tarot and Astrology* (Woodbury, MN: Llewellyn Publications, 2011), p. 199.

after the season has reached full bloom and oversee the season's decline and breakdown, which allows for a new season to begin. The Knights pass the baton to the Queens, who oversee the onset of the next season.

- The Waite Kings/Thoth Princes comprise the *airy* part (moist and hot, of sanguine temperament) of their respective suits. The Kings/Princes behave like beneficent Jupiter and the powerful Sun. Air represents social interaction and the flow of thought. Sharp and analytical, airy people readily perceive connections between ideas. Because they have known suffering, they are able to detach from their emotions and take a broader view. The Air signs are Gemini, Libra, and Aquarius. The Golden Dawn assigned the Kings to the last decan of cardinal signs and the first two decans of fixed signs, and to the pip cards associated with those decans. The Kings govern the period during which the season, recently initiated by the Queens, comes into full bloom. The Kings pass the baton to the Knights, who oversee the season's decline.

The accompanying table summaries some attributes of the court cards based on their elemental associations.

Court Card Symbolism and the Four Elements		
Court Card	Element	Associations
Knights	Fire	Adult males, military personnel, warriors; action, energy, motion, comings and goings, travel, quest, movement, inspiration, enthusiasm, assertion, sex drive, thrust, creativity, opportunity
Queens	Water	Adult females, mother figures, mature accomplished women, influential friends; emotions, empathy, receptivity, caring, loving, nurturing, support, mothering, reconciling, forgiving
Waite Kings/ Thoth Princes	Air	Older adult males, father figures, mature men; wisdom, authority, clear thinking, rationality, decision making, power, leadership, organization, strategy, recognition, accomplishment
Waite Pages/ Thoth Princesses	Earth	Young persons, children, messengers, students, helpers; news, messages, opinions, communications, new learning, inexperience, apprenticeship, acquisition, skill building, material reality

A Note on Airy People versus Airy Situations

Tarot symbolism has many fonts. In this chapter, we focus on the use of the four elements to characterize the court cards of each suit. This method works well with regard to court cards as people but may seem less convincing when we attempt to describe situations related to an element, especially the element Air as it relates to the Swords suit. The Swords court cards are of an *airy* temperament (wet and hot, or sanguine) and show traits of the Air signs Gemini, Libra, and Aquarius. They live in their heads and excel at talking, planning, connecting the dots, theorizing, and strategizing. Indecision and worry sometimes plague their existence.

On the other hand, "Air situations," as depicted in the Swords pips, partake of the symbolism of the sword as a weapon that can cut and injure. Warriors carry swords. The Ten of Swords, for example, could well depict the proverb, "He who lives by the sword, dies by the sword." Just as fish live in water, people live in air, and human social interactions ("air situations") are sometimes painful.

The Wet-Dry Spectrum among the Court Cards

Another important distinction derives from where the court cards fall along the wet-dry spectrum. Recall that dryness relates to self-definition, that is, the determination of form according to one's inner nature. Wetness represents fluidity. Wet things assume the form of their containers and are defined by their surroundings. Of the court cards, the Pages and Knights, as pure types, possess inherent dryness and are more capable of self-determination. The Queens and Kings, as pure types, lack inherent dryness and must depend on their environment to define their form. Consider King Edward VIII of England; he was forced to abdicate the throne to marry the woman he loved. Edward could not continue to be king if he wished to decide upon his own bride. One might say that as a king, Edward was lacking in dryness, but, as a man, he made up for it in heat.

The wet-dry distinction also applies to male and female stereotypes in a patriarchal society. The court cards, after all, represent roles and stereotypes rather than real people. In Western society, these stereotypes derive largely from the Book of Genesis. In the beginning, from the dust of the Earth, God created man in His own image and likeness and gave man dominion over all of creation. On the sixth day, God realized that Adam needed a "helpmate," so God fashioned a woman from one of Adam's ribs. Being hot and dry, Adam provided the creative spark and determination of form to the cold and wet female who molded herself after Adam and depended entirely on him for her self-definition. "And Adam said, This is now bone of my bones, and flesh of my flesh; she shall be called Woman, because she was taken out of man." [156]

....
156   Genesis 2:23 (King James Bible).

Dry, Cold, Earthy Pages/Princesses: DD C

During the Middle Ages, at the age of seven the son of a noble family could begin his training as a page in order to become a knight. Pages had to follow detailed sets of rules as they methodically began to master the skills of knighthood. At age fifteen, the page graduated to the rank of squire. The diligence and meticulous training of these youngsters is characteristic of the element Earth.

Earthy individuals partake of the melancholic (dry and cold) temperament, classically associated with black bile, feces, and the cooling planet Saturn.[157] Earth is a passive, receptive, heavy, inner-directed element that serves the other elements by providing a firm foundation on which life can exist. Being earthy, Pages tend to be studious, practical, frugal, efficient, service-oriented, subservient, a bit plodding, and attentive to detail. Their thinking can at times be rigid or rule-bound, and they may have difficulty seeing the big picture. The basic nature of each tarot Page is tempered by the element corresponding to the suit to which it belongs, yet each Page possesses sufficient dryness to maintain an inner sense of identity.

Modern tarot readers often see pages as messengers as well as the news they carry. The Golden Dawn believed that pages can represent opinions, thoughts, and ideas about a topic. The nature of the opinion is revealed by whether the Page is facing or looking away from another card. This directionality reveals whether the Page agrees with or opposes the subject matter reflected in the other card(s).

Just as the elements Earth (DD C) and Air (WW H) form a complementary pair, the melancholic, earthy pages and the sanguine, airy princes/kings complement each other. Each possesses qualities the other lacks.

Page of Pentacles: DDDD CC

The purest expression of Earth is found in the Page of Pentacles (the earthy part of Earth—DDDD CC). The element Earth refers to that which is stable, enduring, tangible, and "down-to-earth." Earth is dependable and sustaining; it forms the ground beneath our feet and provides the foundation of our existence. We count on the earth simply to be there. Being the earthiest

---

157 For associations of the temperaments with astrological factors, see William Lilly, *Christian Astrology*, *(1647)* (London: Regulus Publishing, 1985), p. 47.

of her group, the Page of Pentacles is calm, studious, detail-oriented, methodical, practical, disciplined, and hard-working. She is a good student who loves to learn and master new skills.

In his classic 1911 text, Arthur Edward Waite linked the Page of Pentacles to application, study, scholarship, reflection; news, messages, and the bringer thereof; rule, and management.[158] *Reversed:* Prodigality, dissipation, liberality, luxury; unfavorable news. Etteilla saw the Page of Pentacles as a "dark youth."

Page of Swords: WW DD H C

The most complex, versatile, and subtle of the pages is the clever Page of Swords (the earthy part of Air—WW DD H C). Because the Page of Swords contains all four elemental qualities, she has something in common with everyone. As wet as she is dry, and as hot as she is cold, this Page is like a chameleon that can be whatever she needs to be in any situation. Such versatility and universality may make the Page of Swords (WW DD H C) a good spy. Being an Air card, she is quick, verbal, analytical, resourceful, and vigilant. She values a no-nonsense understanding of what's going on around her; she loves to communicate, strategize, and connect the dots. Being of Earth, she can be quite determined and persistent in pursuing her goals.

Waite saw the Page of Swords as lithe, active, swift, and alert, as if expecting an enemy to appear at any moment. His keywords include: authority, overseeing, secret service, vigilance, spying, examination, and the qualities thereto belonging. *(R):* The more evil side of these qualities; what is unforeseen, a state of unprepareness; sickness. Etteilla regarded the Page of Swords as a "spy."

Page of Wands: DDD HH C

The spirited Page of Wands (the earthy part of Fire—DDD HH C) has three of four elemental qualities but is lacking in wetness. Thus, she is the least moist, soft, flexible, easy- going, open to change, and susceptible to outside influence of the four Pages. Being very dry and somewhat hot, the Page of Wands partakes of the nature of Mars, the warrior who likes to pursue and conquer. She is active, daring, energetic, outgoing, action-oriented, impatient, and unyielding. Lacking "wetness," she can at times be tense and insensitive, capable of hostility when she

....

158 All citations from Waite in this chapter are paraphrased from *The Pictorial Key to the Tarot* online.

doesn't get her way. Her "dryness" allows her to define clearly what she wants, and her "hotness" gives her the oomph to put her ideas into action.

Waite viewed the Page of Wands as a dark young man, faithful, a lover, an envoy, or a postman. When this Page falls next to a man in a spread, he will bear favorable testimony concerning him, but followed by the Page of Cups, he is a dangerous rival. He bears the qualities of the suit of Wands and may signify family intelligence. *(R):* anecdotes, announcements, evil news; indecision and the instability that accompanies it. Etteilla viewed the Page of Wands as a "foreigner."

Page of Cups: CCC DD W

The cool dry Page of Cups (the earthy part of Water—CCC DD W) has three of four elemental qualities but is lacking in heat. Thus, she is the least expansive of the Pages and displays less oomph and less drive for freedom and adventure than the others. Being predominantly cold and moderately dry, the Page of Cups can be withdrawn, inhibited, inner-directed, slow to react, sensitive to criticism, and resistant to change. Being watery, she is a poet at heart who lives in her imagination and seeks to share her fanciful visions with others.

Waite saw the Page of Cups as a pleasing, somewhat effeminate youth, of studious and intent aspect. His keywords include: a fair young man, impelled to render service and with whom the querent will be connected; a studious youth; news, messages; application, reflection, meditation; also these things directed to business. *(R):* taste, inclination, attachment, seduction, deception, artifice. Etteilla saw the Page of Cups as a "blond youth."

Hot, Dry, Fiery Knights: HH D

Fiery individuals partake of the choleric (hot and dry) temperament, classically associated with yellow bile, urine, and the drying planet Mars. Fire is a positive, active, proud, mobile, light, energizing, outer-directed element that expands and rises to great heights. Fiery radiant energy is able to leave the Earth's gravitational pull and travel throughout the solar system. Wanderlust is an essential feature of the fiery Knights. Constantly on the move, they are portrayed on horseback in search of romance and adventure as befits their "hot" nature. The mode of the knights' travel is often related to the element of their suit: Air (by plane), Water (by boat), Earth (land-based), or Fire (exciting long-distance travel).

Being basically fiery, the knights (HH D) tend to be high-spirited, virile, active, daring, passionate, impatient, expansive, idealistic, pioneering, visionary, and always on the go. The Golden Dawn believed Knights also represent arrivals and departures, or the comings and goings of matters, depending on which way their horse is heading. The dry heat of the Knights makes them capable of fierce action and emotion, though this trait is modified by the element of their suit. Expansive almost without limit, the Knights tend to become fearless leaders, champion athletes, crusaders with or without a cause, type-A personalities, and those who command respect for their breadth of vision and ability to inspire. Unlike the earthy Pages, the Knights see the big picture and seize the opportunity to pursue what they desire, sometimes in an arrogant or overly expansive way. The Knights believe that they must "boldly go where no man has gone before." The nature of each Knight is tempered by the element of the suit to which it belongs, yet each Knight possesses sufficient dryness to maintain an inner sense of identity.

Just as the elements fire (HH D) and water (CC W) form a complementary pair, the choleric, fiery Knights and the phlegmatic, watery Queens complement each other. Each possesses qualities the other lacks.

Knight of Wands: HHHH DD

The purest expression of Fire lies in the passionate Knight of Wands (the fiery part of Fire). Being particularly hot and dry, the Knight of Wands (HHHH DD) is lively, motivated, expansive, impatient, self-confident, charismatic, abrupt, and vehemently energetic. His nature is to go for the gold. He exhibits a fiery zeal for freedom, independence, and the right to creative self-expression; he resents constrictions and limitations. The Knight of Wands tends to be extroverted, assertive, fun-loving, passionate, adventurous, amorous, and inspiring. Fire represents the spark of life. Fiery individuals want to experience life to the fullest without restriction.

Waite regarded the Knight of Wands as a dark young man whose mobility is associated with departure, absence, flight, alienation, emigration, and changes of residence. He is on a journey past mounds of pyramids, perhaps a reference to Aaron, brother of Moses in the Bible, whose staff "sprouted, budded, blossomed, and produced ripe almonds."[159] Despite this knight's upraised Wand, he appears to be friendly and not on a warlike errand. The motion of his horse matches his

....

159 Numbers 17:8 (New Living Translation).

precipitate mood. *(R):* rupture, division, interruption, and discord. Etteilla delineated the Knight of Wands as "departure."

Pratesi's cartomancer (circa 1750) delineates the Knight of Wands as a "door knocker," causing Paul Huson to exclaim: "Why eighteenth-century Bolognese cartomancers should have considered the Knight of Batons a door knocker is beyond my comprehension." [160] Huson speculates that perhaps this knight is one who slams the door on the way out—an action consistent with Etteilla's delineation of "departure" for this card. The high levels of heat and dryness (HHHH DD) associated with this card are consistent with the abrupt and forceful energy used to strike a metal knocker against the door.

The significance of Pratesi's delineation of the Knight of Wands as a door knocker struck home when I drew this as my daily card before leaving for work. I often select a card at random in the morning to see what synchronicities arise during the day. I work in a psychiatric hospital and, on this particular day, the first meeting I attended was a review of the patients' behaviors the night before. The nurse described how a particular patient got upset and was pounding hard on the door of the ward to express his frustration at being confined. The Knight of Wands immediately sprang to mind, as did the eighteenth-century delineation "door knocker."

Apparently, door knockers originated in ancient Greece where they were used to fasten slaves to metal rings attached to the slave owner's entryway. Like the slaves of ancient Greece, the psychiatric patient mentioned above felt trapped by being committed to a psychiatric hospital. Like a Knight of Wands, he pounded on the door to express his desire for freedom. Bearing in mind that the Greek slaves were captives of war, we see new meaning in Waite's association of the Knight of Wands with alienation, departure, emigration, flight, absence, and departure. Like Patrick Henry, the fiery Knight of Wands values freedom above all else.

On a recent trip to Italy, I was impressed by the beautiful door knockers that decorate the outer doors of buildings in historic cities like Florence. In eighteenth-century Italy, the image of a knight was sometimes used in finely crafted door knockers. Perhaps this decorative aspect of the errant Knight of Wands as a door knocker explains why this card often shows up in readings related to travel, relocating, and to buying, renovating, or redecorating a home.

....

160 Huson, *Mystical Origins*, p. 241.

Historically the most common form of Italian door knocker was a lion's head, a symbol of power, strength, and protection. The lion refers to the Fire sign Leo and is also a symbol of Saint Mark the Evangelist, who was petitioned for divine protection. Statues of lions as guardians can be found throughout Italy. The Fire sign Aires is connected to battering rams used to smash doors in. Ornate Italian door knockers were also symbols of nobility, prestige, power, and majesty. The Christian influence in Italy calls to mind the biblical saying: "Ask and it shall be given you; seek and ye shall find; knock and it shall be opened unto you."[161] Perhaps when the eighteenth-century cartomancers defined the Knight of Wands as a door knocker, they had such associations in mind.

When the Knight of Wands appears in a reading, themes may emerge related to the pip cards associated with the three decans the Knight governs. These are the Seven of Cups and the Eight and Nine of Wands.

Knight of Cups: CC HH D W

The most complex, versatile and subtle of the Knights (HH D) is the romantic Knight of Cups (the fiery part of Water—CC HH D W) because he contains all four elemental qualities and has something in common with everyone. Like a chameleon, the Knight of Cups can blow hot or cold, wet or dry, depending on the situation. Like all Knights, he can be passionate, assertive, and ambitious, but as a Knight of watery Cups, he has a dreamy, poetic, secretive side as well. Some authors view the versatile Knight of Cups as a dissembling Don Juan whose words and promises are not always to be trusted.

Waite described the Knight of Cups as graceful and imaginative, a dreamer. His keywords include: arrival, approach (e.g., of a messenger), advances, propositions, demeanor, invitation, incitement. *(R):* trickery, artifice, subtlety, swindling, duplicity, fraud. Etteilla delineated the Knight of Cups as "arrival" in contrast to the "departure" of the Knight of Wands.

When the Knight of Cups appears in a reading, themes may emerge related to the pip cards associated with the three decans the Knight governs. These are the Seven of Swords and the Eight and Nine of Cups.

....
161 Matthew 7:7 (King James Bible).

Knight of Swords: HHH WW D

The high-spirited Knight of Swords (the fiery part of Air—HHH WW D) has three of four elemental qualities but is lacking in coldness. Without "cold," there is little to slow him down. Being overly hot, he is the least passive, calm, practical, contemplative, inner-directed, energy-conserving, and slow to react of all the Knights. As a Knight of Air, he tends to be verbal, strategic, communicative, and caught up in his mind. The excess heat without the balance of cold makes him prone to impractical, overly abstract, or scattered thinking. Being hot and moderately wet, the Knight of Swords can be an exciting ball of fire who rushes off impetuously without a clear focus. He is reminiscent of the animated character Crusader Rabbit of the early days of television.

Waite depicted the Knight of Swords riding in full course, as if scattering his enemies, and viewed him as a hero of romantic chivalry whose sword is swift and sure because he is clean of heart. Waite's keywords include: skill, bravery, capacity, defense, address, enmity, wrath, war, destruction, opposition, resistance, ruin. He sometimes signifies death, but only in proximity to other cards of fatality. *(R):* imprudence, incapacity, extravagance. Etteilla's keyword for the Knight of Swords was "military."

When the Knight of Swords appears in a reading, themes may emerge related to the pip cards associated with the three decans the Knight governs. These are the Seven of Pentacles and the Eight and Nine of Swords.

Knight of Pentacles: DDD HH C

The obstinate Knight of Pentacles (the fiery part of Earth—DDD HH C) has three of four elemental qualities but is lacking in wetness. Thus, he is the least flexible, soft, moist, easygoing, open to change, and susceptible to outside influence of the four Knights. Lacking the fluidity of wetness, his greatest strength is his capacity for unwavering application of effort. Being dry and moderately hot, the Knight of Pentacles can be enthusiastic and energetic but also stiff, rigid, inflexible, obstinate, uncomfortable with feelings, overly pragmatic, and resistant to change. Being so "dry," he likes to prune things down to their bare essentials: "just the facts, ma'am."

Waite saw the Knight of Pentacles as slow, enduring, and heavy. His keywords include: utility, serviceableness, interest, responsibility, rectitude. *(R):* inertia, idleness, repose of that kind, stagnation; also placidity, discouragement, and carelessness. Etteilla delineated the Knight of Pentacles as "usefulness."

When the Knight of Pentacles appears in a reading, themes may emerge related to the pip cards associated with the three decans the Knight governs. These are the Seven of Wands and the Eight and Nine of Pentacles.

Cold, Wet, Watery Queens: CC W

Watery individuals partake of the phlegmatic (cold and wet) temperament, classically associated with phlegm and the moistening planet Venus. Water is a patient, receptive, heavy, inner-directed element that flows, molds itself to its container, and sinks toward the center of the Earth. Being watery, Queens (CC W) are sensitive, empathic, patient, calm, energy-conserving, devoted, faithful, nurturing, and compassionate. Like water, the Queens are quite powerful but may take their time, much like the Colorado River in excavating the Grand Canyon. The Queens are at times too subjective and overly influenced by emotion and sentiment. They can put a damper on the impatient, hasty expenditure of fiery energy by the Knights. Because Queens are inherently lacking in dryness, the basic nature of each Queen is strongly tempered by the element of the suit to which she belongs. This is most pronounced in the Queen of Swords who is basically quite fluid ("wet") but must conform to the stern, objective, detached suit of Swords, which is steeped in the school of hard knocks.

Queen of Cups: CCCC WW

Among the court cards, the purest expression of Water is found in the inner-directed Queen of Cups (the watery part of water—CCCC WW). Despite the fact that Fire provides the spark of life, nothing can grow without water. The heat of the sun evaporates water, which returns to the earth in the form of rain, causing seeds to germinate and crops to grow. Water in motion is tremendously powerful and can hollow out canyons on the surface of the earth. Symbolically water represents our emotions and inner life. Watery people have a strong need for close emotional relationships. As a universal solvent, water is linked to the dissolution of boundaries and a sense of oneness, as occurs during sexual ecstasy, in certain spiritual experiences, or through great works of music, poetry, and art. The Queen of Cups is typically a kind and dreamy woman who feels most at home in the boundless world of imagination, illusion, and intuition. She has a special fondness for the tarot. Being extremely watery and fluid, she may waver and become duplicitous when ill-dignified.

Waite regarded the Queen of Cups as beautiful, fair, dreamy—a good woman, honest and devoted, who will do service to the querent. His keywords include: loving intelligence, the gift of vision; success, happiness, pleasure; also wisdom, virtue; a perfect spouse and a good mother. *(R):* a good woman; otherwise, a distinguished woman but not to be trusted; a perverse woman; vice, dishonor, depravity. Etteilla saw the Queen of Cups as a "blond lady."

When the Queen of Cups appears in a reading, themes may emerge related to the pip cards associated with the three decans that the Queen governs. These are the Ten of Swords and the Two and Three of Cups.

Queen of Wands: HH CC D W

The most complex, versatile and subtle of the Queens (CC W) is the dynamic Queen of Wands (the watery part of Fire—HH CC D W) because she contains all four elemental qualities and thus has something in common with everyone. Like a chameleon, she can blow hot or cold, wet or dry, depending on the situation. Some authors view the Queen of Wands as a bundle of energy who thrives on multitasking and always keeps multiple irons in the fire. Her predominant qualities are heat and cold in perfect balance; thus, she can be ambitious and enterprising but at the same time calm and undeterred in the steady pursuit of her goals.

Waite described the Queen of Wands as the Queen of the suit of life and animation. Her personality corresponds to that of the King, but is more magnetic. His keywords include: a dark woman, a countrywoman, friendly, chaste, loving, honorable. If the card next to her signifies a man, she is well disposed towards him; if a woman, she is interested in the querent. Also, a love of money, or a certain success in business. *(R):* good, economical, obliging, serviceable. With other cards of similar meaning, she can also signify opposition, jealousy, deceit, and infidelity. Etteilla regarded the Queen of Wands as a "rural lady."

When the Queen of Wands appears in a reading, themes may emerge related to the pip cards associated with the three decans the Queen governs. These are the Ten of Cups and the Two and Three of Wands.

Queen of Swords: WWW CC H

The composed Queen of Swords (the watery part of Air—WWW CC H) has three of four elemental qualities but is lacking in dryness. Thus, she is the least rigid, inflexible, self-contained, firm, and unyielding of the four Queens; she is able to be flexible, perceptive, and reasonably balanced in her opinions. Because she lacks "dryness," her form is predominantly determined by the analytical, emotionally detached suit of Swords. Being wet, she can call upon the "moistening" qualities of Venus, the love goddess, to help her reconcile differences and deal empathically with others. Despite her considerable wetness, she is moderately cold and likely to have suffered Saturn's chill in her emotional life.

Waite (1911) wrote that the countenance of the Queen of Swords is severe but chastened, suggesting familiarity with sorrow but not representing mercy. Her sword notwithstanding, this Queen is scarcely a symbol of power. Waite's keywords include: widowhood, female sadness and embarrassment, absence, sterility, mourning, privation, and separation. *(R):* malice, bigotry, artifice, prudery, bale, deceit. Etteilla delineated the Queen of Swords as "widowhood."

When the Queen of Swords appears in a reading, themes may emerge related to the pip cards associated with the three decans that the Queen governs. These are the Ten of Pentacles and the Two and Three of Swords.

Queen of Pentacles: CCC DD W

The pragmatic Queen of Pentacles (the watery part of Earth—CCC DD W) has three of four elemental qualities but is lacking in heat. Thus, she possesses the least oomph, expansiveness, and phallic drive for freedom and adventure of the four Queens. Being cold and moderately dry, she is a down-to-earth, pragmatic organizer who is skilled at reducing matters to their essentials to produce tangible results. The predominance of cold makes her sensible and hardworking; the total lack of heat can render her unimaginative and prone to melancholy—the chill of Saturn.

Waite viewed the Queen of Pentacles as a dark woman, one of greatness of soul and a serious cast of intelligence. His keywords include: opulence, generosity, magnificence, security, liberty. *(R):* evil, suspicion, suspense, fear, mistrust. Etteilla viewed the Queen of Pentacles as a "dark lady."

When the Queen of Pentacles appears in a reading, themes may emerge related to the pip cards associated with the three decans that the Queen governs. These are the Ten of Wands and the Two and Three of Pentacles.

Wet, Hot, Airy Princes/Kings: WW H

Airy individuals partake of the sanguine (wet and hot) temperament, classically associated with life-affirming blood and the warming planet Jupiter. Air is a positive, active, light, outer-directed element that flows and tends to rise upward. Unlike Fire, Air is contained within the Earth's gravitational pull.

Being airy, the sanguine Princes (Waite's Kings) tend to be sociable, optimistic, cheerful, pleasure-loving, expansive, logical, and analytical. Like the Knights, the Kings (WW H) are able to grasp the big picture but, being less hot and impetuous than the Knights, the Kings display better judgment through the use of their synthetic intellect. The Kings' social skills, ability to connect the dots, and facility with relationships make them good strategists, chief executives, and administrators. Being of sanguine temperament, the Kings know how to have a good time and enjoy the finer things in life. As a type, Kings lack "cold" and thus tend to be more outer- than inner-directed. Kings also inherently lack dryness, so the basic nature of each King is strongly tempered by the element of the suit to which it belongs.

King of Swords: WWWW HH

Among the court cards, the purest expression of Air is found in the fluid and energetic King/Prince of Swords (the airy part of Air—WWWW HH). The element Air is linked to language, thought, and communication. Indeed, the answer is sometimes found blowing in the wind. Air in motion can scatter seeds and spread plants to new locations. Currents of air can transport a tiny spider from one continent to another.

People who partake of the Air temperament readily link ideas, create a relational web, and formulate effective strategies and abstract theories. Air is impartial; it blows on everyone equally without discrimination, like justice fairly applied. Air circulates above the water and the earth and thus has a broad view of human affairs. A stiff wind can disperse the clouds and clear the air, allowing a better view of a situation. On a clear day, we can see forever.

The King of Swords lacks both cold and dryness. Being hot without cold, he is expansive, forceful, and outgoing. Being wet without dryness, he depends on his surroundings to define his form. This King's environment is the analytical, perceptive, emotionally detached suit of Swords which deals with the conflicts and cruelties of daily life.

Waite tells us that the King of Swords sits in judgment, reminiscent of the Justice trump. He has power over life and death by virtue of his office. His keywords include: judgment, power, command, authority, militant intelligence, law, and offices of the crown. *(R):* cruelty, perversity, barbarity, perfidy, evil intention. Etteilla saw the King of Swords as a "lawyer."

When the King of Swords appears in a reading, themes may emerge related to the pip cards associated with the three decans the King governs. These are the Four of Pentacles and the Five and Six of Swords.

King of Pentacles: DD WW H C

The most complex, versatile, and subtle of the Kings (WW H) is the focused yet flexible King of Pentacles (the airy part of Earth—DD WW H C), because he contains all four elemental qualities and thus has something in common with everyone. Like a chameleon, he can call upon whichever quality he needs, depending on the situation. Some authors view the King of Pentacles as the most well-rounded, stable, sensible, and hardworking of all the Kings. His predominant qualities are dryness and wetness in equal balance; thus, he can reduce matters to their essentials and deal with them flexibly to achieve his goals.

Waite linked the King of Pentacles to courage, lethargy, money (sometimes), valor, realizing intelligence, business and normal intellectual aptitude, and occasionally mathematical gifts and attainments. *(R):* vice, weakness, ugliness, perversity, corruption, peril. Etteilla viewed the King of Pentacles as a "dark man."

When the King of Pentacles appears in a reading, themes may emerge related to the pip cards associated with the three decans the King governs. These are the Four of Wands and the Five and Six of Pentacles.

King of Wands: HHH WW D

The energetic and peaceable King/Prince of Wands (the airy part of Fire—HHH WW D) has three of four elemental qualities but is lacking in coldness. Thus, he is the least passive, calm, practical, contemplative, inner-directed, energy-conserving, and slow to react of the four Princes/Kings. Being very hot, the King of Wands tends to be enterprising, impulsive, direct, enthusiastic, energetic, and charismatic in his dealings with others.

Waite viewed the King of Wands as a dark man, ardent, lithe, animated, impassioned, and noble, much like the lion emblazoned on his throne. His keywords include: friendly, a countryman, generally married, honest, and conscientious. The card always signifies honesty. It may mean impending news of an unexpected inheritance. *(R):* Good, but severe; austere, yet tolerant. Etteilla viewed the King of Wands as a "rural gentleman."

When the King of Wands appears in a reading, themes may emerge related to the pip cards associated with the three decans that the King governs. These are the Four of Cups and the Five and Six of Wands.

King of Cups: WWW CC H

The empathic and pragmatic King/Prince of Cups (the airy part of Water—WWW CC H) has three of four elemental qualities but is lacking in dryness. Thus, he is the least rigid, inflexible, self-contained, tense, and unyielding of the four Kings because his form is determined by the receptive, nurturing suit of Cups. Being very wet, the King of Cups has the help of Venus in reconciling differing viewpoints and empathically appreciating the emotional undercurrents of any situation. The excess wetness with no counterbalancing dryness can render him sensitive, imaginative, spiritual, obliging, and compassionate, but at the same time somewhat passive and indolent.

Waite, noting that Cups refer to water, observes that the throne of the King of Cups is set upon the sea; on one side a ship is riding and on the other a dolphin is leaping. His keywords include: a fair man; a man of business, law, or divinity; responsible, disposed to oblige the querent; also equity, art, and science, including those who profess science, law, and art; creative intelligence. *(R):* Dishonest, double-dealing; roguery, exaction, injustice, vice, scandal, pillage, considerable loss. Etteilla delineated the King of Cups as a "blond man."

When the King of Cups appears in a reading, themes may emerge related to the pip cards associated with the three decans the King governs. These are the Four of Swords and the Five and Six of Cups.

Crowley's Astrological Attributions of the Court Cards

According to Crowley, the Thoth Princesses (Waite-Smith Pages) do not have any zodiacal attribution. Instead, they are assigned to the four quadrants of the heavens around the North Pole with a meridian through the Great Pyramid of Giza. Hellenistic astrology developed in the same region as the Great Pyramid, and the meridian of the *Thema Mundi*, the Hellenistic horoscope for the creation of the universe, passes through the Fire sign Aries, which corresponds to the suit of Wands. Each Page/Princess is said to cover a quarter of the Earth's surface as measured eastward around the equator, starting at the longitude of the Great Pyramid (about 30°N, 31°E) and proceeding in seasonal order: Fire/Wands (spring), Water/Cups (summer), Air/Swords (autumn) and Earth/Pentacles (winter). For what it's worth, Crowley regarded the Page of Wands as covering Asia; of Cups, the Pacific; of Swords, the Americas; and of Pentacles, Europe and Africa. How like Crowley, a Brit, to view America as the Page of Swords, a quintessential problem child!

A simple metaphor may help clarify this idea. Even if you are not a New Yorker, picture the universe as a perfectly formed giant apple. The Earth lies at the center of this apple, and its North Pole points directly upward toward the apple's stem. Now take a knife and slice the giant apple vertically through its stem into four identical quarters. Each quarter belongs to one of the earthy Pages; they are earthy because collectively they govern the entire universe, and Earth is the element of manifestation. God asks each Page to act as a portal or "throne" for one of the four Aces he has up his sleeve, each Ace representing an idea of a distinct element in the mind of God.

The four Aces link the tarot pip cards of each suit to the corresponding Pages "who rule the Heavens around the North Pole" and serve as seats of power for the Aces.[162] The four Aces, which represent the spiritual root-forces of the four elements, are "placed on the North Pole of the Universe, wherein they revolve, governing its revolution, and ruling as the connecting link between Yetsirah and the Material Plane of the Universe."[163] In this fancy-schmancy language of the Golden Dawn, the four Pages constitute the "Thrones of the Powers of the four Aces."

The non-Page court cards are each assigned only 30-degree segments of the zodiac circle. Crowley allots each Knight, Queen, and Prince/King a 30-degree segment consisting of the last decan of one sign and the first two decans of the following sign. Thus, each Knight, Queen, and Prince/King governs three consecutive decans which, taken together, overlap adjacent zodiacal signs. Crowley explains that the Knights, Queens, and Princes/Kings do not rule a single zodiac sign because they represent people, and people inhabit the "realm of the Elements" where "all things are mixed and confused."[164] People are complex; hence, the court cards that symbolize them must refer to a mixture of zodiacal signs and elements.

In Crowley's Thoth deck, the court cards indicate people whose natal Sun or rising sign falls "within the Zodiacal attribution of the card" or people who possess qualities of any of the three included decans.[165] Crowley, for example, was born on October 12, 1875 within an hour of midnight. The Ascendant at this birthplace shifted from Cancer into Leo at 10:57 p.m., an hour and three minutes before midnight. Thus, at Crowley's birth either the last decan of Cancer or the first decan of Leo was rising. The first decan of Leo is associated with the Thoth Prince of Wands, a card Crowley strongly identified with. In one of the rare instances where Crowley cites a practical example in *The Book of Thoth*, he comments about his own birth chart: "A person born on 12 October might possess many of the qualities of the Queen of Swords; while if, he were born shortly before midnight, he would add many

....

162 Crowley, *The Book of Thoth*, p. 179.

163 Regardie, *The Golden Dawn*, p. 542.

164 Crowley, *The Book of Thoth*, p. 149.

165 Crowley, ibid., p. 149.

of the characteristics of the Prince of Wands."[166] Crowley would rather be a Prince than a Queen, or would he?

Paul Hughes-Barlow believes that the Thoth Prince of Wands is "the Great Beast himself, Aleister Crowley."[167] Hughes-Barlow notes that the Greek inscription on the breastplate of the Thoth Prince of Wands translates as "the great beast," a term that Crowley reserved for himself. Biographer Richard Kaczynski explains that Crowley grew up in a Bible-reading religious household and his mother "in moments of exasperation with her son … would say he was the beast prophesied in the Book of Revelation."[168] In Crowley's notorious 1934 libel trial, he explained that he called himself "Master Therion" because *Therion* means "great wild beast," a reference to Beast 666 of the Apocalypse. Crowley told the magistrate that 666 is the number of the sun and added, "You can call me 'Little Sunshine.'"[169] The British tabloids were less kind and called Crowley "the wickedest man in the world," an appellation that stuck.

As an astrologer, Crowley was aware that the rising sign of his birth chart was either late Cancer or early Leo (the royal sign)—a region of the zodiac associated with the Prince of Wands. Paul Hughes-Barlow notes that Crowley's description of this card in *The Book of Thoth* sounds autobiographical. Crowley described the Prince of Wands as a warrior who is swift and strong (Crowley was an avid mountaineer), inclined to act on impulse, noble and generous, an extravagant boaster (Crowley's narcissism is legendary), dynamic, energetic, romantic (Crowley was bisexual and promiscuous), violent in the expression of an opinion, just, proud, courageous, a practical joker, contemptuous of the world at large, and a symbol of terror (the Great Beast).[170] As the airy part of Fire, the Prince of Wands

166 Crowley, *The Book of Thoth*, p. 149.

167 Paul Hughes-Barlow, "Knight of Wands Definitions" in "A Compendium of Tarot Card Meanings," *Super Tarot* blog, http://supertarot.co.uk/minor-wands/knight.htm (accessed 5 Jan. 2012).

168 Richard Kaczynski, *Perdurabo, The Life of Aleister Crowley* (Berkeley, CA: North Atlantic Books, 2010), p. 16.

169 Kaczynski, ibid., p. 474.

170 In *Understanding Aleister Crowley's Thoth Tarot* (San Francisco: Weiser Books, 2003), author Lon Milo Duquette notes that Crowley had "an outrageously twisted sense of humor," p. 316.

combines the intelligence of Air with the enthusiasm and intuition of Fire. Anyone familiar with Crowley's biography will recognize him in the Prince of Wands.

The Confusion Caused by the Golden Dawn

The Golden Dawn manuscripts created confusion about the court cards because they began with the idea that a King correlates with Fire and with the first letter of God's name, *Yod* of the tetragrammaton (*Yod—Heh—Vau—Heh*). Kings were viewed as patriarchal father-gods endowed with huge creator-phalluses, symbolized by the powerful stallions between their legs. The Golden Dawn's obvious choice for King was the horse-riding Knight of the Marseille deck. Despite the fact that Colman Smith depicted her Kings as mature older men, Waite in his 1911 *Pictorial Key to the Tarot* referred to the seemingly youthful steed-riding Knights as men older than forty. This confusion resulted from an attempt to impose the patriarchal system of the Kabbalah on the traditional imagery of the classic Marseille deck.

The Golden Dawn correlated the Princes with the element Air and the Hebrew letter *Vau*, the third letter of the tetragrammaton, but the Golden Dawn at times also referred to the Princes as Kings. To confound matters further, the Prince of Wands (Fire) was assigned to the first two decans of Leo, the most regal sign of the zodiac. The originators of the Golden Dawn kept flip-flopping about who would be King: their Knights or their Princes.

If we ignore the Golden Dawn's attempt to force the tarot to conform to the Kabbalah, a sound argument can be made that Knights are of the element Fire, and Kings of the element Air. Like Fire, the Knights are dynamic, energetic, impetuous, daring, adventurous, and passionate. They are bold, aggressive warriors who dash off on a quest at a moment's notice. Knights have the flexibility and volatility of the mutable signs of the zodiac.

Kings, on the other hand, are logical, tactical, thoughtful, discriminating, settled, and orderly. They resemble the stable fixed signs of the zodiac. As author Nevill Drury explains, "The allocation of Air to the King and Fire to the Knight may seem to be contradictory, but in medieval times the Knights were the aggressors and warriors, and the Kings more commonly the administrators or rulers." [171] Tarot experts Ruth Ann and Wald Amberstone follow these elemental attributions as well and note that the King of Wands "combines Air, associated with the rank of King, and Fire, associated with the suit of Wands." [172] My own preference is also to view Kings as older, experienced men of the element Air, and Knights as younger, impetuous men of the element Fire.

Correlations among Court Cards of Waite, Thoth, and Golden Dawn Decks					
Family Relationship	Waite-Smith	Thoth (Crowley)	Golden Dawn	Element	Hebrew Letter
Father (with a huge stallion-phallus)	Knight (men over forty)	Knight (Fire)	Lord/King/ Knight	Fire	Yod
Mother	Queen (women over forty)	Queen (Water)	Queen	Water	1st Heh
Son (with a smaller phallus)	King (men under forty)	Prince (Air)—the "Little King" symbolized by the royal star Regulus in Leo	Prince/King	Air	Vau
Daughter	Page (women under forty)	Princess (Earth)	Princess/Knave	Earth	2nd Heh

....
171 Nevill Drury, *The Tarot Workbook* (San Diego: Thunder Bay Press, 2004), p. 30.
172 Ruth Ann and Wald Amberstone, *Tarot Tips* (Woodbury, MN: Llewellyn Publications, 2003), p. 42.

In Crowley's attributions, the Thoth Queens refer to the first decan of the cardinal signs and the two adjoining decans. In other words, the Queens oversee the birth of each new season as follows: Queen of Wands, spring; Queen of Cups, summer; Queen of Swords, autumn; and Queen of Pentacles, winter. The Thoth Princes (Waite-Smith Kings) correspond to the first decan of the fixed signs and the two adjoining decans, and the Thoth Knights are linked to the first decan of the mutable signs and its adjacent decans. In addition to zodiacal attributions, Crowley assigned elemental properties to the court cards and, in this sense, regarded the court cards as representing the elements themselves. See appendix C for further details.

EIGHT

The Major Arcana

Myth is something that never was true, but always will be. [173]

SALLUSTIUS

The term "major arcana" was coined by the nineteenth-century French occultist Jean Baptiste Pitois (aka Paul Christian). *Arcana* means "secrets" and refers to Pitois's belief that the tarot trumps display images containing hidden spiritual wisdom. We have spent little time thus far discussing the major arcana cards. In this chapter, we will turn our attention to the trump cards because they often highlight major life issues, as the following reading illustrates.

Kevin's Gig

We met Kevin earlier when he was looking for work as an English teacher in Japan. In July 2011, Kevin asked my opinion of a three-card reading he had done for the question: "How will the gig go on Saturday night?" Kevin is an amateur musician and a talented guitar player. After months of feeling isolated in a foreign country, he found a job teaching English and began to meet people who shared his interests. To Kevin's delight, one of his new friends invited him to play at a gig the

---

173 Sallustius (fourth century CE), quoted in "The Origin of the Book of Mormon," *MormonMatrix* blog, http://faculty.gvsu.edu/websterm/Mythdefinitions.htm (accessed 4 March 2013).

coming weekend. Because he was nervous about being out of practice with his guitar, Kevin did a three-card reading about the upcoming performance. Two of the three cards were major arcana:

VII Chariot—XX Judgment—Page of Pentacles

Kevin saw the Chariot as a sign of victory, Judgment as winning favor with the audience and perhaps "knocking them dead," and the Page of Pentacles as "new education." His email went:

The man in the Chariot has stars all over his wagon and on his head. The two lions at his feet resemble protective females. Women are usually great at social scenes and knowing the right people. I would like to play more seriously once I meet the right people and make the right connections. I have found that women make the most loyal and dedicated friends when they find out I play and they believe in my talents.

Gabriel is blowing his horn. It looks to me like he's playing music. The dead are rising to the sound of the tune, as if they have never heard anything so sweet before. Their arms are open, receiving the gift of music. It's like they have been dead until they heard this and now they are alive.

The Page of Pentacles has just risen. This is a new dawn, the beginning of the day. He cups his hands and appears to be holding the Sun. Perhaps someone will take me under their wing and further my musical education or want to work with me?

I'm most likely reading into these cards what I am hoping for and this is to do a damned good job at the club on Saturday night. There is just no way in hell that I would want to get out there and make a fool of myself, or lay an egg in front of all these new people and my new coworkers. This is a big risk. I'm not a professional musician and I don't have a band.

Having little to add to Kevin's insightful interpretation, I sent him a brief reply:

The three cards are all upright, so it looks like smooth sailing. Two out of three cards being trumps suggests that this is a meaningful occasion. The charioteer has gotten all his ducks in a row and is able to steer his chariot where he wants to go. The Judgment card refers to the Last Judgment in the Bible. Souls are ready to rise from the dead and enter into heaven. They are awakening to a new life. The angel is blowing his horn to announce this important event. The Page of Pentacles is a studious young person who is humble, sincere, and serious about learning something new. He is someone who does his homework.

Since you were asking about the performance, the cards seem to be saying it will go well. The Chariot and the Page suggest that you need to prepare by practicing and getting all your abilities aligned in the right direction. I think the Judgment card means you will blow them away. You will wake the dead with your music. So keep practicing this week and just have fun on Saturday night.

With Judgment as the central card, I felt that Kevin was embarking on a period of renewal in his life. The angel on the card is calling dormant souls to a new realm of existence. Kevin's musical interest, which had lain dormant for a long time, was coming to life. It crossed my mind that the Chariot trump often literally signifies a vehicle or means of transportation. Knowing that Kevin had no car in Japan, I dismissed the possibility and did not mention it. To my surprise, when Kevin responded, he reported that his new boss owned an extra car and offered to rent it to him for a nominal fee.

Sir Francis Bacon's comment about the "thoughts of the moment" came to mind, "those that come unsought for are commonly the most valuable." I had ignored my own advice to pay attention to unbidden intuitions. Making note of such subtle fleeting impressions without analyzing or dismissing them often provides important clues to the reading. One author advises leaving these unbidden intuitive flashes in their "ambiguous, undefined, and unanalyzed state, until their meaning develops in its own way … even putting these delicate impressions into words runs the risk of distorting them."[174]

As the cards suggested, Kevin's gig went well and he was warmly accepted by the audience. What's more, he was about to rent a car (his new chariot) and would be able to travel easily to his new job.

---

174 Belleruth Naparstek, *Your Sixth Sense* (San Francisco: HarperSanFrancisco, 1997), p. 82.

Ways of Arranging the Major Arcana

The tarot trumps (from the Italian *trionfi,* meaning "triumphs") allude to an ancient Roman ceremony involving a triumphal march, the "entering of Rome by a general who had won a decisive victory over a foreign enemy." [175] The origin of the Roman triumph dates back into the mythical history of Rome. During the Roman Empire, only the Senate was empowered to grant a triumph. Dressed like a divine king, the victorious general rode in a chariot drawn by two or four horses in the triumphal march, the procession weaving through the streets of Rome. The general was accompanied by his army and the spoils of war. The triumphal procession typically included exotic animals, musicians, and slaves carrying images of conquered cities and names of vanquished populations. When the general arrived at Jupiter's temple on Capitoline Hill, he sacrificed bulls and offered tokens of his victory to the chief Roman god.

The Roman triumphal march captured the imagination of the Renaissance. The Italian poet Petrarch (1304–1374), the "Father of Humanism," wrote a poem called "Trionfi" patterned after the triumphal marches, in which he presented "the story of the human soul in its progress from earthly passion toward fulfillment in God." [176] In the 1400s, Renaissance artists of Christian Italy combined the idea of the Roman triumphal procession with the spiritual interpretations of Petrarch to create the original tarot trumps. Early tarot decks had varying numbers of trump cards with a variety of orderings. The modern arrangement and number of tarot trumps was settled on later in the history of the cards and owes its conceptual foundation to a combination of Roman tradition, Platonic philosophy and Christian theology.

Because the tarot trumps represent a triumphal procession in hierarchical order, each higher-numbered card in the sequence will trump all the cards that come before it. In the game of tarot, the High Priestess (II) is more powerful than the Magician (I), the Empress (III) outranks the High Priestess (II), the Pope or Hierophant (V) beats the Emperor (IV), and so on. The Fool, generally not numbered in early decks, is *not* part of the sequence of trumps but instead is an outsider, a spectator who observes the triumphal march. In the north-Italian card game played

....

175 *Miriam-Webster Dictionary,* s.v. "triumph," http://www.merriam-webster.com/dictionary/triumphs ?show=0&t=1312996330 (accessed 5 Jan. 2012).

176 *Encyclopedia Britannica,* s.v. "triumphs," http://www.britannica.com/EBchecked/topic/606113/Triumphs (accessed 5 Jan. 2012).

with the trionfi deck, the Fool acts like a wild card that can be played instead of a trump.[177] Using history as our guide, we can thus divide the tarot deck into four unequal parts:

- The observing Fool, unnumbered, a single card in a class by itself.

- The twenty-one trumps (21 is a triangular number, $21 = 1 + 2 + 3 + 4 + 5 + 6 = 3 \times 7$) that constitute the triumphal march.

- The forty pips (4×10), consisting of the four Aces or root cards and the thirty-six pips that develop from initial spark of the Aces (36 is a triangular number).

- The sixteen court cards (4×4).

Those involved in establishing the number and pattern of the tarot deck were likely influenced by Pythagorean beliefs about numbers and the all-encompassing worldview of classical astrology, which explains reality in terms of twelve signs of the zodiac and ten essential chart points (the Earth, the seven visible planets, and the two nodes of the Moon where eclipses occur). Of course, $12 + 10 = 22$, the number of trump cards in the tarot.

Arranging the Major Arcana by the Four Cardinal Virtues

Author Gareth Knight organizes the major arcana around the four cardinal virtues: Justice, Strength, Temperance, and Prudence.[178] He envisions the Fool (0) and the Magician (I) as two aspects of the same character, the living spirit of the tarot who must explore a set of four halls, each governed by a different virtue. Knight associates the pips and court cards of each suit with the Renaissance categories of human life: "executive power, organization (Wands); opposition, external forces (Swords); love, social relationships (Cups); and wealth, gain, physical well-being (Coins)."[179]

---

177 Place, *The Tarot: History, Symbolism*, p. 188.

178 Knight, *Magical World*, p. 15.

179 Knight, ibid., p. 92.

- The Hall of Justice (VIII) represents fairness and balanced judgment. This hall contains the Hanged Man (XII), a different perspective; Death (XIII), inevitable endings; the Devil (XV), bondage; the Tower (XVI), sudden disruption; and the entire suit of airy Swords.

- The Hall of Strength or Fortitude (XI) represents power and authority. Within this hall one finds the High Priestess (II), higher wisdom; the Empress (III), maternal fertility; the Emperor (IV), temporal authority; the Pope or Hierophant (V), moral authority; and the entire suit of fiery Wands.

- The Hall of Temperance (XIV) represents moderation, harmonious blending, and synthesis. It consists of the Lovers (VI), personal commitment; the Chariot (VII), triumph over opposing forces; the Hermit (IX), sage guidance; the Wheel of Fortune (X), inevitable change; and the entire suit of watery Cups.

- Finally, the Hall of Prudence or the World (XXI) represents wise action that leads to completion and fulfillment. This hall's members include the Star (XVII), hope; the Moon (XVIII), hidden forces; the Sun (XIX), vitality; the Last Judgment (XX), awakening and renewal; and the entire suit of earthy Pentacles/Coins. Unlike Knight, the thirteenth-century theologian Thomas Aquinas called Prudence the charioteer of the virtues (Latin: *auriga virtutem*) because it guides all other virtues by providing them with their rule and measure. No doubt Aquinas would have identified Prudence with the Chariot had the tarot existed in his day.

Arranging the Major Arcana by Plato's Three Levels of Soul

Robert Place advocates dividing the major arcana according to Plato's three-part nature of the human soul.[180] Drawing on the ideas of his teacher Socrates, Plato believed the soul represented the essential part of a person and determined how that person behaved. He subdivided the soul into three main functions—thinking, willing, and feeling:

....

180 Place, *The Tarot: History, Symbolism,* 2005

- The Rational Soul of the thinking mind or intellect (*logos*) is related to the virtue of Wisdom or Prudence needed to use reason in a morally proper way.

- The Spirited Soul of will or volition (*thymos*) is related to the virtue of Strength, Fortitude, or Courage, which is needed to exercise one's will effectively.

- The Appetitive Soul of feeling or desire (*eros*) is related to the virtue of Temperance, which is needed to control one's natural appetite for sensual satisfaction.

The basest level is the appetitive soul, and the loftiest level is the rational soul. When all three parts of the human soul act virtuously and harmoniously together, the person behaves according to the fourth cardinal virtue of Justice. In Place's view, it is no accident that the four cardinal virtues play such a prominent role in the major arcana. He believes that the trump cards were deliberately designed to convey the views of Plato and the neo-Platonists.

In the Platonic view, the unnumbered Fool stands apart from the twenty-one numbered trumps, which represent the spiritual lessons that the Fool must learn. Because 21 = 3 x 7, each of the three levels of the soul is alloted seven trump cards, as follows:

The base Appetitive Soul (feeling) is apportioned trumps I through VII: the Magician, High Priestess, Empress, Emperor, Hierophant, Lovers, and Chariot. These cards relate to human desire and temporal power. Plato used the image of the Chariot as a metaphor for the soul. The driver represents the rational mind acting prudently. The two horses, one black and one white, signify the cravings of the Appetitive Soul (in need of Temperance) and the will of the Spirited Soul (in need of Strength or Fortitude).

The middle Spirited Soul (the will) is granted trumps VIII through XV: *Strength*, the Hermit, the Wheel of Fortune, *Justice*, the Hanged Man, Death, *Temperance,* and the Devil. These cards deal with various aspects of the human will, including things that occur outside our volition.

Finally, the lofty Rational Soul (reason) is allotted trumps XVI through XXI: the Tower, Star, Moon, Sun, Judgment, and the World trump, which is associated with the virtue of *Prudence*. The characters that appear on the cards following the Tower trump are naked, suggesting a focus on lofty, nonmaterial or spiritual reality. The Catholic theologian Thomas Aquinas (1225–1274 CE) reworked Plato's ideas about the cardinal virtues and concluded that Prudence, rather than Justice, was the highest or ultimate virtue.

L. Frank Baum's children's tale, *The Wonderful Wizard of Oz,* is a modern retelling of Plato's dialogue. The three characters whom Dorothy (a modern Fool) meets on her journey represent the three aspects of the Platonic soul. The Scarecrow, the Cowardly Lion, and the Tin Man respectively lament their lack of a brain (a prudent mind), courage (strength of will), and a heart (temperate desire). Dorothy shows the Scarecrow that he has good ideas (a rational soul behaving with *Prudence*), the Cowardly Lion that he can be brave in spite of his fear (a spirited soul behaving with *Strength*), and the Tin Man that he can act kindly in the face of desire (an appetitive soul behaving with *Temperance*). Acting in concert, the three friends of Dorothy secure *Justice* from the Wizard, who then returns Dorothy to Kansas, which corresponds to the World trump. Only a Fool would regard Kansas as the ultimate, most cherished destination of the journey of life!

In discussing the Marseille pattern tarot, author Lee Bursten adds an interesting twist to Robert Place's view of the role of Plato's three-part soul in tarot interpretation. [181] When reading the tarot of Marseille, Bursten advocates visually dividing each card into thirds, one third for each part of the soul. The lower third of a card represents the soul of appetite; the middle third, the soul of will; and the upper third, the soul of reason. Then, the images in each section of a Marseille card are interpreted in the context of the part of the soul where they fall.

Arranging the Major Arcana as a Mandala

In *Tarot and Psychology,* Jungian psychologist Arthur Rosengarten suggests that the major arcana can be arranged in a "circle of interbeing" with the Fool at the center. [182] In this way he avoids the idea of the Fool's journey as a linear, step-by-step progression in time through the major arcana. Instead, the Fool has access to all the lessons of the major arcana cards simultaneously. These lessons are thus interdependent and interrelated, just as in real life.

....

181   Lee Bursten, *Universal Tarot of Marseille* (Torino, Italy: Lo Scarabeo, 2006), p. 57.

182   Arthur Rosengarten, *Tarot and Psychology* (St. Paul, MN: Paragon House, 2000), pp. 168–170.

The Individual Cards of the Major Arcana

The next section will look at each of the major arcana individually. The names of the cards presented here are drawn from several traditions including the classic Marseille deck, Crowley's Thoth tarot, the Waite-Smith deck, Gainsford's Wiccan Tarot of the Old Path, and the Osho Zen Tarot. Juno and Jupiter are alternative names for the Popess (trump II) and Pope (trump V), respectively from the Swiss 1JJ tarot deck. [183] The names "Popess" and "Pope" were apparently offensive to the Vatican because they implied the heretical notion that a woman could be Pope. God forbid!

For political reasons, the Emperor and Empress were renamed "Grandfather" and "Grandmother" during the French Revolution. [184] Fortunately, this idea did not catch on. Can *you* imagine Gramps as a hot stud and Granny as a symbol of sensual delight? On the other hand, these cards may refer to one's grandparents in an actual reading. For example, author Wilma Carroll discusses a Celtic Cross spread that a young man did for his mother. The Empress appeared in position 2, "crossing" the querent (his mother) and represented his sick grandmother who was in his mother's care. [185]

The order of the trumps presented here is from the Marseille deck of the 1700s. Waite switched the Marseille positions of Strength and Justice so the trumps in his deck would correspond to the signs of the zodiac, in which Libra (the seventh sign) comes later than Leo (the fifth). The astrological correspondences in parentheses are those of the Golden Dawn. There are variations of these correspondences in the tarot literature. Because Waite's *Pictorial Key to the Tarot* has been so influential in modern thinking about the major arcana, I have included Waite's keywords at the beginning of the discussion of each card. [186]

0—The Fool—The Foolish Man—The Madman—Lunatic (Air)

Waite: ZERO. THE FOOL.—Folly, mania, extravagance, intoxication, delirium, frenzy, bewrayment [betrayal]. *Reversed:* Negligence, absence, distribution, carelessness, apathy, nullity, vanity.

---

183   A derivative of the Tarot de Besançon.

184   *Wikipedia*, s.v. "Tarot of Marseilles," http://en.wikipedia.org/wiki/Tarot_de_Marseille (accessed 10 Mar 2012).

185   Carroll, *2-Hour Tarot Tutor*, p. 41.

186   Unless otherwise noted, all quotations from Waite in this chapter are from *The Pictorial Key to the Tarot* online.

The Golden Dawn assigned the Foolish Man to the element Air and warned that with regard to practical matters of ordinary life, this card suggests folly, stupidity, and odd behavior. Modern writers have connected the Fool with Uranus, the planet of novelty and unexpected events. Air belongs to the sanguine temperament, so we can expect the Fool to be sociable, relationship-oriented, optimistic, playful, happy-go-lucky, impulsive and pleasure-seeking. Sanguine individuals enjoy being with people and circulating in social circles. They see life as pregnant with possibilities.

Because of the connection with the element Air, sanguine people are fond of travel, both physical and mental. Like a newborn child, the tarot Fool is starting out on a journey of self-discovery. In the Waite-Smith deck, the Fool is perched at the edge of a precipice, preparing for a leap of faith. In older decks, the Fool looks like a wandering jester, possibly schizophrenic, who is capable of both lunacy and profound insight into the human condition. Gareth Knight regards the Fool as the genuine spirit of the tarot.

The youthful Pages of the tarot deck can be viewed as sub-personalities of the Fool. Like the Fool, the Pages possess a childlike openness and sense of wonder as they set forth to learn the lessons of their respective suits. Sometimes young people act like fools, rushing in where angels fear to tread. The Fool may appear in a reading to warn us that we are acting foolish in a practical situation of everyday life.

A Fool Reading

A woman in her midthirties asked whether she would be able to get pregnant. She had been through a divorce a few years earlier and recently remarried. She very much wanted to have a child with her new husband but had been unable to conceive. We did a three-card spread with the Waite-Smith deck:

The Fool—Eight of Wands—Four of Cups

The presence of a major arcana card implied that her question was a matter of importance. We reflected jointly on the cards and arrived at the following possible interpretations. The Fool represented her recent marriage, a fresh start in her life, and her desire to bring a new child into the world. The Eight of Wands, a card of haste, indicated that she felt that time was passing quickly and her biological clock would soon make conception impossible. The Four of Cups, a card of weariness and discontent, suggested that despite her happy marriage and comfortable circumstances, the thing she desired most—a new child—felt unattainable.

The reading seemed equivocal about whether she would be able to conceive. Looking at the pensive figure on the Waite-Smith Four of Cups, I felt that at best there would be a delay and at worst she would learn that pregnancy was not possible. The most promising aspects of the reading were the hand offering a fourth cup out of the clouds and the astrological connection of the Four of Cups with the Moon decan of Cancer. Crowley named this card "Luxury." The Moon and Cancer are astrological symbols of female reproduction, pregnancy, and motherhood. About a year after the reading, I heard from a mutual acquaintance that she had finally managed to conceive.

I—The Juggler—Trickster—Magician— Magus—Mountebank—Existence (Mercury)

Waite: THE MAGICIAN.—Skill, diplomacy, address, subtlety; sickness, pain, loss, disaster, snares of enemies; self-confidence, will; the querent, if male. *(R):* Physician, magus, mental disease, disgrace, disquiet.

In early tarot decks, the character on this card was a traveling street performer whose skill at legerdemain allowed him to con his audiences out of their hard-earned money. The Magician in older decks is a dissimulating juggler, caster of dice, mountebank, and trickster. The Waite-Smith deck corrupted this classic image into a goody-two-shoes manipulator of cosmic forces. The Golden Dawn saw this card as a symbol of skill, craft, cunning, and, at times, occult wisdom.

Swift-footed Mercury/Hermes, who is associated with this trump, came into this world a cunning thief. Within hours of his birth, Mercury managed to slip out of his cradle and steal the oxen of his brother Apollo. When his brother denounced him before their divine father Jupiter/Zeus the next day, Mercury asked naively, "What sort of animal is an ox?" and added, "How could I have stolen his oxen? I was only born yesterday!" When the Magician appears in a reading, we are being reminded that we were *not* born yesterday and that we do possess the skills and cunning to achieve our goals and win others to our point of view.

The Knights of the four suits can be viewed as sub-personalities of the Magician. Like the Magician, they are youthful adults on their way to maturity. As Pages, they learned the skills of a knight and honed their ability to manifest their desires. Now they are setting out to put their skills to the test in search of new adventures.

II—The Female Pope (Joan)—La Papessa— Juno—The High Priestess—Inner Voice (the Moon)

Waite: THE HIGH PRIESTESS.—Secrets, mystery, the future as yet unrevealed; the woman who interests the querent, if male; the querent herself, if female; silence, tenacity; mystery, wisdom, science. *(R)*: Passion, moral or physical ardour, conceit, surface knowledge.

This card reminds me of the legend of Pope Joan, the fictitious ninth-century female pope of the Roman Catholic Church. As the story goes, Joan was a brilliant and talented woman who realized there were few opportunities for members of her gender in a patriarchal society. Having learned the lesson of the Magician (trump I), Joan disguised herself as a man and entered the priesthood. Her remarkable abilities were quickly recognized and she was eventually elected to the papacy, all the while concealing the fact that she was a woman. Her lonely secret was finally revealed when she gave birth to a child, following which her sanctimonious colleagues stoned her to death. That'll teach them uppity women to presume they could be pope!

A real-life parallel can be found in the story of Sister (Sor) Juana Inés de la Cruz (1651–1695), probably the most brilliant mind in seventeenth-century Mexico. Sor Juana was self-taught because she was not permitted to attend the all-male university in Mexico City. Envious of her outstanding intellect and independent ideas, high-ranking church officials schemed to silence her and fostered her early demise.

The inspiration for Pope Joan, the Popess of the tarot, was most likely Pope John VIII (c. 825–882), a brilliant administrator noted for his effeminacy. John's supporters referred to him as "Pope John the Manly" in an effort to counteract the "stigma of effeminacy."[187] Pope John's detractors, however, were not so kind and referred to him behind his back as "Pope Johanna." An important lesson of the Female Pope trump is that something remains hidden and things may not be all that they seem.

....

187 *The Catholic Encyclopedia,* http://www.newadvent.org/cathen/08407a.htm (accessed 10 Mar. 2012), notes: "Photius of Constantinople (De Spir. Sanct. Myst., lxxxix) refers emphatically three times to this pope as 'the Manly', as though he would remove from him the stigma of effeminacy."

Not surprisingly, the Female Pope (High Priestess) has come to represent feminine wisdom, maternal intuition, spiritual awareness, mystery, hidden knowledge, and the revelation of the secrets behind the veil. The Golden Dawn associates the Popess with Luna the Moon, Queen of the Night, a symbol of change and fluctuation. Given her possible origins in the legend of Pope Joan, she may also refer to women's rights, the glass ceiling, oppression of minorities by the ruling class, and the isolation and loneliness of gifted, ambitious women in a patriarchal society.

III—The Empress—Grandmother—Creativity (Venus)

Waite: THE EMPRESS.—Fruitfulness, action, initiative, length of days; the unknown, clandestine; also difficulty, doubt, ignorance. *(R):* Light, truth, the unraveling of involved matters, public rejoicings; according to another reading, vacillation.

The ancient astrologer Ptolemy wrote that the Moon and Venus represent one's mother in a birth chart. The intuitive lunar aspect of the mother appeared in the High Priestess. In the Empress we find the Great Earth Mother and goddess of grain, Demeter, who makes the crops grow and nourishes mankind. The Empress is also Venus, the "lesser benefic," the goddess of love, luxury, and sensual delight. When the Empress appears in a reading, she often has to do with fertility, pregnancy, abundance, creativity, sensuality, marriage, and the assumption of the roles of wife and mother. When connected with stressful cards, the Empress may represent the earth goddess Demeter pining for her abducted daughter, Persephone, and consequently neglecting her divine task of tending the earthly garden.

The Queens of the four suits can be viewed as sub-personalities of the Empress. Like the Empress, they are the wives and mothers of the tarot. Queens hold positions of power and authority from which they are able to love and nurture those in their care.

IV—The Emperor—Grandfather—the Rebel (Aries)

Waite: THE EMPEROR.—Stability, power, protection, realization; a great person; aid, reason, conviction; also authority and will. *(R):* Benevolence, compassion, credit; also confusion to enemies, obstruction, immaturity.

All the trump cards that precede the Emperor have been associated with individual planets (the Fool, Uranus; the Magician, Mercury; the High Priestess, the Moon; and the Empress, Venus). Uranus lies outside the bounds of the solar system of traditional astrology in which Saturn was the ultimate frontier. Venus, Mercury, and the Moon are personal "inner planets" because their orbits lie within that of the Sun in the geocentric universe. The Emperor is the first of the major arcana to be linked to the zodiac belt, specifically to the first sign Aries, where Mars rules and the Sun is exalted. The war god Mars and the regal Sun are fitting symbols for the commanding Emperor. The Golden Dawn views this card as one of ambition, conquest, victory, and strife.

Aries the Ram is a cardinal, masculine Fire sign that marks the beginning of spring in the tropical zodiac and a new cycle of life. Aries energy is independent, pioneering, direct, assertive, courageous, and self-expressive. Mars, the ruler of Aries, loves competition and conquest; you can feel safe and well protected when Mars is on your side. The red planet, however, can be impatient and insensitive to the feelings of others. The Sun, which is exalted in Aries, is the center and king of the solar system. As such, the Sun symbolizes authority, fatherhood, pride, recognition, generosity, ambition, and the human will. The Emperor is numbered IV, a number Crowley associates with the Rule of Law.

The Kings of the four suits can be viewed as sub-personalities of the Emperor. Like the Emperor, the Kings are father figures who hold positions of power and authority, from which they are able to establish and maintain societal structures geared toward maintaining the welfare of their wards.

V—The Pope—Jupiter—The Hierophant—No-thingness (Taurus)

Waite: THE HIEROPHANT.—Marriage, alliance, captivity, servitude; by another account, mercy and goodness; inspiration; the man to whom the Querent has recourse. *(R):* Society, good understanding, concord, over-kindness, weakness.

For years I was not particularly fond of this card, probably because of my distrust of orthodoxy and of those who claim to speak infallibly on God's behalf. My attitude changed, however, when a friend lost his son to a neurological disorder. I attended the young man's funeral and was at a loss for words. Fortunately the rabbi, a kind and compassionate man, guided the congregation in a moving ceremony rooted in thousands of years of Jewish culture. I was extremely grateful to this modern hierophant who, steeped in his tradition, knew exactly what to say and do. My attitude toward the Hierophant card changed after that funeral service.

The original hierophant of ancient Greece was a priest elected for life to guide his congregation in the rituals of the Eleusinian mysteries. The hierophant was typically an older celibate male with a powerful voice. His principal function was to explain to the initiates the secret meanings of the sacred objects used in the celebration of the mysteries. He was a teacher of divine wisdom who was granted the authority to separate the clean from the unclean among the parishioners so that the unclean would not debase the sacred ceremony.

The Eleusinian mysteries are a set of religious rites based on the myth of Demeter/Ceres, the corn goddess of fertility and the harvest. Demeter is Mother Earth who is associated with trump III, the Empress. One day Demeter's daughter Persephone disappeared; Hades/Pluto had abducted the young lady to be his unwilling bride in the underworld. The distraught Demeter went to Eleusis in search of her daughter and there she befriended the royal family, which built a temple in her honor.

In her grief, Demeter ceased making the crops grow. The earth was plunged into winter, earning for Demeter the appellation of "bringer of seasons." Eventually Zeus intervened and struck a deal with Hades in which Persephone would spend the winter months in the underworld and the rest of the year above ground with her mother. Persephone might have escaped entirely but Hades tricked her into eating some pomegranate seeds, which served to forever bind the fair maiden to spending some time with Hades during an annual sojourn in the underworld.

The Golden Dawn paired the Hierophant with the sign Taurus, the home of Venus, the tarot Empress. Opposite Taurus one finds Scorpio, the home of Mars and Pluto/Hades. Taurus governs the lush vegetation that grows at the height of spring. Scorpio, in contrast, rules the death and decay of living things that occurs during the autumn and heralds the impending winter.

The Hierophant understands this cycle of birth and death, light and dark, Demeter and Hades, Taurus and Scorpio, spring and autumn, fecundity and barrenness. As the high priest of the Eleusinian mysteries, the hierophant has witnessed this cycle play itself out countless times. When the Hierophant appears in a reading, he helps us to understand our place in the cycle of life and death and how that cycle applies to our lives, often in the context of a traditional religious ceremony such as a marriage, funeral, baptism, bris, etc.

VI—Love—The Lovers (Gemini)

Waite: THE LOVERS.—Attraction, love, beauty, trials overcome. *(R):* Failure, foolish designs. Another account speaks of marriage frustrated and contrarieties of all kinds.

Author Dusty White writes that the Golden Dawn association of the Lovers trump with Gemini provokes him to "violent fits of hysterical laughter."[188] He prefers to link this card to the planet Venus, the goddess of love. What, then, does the mental Air sign Gemini, ruled by swift Mercury, have to do with love? And how did the Golden Dawn arrive at this seemingly odd connection?

The sign Gemini is named after the twins Castor and Pollux, the so-called Dioscuri of ancient Greece. These twin sons of Leda were the protectors of sailors through their ability to control the winds. One day the philandering Zeus disguised himself as a swan to approach and rape the beautiful Leda. That same night, Leda had sex with her husband Tyndareus. As a result, she got pregnant with two sets of twins: the mortals Castor and Clytemnestra from the egg inseminated by her mortal husband, and the immortals Pollux and Helen of Troy from the egg inseminated by immortal Zeus. She gave birth to quadruplets, two boys and two girls, produced from the mixed sperm of two dads, one mortal and the other a god.

Leda's two sons, fraternal twins, became inseparable. In fact, Castor and Pollux so loved each other that when the mortal Castor died, his divine brother Pollux chose to sacrifice his immortality to reunite with his dead twin. Love often involves making difficult choices. Zeus permitted Pollux to share his immortality with mortal Castor by transforming them jointly into the constellation Gemini. Ever since, Gemini has been a testament to undying brotherly love. "Greater love hath no man than this, that a man lay down his life for his friends."[189] The creator of the fifteenth-century Visconti-Sforza deck may have had the Gemini twins in mind when he painted the World card, displaying twins with angelic wings holding up the New Jerusalem. The Fool must learn to love his fellow humans, as Pollux loved Castor, to enter the kingdom of heaven.

---

188 Dusty White, *The Easiest Way to Learn Tarot—Ever!* (Charleston, SC: BookSurge Publishing, 2009), p. 8.
189 John 15:13 (King James Bible).

In older versions of the Lovers trump, the winged Eros/Cupid, the mischievous god of passion and fertility, hovers above the two lovers. The mother of Eros is none other than Venus/Aphrodite, the goddess of sexual love and beauty. Eros is often depicted as blindfolded because there is no telling where his arrows may fall.[190] Love is blind and can strike without warning. In some versions of the card, the young man is deciding between two women, one pure and innocent and the other mature and experienced in carnal affairs. Some authors view the Lovers trump as alluding to the mythical judgment of Paris, which initiated the Trojan War. Choices have consequences.

In the Lovers trump of the sanitized Waite-Smith deck, the archangel Raphael, rather than erotic Eros/Cupid, hovers above the two lovers. The name Raphael means "it is God who heals." In the Old Testament, God sends his angel Raphael, the matchmaker, to heal Tobit of blindness and to help Tobit's son Tobias hook up with the unfortunate Sarah, who is being tormented by a demon that kills every man she weds before the marriage can be consummated. What a wedding night!

By the time Raphael appears in Sarah's life, the vile demon has slaughtered seven of Sarah's husbands before they are able to climax. Inspired by God to help Sarah, Raphael casts out the nasty demon. No longer possessed, Sarah is able to consummate her union with Tobias, who is glad to be still alive the morning after. Perhaps the Golden Dawn was thinking of Sarah when it taught that the Lovers card refers to "motive, power, and action arising from inspiration."[191]

Among Roman Catholics, Archangel Raphael has become the patron saint of physicians, nurses, healers, travelers, happy encounters, matchmakers, and the blind (love is blind, after all). Inspired by the story of Tobias and Sarah, Catholic singles now pray to Saint Raphael for help in finding a spouse.[192] It's cheaper than a dating service and at least as effective as the rhythm method. Arthur Edward Waite, who grew up Catholic, was aware of the symbolism of Raphael as a Christianized version of Eros/Cupid. Waite was also aware that the six-pointed Star of David is a symbol of the loving union of Adam and Eve, whom God created

190 The airborn wands on the Waite-Smith Eight of Wands are sometimes interpreted as Cupid's arrows.

191 Israel Regardie, *The Golden Dawn*, p. 584.

192 See "Saint Raphael Patron Saint" at http://www.saintraphael.webhero.com/patron.htm (accessed December 22, 2011) and "Saint Raphael Patron of Catholic Singles" at http://www.straphael.net/saint-raphael-catholic-singles-patron.php (accessed December 22, 2011).

to be Adam's companion on the sixth day of creation, the same in number as the sixth trump, the Lovers (VI).

Given that the Lovers trump follows and therefore trumps the four temporal rulers (the female Popess, the Empress, the Emperor, and the male Pope), we are reminded of the biblical passage:

> Though I speak with the tongues of men and of angels and have not love, I am become as sounding brass or a tinkling cymbal…And though I bestow all my goods to feed the poor…and have not love, it profiteth me nothing…And now abideth faith, hope, love, these three; but the greatest of these is love. [193]

VII—The Chariot—Winged Victory—Mastery—Awareness (Cancer)

Waite: THE CHARIOT.—Succour, providence; also war, triumph, presumption, vengeance, trouble. *(R):* Riot, quarrel, dispute, litigation, defeat.

Cancer is the rising sign of the *Thema Mundi*, the mythical Hellenistic birth chart of the universe. In the modern natural zodiac with Aries rising, Cancer lies at the bottom of the chart in a location analogous to the fourth house, representing our roots, foundations, ancestry, family, and home life. Cancer is the sign of the crab that carries a protective shell on its back, bringing a secure interior environment wherever it goes. By pairing Cancer with the Chariot trump, the Golden Dawn suggests that this card has to do with creating a safe environment that will allow our sensitive inner self to survive and flourish.

Plato used the chariot as a metaphor for the three parts of the human soul: appetite, will, and reason. In Plato's view, the function of the "soul of reason" is to harness the strength of the headstrong horses of appetite and will, that is, those inner contradictions that pull in different directions, in order to maintain focus and direct the person one-pointedly toward the good. This Platonic metaphor is reflected in the Golden Dawn's interpretation of the Chariot as success, health, victory, and triumph.

---

193   1 Corinthians 13:1–13 (King James Bible) with "charity" rendered as "love."

As mentioned previously, Thomas Aquinas (1225–1274) viewed Prudence as "the cause, measure, and form of all virtues … the *auriga virtutum* or the charioteer of the virtues." [194] Without prudent judgment, we would be unable to exercise the virtues of strength, justice, or temperance. According to Aquinas, prudence (the charioteer of the virtues) is primary because it tells us when and under what circumstances it is wise to act with courage, fairness, or moderation. The primacy of Prudence may explain why Renaissance artists, who were familiar with Thomas Aquinas, placed the Chariot in the sequence of trumps before the other cardinal virtues. They were merely following the lead of Aquinas, who structured his discussion of the cardinal virtues in his *Summa Theologica* in the order Prudence, Justice, Fortitude, and Temperance—the same order in which the tarot trumps the Chariot (VII), Justice (VIII), Fortitude (XI), and Temperance (XIV) would later appear in fifteenth-century tarot decks. [195] Some authors believe that the World card represents prudence. If so, Prudence also comes last—an idea consistent with Aquinas's teaching that Prudence is the alpha and the omega of all virtues.

The Chariot may appear in a reading when we are being pulled in many directions and need to maintain a straight course by allowing our rational mind to take charge of the conflicting desires of will and appetite (Plato's white and dark horses). The Chariot calls on us to use our "wise mind" to act prudently with justice, fortitude, and temperance. It advises us to remain in the driver's seat and steer clear of emotional pitfalls, dead ends, and addictive behaviors. If Paris had exercised prudence when he was asked to judge which goddess deserved the golden apple for her beauty, the Trojan War might have been averted.

Sometimes a cigar is just a cigar. The Chariot may simply refer to a vehicle for transportation or to the journey itself. How prudent can you get?

VIII or XI—Justice—Adjustment—Breakthrough (Libra)

Waite: JUSTICE.—Equity, rightness, probity, executive; triumph of the deserving side in law. *(R):* Law in all its departments, legal complications, bigotry, bias, excessive severity.

For Plato (unlike Aquinas), Justice was chief among the four cardinal virtues. In older decks, Justice was numbered VIII, but Waite renumbered Justice XI to make it central among the major

194 *Wikipedia*, s.v. "Prudence," http://en.wikipedia.org/wiki/Prudence (accessed 10 May 2013).

195 Ronald Decker, *Art and Arcana*, p. 36.

arcana in correspondence with the sign Libra. In Greek mythology, Themis was the goddess of justice. She was the daughter of Ouranos and Gaia and the sister of Cronos/Saturn. Themis, who embodied divine law and order, sat beside Zeus as his advisor. Themis was the first divine being in charge of the Delphic Oracle, who helped visitors gain a clearer perspective on their lives—a role that tarot readers play today. [196] Themis was also charged with deciding whether the dead would enter the Elysian Fields or the Pit of Tartarus, the ancient equivalents of the Christian heaven and hell.

The Roman name for Themis was Iustitia—the origin of our English word "justice." Iustitia is depicted as a blindfolded goddess holding the scales of justice in her left hand and a double-edged sword in her right to symbolize reasonableness and fairness. The blindfold represents her impartiality. The façade of many courthouses today is graced by a statue of Iustitia. When the Justice trump appears in a reading, the goddess may be inviting us to stop by and say hello to her on our way to court.

Themis had a daughter, Astraea/Dike, the celestial virgin who symbolizes purity and innocence. Like Themis, her daughter Astraea/Dike was associated with moral order and fair judgment. According to Ovid, Astraea got fed up with human greed and wickedness and fled to the heavens where she became the constellation of Virgo the Virgin. The scales of justice carried by Astraea then became the adjacent sign Libra, which at times was also viewed as the claws of the Scorpion.

In ancient Egypt, the goddess Maat carried a sword of justice, but no scales. Maat wore an ostrich feather in her hair to symbolize truth, and she assisted Anubis in judging the dead by weighing their hearts against a feather. The Egyptians believed that the soul resided in one's heart and a good soul was lighter than a feather. Maat's function was to provide lawful orderliness to the universe so that the world would not return to the chaos of the moment of creation.

When Justice appears in a reading, the querent may be dealing with a legal matter or an appearance in court. Say hi to Iustitia on the way in! Mythology suggests that the Justice trump relates to law, order, fairness, impartiality, morality, purity, innocence, virginity, clear thinking, balanced judgment, the consequences of one's behavior, the avoidance of chaos, the orderly

---

196 Eventually the administration of Delphi was given over to the god Apollo.

workings of society, escape from greed and wickedness, and perhaps also the need to consult the oracle to put things in perspective.

IX—Father Time—The Hermit—The Wise One—Aloneness (Virgo)

Waite: THE HERMIT.—Prudence, circumspection; also and especially treason, dissimulation, roguery, corruption. *(R):* Concealment, disguise, policy, fear, unreasoned caution.

> *Far from the madding crowd's ignoble strife*
> *Their sober wishes never learn'd to stray;*
> *Along the cool sequester'd vale of life*
> *They kept the noiseless tenor of their way.*
> —Thomas Gray [197]

By definition a hermit is a person who withdraws from society and lives a solitary existence in search of wisdom, usually in a remote location isolated from human contact. The English word "hermit" comes from the Greek *eremia* meaning "desert" and *eremos* meaning "solitary"— the original hermits lived alone in the desert in search of spiritual enlightenment. In our discussion of the Justice trump, we saw how Astraea, a Greek virgin goddess of justice, fled to the heavens as the constellation Virgo to escape human corruption and wickedness. Her scales of justice became the adjacent sign Libra. The Golden Dawn assigned the Hermit trump to Virgo because Astraea/Dike—the goddess of purity, innocence, and moral law and orderliness—preferred a hermitlike existence in the night sky to living amidst human corruption on earth.

The early Christian hermits devoted themselves to asceticism, celibacy, fasting, prayer and works of piety. Traditional decks depict the Hermit as an old man with a walking stick. He holds an hourglass in his hand rather than the lantern seen in modern decks. Centuries ago this card was sometimes referred to as Time, the Old Man, or the Hunchback. The Hermit with the hourglass is none other than Father Time, a personification of Saturn/Cronos of mythology. A closer look at Saturn may deepen our understanding of its meaning.

....

197 Thomas Gray, "Elegy Written in a Country Churchyard," Thomas Gray Archive, http://www.thomasgray .org/cgi-bin/display.cgi?text=elcc (accessed 19 Dec. 2012).

William Lilly, in his 1647 text *Christian Astrology*, wrote that Saturn "is profound in imagination, in his acts severe, in words reserved, in speaking and giving very spare, in labor patient, in arguing or disputing grave, in obtaining the goods of this life studious and solicitous, in all manner of actions austere." Lilly also said that Saturn represents "husbandmen, clowns, beggars, day laborers, old men, fathers, grandfathers, monks, Jesuits, sectarists [members of a sect]." In many ways Saturn is like the tarot Fool, for he can be as childlike as a clown or as wise as a respected elder. Robert Place speculates that the Hermit may represent the "missing" cardinal virtue of Prudence in the major arcana.

When the Hermit appears in a reading, he is suggesting that we remove ourselves temporarily from the madding crowd to put our lives in order and see things from a better perspective. In some older decks, the Hermit can be seen at the bottom of the Wheel of Fortune as the figure who has renounced worldly ambition and rules nothing. The Hermit withdraws from the world in search of the clarity and understanding that only quiet contemplation can bring. In his solitude, the Hermit partakes of the analytical Virgo archetype to help him discern what really matters.

X—Fortuna—Dame Fortune— The Wheel of Fortune—Change (Jupiter)

Waite: WHEEL OF FORTUNE.—Destiny, fortune, success, elevation, luck, felicity. *(R):* Increase, abundance, superfluity.

In astrology, the planet Jupiter is called the "greater benefic." Jupiter is said to confer good fortune and to mitigate negative factors in a birth chart. In Greco-Roman mythology, Zeus/Jupiter was lucky from the get-go. Zeus was the son of the infanticidal Cronos and the grandson of Ouranos, the original sky god. When Cronos/Saturn wrested power from his dad Ouranos, Cronos was warned that his own son would one day depose him. To maintain his grip on power, Cronos began to swallow his own children as soon as they were born.

Cronos's wife Rhea got fed up, so to speak, with her husband's postpartum antics. After losing her first five children to Cronos's gullet, Rhea decided to hide her sixth newborn, Zeus, from her devouring husband. In place of Zeus she fed Cronos a stone, which he promptly swallowed. As predicted, Zeus came of age and overthrew his father Cronos, kicking him so hard in the gut that Cronos vomited up Rhea's five other undigested children—the gods Demeter/Ceres, Hades/Pluto, Hestia/Vesta, Hera/Juno, and Poseidon/Neptune.

The recently regurgitated Hera, sister of Zeus, was so beautiful that Zeus decided to marry her. Apparently there was no incest taboo on Olympus. Hera, the sister and wife of Zeus, became the goddess of marriage. She was a jealous and vengeful goddess, embittered by Zeus's infidelity and his many one-night stands. Hera never could get over the way Zeus turned himself into a swan to goose Leda and father a pair of immortal twins. One way or another, Zeus always "got lucky" when he pursued women who interested him. The "luck" of Zeus was Hera's misfortune.

The story of the succession of power from Ouranos to Cronos to Zeus is reflected in the fifteenth-century Visconti-Sforza deck's Wheel of Fortune trump, which depicts the goddess Fortuna in the center of her ever-turning wheel. The goddess of fortune is blindfolded (like Cupid in the Lovers card) because luck, like love, can strike randomly and without warning. Four figures appear at the cardinal points of the wheel, each with a caption appropriate to its position in the cycle:

- at the left, ascending, "I shall rule"

- at the top, "I do rule"

- at the right, descending, "I have ruled"

- at the bottom, "I am without rule"

When the Wheel of Fortune appears in a reading, it suggests that our luck is about to change. We are also reminded of the randomness of life. The meaning of "luck" is in the eye of the beholder. There are many stories of people winning the lottery, only to end up feeling miserable because of unexpected and unwelcome changes in their lives. Zeus was lucky in love, but one must consider what his intoxication with amorous adventure did to his marriage. His wife Hera ended up an embittered, often vengeful goddess of marriage, akin to an ill-dignified Queen of Swords.

The Wheel of Fortune can also refer explicitly to gambling and games of chance. As I was writing this section about trump X, an interesting synchronicity occurred. I turned on the radio and heard a story about how a Kenny Rogers song had become the theme song of the Libyan revolution of the Arab Spring. The radio journalist reported: "One of the lessons the Libyan driver takes from the song is that your fate is really in your own hands, your luck is largely of your own making, and it's all about making the right choices."[198] The Libyan driver would make a great tarot reader.

XI or VIII—Fortitude—Strength—Lust—Courage (Leo)

Waite: FORTITUDE.—Power, energy, action, courage, magnanimity; also complete success and honors. *(R):* Despotism, abuse of power, weakness, discord, sometimes even disgrace.

Strength (fortitude, courage) is one of the four cardinal virtues. It is associated with the sign Leo the Lion, the domain of the radiant and powerful Sun. Leo symbolizes strength, dignity, nobility, leadership, individuality, creativity, masculine prowess, procreation, sexuality, generativity, and self-expression. The Sun is the life force of the solar system and is tied symbolically with the production of offspring, both physical and mental. The Sun, exalted in Aries, has an association with tarot trump IV, the Emperor, which embodies its solar paternal qualities.

Some older decks illustrate this card with the story of Hercules and the Nemean lion. Hercules had to slay the evil lion as the first of his twelve labors. The Nemean lion, of divine origin, had golden fur that was impervious to attack; its claws were sharper than any blade known to man. The sneaky lion would abduct beautiful maidens in hopes that brave warriors would try to rescue the damsels in distress.

Unaware that the lion had already eaten the beautiful maidens, the warriors were lured into the den of the beast, which had shape-shifted into a damsel. Believing they were seeing a distraught woman, the men would approach the disguised lion. The "maiden" then suddenly assumed its original form and devoured the poor chaps, spitting out their bones as a gift for Hades. Hercules, calling on his inner strength, was able to corner the lion, stun it with his wooden club, and choke the beast to death with his bare hands.

There is yet another depiction in older decks of a woman standing next to a broken pillar, a reference to the story of Samson and Delilah. Samson was one of the Judges of the ancient Israelites to whom God granted supernatural powers in exchange for a promise never to shave, get a haircut, or use deodorant. Apparently, God dug the hippie look.

....

198   Lourdes Garcia-Nararro, "For a Libya in Flux: A Theme Song," NPR News, http://www.npr
.org/2011/12/24/144219468/for-a-libya-in-flux-a-theme-song (accessed December 24, 2011).

In Hebrew, Samson means "man of the Sun" (the Sun rules Leo the Lion, the sign associated with this card). With his bronzed body, budging muscles, untrimmed beard, foul stench, and unshorn head, Samson must have looked (and smelled) a lot like the Nemean lion. Like Hercules, Samson killed the vicious lion with his bare hands; but, unlike Hercules, Samson found bees and honey inside the beast. Samson was a notoriously hot-tempered man who had trouble integrating his animal passions with the norms of society. He clearly lacked the virtue of temperance. One day Samson found the Philistines to be particularly annoying and felt justified killing a thousand of them with the jawbone of an ass.

Being a divinely appointed superstud, Samson enjoyed sex with multiple women, including the ladies of his enemy tribe, the Philistines. Unfortunately, Samson tended to hook up with women who got him to reveal things he should have kept private. One of his many lovers, the voluptuous Philistine Delilah, managed to trick the lustful hero into telling her the secret of his strength. Delilah then had a servant cut Samson's hair while he slept, rendering him powerless against the Philistines who quickly captured him and plucked his eyes out—just punishment for his lecherous ways. Soon Samson's hair began to grow back and one fine day he convinced the Philistines to chain him between the two main support columns of their temple, which was crowded because it was a feast day. The Philistines weren't too bright. Samson pulled the pillars together, collapsing the temple and killing himself and oodles of surprised Philistines in the process.

The stories of Hercules and Samson have in common a strong man, a powerful lion, and a wily woman or beast. In both tales, things are not what they seem. Samson's lion is filled with bees and honey. Delilah's protestations of love are but a ruse to discover Samson's secret. Hercules' Nemean lion is able to disguise itself as a beautiful damsel to ensnare the unsuspecting warriors who lusted after her. Thus, in the Strength trump, we learn lessons about trust and betrayal, clarity and illusion, friends and enemies, male-female relationships, strategy, cunning, deception, false appearances, brute strength, courage, fortitude, animal passion, lust, inner strength, powerful urges, the ability of words to deceive, and the potential for passion to corrupt our better judgment. Aleister Crowley was so impressed with the erotic nature of this card that he renamed it "Lust." Crowley was aware that sexual desire is as powerful as the lion on the Strength trump—a card that teaches us about taming the wild beast within.

A Strength/Lust One-Card Reading

A few years ago, I took a Spanish course in a Latin American country where a local high school student and I were paired as conversation partners. Alejandro would help me with Spanish and I would help him with English. After I returned to the United States, we kept in touch periodically by email. In one of his messages, Alejandro said he wanted to talk about an important issue, so we arranged to chat via Skype. Before our conversation, I decided to reflect a bit with the tarot and drew a single card, the Strength/Lust trump.

When we connected on Skype, Alejandro told me that he believed he was bisexual and did not feel comfortable talking about it with the adults he knew locally. He was sexually inexperienced with members of either gender but had recently met a young man who was pressuring him for sex. He felt confused about his feelings and conflicted about what to do, partly because he was unsure of this young man's intentions. Although I didn't mention that I had consulted the tarot, we had a frank discussion about the issues raised by the Strength/Lust card. Alejandro felt clearer about his situation and was grateful to me for listening.

Follow-up to the Strength One-Card Reading

Several months had passed when I received another email from Alejandro. He again wanted to talk and informed me that he had attended several sessions with a psychologist and was now clear in his own mind that he was gay. He had recently "come out" to his father, who expressed surprise but was supportive and understanding. When he told his mother, however, she "freaked out" as she had a conservative upbringing. Whenever he tried to talk to her about his sexuality, she would burst into tears.

Alejandro's mother decided to take him to a different psychologist, one whom she believed would cure him of his "crazy ideas" and restore him to the "normal" sexual orientation that God intended for him. We discussed what psychologists could and could not do, the current thinking in psychiatry about sexual orientation, and how I would deal with this situation in my own psychiatric practice—namely, meet with the family and have a frank, open discussion. Again Alejandro was grateful for my willingness to listen.

After our conversation, it occurred to me to do a Celtic Cross spread about Alejandro's impending visit with the new psychologist. After shuffling and cutting the deck, I drew ten upright cards, the first of which was the Strength trump, just as in the initial reading. This coincidence confirmed in my mind that the reading was likely to be valid. Here are all the cards with some keywords I considered in my interpretation:

1. This covers you: Strength. Lust. Issues related to sexual desire. The need to act with courage and fortitude.

2. This crosses you: The Ace of Swords. The need for clarity, setting limits, and defining who you are and what you want. All the Aces are cards of strength.

3. This is beneath you: The Five of Swords. Failure of communication. Behavior that focuses on one's own needs at the expense of others. Feelings of defeat or humiliation.

4. This is behind you: The Six of Swords. Movement away from a troubling situation.

5. This crowns you: The Ace of Wands. Desire to move boldly and creatively toward one's goals.

6. This is before you: The Hanged Man. Adopting a new perspective. A change of attitude. Surrender. Shame. Self-sacrifice. Feeling betrayed or victimized. Life in suspension.

7. You in this situation: The Four of Pentacles. Holding on tightly to feel secure. Not taking risks with one's emotions or resources.

8. Those around you: The Moon. Powerful unconscious forces. Childhood conditioning. Not seeing things clearly. Hecate, the three-faced Moon goddess of the crossroads, who aided women in raising young men. Uncertainty about which path to follow.

9. Your hopes and fears: The Tower. Collapse of a traditional structure. Conflict between parents and children that requires a bolt from the blue to resolve.

10. The outcome: The Queen of Pentacles. Taking care of one's physical needs and material security. Assistance from a learned or financially secure woman. Could this be the new psychologist? Would Alejandro's

mother have a change of heart? Because this is a court card, I drew a clarification card for the outcome.

11. Clarification: The Sun. Success, optimism, individuation, a bright future. The freedom to be who you are. Because I viewed the Moon in position 7 as reflecting his mother's conservative conditioning, I thought that the Sun in this position meant his mother would finally see the light. Perhaps the new psychologist would help Alejandro's mother to understand her son rather than try to cure Alejandro of his non-illness.

A few days after this reading, I got a message from Alejandro. He said that our discussion had given him the courage to have a heart-to-heart talk with his mother. Although it was emotionally draining, he told his mother that he was still the same son she always knew. The only difference was that he realized he liked guys and he did not think he was going to change. His mother said it was difficult for her to accept but she was willing to step back and "give him his freedom." She also dropped her insistence that he see a new psychologist to attempt a cure. Alejandro felt both relieved but strangely "down" after the talk with his mother.

XII—The Hanged Man—The Traitor— The Lone Man—New Vision (Water)

Waite: THE HANGED MAN.—Wisdom, circumspection, discernment, trials, sacrifice, intuition, divination, prophecy. *(R):* Selfishness, the crowd, body politic.

The Golden Dawn assigned the Hanged Man (aka the Drowned Man) to the element Water. Modern writers have connected this card to Neptune, the modern ruler of watery Pisces. Water belongs to the phlegmatic temperament, so we can expect this trump to refer to situations that are relaxed, quiet, calm, passive, and reflective. Phlegmatic (cool and moist) individuals tend to be observers rather than doers; they let things happen rather than make things happen. Unlike members of the hotter temperaments who would rather fight than surrender, the cooler phlegmatic individuals expend the least amount of energy possible, distancing themselves from the fray and accepting what comes their way. A danger of this stance is the possibility of going through life as a victim or martyr, making sacrifices for the wrong reasons. Sometimes the sacrifice implied by the Hanged Man is not of one's choosing, as when one suffers loss, deception, punishment, or involuntary confinement.

The Waite-Smith Hanged Man is seen peacefully reflecting in a state of suspended animation. He hangs by one foot, a reference to the zodiacal sign Pisces, which rules the feet. Pisces is associated by modern astrologers with the twelfth house of confinement, limitation, and self-undoing. The Pisces/Neptune connection suggests that the Hanged Man has performed an act of sacrifice or self-surrender, perhaps out of faith that God or the universe will provide. His upside-down stance suggests that he is viewing the world from a unique perspective.

In fifteenth-century Italy where the tarot was invented, ruling class Italians displayed "shame paintings" that portrayed their enemies hanging by one foot as a form of public ridicule. The original name of the Hanged Man was "the Traitor." A man hanging by one foot was viewed as a traitor whose values were at odds with the prevailing society. The fifteenth-century prototype for this card was likely Muzio Atendolfo Sforza who opposed ("betrayed") the pope. The irate Holy Father subsequently humiliated his enemy by posting shame paintings of Muzio around Rome. Even today churches in Italy display pictures of the Last Judgment in which the figures in hell are hanging by one foot. The Italian leader Mussolini was reportedly hanged by one foot at the end of the war to shame him for betraying the Italian people.

"Betrayal" as a keyword for the Hanged Man often applies. According to the Gospel of Matthew, the apostle Judas hanged himself after betraying Jesus. The Acts of the Apostles, however, says that Judas fell headlong and died. The Hanged Man may be a reference to both these stories about Judas' betrayal of Christ and his subsequent death by hanging. In her book *Easy Tarot Reading,* Josephine Ellershaw describes a reading she did for a woman who was betrayed by a friend who later sued the querent in court. The Hanged Man appears as the key card in the future area of the Life Spread at a time when the pending court case was uppermost on the querent's mind. [199]

"Shame" is another useful keyword for the Hanged Man, which may appear when the querent has to confront or rectify (set upright) a situation that involves shameful behavior or a deep sense of humiliation. For example, in the reading for Alejandro, the gay adolescent who had trouble coming out to his mother, the Hanged Man showed up in the near-future position,

....

199   Josephine Ellershaw, *Easy Tarot Reading* (Woodbury, MN: Llewellyn Publications, 2011), pp. 62–63.

indicating that Alejandro needed to confront the profound sense of shame his mother felt about his homosexuality. He himself felt "betrayed" by his mother's demand that he see a psychologist to change his sexual orientation.

A Hanged Man Reading

A man in his sixties approached me for a reading. We happened to meet while I was vacationing at a summer resort. He noticed me sitting on the lawn, reading Paul Huson's book and looking though the companion tarot deck. The man introduced himself and asked if I knew how to read the cards. I'll refer to him as Jake. When I responded in the affirmative, Jake sheepishly told me something was going on in his life and he wanted to know what the cards might have to say about it. We found a place to meet in private.

Even though we would probably never meet again, Jake was reluctant to tell me directly what was on his mind. Instead, he asked me to look at the cards and tell him what they said about his situation. I decided to do a three-card Past, Present, Future spread. At the time, I had with me Paul Huson's Dame Fortune's Wheel Tarot, based on the mid-eighteenth-century Etteilla divinatory meanings rather than the more modern Golden Dawn and Waite-Smith traditions. Using only upright cards, I drew the following from Huson's Dame Fortune's Wheel deck:

Seven of Coins, King of Swords, and The Hanged Man *(Dame Fortune's Wheel Tarot).*

Etteilla viewed the Seven of Coins as a card of money and riches but also candor, honesty, whiteness, and purity. Huson's card shows a woman dressed in white. She is holding a lamb, also white, and standing in front of the table of a man who looks like a money-lender or merchant. Gold coins are piled on his table. It is not clear whether the woman has just bought the lamb or wants to sell it. The money-lender looks like someone who values his money and would drive a hard bargain. I said to Jake that the card in the past position suggested that he had been dealing with an issue involving money or riches as well as the importance of candor and honesty. The phrase "Mary had a little lamb whose fleece was white as snow" ran through my mind, but I didn't know what to make of it, so I didn't mention it.

In Etteilla's system, the King of Swords represents "a man of law" such as a judge, lawyer, or legal expert. Huson illustrates the King of Swords as King David of the Bible with an upright sword in his right hand, representing justice, and a lyre in his left hand with which he was able to compose the Psalms and soothe King Saul, who was tormented by an evil spirit. I explained Etteilla's interpretation and asked Jake if he was currently feeling "tormented" (like King Saul) by legal matters (King of Swords) involving money (Seven of Coins). He nodded yes and asked me to continue.

The third card, in the future position, was the Hanged Man. According to Paul Huson, Etteilla relates the Hanged Man to constraint, treachery, punishment, and a reversal of values. As mentioned above, the Hanged Man has links to Neptune, Pisces, and the twelfth house of confinement and undoing. The Dame Fortune's Wheel Hanged Man appears to be modeled after Judas, who hangs like a traitor in an Italian "shame painting." Judas feels guilty for having accepted bags of money to betray Jesus. I explained these meanings to Jake and linked the Hanged Man to the first two cards, saying that there was most likely an issue about money and honesty that had become a legal matter that was heading toward some sort of constraint or punishment.

Jake then told me his story. He was in his midsixties and nearing retirement. Several years ago he was struggling financially. During that time, his father died. Rather than notify the proper government offices of his father's death, Jake continued to collect his deceased father's benefits and did so for years. I thought back to the white lamb on the first card and the idea of "fleecing the government" went through my mind, but I did not say it aloud. Suddenly I understood why the lamb's fleece had caught my attention.

When the feds finally caught up with Jake, he engaged the services of an attorney who was trying to negotiate a settlement. His lawyer told him that even if he were to reimburse all of the money with penalties, a prison term seemed inevitable. Jake was taken with the reading and amazed that just three cards could capture his situation and inner state so accurately. He seemed relieved that the cards had confirmed what his lawyer was telling him and he appeared ready to accept his punishment. Jake added that he had awakened every day since his father's death with the worry that today would be his day of reckoning. He was embarrassed that his misdeeds had been published in his local newspaper but also glad to have reached the end of the road.

We did another three-card reading regarding the likely outcome of his prison term. Jake drew the following:

Eight of Swords—The World—Three of Cups

I viewed this spread as positive. The Eight of Swords probably referred to his impending censure and imprisonment, which would paradoxically free him. The World suggested coming to the end of the road and achieving a sense of finality for which he was grateful. The Three of Cups suggested a happy outcome. He would emerge from prison free of the burden of torment that had plagued him for years. He would be free to celebrate the remainder of his life without a guilty conscience. Despite the "bad news" delivered by the cards, Jake was relieved and grateful for the reading.

XIII—Death—The Close—Transformation (Scorpio)

Waite: DEATH.—End, mortality, destruction, corruption; also, for a man, the loss of a benefactor; for a woman, many contrarieties; for a maid, failure of marriage projects. *(R):* Inertia, sleep, lethargy, petrifaction, somnambulism; hope destroyed.

Tarot authors often state that the Death trump does not literally mean death, but to my mind denial of death is merely an attempt to assuage a fearful public. Death is death; it is an essential part of life. We begin to die from the moment we are born. Death is one of the most profound images in the tarot. The Death trump refers to the cycle of birth, maturation, decline, decay, and final endings.

The Death card often marks a transition to a new phase of existence. Waite says this card represents "the natural transit of man to the next stage of his being."[200] The Golden Dawn views Death as an "involuntary change" and contrasts it with the voluntary change implied by the Moon trump. Death is associated with Scorpio, the zodiac sign connected with deep-seated emotions and profound transformation. Mars, the god of war, traditionally rules Scorpio and is associated with the Tower trump, another card of radical change and potential destruction.

World mythologies abound with personifications of death as the Grim Reaper or the Angel of Death. In some readings, Death will refer to the physical death of someone; the surrounding cards will make this clear. More commonly, the Death trump refers to a major transition or letting go, closing the door on one chapter of life and moving on to something new. Not uncommonly Death appears in readings for people who are about to retire from a job they have held for many years. The classic poem by Emily Dickinson captures a core meaning of the card:

My life closed twice before its close;
It yet remains to see
If Immortality unveil
A third event to me,
So huge, so hopeless to conceive,
As these that twice befell.
Parting is all we know of heaven,
And all we need of hell.[201]

When Death appears in a reading, we would do well to view life as a novel with many chapters. The Death trump acts like a bookmark, signaling the end of one chapter and the beginning of the next. Like any novel, life has a final chapter, and when the Death card reaches the last page of our story, we have come to "the end." Generally, however, the Death trump signals an important transition. Part of our life has come to an end, and it's time to move on to something new. The Death card advises us to accept change as inevitable and allow the metamorphosis to begin.

....

200 Waite, *Pictorial Key*, p. 120.

201 Emily Dickinson (1830–1886), "My Life Closed Twice Before Its Close," About.com Quotations, http://quotations.about.com/cs/poemlyrics/a/My_Life_Closed_.htm (accessed 10 Dec. 2012).

XIV—Temperance—Art—The Guide—Integration (Sagittarius)

Waite: TEMPERANCE.—Economy, moderation, frugality, management, accommodation. *(R):* Things connected with churches, religions, sects, the priesthood, sometimes even the priest who will marry the Querent; also disunion, unfortunate combinations, competing interests.

Temperance—Aristotle's golden mean, Buddha's middle way—is one of the four cardinal virtues. Many authors believe the figure on the Temperance trump to be the archangel Michael, whose name derives from the Hebrew phrase *Mikha'el.* To utter the name Michael is to ask the question: "Who is like unto God?" This rhetorical inquiry was the battle-cry of a legion of angels whom Michael led against Satan and his minions. Satan, convinced that he himself was like unto God, had answered the question arrogantly, committing the sin of pride. Satan's self-glorification apparently irked the Old Testament deity who reacted by assigning the devil to eternal hell; hence, Waite's suggestion that Temperance inverted signifies disunion, unfortunate combinations, and competing interests. Interestingly, the angel of the Apocalypse has one foot in water and the other on land, perhaps an allusion to Michael fighting the puffed-up devil till the end of time.

The Church looked to Michael for protection from the wickedness and snares of the devil (card XV). Michael's strength lay in his ability to balance the recognition of his likeness unto God with his humility and reverence toward the Creator. Archangel Michael is neither overly humble nor excessively proud; he has achieved a position of harmony and balance between these contrasting emotional states. A person who exhibits the virtue of temperance displays the fiery energy of Michael but is also able to patiently maintain his balance. The blending of water and wine in the two goblets on the card links the virtue of temperance to the suit of Cups.

The Greek idea of temperance as a virtue dates back at least as far as the age of the Seven Sages (c. 650–c. 550 BCE). In his *Rhetoric,* Aristotle attributes this idea to Chilo, one of the ancient Greek sages. The saying *meden agan* ("nothing in excess") was inscribed on the temple of Apollo at Delphi. The moral is to maintain a balance among the disparate and conflicting elements of one's life to preserve one's health and act with virtue.

Cultivating the virtue of temperance was particularly important for the centaur of Sagittarius. Half-man, half-horse, he was always struggling with the tension between his animal instincts and his human nature. Satisfying either of his natures to the exclusion of the other would have prevented him from fulfilling his destiny as a man-horse. Only by integrating the warring demands of his various parts could the centaur be sure that all his needs would be met. Crowley renamed the Temperance card "Art" and saw it as representing the creative synthesis and integration of incomplete elements with their equal but opposite counterparts.

When Temperance appears in a reading, we are being asked to review our actions for any imbalance, incompatibility, or excess that may be negatively affecting our well-being and sense of fulfillment. We are advised to step back, put things in perspectives and take the time to synthesize the conflicting aspects of our lives. By harmonizing our forces temperately, we can reach great heights. Otherwise, we are plagued by troublesome inconsistencies that create discord in our lives. The inverse of Temperance suggests a bad mix. In the next chapter, we will consider a reading in which the querent asked whether a certain book was right for her. Temperance, reversed, appeared in the outcome position. The querent found the book to be incompatible with her needs. She was unable to find a harmonious middle ground between the author's approach and what she wanted to learn.

XV—The Devil—Temptation—Pan— The Horned God—Conditioning (Capricorn)

Waite: THE DEVIL.—Ravage, violence, vehemence, extraordinary efforts, force, fatality; that which is predestined but is not for this reason evil. *(R):* Evil fatality, weakness, pettiness, blindness.

Satan is often called the Prince of Darkness. It is no accident that the Devil trump is assigned to Capricorn, which marks the beginning of winter in the northern hemisphere when the days are short and the world is bathed in maximum darkness. Capricorn is the sign of the goat. Perhaps the most famous goat of mythology is Amalthea, the she-goat who suckled baby Zeus in the cave where he was hiding from his father's murderous rage. When Zeus accidentally broke off one of Amalthea's horns, he remorsefully promised his nurse-goat that her broken horn would thenceforth be filled with whatever she desired. The horn became known as the cornucopia or horn of plenty. The Devil trump has to do with our wish to possess the cornucopia, to have whatever we want regardless of the spiritual cost.

Satan committed the sin of pride when he proclaimed that he was "like unto God." He serves as a reminder of what can happen when we fail to practice the virtue of temperance (card XIV). Lacking humility and reverence, we become "puffed up" and go to extremes—be it with alcohol, drugs, sexual addition, thirst for knowledge and power, or other compulsive behaviors. Without balance (the virtue of temperance) we lose our spiritual bearings and become slaves, addicted to the material world. Puffed up by greed or desire, we fall prey to our obsessions and temptations, which are ultimately harmful to ourselves and others. "For what is a man profited, if he shall gain the whole world and lose his own soul?" [202]

In the Germanic legend of Doctor Faust, a gifted and successful scholar sells his soul to the devil in exchange for unlimited knowledge, magical power, and worldly pleasure. Having made his pact with the devil, Faust found himself unable to find true love. Faust's predicament was of his own making. His undoing was his bondage to his material ambitions and unchecked lust for power.

The Devil sometimes appears in the guise of a power-hungry Pope or Hierophant. The Waite-Smith Hierophant with its two acolytes bears a striking resemblance to the Devil trump with its two demonic minions. Many cults and religions seek to control people with superstitious beliefs and fears of damnation. Religion becomes an opiate to intoxicate the faithful into blind submission. Enslavement to extreme views about the sinfulness of the flesh is as much a manifestation of the Devil trump as its complementary opposite of sexual addiction.

The Renaissance creators of the Devil trump were familiar with a famous tale about the devil from the *Decameron* by the Italian poet Boccaccio (1313–1375). In this story a fourteen-year-old heathen girl, a virgin, is so impressed by her Christian neighbors' faith that she runs off to the woods populated by Christian hermits to experience the strange new religion. There she encounters a naked hermit [tarot trump IX] who hasn't seen a woman in ages and quickly gets aroused. Startled by the hermit's phallic response, the girl asks about his upright organ. The hermit explains that God gave men a phallus to remind them of the evils of Satan. When the girl expresses relief that God did not give women such an appendage, the hermit explains that God instead gave women a special opening to symbolize the hell where Satan resides.

It is the duty of every Christian, explains the hermit, to practice thrusting Satan back into hell. The girl, eager to participate in her new religion, willingly obliges. At first she finds the process painful and says that she now understands the suffering caused by the evils of Satan. With further practice, however, the ritual becomes more pleasurable. The maiden finally realizes

....
202   Matthew 16:26 (King James Bible).

the truth of what her neighbors have been telling her—that to serve God as a good Christian is the greatest of delights. Boccaccio ignores the sexually exploitative nature of the hermit's relationship with his underage student as he leads her into temptation. Not uncommonly in a tarot reading, the Devil trump refers to themes of temptation, greed, self-gratification, abuse, or exploitation. In the words of an Italian proverb: *Dio non fa mai chiesa, che il diavolo non ci voglia la sua capella*—God never builds a church where the devil does not want a chapel of his own.

Some modern decks have renamed the Devil "Pan" after the Greek god of sexual abandon. Unencumbered by puritanical ideas about the body, the hairy goat-god Pan taught his followers to enjoy their sexuality without guilt. The Golden Dawn assigned the Devil to the sign Capricorn, which is linked to the goat-god Pan and Capricorn's goat-fish. Venus, the goddess of love, when in the sign Capricorn was traditionally believed to indicate a hearty sexual appetite. By redefining Pan as the Devil, the Christian tradition added the idea that indulgence in material pleasure (sex, drugs, food, money, shopping, video games, etc.) ultimately harms the soul. The Devil tempts us to put immediate gratification above our best interests. He whispers in our ear, "If it feels good, do it!"

XVI—The Lightning-Struck Tower—The House of the Devil— The House of God—The Arrow—The Thunderbolt (Mars)

Waite: THE TOWER.—Misery, distress, indigence, adversity, calamity, disgrace, deception, ruin. It is a card in particular of unforeseen catastrophe. *(R):* According to one account, the same in a lesser degree; also oppression, imprisonment, tyranny.

This card reminds me of Buddha confronting the demon Mara during his meditation under the Bodhi tree. Mara, whose name means "destruction," was the Lord of Death. Like the Devil of the previous card, Mara snares and deludes by stirring our passions. By maintaining a virtuous course, Buddha was able to defeat Mara and achieve enlightenment, which is *Bodhi* in Sanskrit, a term that means "awakening and understanding." The three cards that follow the Tower trump show increasing degrees of illumination, ranging from stars, to the Moon, and finally the Sun. After the Sun, there is an awakening in the Final Judgment followed by the ultimate arrival at the New Jerusalem in card XXI. The humans on these final trumps in the Waite-Smith deck are all without clothing.

The Golden Dawn attributed the Tower card to the planet Mars, god of war, and associated it with ambition, fighting, courage, danger, and destruction. Mars is ruler of Scorpio, a sign closely associated with death through the sting of the scorpion. The scorpion's sting shakes us out of our rut and demands our immediate attention. When the Tower appears in a reading, we often feel under attack by forces beyond our control. Outmoded structures come crashing down, clearing the way for radical transformation if we are open to it. The universe is making us an offer we can't refuse.

Paul Huson tells us that a sixteenth-century name for this card was the "House of the Devil," a house that needs to be destroyed to liberate its inhabitants who are trapped by Satan's power.[203] Older names also include "the Arrow" and "the Thunderbolt," which was sent by heaven to destroy Satan's dwelling. These depictions are similar to Buddha freeing himself from Mara's illusions about the nature of reality. Liberation and enlightenment can be jolting and disruptive (like lightning), but prove beneficial in the long run.

Given the Christian context in which the tarot developed, the Tower could be a reference to the biblical Tower of Babel, a symbol of human pride gone wild, which God punished by making everyone on Earth speak different languages. In fact, I have done readings in which the Tower card appeared when the people involved might as well be speaking in tongues and only a bolt from the blue would get them communicating again. The Tower might also relate to the destruction of Babylon in the New Testament Book of Revelation (18: 1–8), aka the Apocalypse, from a Greek word meaning "unveiling" or "revelation." The destruction of Babylon will release humankind from its bondage to evil and make way for the kingdom of heaven.

Another name for the Tower is the "House of God," a likely reference to the legend of the third-century Christian martyr Barbara (who probably never existed).[204] The tarot, fortunately, deals with mythology and intuition rather than historical fact. The cult of Saint Barbara began in the ninth century and was popular during the Renaissance when the tarot was invented. As the story goes, Barbara became a Christian against the wishes of her powerful father, a pagan fundamentalist. Rejecting sex and marriage, she lived in a tower and devoted her life to prayer. As a sign of her Christian faith, Barbara had three windows constructed in her tower to honor

....

203 Huson, *Mystical Origins*, p. 130.

204 Harry F. Williams, "Old French Lives of Saint Barbara," *Proceedings of the American Philosophical Society* 119.2 (16 April 1975:156–185).

the Holy Trinity. Barbara's three windows are depicted on the Tower trump of many Marseille pattern decks, and this same pattern is repeated in the influential Waite-Smith deck.

When Barbara's father realized the Christian significance of her three windows, he followed the dictates of his pagan fundamentalism and chopped his daughter's head off. That'll teach her to worship the Trinity! The triune God, however, got the last laugh—he struck her dad with lightning, which consumed him in flames. The Tower card thus alludes to conflicting values between parent and child, or perhaps between generations, as well as the various and sometimes jolting ways by which we achieve enlightenment. When irreconcilable differences appear in a relationship, it is often necessary to think outside the box (or tower, as the case may be). In Barbara's case, we might say that her father, despite his resistance to her differing religious views, was finally made to see the light in a way he couldn't refuse. Isn't that what the Tower card is all about?

XVII—The Star—Silence (Aquarius)

Waite: THE STAR.—Loss, theft, privation, abandonment; another reading says—hope and bright prospects. *(R)*: Arrogance, haughtiness, impotence.

Modern tarot readers generally ignore Waite's negative meanings for the Star and go with "hope and bright prospects." This latter opinion is consistent with the Golden Dawn's view of the Star as a card of hope, faith, and unexpected help. Theories vary about the origins of this card. Because the tarot developed in Christian Italy, the Star may well refer to the star of Bethlehem, which guided the three wise astrologers to the newborn Redeemer. The Star is the first glimmer of light after the destruction of the House of the Devil.

The light of the Star is also reminiscent of the opening lines of the Gospel of John: "In the beginning was the Word and the Word was with God and the Word was God ... In him was life; and the life was the light of men. And the light shineth in darkness; and the darkness comprehended it not." [205] The Star card can indeed be a light that shines in the darkness. For generations stars have guided ships at sea and indicated to farmers the best times to plant their crops. Sometimes when the Star card appears in a reading we are being advised to let

....
205 John 1:1–12 (King James Bible).

ourselves shine, as in the famous biblical passage: "Let your light so shine before men, that they may see your good works and glorify your Father which is in heaven." [206]

Another biblical reference, the Book of Revelation (10:1–11), speaks of an angel with one foot on the sea and the other on land, with a small open book in hand. Upon the cry of this angel, the seven thunders utter secrets that are not to be put in writing. No doubt this apocalyptic angel, with one foot on land and the other on water, served as an inspiration for the woman of the Star card. Pamela Colman Smith even split the woman's poured water into five small streams as an allusion to the five wounds of Christ that offer hope of salvation. The apocalyptic angel is also reflected in the angel of the Temperance trump.

The Renaissance artists who created the tarot were also conversant with ancient Greek mythology. Historians of religion believe that some worshipers of the mysteries of Eleusis regarded those rites as spells to induce fertility. Artist Jean-Claude Flornoy notes that the woman in the Star card of the Nicolas Conver eighteenth-century Tarot of Marseille is pregnant. [207] Conver viewed the Star trump as representing fertility, hope, optimism, promise, and the expectation of a better future.

Author James Hastings tells us that primitive religions often included a ritual of pouring water on the ground to produce rain. He adds: "At Eleusis, in the great mysteries, the votaries emptied two vessels filled with water, turning to east and west and repeating the sacred formula, 'Sky pour rain; earth bear grain,'…directed to earth and sky…a survival of an ancient magical formula for the production of rain." [208] With rain comes the possibility of new life.

As mentioned previously, the Eleusinian mysteries commemorate the story of the grain goddess Demeter's search for her abducted daughter Persephone. Preoccupied with the loss of her daughter, Demeter ceased watering the earth with life-giving rain. The earth became barren, and humanity faced extinction. Through the rituals of the Eleusinian mystery religion, the faithful appreciated the cycle of life, death, and rebirth and came to appreciate their own immortality and divinity. The majority of initiates at Eleusis were women, much like

....

206 Matthew 5:16 (King James Bible).

207 Jean-Claude Flornoy, "History," *The Tarot of Marseille,* http://www.tarot-history.com/History/pages/history -page-2.html (accessed 7 Jan. 2012).

208 James Hastings, *Encyclopedia of Religion and Ethics,* Part 23, "Symbolism," (Whitefish, MT: Kessinger Publishing, 2003), p. 139.

the woman on the Star trump who is pouring water from two urns as part of a sacred ritual of spiritual renewal.

Perhaps Cicero, the great Roman statesman, summed up the meaning of the Star card when he said of the mysteries of Eleusis: "For by their means we have been brought out of our barbarous and savage mode of life and educated and refined to a state of civilization; and as the rites are called initiations, so in very truth we have learned from them the beginnings of life and have gained the power not only to live happily, but also to die with a better hope." [209]

And what do we make of the Golden Dawn attributing the Star trump to the sign Aquarius, the Water Bearer? Some authors see a connection between the Star and the Egyptian mother-goddess Isis. The annual reappearance of the Star of Isis was a harbinger of the rainy season, which replenished the dry lands and the rivers of Egypt, making possible the maintenance of human life. Perhaps the naked woman on the Star trump is the goddess Isis pouring life-giving water onto the land and rivers of Egypt, thus offering hope for a better future.

XVIII—The Moon—Luna—Illusion—Past Lives (Pisces)

Waite: THE MOON.—Hidden enemies, danger, calumny, darkness, terror, deception, occult forces, error. *(R):* Instability, inconstancy, silence, lesser degrees of deception and error.

Most authors remind us that the English word "lunatic" derives from the Latin word *luna* for "moon." Unable to think rationally, lunatics are driven by their unregulated fluctuating emotions and they act in crazy ways. Historian Franco Pratesi, however, tells us that the earliest recorded divinatory meaning for the Moon trump dates back to 1750. At that time, the Moon card was simply delineated as "night." Similarly the Sun trump was interpreted as "day." Although modern tarot readers sometimes feel confused about how to interpret the Moon card, the 1750 divinatory significance of the Moon (XVIII) and the Sun (IX) was as clear as night and day. If the Moon means "night," then to understand this card we must ask ourselves what sort of things happen in the darkness of the night:

....

209 Cicero quoted in "The Shrine of Mysteries at Eleusis," *A Roman Lover's Webpage,* http://romeartlover
.tripod.com/Eleusi.html (accessed 15 Jan 2012).

From goulies and ghosties and long-leggedy beasties
And things that go bump in the night
Good Lord, deliver us! [210]

We all know that the gravitational field of the moon is responsible for the ocean tides. Researchers at Texas State University discovered that on January 4, 1912, the moon made its closest approach to the Earth in 1,400 years. They theorized that the close proximity of the moon early in 1912 dislodged the iceberg that sank the Titanic. [211] The increased gravitational attraction of the moon caused unusually high tides, which dislodged icebergs off the coast of Greenland, carrying them south into standard Atlantic shipping lanes. The captain of the Titanic, who was convinced he knew the route well, believed the warnings about icebergs to be false and proceeded full speed ahead. The rest is history. Tarot readers know that the Moon trump can be a warning to slow down, heed the warnings of our intuition, and be on the lookout for unseen peril. The Moon card often appears when we are unsure how to proceed along a route we have taken.

The Moon trump is numbered XVIII, which happens to be the number of years in the Saros cycle of solar and lunar eclipses. The cycle more accurately lasts about 18 years, 11 days, and 8 hours. Known to ancient astrologers as the period when nearly identical eclipses recur, the Saros cycle was used to predict dire fated events that generations of astrologers had correlated with eclipses of the sun and moon.

Another fascinating astronomical fact is that the moon is always facing us on Earth. We never see her back side, and her front side is constantly changing. When the Moon appears in a reading, it frequently means that something about the situation remains unseen at the moment. An important fact may be hidden from view; it might as well be on the dark side of the moon. If we wait a little while, what we see will look different. Inebriated college students sometimes "moon" passers-by. The Moon is symbolically linked to inebriation, alcohol, and

....

210 From *The Cornish and West Country Litany* (1926), quoted in The Phrase Finder, http://www.phrases.org .uk/meanings/378900.html (accessed 4 Jan. 2012).

211 Donald W. Olson, Russell L. Doescher, and Roger W. Sinnott, "Did the Moon Sink the Titanic?," *Sky and Telescope*, April 2012.

imagination through its association with the sign Pisces, whose modern ruler Neptune is the planet of illusion.

Aleister Crowley, with his hypersexual imagination, pondered the moon's concealed back-side and connected it with anal intercourse. (No wonder people called him the wickedest man in the world.) Crowley referred to the waning moon on his Thoth trump as "the moon of witchcraft and abominable deeds … the poisoned darkness which is the condition of the re-birth of light … a drunkenness of sense, after the mind has been abolished by the venom on this Moon."[212] Crowley is not alone in comparing the Moon to hidden parts of the human anatomy and "abominable deeds" that may occur there. One tarot blog links the Moon trump in a sexual reading to "naïve indulgences in the perverse" and "hideous sexual tendencies."[213] The Osho Zen Tarot views the Moon as a depicting the vaginal orifice of the cosmic mother through which we perceive the "karmic patterns of our lives and their roots in an endless repeti-tive cycle that traps us in unconscious behavior."[214]

Many authors regard the Moon as threatening or alarming. The Golden Dawn delin-eated this card to mean falsity, lying, error, deception, dissatisfaction, and voluntary change. The images on the Waite-Smith Moon trump remind us of the mythology of the Greek Moon goddess Hecate, at whom hounds bayed at night. Hecate was the three-faced goddess of the crossroads and mistress of the night; she was also associated with witchcraft. In his poem *Medea*, the Roman poet Seneca describes how the witch Medea cast a spell by appeal-ing to Hecate and chanting: "Now summoned by my sacred rites, do thou Hecate, orb of the night [the Moon], put on thy most evil face and come, threatening in all thy forms."[215] As goddess of the crossroads, Hecate may warn us of potential dangers that lie ahead, depending on which route we take.

....

212 Crowley, *The Book of Thoth*, pp. 112–113.

213 Shannon Rae, "Sexual Key to the Tarot: XVIII The Moon," *The Tarot Guild,* http://www.tarotguild.com/profiles/blogs/sexual-key-to-the-tarot-xviii (accessed 31 Mar. 2013).

214 Osho, *Osho Zen Tarot* (New York: Saint Martin's Press, 1995), p. 38.

215 Seneca, *Medea 750*, quoted in "Triad of Hekate, Artemis & Selene," *Hekate Goddess,* http://www.theoi.com/Khthonios/HekateGoddess.html (accessed 13 Feb. 2012).

The hounds of Hecate remind me of a Cherokee proverb, often displayed on a poster that shows two wolves baying at the moon. An old Cherokee is explaining to his grandson that there is always a battle being fought between two wolves that live inside us. One wolf spurs us to anger, greed, hatred, envy, arrogance, and deceit. The other encourages love, humility, compassion, truth, and generosity. The grandson asks, "How do you know which wolf will win?" The grandfather replies, "The one you feed."

Because of the Moon's association with intoxication and the darkness of night, this card often implies feeling uncertain or confused, not seeing things clearly, having insufficient information, being unsure which way to turn, or deciding on the basis of illusion or outright deception. The moon has no source of illumination of its own but shines only by reflecting the light of the sun. When the Moon card appears in a reading, it may be a warning to delay making a major decision until matters become better illuminated. Astronomically, it takes us almost twenty-eight days to get a full picture of a lunar cycle. Forcing an issue in a state of "lunar" dimness and uncertainty can have untoward consequences.

A Moon Card Reading

A young man from Indonesia had read an article I wrote about tarot and emailed me to ask the cards whether he would be able to fulfill his childhood dream of traveling to the United States. His uncle, who lived in New York, had promised to help him with his documentation so that he could legally enter America. I did a three-card spread and drew the following cards:

Page of Swords—The Moon—The Tower

The presence of two trump cards highlighted the importance of this matter for the querent. Because of the pairing of the Moon (confusion) and the Tower (disruption), I told him that the spread did not look promising and he might have some conflict (Page of Swords) with his uncle, who may have promised more than he could deliver (the Moon). I cautioned that he might feel a bit shocked (the Tower) by the outcome.

About a month later, I received another email with his response to the reading. Initially he did not believe my comments and thought I must have read the cards wrong. He contacted his uncle to say that he was now old enough to journey to America. His uncle told him that he was not in a position to help him move to the USA and would not be able to sponsor his travel. The two of them got into a bitter argument. The querent ended up feeling misled and betrayed by his uncle's promises of help. It came as a shock to him that someone he thought he could trust had so utterly let him down. The symbolism of the illusory Moon trump caught between a Sword and the Tower seemed to capture this event quite accurately.

Another quote relevant to the Moon comes from the New Testament: "For now we see through a glass darkly; but then face to face: now I know in part; but then shall I know even as also I am known."[216] Here the Moon is a metaphor for the spiritual darkness in which humanity exists. When the Moon trump appears in a reading, it suggests that we are seeing through a glass darkly and we know only in part. Only when we encounter the next trump, the Sun, are we able to see clearly, face to face.

XIX—The Sun—Innocence (Sun)

Waite: THE SUN.—Material happiness, fortunate marriage, contentment. *(R):* The same in a lesser sense.

When I was a college student, one of my favorite plays was *The Fantasticks* by Harvey Schmidt and Tom Jones. I saw the play several times and listened to the album so often that the vinyl recording wore out. Now, whenever the Moon or the Sun trump appears in a reading, the words of El Gallo, the narrator of the play, come to mind, reminding me that life does not end in the moonlit night, "For the story is not ended and the play never done until all of us have been burned a bit and burnished by the sun."[217]

In the tarot, the Sun rarely burns and burnishes the querent. Most authors interpret this card as positive, even in its reversed position. Thus, we find keywords such as hope, faith, good health, vitality, illumination, clarity, unexpected help, success, warmth, positive energy, growth, achievement, honors, recognition, optimism, joy, happiness, a vacation in the sun, and so on.

---

216 I Corinthians 13:12 (King James Bible).

217 Harvey Schmidt and Tom Jones, *The Fantasticks,* 1960, at *Hallmark Hall of Fame,* http://www.imdb.com /title/tt0595374/quotes?qt0539641 (accessed 10 Jan. 2012).

An Unusual Sun Card Reading

A university student, who was just learning to read the tarot, asked my opinion of a reading he had done regarding study abroad. The first two cards of his Celtic Cross spread were the Fool (0) and the Sun (XIX). I pointed out that the Fool signifies the beginning of a journey of exploration, learning, and personal development. When I looked at the Sun trump, an image of the flag of Japan ("the Land of the Rising Sun") came to mind. The student had recently won a scholarship to study in Japan and was asking about what that experience would be like. He had not associated the Sun card with the country where he would be studying. The kanji characters that spell Japan (日本) literally stand for "sun origin" and connote the Land of the Rising Sun. The tarot was being quite literal: the Fool is the origin, and the Sun card obviously stands for the sun.

XX—Judgment—The Last Judgment— The Angel—Karma—The Aeon—Beyond Illusion (Fire)

Waite: THE LAST JUDGMENT.—Change of position, renewal, outcome. Another account specifies total loss though lawsuit. *(R):* Weakness, pusillanimity, simplicity; also deliberation, decision, sentence.

The dictionary defines "judgment" as "the ability to judge, make a decision, or form an opinion objectively, authoritatively, and wisely, especially in matters affecting action; good sense; discretion."[218] The Golden Dawn stuck closely to the dictionary definition in choosing keywords for the Judgment trump such as a final decision, sentence, or the determination of a matter.[219] Judgment appears when we need to judge a situation wisely or when we ourselves face being evaluated. The result of this process can be transformative, often by eliminating what is no longer of benefit.

Modern authors link the Judgment card to the dwarf planet Pluto, which happens to rule purgatives, laxatives, and bowel movements. The Golden Dawn linked Judgment to the element Fire, which is associated with purification by fire and the choleric temperament. When this card appears in a reading, we may be dealing with a situation involving people who are

---

218 *Dictionary.com*, s.v. "Judgment," http://dictionary.reference.com/browse/judgment (accessed 10 Jan. 2012).

219 "Sentence" in the sense of a conclusion reached after deliberation or a legal sentence pronounced by a judge.

passionate, assertive, charismatic, hot-tempered, or domineering. Choleric individuals like to lead and to be obeyed. They tend to go to extremes and exhibit wide swings in mood.

The planet Pluto is the modern ruler of Scorpio, the sign associated with elimination, death, transformation, and rebirth—like the phoenix rising from its ashes. Just as fire burns away impurities, Pluto purges from our lives situations and relationships that no longer serve a useful purpose. In astrology, the major transits of Pluto are said to divide our lives into "before and after." In discussing the four elements, Aristotle stated that Fire brings together matter of the same nature by burning away the dross so that only the purest form of the substance remains.

At this point in the Fool's journey, he has been through his ordeal and has eliminated that which no longer serves his spiritual purpose. The Fool has been purified and transformed. He is ready for his rebirth in the New Jerusalem of trump XXI. In Christian mythology, the great herald angel blows his horn to awaken our souls to new life if we've been good, or to burn eternally in hell if we haven't. Perhaps this biblical allusion explains why Waite relates the Judgment trump to lawsuits, outcomes, decisions, and sentencing. The Judgment card in a reading is often a wake-up call. We are being aroused from our slumber so we can enter a new phase of existence. Renewal and transformation are at hand. It's time to wake up and smell the coffee.

XXI—The World—The Universe— The New Jerusalem—Completion (Saturn)

Waite: THE WORLD.—Assured success, recompense, voyage, route, emigration, flight, change of place. *(R):* Inertia, fixity, stagnation, permanence.

Robert Place and Gareth Knight identify the World card with Prudence, one of the four cardinal virtues. My own belief is that Renaissance artists automatically saw the Chariot as Prudence because of the popularity of Thomas Aquinas, who made Prudence synonymous with the charioteer (*auriga virtutem*) in the culture of the time. Regardless of which trump represents Prudence, the tarot is fundamentally a Christian allegory and the Fool's journey appropriately ends at the New Jerusalem "where believers in Christ will spend eternity…the ultimate fulfillment of all God's promises…heaven, paradise, God's goodness made fully manifest."[220] The Fool has labored long and hard and has reached his ultimate destination.

A depiction of the New Jerusalem from the Bamberg Apocalypse (c. 1000) bears a striking resemblance to the World card. In the Bamberg image, an angel is showing John the New Jerusalem in which Christ, as the Lamb of God, stands at the center.[221] In the Waite-Smith World trump, the symbols of the fixed signs of the zodiac appear in the four corners (the Taurus Bull, Leo Lion, Scorpio Eagle, and Aquarius Water Bearer).[222] These four figures are also a reference to the wounds in the hands and feet of Christ and the Four Horsemen of the Apocalypse (Revelation 6: 1–8), who were unleashed after Christ opened the first four of the Seven Seals. The four horsemen symbolize events at the end of time (conquest, war, famine, and death). The central figure of the World card is Christ whose heart was pierced to save humankind: "For God so loved the world that he gave his only begotten Son, that whosoever believeth in him should not perish, but have everlasting life."[223]

Just as Saturn, the outermost visible planet, marks the ancient boundary of the solar system, the World card indicates the final destination of the Fool's travels. The World is the Promised Land, heaven on earth, the end of the journey, the goal that the Fool has been striving to attain. The Fool has journeyed far and wide to experience life and learn what he needs to know. His life is now complete. Paradoxically the circular wreath on the World trump, like the 0 on the Fool card, suggests that the Fool has returned to where he started from. Dorothy has come back to Kansas. Welcome home!

Although the World can represent the pot of gold at the end of the rainbow, the Golden Dawn makes an interesting suggestion about interpreting this trump in a reading. It is possible to use keywords such as kingdom, world, or synthesis, but in the Golden Dawn view the World

....

220   "What is the New Jerusalem?," gotQuestions?.org, http://www.gotquestions.org/new-jerusalem.html (accessed 4 Feb. 2012).

221   An image of the New Jerusalem of the Bamberg Apocalypse can be viewed at http://en.wikipedia.org/wiki /File:BambergApocalypseFolio055rNew_Jerusalem.JPG (accessed 6 Jun. 2012).

222   These same figures appear in the four corners of the Waite-Smith Wheel of Fortune trump, probably to signify the good fortune of the human race to be saved by the sacrifice of Christ.

223   John 3:16 (King James Bible).

trump usually refers to the matter itself, "denotes the actual subject of the question, and therefore depends entirely on the accompanying cards." [224] The following reading illustrates this idea.

El Profesor de Español

This reading took place in Central America where I was taking an intensive Spanish course. My teacher, whom I will call Carlos, was an enthusiastic university graduate in his mid-twenties who had asked me to speak in Spanish about my hobbies. When I mentioned the tarot, he became intrigued but was skeptical that tarot had any validity. Carlos requested a demonstration, so the next day I brought my Waite-Smith deck to class. He had no specific question but simply wanted to see what the cards might say about his life. I gave Carlos the deck and asked him to shuffle until he felt comfortable that he had sufficiently mixed the cards. After having him cut the deck, I proceeded with a Celtic Cross spread, turning one card over at a time and discussing each card before moving on to the next. Although I did not use a significator, in my mind Carlos was the diligent, studious Knight of Pentacles.

1. The first card ("this covers you") was the World trump. This surprised me because the World, a major arcana card, represents the end of the Fool's long journey—a completion—yet here it appeared at the beginning of the spread. I thought for a minute and said (in Spanish): "The World represents an important goal that you want to achieve, something that you must work toward and that will make your life feel more complete. I think this reading has to do with a goal that has major importance for you. The World card can also be associated with a journey, possibly abroad." My teacher's face lit up with recognition.

....
224 Regardie, *The Golden Dawn*, p. 585.

2. The second card ("this crosses you") was the Wheel of Fortune. I explained that the Wheel was also a major arcana card that represented significant changes in one's luck. It often heralds an important turning point. Because the Wheel was in the crossing position, he would have to pass through a change in his fortune to be able to accomplish the long-range goal indicated by the World trump. The Wheel of Fortune suggested that his luck would soon change for the better, making it possible for him to pursue his goal. He smiled.

3. The third card ("the foundation"), beneath the initial cross, was the Queen of Pentacles. I described the Queen of Pentacles as a woman who was hard-working, mature, and industrious. She might be a businesswoman, a person of means, or someone accomplished in her field—a person who could help him to pursue his goals, possibly financially. Because he was a teacher, I added that the Queen of Pentacles might also be well-educated or connected with education. A look of amazement crossed his face. As the foundation card, she would play a key role in his question.

4. The fourth card ("the recent past"), just to the left of the initial cross, was the Knight of Pentacles. In my mind I had already pictured Carlos as the Knight of Pentacles, very studious and hard-working. I said I thought this card represented him and indicated that he had recently taken some action regarding his goal. I did not know what kind of action, but Knights often suggest movement or travel and Pentacles generally relate to money, finances, and education. In addition, because the Queen of Pentacles appeared in the foundation position of the reading, perhaps the recent past event had to do with his relationship with a woman represented by the Queen—the Knight of Pentacles in relation to the Queen of Pentacles.

5. The fifth card ("this crowns you"), above the initial cross, was another major arcana card—the Empress. This position often suggests a potential or idealized outcome or some conscious goal of the querent. What immediately came to mind were thoughts of fertility, pregnancy, and childbirth. I wondered aloud whether Carlos was thinking about getting married and starting a family. Perhaps the Queen of Pentacles was the woman he wanted to marry. Carlos kept silent but his face continued to register recognition and a bit of amazement.

6. The sixth card ("the near future"), to the right of the initial cross, was also a trump card—the Chariot. I explained that sometimes this card refers literally to a trip or a means of transportation such as an automobile (a modern chariot), but metaphorically it represents an important journey in which the querent must balance contradictory forces to remain "in the driver's seat." I added that because the first card, the World, signifies an important goal, the Chariot might refer to a step he was about to take on his journey toward that goal. I also commented that this was the third "travel" card to appear in the spread (i.e., the World, the Knight of Pentacles, and the Chariot), so that travel related to his goal might be in the offing. Up to this point Carlos had continued to listen attentively without making any comments. His body language continued to suggest that the cards were making sense to him.

7. The seventh card ("this represents you in this situation"), at the base of a column to the right of the wreathed cross, was yet another major arcana card—the Pope or Hierophant. I was surprised because in my mind the Hierophant is traditional and conservative, which was the opposite of my impression of Carlos, who seemed open, tolerant, and flexible in his views. Because we were in a Latin country, I assumed he was Roman Catholic and said, "Perhaps the Pope here means you are thinking about something related to religion, like a church ceremony." Thinking back to the Empress and the symbolism of starting a family, I added, "Sometimes this refers to a church wedding." Carlos chuckled.

8. The eighth card ("those around you"), above the seventh card, was the Four of Wands. I noted that this card usually marks an important rite of passage such as a graduation or a wedding in which family and friends participate. Carlos began to chuckle even harder and for the first time gave feedback on the reading. He asked me to keep my voice down so that his fellow teachers outside the classroom would not hear our discussion. He confided that he had been thinking about getting married but had not yet proposed to his girlfriend, who was another teacher at the school. He didn't want her to overhear our conversation.

9. The ninth card ("your hopes and fears"), above the eighth, was the Ten of Wands. I explained that his card shows someone carrying a heavy load, symbolically laden with responsibility, and suggested that perhaps the idea of getting married and starting a family might seem like more than he could manage at this time. He nodded in agreement.

10. The tenth card ("the likely outcome"), at the top of the column, was the Page of Wands. I was a bit puzzled by this as a final card because it usually represents the initial impulse to create something new in one's life. I wondered aloud whether this Page might represent Carlos, who was about to embark on a new phase of life, or perhaps it referred to a young person who would play a key role in the outcome. I added that Pages can represent important messages and that Wands often pertain to career ambitions, so that perhaps he would be receiving some significant news about career plans in the near future.

Carlos was amazed by the reading. He said that although he was very skeptical about the tarot, the reading had been quite accurate. He was thinking of getting married but was not sure that this was the right time for it. His overarching ambition was to go to medical school, possibly in a foreign country, and become a pediatrician. The young Page in the outcome position suddenly made more sense. On his teacher's salary, he could not afford medical school and had contacted an aunt who owned her own business to ask whether she could help with the tuition. He wanted to talk to his aunt in person and was planning a trip to visit her in a month's time.

Carlos was worried about the cost of medical school in terms of money, his personal life, and his ability to marry at this time. If his aunt could help him, it would represent a major change in his financial fortunes. He was also contemplating moving closer to the school where he teaches to reduce the cost and amount of time he spent commuting. He was considering buying a car but, because of the expense, he had put off that decision until he was clear about medical school. Virtually every symbolic meaning of the cards made sense to him in light of his current situation.

NINE

The Anatomy
of the Four Suits

We never see anything in nature as an isolated entity,
but rather we see everything in connection with something else
which lies before it, beside it, behind it, beneath it, or above it. [225]
JOHANN WOLFGANG VON GÖETHE

Appendix A of this text presents the anatomy of the four tarot suits with a focus on the symbolism underlying each card in the systems used by Waite, Crowley, and the Golden Dawn. These approaches had a major impact in Great Britain and the United States, and the modern meanings of the tarot cards in the English-speaking world are highly influenced by their teachings. My method will be to consider common keywords for each card.

Each set of keywords acts like an x-ray, revealing the inner structure of a card, which may not be visible to the naked eye. Keywords ignite the reader's imagination regarding possible

---

225 My translation of Göethe's quote from *Göethes Gespräche mit J.P. Eckerman*: "Wir sehen in der Natur nie etwas als Einzelheit, sondern wir sehen alles in Verbindung mit etwas anderem, das vor ihm, neben ihm, hinter ihm, unter ihm und über ihm sich befindet," at "Biografien: Johann Wolfgang von Goethe," http://www.wissen -im-netz.info/literatur/goethe/biografien/eckermann/3-1826/18260605.htm (accessed 10 Feb. 2012).

meanings. Appendix A lists keywords as they relate to number symbolism, suits, elements, qualities, astrological associations, and the *I Ching,* if applicable. Because the meanings of the astrological decans heavily influenced the Golden Dawn delineations of the pip cards, I have quoted descriptions of the decans from Agrippa and also from my own rendering into English of a German edition of *Picatrix* translated from the original Arabic. [226, 227]

Also included is a synopsis of divinatory meanings used in the eighteenth century by Etteilla, in the nineteenth by the Golden Dawn, in the twentieth by Aleister Crowley, and in the twenty-first century by a variety of contemporary authors. In this way the reader can follow the historical progression of ideas to see how they have changed over time. Waite's keywords for the pips can be found in the chapter on number symbolism, and for the court cards in the chapter on court card personalities.

About half of the pip card meanings used by the Golden Dawn and by A. E. Waite come directly from Etteilla (Jean-Baptiste Alliette, 1738–1791), who learned the art of divination in Paris in the mid-1700s. According to Ronald Decker, as a boy of fifteen, Etteilla "began recording the meanings of common French cards as they were being used by elderly fortune-tellers in Paris." [228] In his late teens, he studied tarot with a cartomancer named Alexis from the Piedmont region of Italy. Etteilla carried forward the tradition of these Parisian and Italian diviners and, as Paul Huson in Dame Fortune's Wheel Tarot notes: "Aside from putting cartomancy on the map as a divination method, Etteilla and his pupils provided what would henceforth become *the 'canonical' European interpretation of the suit cards*" (italics mine). [229]

The keywords presented reveal what the creators of many decks had in mind when they assigned meanings to their cards. Each reader, however, must develop a personal feel for the symbolism of a given deck to read the cards comfortably. Keywords are simply tools that aid

....

226 Descriptions of the decans are from the 1651 edition of Henry Cornelius Agrippa of Nettesheim, *Three Books of Occult Philosophy,* translated out of the Latin into the English tongue by J.F., London, printed by R.W. for Gregory Moule, http://www.esotericarchives.com/agrippa/agrippa1.htm (accessed 11 Jun. 2012).

227 The notes on *Picatrix* are based on my translations from the German edition of *"Picatrix" Das Ziel des Weisen von Pseudo-Magriti, Studien der Bihliothek Warburg,* Vol. 27, 1962, translated into German from the original Arabic text by Hellmut Ritter and Martin Plessner in 1933, http://warburg.sas.ac.uk/pdf /FBH295P31zg.pdf (accessed 13 Jun. 2012).

228 Decker, *Art and Arcana,* p. 74.

229 Paul Huson, LWB of *Dame Fortune's Wheel Tarot* (Torino, Italy: Lo Scarabeo, 2008), p. 3.

us in interpreting the cards. Ultimately, as Gareth Knight suggests, "We should not be tied to Golden Dawn or other traditional formulations. The inner world is a free country!"[230] Lee Bursten gives additional advice: "Whichever meanings you choose, you should be able to feel a certain tone, a set of emotions and associations, for each number and each suit."[231]

The Keyword Kaleidoscope

Tarot beginners sometimes feel overwhelmed by the huge number of available keywords. In their introductory text on tarot, Marcus Katz and Tali Goodwin present a useful technique for working with such a wealth of meanings. Starting with a handful of keywords from different sources, they pair words or phrases, two at a time, to see what expanded meanings and feeling states can be generated by linking the different words, concepts, or phrases.[232] The authors provide a template to aid in the process. In addition, Angelo Nasios has posted a YouTube video to illustrate the kaleidoscope method.[233]

Tyson's 1*2*3 Keyword Method

Whereas Katz and Goodwin show us how to expand and flesh out keywords with their kaleidoscope method, Donald Tyson takes an opposite tack and teaches us to condense the plethora of keywords into a simple three-part sentence.[234] Basing himself in the Golden Dawn tradition, Tyson summarizes the core meaning of each card into a key sentence consisting of (1) a subject (the nature of the card), (2) a verb (the action of the card), and (3) an adverb (how the action is carried out). Such sentences have an oracular quality and sound a bit like the Jedi Master Yoda of *Star Wars*.

230 Knight, *Magical World*, p. 52.

231 Bursten, *Universal Tarot of Marseille*, p. 57.

232 Marcus Katz and Tali Goodwin, *Around the Tarot in 78 Days: A Personal Journey through the Cards* (Woodbury, MN: Llewellyn Publications, 2012), p. 21.

233 Angelo Nasios, *Keyword Kaleidoscope—Creating Tarot Meanings—Method*, on YouTube at http://www .youtube.com/watch?v=ArCOsSGbwIg (accessed 19 Jan. 2013).

234 Tyson, *1*2*3 Tarot*.

For example, the Golden Dawn teaches that the Two of Swords relates to restoring peace by balancing opposing ideas or forces in an equitable manner. Tyson condenses this idea into the sentence, "Peace balances with equality." [235] Reversing a card can impair the pure expression of its subject; hence, instead of restoring peace, the flipped card suggests upsetting harmony by affronting someone in an insensitive manner. Thus, the reversed Two of Swords receives the key sentence, "Affront resumes with insensitivity." [236] Whether or not you use the Golden Dawn meanings, Tyson's approach is of value. As he suggests, a useful learning exercise is to take your favorite and most representative keywords for each card and construct a brief sentence that reflects the subject, action, and mode of action of the card.

Tyson extends this idea to a novel method for reading a three-card spread. Using both upright and inverted cards, he proceeds as follows. The subject of the first card becomes the main theme of the three-card spread, the verb of the second card becomes the action of the spread, and the adverb of the third card tells how the action of the spread is carried out. This new three-part sentence embodies the answer to the querent's question in a highly oracular form.

One reviewer, who was looking for an easy approach to tarot reading, used Tyson's method to ask, "Is this book right for me?" Her answer was "Pleasure—endures—with incompatibility," as read from the three-card spread: Six of Cups—Nine of Swords (reversed)—Temperance (reversed). [237, 238] She found the meaning of the oracle inscrutable and decided to give up on the method. A careful reading of Tyson's text, however, reveals that the Six of Cups has to do with enjoyment, the Nine of Swords (inverted) with resigning oneself to one's fate, and Temperance (inverted) with a bad mix that thwarts an agreeable outcome. Ironically, Tyson's method produced an accurate answer: her wish for an easy method to read the tarot was not compatible with his approach. Based on her experience, the reviewer concluded that she and Tyson's book did not mix well (Temperance inverted; union averted). Too bad! Though pithy, it's quite a good book.

....

235 Tyson, *1*2*3 Tarot*, p. 194.

236 Ibid.

237 Review of Tyson's *1*2*3 Tarot* by angirocks at amazon.com, http://www.amazon.com
     /1-2-3-Tarot-Answers-In-Instant/dp/0738705276/ref=cm_cr_mr-title (accessed 21 Mar. 2013).

238 Temperance is associated with Sagittarius, which lies across the wheel from Gemini (study, reading, learning).
     Hence, to solve the difficulty posed by Temperance inverted, she would need to do more reading and study.

Drive Theory Keywords for the Four Suits

Psychologists love to invent theories about what motivates people. For Empedocles, the two basic drives of existence are Love and Strife, which in astrology are embodied by the planets Venus and Mars respectively. Freud expressed a similar idea when he reduced human motivation to the two basic urges: libido (sex) and thanatos, (the death instinct). Jung became fascinated with the four humors, based on the four elements, and came up with four fundamental personality types. Each psychologist has his or her own way of slicing the pie.

In tarot, the idea of viewing the four suits as four basic human drives is helpful in appreciating the significance of the cards. This understanding is rooted in ideas about the four elements and the four primary qualities. By way of review, "hot" and "cold" are active qualities that bring together things that are, respectively, alike or different. "Wet" and "dry" are passive qualities that indicate whether something conforms, respectively, to an outer structure or an inner ideal form. The drives represented by the four suits are morally neutral. Hence, philosophers linked each drive to a cardinal virtue. We might summarize them as follows:

- *Fire/Wands:* the urge to create something new, expand our horizons, express our will, and infuse life into our plans and intentions. Wands do best to act with fortitude, displaying strength of purpose and courage in the face of adversity.

- *Water/Cups:* the urge to merge, to enjoy pleasure, and to experience a sense of unity with others. Cups do best to act with temperance, displaying moderation and self-restraint in feelings and imagination.

- *Air/Swords:* the urge to penetrate and to analyze dispassionately, to separate into distinct parts and perceive the connections between things. Swords do best to act with justice, displaying fairness in disputes and reasonableness when thoughts trouble their mind.

- *Earth/Pentacles:* the urge to make tangible and enduring, to survive and provide security and sustenance. Pentacles do best to act with prudence, displaying discretion in practical affairs and good judgment in managing fiscal and physical health.

When a suit card appears inverted in a reading, its drive may be being put to other than its most virtuous use.

The Two of Swords
(Classic Tarot).

Analyzing a Single Card Using Keywords and Elemental Qualities

As an example, let's consider the Two of Swords.

Meanings: In the eighteenth century, Etteilla associated the Two of Swords with friendship, intimacy, attraction, rapport, and affection, perhaps because two is a number of pairing and bringing into relationship. Crowley and the Golden Dawn related this card to peace or peace restored, as well as quarrels settled and resolved. Modern authors often delineate the Two of Swords as a deadlock or stalemate. To see how all of these meanings are embodied in the symbolism of the card, we need to look at the significance of the number two and the suit of Swords.

Number Symbolism: The number two is associated with balance, choice, partnership, mirroring, and complementary forces.

The idea of forces that are equal and opposite, or balanced and complementary, suggests the notions of peace, stalemate, and resolved quarrels. Because two is an even number, it is considered passive and feminine and is thus related to receptivity, balance, and harmony. Anatomically, two is the number associated with the female genitals, specifically with the set of lips on either side of the vaginal opening.

Elemental Analysis: Swords belong to the element Air (WWH), which is wet and hot. Recalling the "hot dry men and cold wet women" of Renaissance art, we would judge the feminine number two to be cold and wet. The large amount of "wetness" in this card implies a desire to go with the flow and merge with others; hence, Etteilla's emphasis on friendship, rapport, and intimacy. In the Waite-Smith deck, the idea of Air being "hot" is depicted as the woman holding two swords, weapons that are used in the heat of battle. The idea of "coldness" in the feminine two of the Two of Swords is represented by the woman's stillness and frozen posture as well as the cold sea behind her.

Astrology: When we add astrology to the mix, we find ourselves in the Moon decan of Libra. The Moon is a cold, watery, feminine planet that symbolizes our emotional needs. Libra is the sign of balance, peace, justice, harmony, intimate partnerships, the yoke of matrimony, and control of emotional expression. According to Agrippa, the Moon decan of Libra relates to "justifying and helping the miserable and weak against the powerful and wicked." The traditional meanings of the Two of Swords are clearly related to this astrological and elemental symbolism.

Kaleidoscope: If we use Katz and Goodwin's idea of combining keywords to generate a fresh understanding of the card, we might pair Etteilla's "friendship" with the Golden Dawn's "peace restored." To me this combination suggests that friends remain friends because they are able to find a way to iron out their differences. When friends reach an impasse (a modern meaning for this card), they find a way to resolve their conflicting views and restore peace between them.

Homework: As an exercise, the reader may wish to use the tables provided in the appendix to analyze the underlying symbolism of each card. Meditating on a keyword or association while visualizing the image on the card will greatly enhance your personal contact with the archetypal energy involved. This is the approach recommended by Gareth Knight in his instructions on learning the tarot intuitively through meditation on the images. According to Knight, the secret to success is to "use your own visionary imagination to see and maintain the picture for each card," thereby building a personal image of the card in your imagination.[239]

Example Using Keywords: A Woman with a Health Concern

The Question: A woman phoned to ask about a health problem. She awakened a couple days earlier with a pimple on the corner of her lip. During the ensuing two days, the area showed increasing inflammation. Because she was diabetic, she scheduled an appointment with her doctor for later the same day. Meanwhile she called me for a reading about the likely outcome of her health concern. Using the beautiful Tarot of the Old Path (the Classic Tarot appears below), we did a three-card spread:

....
239 Knight, *Magical World*, p. 97.

The Hierophant (V), Ten of Wands, and Three of Pentacles *(Classic Tarot)*.

Card 1: The Hierophant (or High Priest) is associated with the sign Taurus, which happened to be this woman's sun sign. The Hierophant often represents a wise or trusted traditional advisor, in this case her physician and possibly also me. Taurus is a sign related to a fondness for rich foods and luxurious desserts, big no-nos for someone with diabetes.

Card 2: The Ten of Wands shows a man overburdened by ten rods or staves. Wands are a Fire suit, related to energy and vitality. The Ten of Wands is assigned to the Saturn decan of Sagittarius and thus linked to the planet Saturn, which tends to decrease vitality. Perhaps her lip inflammation is related to stress.

Card 3: The Three of Pentacles as the final card suggests that she will team up with someone (her physician) to tackle the problem. Pentacles relate to the body and health matters. The Three of Pentacles is associated with the Mars decan (looking out for number one) of Capricorn (prudence). The craftsman on the Three of Pentacles is a skilled artist who knows how to achieve a successful outcome. In the Tarot of the Old Path, the man on the Three of Pentacles looks like a young doctor sitting at his desk to write a prescription.

Advice: I told the querent that she was wise to have called her doctor so promptly and that the problem might be stress-related (Ten of Wands), possibly connected with the choice of foods in her diet (Taurus, the Hierophant). Being careful to avoid offering a medical diagnosis, I advised her to discuss these ideas with her doctor, who according to the cards appeared to be quite skilled (Three of Pentacles) and capable of giving her proper treatment.

Clarification Card: For further information, I drew a clarification card to see if there was anything else that might be helpful for her to know. The Six of Cups appeared. The astrological region associated with this card is the Sun decan of Scorpio, a sign associated with healing and the medical profession. The Sun symbolizes vitality and good health. The Six of Cups is a card of harmony and pleasure, often related to reconnecting with someone from the past. I was puzzled by this emphasis on pleasure in the context of a medical appointment. The querent explained that she had known her physician for a long time, and going to see him was very much like visiting an old friend. In addition, the doctor had given her the last appointment of his work day because he was about to leave for his summer vacation.

Outcome: The querent had a pleasant visit with her physician. He examined her, did some blood tests, and concluded that no serious infection was present. He instructed her to keep the area clean and apply hot soaks several times a day. Within three days her lip completely healed, the timing possibly reflected in the three of the Three of Pentacles in the outcome position.

Another Health Reading Using Keywords

The querent was a man who had suffered a severe heart attack a few years earlier. He had recently gone into heart failure due to atrial fibrillation, an irregular rhythm of the upper chamber of his heart. He was worried that his new symptoms spelled his impending demise, and he wondered about the outcome of a cardioversion—a procedure to reset the heart's rhythm with electrical shocks—he was about to undergo in the hospital. He was beginning to lose hope for the future. We did a three-card spread in which he selected:

Ace of Cups—Seven of Swords—Ace of Wands

The presence of two Aces looked hopeful. Aces represent new beginnings, Cups often refer to healing, and Wands are symbols of vitality and new life. The Golden Dawn calls the Seven of Swords "unstable effort," which seemed to refer to his heart's inability to pump blood adequately due to the arrhythmia. Swords can also refer to medical or surgical procedures. The Seven of Swords suggests a clever stratagem (electrical shock to the heart) to solve the problem. Etteilla viewed the Seven of Swords as "hope." Overall, the keywords for these cards in the context of his question suggested a successful outcome. His treatment in the hospital went well, his heart rhythm was restored to normal, and he felt a sense of renewed hope for the future as a result.

Epilogue

Prediction is difficult, especially about the future.

Yogi Berra (paraphrasing Niels Bohr)[240]

This book began with a tarot reading about relationships; it seems fitting to end with one. As I was pondering what to include in this final chapter, a college student of my acquaintance contacted me with a question. This young woman is a conscientious student whose social life suffers because of her devotion to her studies. Her friends were encouraging her to go on a blind date with a guy she met on a social networking site, but she was nervous about going out with a stranger. Finally, she agreed to meet him at a local student hangout. She wanted to know how the date would turn out. I thought a three-card reading would give the answer.

Because she was attending a university in a distant city, we did the consultation via Skype. While she was explaining her question, I thoroughly shuffled my Waite-Smith deck and instructed her to stop me when she felt the time was right. I then cut the deck and asked her to pick a number from one to ten. She chose four. I counted to the fourth card of the deck and turned it over: the Nine of Pentacles.

I looked at the card and said what came to mind in the context of her question. Here is a woman, comfortable and nicely dressed, standing in a well-tended garden. A bird sits on her outstretched hand. There she stands, content but alone, except for her avine friend

240 Madison Guy, "Bohr leads Berra, but Yogi closing the gap," *Letter from Here,* December 2, 2006, http://www.peterpatau.com/2006/12/bohr-leads-berra-but-yogi-closing-gap.html (accessed 5 Mar. 2013).

and a solitary snail at her feet. No people accompany her; she does not appear to be in a relationship. This card often refers to solitary pursuits carried out in the luxury of one's personal surroundings.

The Nine of Pentacles describes the querent well: a diligent student who feels somewhat isolated and alone. The astrological association for this card has a similar connotation: the Venus decan of Virgo, the meticulous, analytical Virgin. Given her question, I particularly noticed the two trees in the background. The presence of pairs of objects often suggests the potential or desire for a relationship. The woman in the garden is facing in the direction of the middle card of the spread, perhaps wondering what her future will bring.

We moved on to a second card to see where the lady of the garden was headed. Following the same procedure as with the first card, she selected trump II—the Female Pope or High Priestess. My immediate reaction, which I said aloud, was "another woman alone." The Popess is an intelligent and devoted lady with access to secret knowledge but often misunderstood, especially by the men around her. The two pillars, one black and the other white, reminded me of the two trees of the Nine of Pentacles, again hinting at the potential for a relationship. The myth of Persephone came to mind, her abduction by Hades and separation from her mother Demeter that caused much human suffering. In the context of a blind date, the sequence of two solitary female figures did not look promising. The third and final card would give us of sense of how matters might evolve.

The last card she drew was the Five of Swords. Again I said aloud what I saw in the card. In the foreground is a man standing tall and self-satisfied. He appears to have defeated two men who are walking away with their backs turned to him. They are looking somewhat dejected. The smug man appears to have won the battle but finds himself isolated and alone—a common theme running through all three cards. The Five of Swords is associated with the Venus decan of Aquarius, a sign known for its ability to detach emotionally. Venus is the planet of love and personal relationships. Crowley and the Golden Dawn called this card the "Lord of Defeat." The victorious man on the Waite-Smith Five of Swords, in the outcome position of the spread, is looking back disdainfully at the two lonely women of the first two cards.

**Blind Date Three-Card Spread: Nine of Pentacles,
High Priestess, Five of Swords** *(Universal Tarot).*

Putting it all together, I summarized my take on the sequence of cards: Your studies are going well, but you feel somewhat lonely and long for more of a social life. All three cards speak of isolation. The final card shows an insensitive self-centered man who hurts his colleagues emotionally. As a result, he ends up alone. The tarot is suggesting that the date may not work out as you would like. It is even possible that he won't show up!

I advised her to take the reading with a grain of salt. The cards are not infallible; they merely give us another perspective from which to view a situation. As Dion Fortune was fond of saying, divination is like a weather vane that tells us which way the wind is blowing; it's up to us to trim the sails. At its best, divination does not predict the future; rather it gives us a useful framework from which to make decisions about our lives.

Outcome: She contacted me the day after the blind date. She had gone to the local hangout at the appointed time, but the young man was nowhere to be found. Shortly thereafter he called her cellphone to say that he was running late and would arrive in twenty minutes. She waited a full hour, and he never called or showed up. She went home feeling dejected, but very much wanted to tell me that the cards had been right on target. Perhaps like the fox rejecting the grapes as sour, she added that she would not attempt to see this young man again so she would not have to worry about being kidnapped or attacked by a stranger. The myth of the High Priestess as Persephone abducted by Hades again came to mind, but I chose not to mention it.

The above reading touches on many of the topics covered in this book and raises further questions. We see the importance of listening attentively to the querent's concerns and keeping them in mind as the context for the reading. We see the role played by the directionality of the figures on the cards. We appreciate the need to pay special attention to our intuitive flashes, especially concerning small details on the cards that happen to stand out to us in a particular reading. Shortly after this consultation, I happened to open a book by Dion Fortune and the following line jumped out at me: "The impressions that have value are the spontaneous ones, because these alone well up from subconsciousness."[241]

We can also discern in this example the usefulness of mythology and the Bible, as well as the various systematic approaches that consider the astrology and number symbolism of the cards, though it is easy to feel overwhelmed by the amount of detail such systems provide. We are left wondering what prompted this young woman to contact me for a reading at the very moment I was seeking a useful way to end this book. How is it that the reading turned out as accurately as it did? Was it mere coincidence that I happened to read Dion Fortune's comments about "spontaneous impressions from the subconscious" shortly after doing this reading? How is it that the details of a card, unique to a given deck, so aptly describe the situation of the querent? I don't have satisfactory answers to questions like these. It's not enough simply to label it "synchronicity." What does that really mean, anyway?

I hope that as a reader of this book, you have found the material useful. I learned a lot by reviewing the literature, summarizing it in the various chapters, recording my tarot readings, and trying to explain them in writing. It was especially interesting to trace the history of the ideas that underlie the tarot symbols and to see how they developed and changed over the centuries. An important lesson is that there is no single right way to read the cards; there are many approaches to the tarot and they all can be valuable. Most important is that we respect and learn from each other.

A great deal of information intended for reference is included in this book, both in the chapters and in the appendices. Appendix A summarizes keywords of several systems as they

---

241 Fortune, *Practical Occultism in Daily Life*, p. 27.

apply to the minor arcana cards. There is no need to memorize this detailed information. Its usefulness lies in the ability of different approaches to stimulate our imagination and guide us to a deeper personal understanding of the cards. During actual readings, we do best to take off our theoretical spectacles and pay rapt attention to the querent and the cards. As Wilma Carroll puts it, "All you have to do is look at the cards and say what you see."[242] In a similar vein, Douglas Gibb urges us to keep things simple: "Doing great Tarot readings is about letting things be what they are. The 3 of Swords is sorrow—that's it. It's a simple and elegant idea. Respect that."[243]

I happen to love the astrological associations that underlie Pamela Colman Smith's choice of images, but I am aware that others may not share my enthusiasm. I readily admit that I am a "blind man" who has merely presented what he "sees" when he touches the elephant of tarot. To use a different metaphor, I have offered the reader my own way of slicing the pie. Whatever your preferred method of reading the cards, may your journey through the tarot always be a pleasant and enlightening one.

242 Carroll, *2-Hour Tarot Tutor*, p. 8.

243 Douglas Gibb, "What everyone ought to know about doing great tarot readings," *Tarot Eon* blog, May 28, 2011, http://taroteon.com/tips-and-techniques/what-everyone-ought-to-know-about-doing-great-tarot -readings/ (accessed 01 March 2013).

Appendix A:
Keywords for the Suit Cards

Note that dates in the following tables are given for both the tropical (season-based) and sidereal (star-based) zodiacs. For timing purposes, the Golden Dawn preferred the sidereal zodiac.

Keywords for the Four Suits	
Suit: Wands/Rods/ Batons/Staves/Polo Sticks • **Virtue: Fortitude** • **Temperament: Choleric** • **Element: Fire** (**Hot > Dry**) ****	Career, ambition, will, intention, passion, life force, new growth, budding, the urge to bring forth, self-expression, love of challenge, spirit, creativity, exuberance, enthusiasm, enterprise, action, fun, adventure, desire for achievement, excitement, charisma, animation, movement, progress, sex drive, intuition, sports, pride, competition, risk, opposition. Etteilla equated tarot Wands/Batons with the diamonds of French playing cards.

**** Throughout Appendix A, I have used the mathematical symbol ">" to mean "exceeds" or "is greater than."

Keywords for the Four Suits

Suit: Cups/Chalices • **Virtue: Temperance** • **Temperament: Phlegmatic** • **Element: Water** **(Cold > Wet)**	Caring, empathy, healing, renewal, love, heart, attraction, romance, intimacy, emotion, imagination, female intuition, psychic ability, sensitivity, receptivity, fantasy, dreams, inner life, feelings, fun, pleasure, fertility, soothing, counseling, artistic creativity, spirituality, moderation, conciliation. Etteilla equated tarot Cups with the Hearts of French playing cards.
Suit: Swords/Scimitars • **Virtue: Justice** • **Temperament: Sanguine** • **Element: Air (Wet > Hot)**	Ideas, mind, insight, mental activity, worry, affliction, problems, curiosity, communication, detachment, strategy, authority, decisiveness, fairness, legal matters, invoked force, facing the facts, cutting, surgery, medical procedure, sickness, boundaries, separation, disappointment, conflict, animosity, defense, anger, strife, troubles, cruelty, stress, sadness, trauma, pain, loss. Etteilla equated tarot Swords with the Spades of French playing cards.
Suit: Disks/Coins/Pentacles/Dinars • **Virtue: Prudence** • **Temperament: Melancholic** • **Element: Earth (Dry > Cold)**	Money, income, savings, resources, steady effort, job, achievements, business, labor, power, wealth, property, real estate, possessions, gain and loss, buying and selling, giving and receiving, practical matters, basic needs, survival, material affairs, family, education, training, study, nature, the body, health, physical comforts, inheritance, diligence, tangible results, difficulty expressing emotions. Etteilla equated tarot Coins/Pentacles with the Clubs of French playing cards.

Section 1: The Suit of WANDS, RODS, BATONS, or POLO STICKS	
Ace of Wands	**Keywords & Associations**
Number: 1 (active, masculine)	Initial spark, inspiration, seed, new growth, strength, phallus
Suit: Wands/Rods/Batons	Ambition, zeal, valor, risk, competition, phallus, creative urge
Element: Fire (Hot > Dry)	Vitality, life energy, passion, expansion, enthusiasm
Primary Quality: Hot	Dynamic, expansive, moving up & outward, exuberant
Secondary Quality: Dry	Sharply defined, rigid, decisive, abrupt, self-determined
Crowley/Golden Dawn Labels	Root of the Powers of Fire
Crowley/Golden Dawn Meanings	Solar phallic energy. The seed of the element Fire.
Etteilla Meanings (late 1700s)	Birth, commencement, creation, first fruits, origin, source. *(R):* downfall, decline, failure, dissipation, bankruptcy, ruin.
Some Contemporary Meanings	New life, vitality, initiative, conception, inspiration, an urge to create, the start of something big, confidence, virility, courage, passion, birth of a child, a new career path

Two of Wands (Mars–Aries)	Keywords & Associations
Number: 2 (passive, feminine)	Duality, dialogue, balanced forces, crossroads, decision point, relationship issues, gestation, the vaginal orifice
Suit: Wands/Rods/Batons	Ambition, zeal, valor, risk, competition, phallus, creative urge
Element: Fire (Hot > Dry)	Vitality, life energy, expansion, ambition, enthusism
Primary Quality: Hot	Dynamic, expansive, moving up & outward, exuberant
Secondary Quality: Dry	Sharply defined, rigid, decisive, abrupt, self-determined
Zodiac Sign: Aries	Assertive, pioneering, self-interested, ardent, generative
Analogous House: 1st	Self, body, vitality, sense of identity, temperament
Sign Ruler: *Mars* (malefic)	See *Mars* under Decan Ruler
Exalted Planet: Sun	Dominion, leadership, mastery, honor, triumph, fatherhood
1st Decan (0–10 degrees of Aries: March 21–March 31) Agrippa & [Picatrix]	"…a black man, standing and clothed in a white garment, girdled about, of a great body, with reddish eyes, and great strength, and like one that is angry; and this image signifieth and causeth boldness, fortitude, loftiness and shamelessness" [crass, imperious, arrogant, impudent]
Decan Ruler: Mars (malefic)	Force, fight, virility, phallus, war, cutting, desire to win
Modality: Cardinal	The urge to rouse, lead, put into action, start something new
Crowley/Golden Dawn Labels	Lord of Dominion
Crowley/Golden Dawn Meanings	The will at its most exalted. Influence over another.
Etteilla Meanings (late 1700s)	Sorrow, dark thoughts, sadness, disagreement, displeasure. *(R):* surprise, unexpected event, fear, domination, miracle.
Some Contemporary Meanings	Taking charge of realizing goals, creative tension, a period of waiting, a decisive action, leaving the winter behind, the need to choose a future path, desire to see the world

Three of Wands (Sun–Aries)	Keywords & Associations
Number: 3 (active, masculine)	Trinity, gaiety, group effort, creative expression; to plan, direct, consult, bear fruit; the first triangular number
Suit: Wands/Rods/Batons	Ambition, zeal, valor, risk, competition, phallus, creative urge
Element: Fire (Hot > Dry)	Vitality, life energy, expansion, ambition, enthusiasm
Primary Quality: Hot	Dynamic, expansive, moving up & outward, exuberant
Secondary Quality: Dry	Sharply defined, rigid, decisive, abrupt, self-determined
Zodiac Sign: Aries	Assertive, pioneering, self-interested, ardent, generative
Analogous House: 1st	Self, body, vitality, sense of identity, temperament
Sign Ruler: Mars (malefic)	Force, fight, virility, phallus, war, cutting, desire to win
Exalted Planet: *Sun*	See *Sun* under Decan Ruler
2nd Decan (10–20 degrees of Aries: March 31–April 11) Agrippa & [Picatrix]	"…a woman, outwardly clothed with a red garment, and under it a white, spreading abroad over her feet, and this image causeth nobleness, height of a Kingdom, and greatness of dominion." [high rank, nobility, lordship, greatness]
Decan ruler: Sun	Dominion, leadership, mastery, honor, triumph, fatherhood
Modality: Cardinal	The urge to rouse, lead, put into action, start something new
Crowley/Golden Dawn Labels	Lord of Virtue. Established Strength.
Crowley/Golden Dawn Meanings	Pride, arrogance, power, virtue, established strength
Etteilla Meanings (late 1700s)	Enterprise, boldness, audacity, effort. *(R):* interruption of misfortunes, repose, cessation, intermission.
Some Contemporary Meanings	Early success in pursuing goals, accomplishment, planning, foresight, enterprise, commerce, collaboration, teamwork, seeking direction, awaiting results of prior actions

Four of Wands (Venus–Aries)	Keywords & Associations
Number: 4 (passive, feminine)	Steady, stable, safe, structured; to solidify, order, manifest, establish, lay foundations; the transition from 3 to 5
Suit: Wands/Rods/Batons	Ambition, zeal, valor, risk, competition, phallus, creative urge
Element: Fire (Hot > Dry)	Vitality, life energy, expansion, ambition, enthusiasm
Primary Quality: Hot	Dynamic, expansive, moving up & outward, exuberant
Secondary Quality: Dry	Sharply defined, rigid, decisive, abrupt, self-determined
Zodiac Sign: Aries	Assertive, pioneering, self-interested, ardent, generative
Analogous House: 1st	Self, body, vitality, sense of identity, temperament
Sign Ruler: Mars (malefic)	Force, fight, virility, phallus, war, cutting, desire to win
Exalted Planet: Sun	Dominion, leadership, mastery, honor, triumph, fatherhood
3rd Decan (20–30 degrees of Aries: April 11–April 21) Agrippa & [Picatrix]	" …a white man, pale, with reddish hair, and clothed with a red garment, who carrying on the one hand a golden Bracelet, and holding forth a wooden staff, is restless, and like one in wrath, because he cannot perform that good he would. This image bestoweth wit, meekness, joy and beauty." [femininity, delicacy, fairness, kindness, games, music, adornment]
Decan Ruler: Venus (benefic)	Love, attraction, beauty, fun, friendship, sensual pleasure
Modality: Cardinal	The urge to rouse, lead, put into action, start something new
Crowley/Golden Dawn Labels	Lord of Completion. Perfected Work.
Crowley/Golden Dawn Meaning	Settlement
Etteilla Meanings (late 1700s)	Social success, association, alliance, liaison, society, community, pact. (R): Increase, good luck, success, happiness, prosperity.
Some Contemporary Meanings	A safe haven, happy home, settling down, contentment, laying foundations, a milestone, life transition, wedding, rite of passage, good harvest, relocation, changes in the home

Five of Wands (Saturn–Leo)	Keywords & Associations
Number: 5 (active, masculine)	Disruption, crisis, challenge, instability, uncertainty, break in routine, adjustment, the five senses, the human body
Suit: Wands/Rods/Batons	Ambition, zeal, valor, risk, competition, phallus, creative urge
Element: Fire (Hot > Dry)	Vitality, life energy, expansion, ambition, enthusiasm
Primary Quality: Hot	Dynamic, expansive, moving up & outward, exuberant
Secondary Quality: Dry	Sharply defined, rigid, decisive, abrupt, self-determined
Zodiac Sign: Leo	Creative, regal, proud, fun-loving, fond of children, bossy
Analogous House: 5th	Pleasure, romance, pregnancy, children, fun, creative self-expression, competition, sport, gambling
Sign Ruler: Sun	Dominion, leadership, mastery, honor, triumph, fatherhood
1st Decan (0–10 degrees of Leo: July 23–August 3) Agrippa & [Picatrix]	"…a man riding on a Lion; it signifieth boldness, violence, cruelty, wickedness, lust and labours to be sustained." [power, nobility, vigor, joy, imperiousness, domination]
Decan Ruler: Saturn (malefic)	Structure, limits, delay, duty, fear, loss, obstacle, burden
Modality: Fixed	The urge to sustain, stabilize, and make lasting; purposeful, firm, enduring, self-contained, slow to change
Crowley/Golden Dawn Labels	Lord of Strife
Crowley/Golden Dawn Meanings	The element of Fire weighed down and embittered by Saturn. Quarreling, fighting.
Etteilla Meanings (late 1700s)	Gold, abundance, riches, luxury, fortune, brilliance. (R): wrangles, disputes, oppositions, bickering, litigation.
Some Contemporary Meanings	Competition, strife, conflict, debate, challenge, struggle, total involvement, assertion of desire, confrontation, rivalry, sport, sexual play, male bonding, group activity

Six of Wands (Jupiter–Leo)	Keywords & Associations
Number: 6 (passive, feminine)	Sharing, generosity, kindness, balance, equilibrium, smooth sailing, transition; the second triangular number
Suit: Wands/Rods/Batons	Ambition, zeal, valor, risk, competition, phallus, creative urge
Element: Fire (Hot > Dry)	Vitality, life energy, expansion, ambition, enthusiasm
Primary Quality: Hot	Dynamic, expansive, moving up & outward, exuberant
Secondary Quality: Dry	Sharply defined, rigid, decisive, abrupt, self-determined
Zodiac Sign: Leo	Creative, regal, proud, fun-loving, fond of children, bossy
Analogous House: 5th	Pleasure, romance, pregnancy, children, fun, creative self-expression, competition, sport, gambling
Sign Ruler: Sun	Dominion, leadership, mastery, honor, triumph, fatherhood
2nd Decan (10–20 degrees of Leo: August 3–August 13) Agrippa & [Picatrix]	"…an image with hands lifted up, and a man on whose head is a Crown; he hath the appearance of an angry man, and one that threateneth, having in his right hand a Sword drawn out of the scabbard, & in his left a buckler; it hath signification upon hidden contentions, and unknown victories, & upon base men, and upon the occasions of quarrels and battles" [innovation, folly, confusion, the rising up of the reckless and stupid, the drawing of swords, battle]
Decan Ruler: Jupiter (benefic)	Expansion, excess, luck, protection, gain, profit, adventure
Modality: Fixed	The urge to sustain, stabilize and make lasting; purposeful, firm, enduring, self-contained, slow to change
Crowley/Golden Dawn Labels	Lord of Victory
Crowley/Golden Dawn Meaning	Stable victory, gain, success
Etteilla Meanings (late 1700s)	Domestic, housework, servant, attendant, lackey, messenger. *(R):* expectation, hope, trust, foresight, apprehension.
Some Contemporary Meanings	Victory in battle, triumph, success, acclaim, recognition, popularity, pride, optimism, good news, heroism, confidence, smooth progress, advancement

Seven of Wands (Mars–Leo)	Keywords & Associations
Number: 7 (active, masculine)	A boundary or threshold, assessment, reflection, challenge, solitary action, sabbatical, sacredness, wisdom, mystery
Suit: Wands/Rods/Batons	Ambition, zeal, valor, risk, competition, phallus, creative urge
Element: Fire (Hot > Dry)	Vitality, life energy, expansion, ambition, enthusiasm
Primary Quality: Hot	Dynamic, expansive, moving up & outward, exuberant
Secondary Quality: Dry	Sharply defined, rigid, decisive, abrupt, self-determined
Zodiac Sign: Leo	Creative, regal, proud, fun-loving, fond of children, bossy
Analogous House: 5th	Pleasure, romance, pregnancy, children, fun, creative self-expression, competition, sport, gambling
Sign Ruler: Sun	Dominion, leadership, mastery, honor, triumph, fatherhood
3rd Decan (20–30 degrees of Leo: August 13–August 23) Agrippa & [Picatrix]	"…a young man in whose hand is a Whip, and a man very sad, and of an ill aspect; they signify love and society, and the loss of one's right for avoiding strife" [love, social equality, mutual affection, cooperation, peacefulness]
Decan Ruler: Mars (malefic)	Force, fight, virility, phallus, war, cutting, desire to win
Modality: Fixed	The urge to sustain, stabilize, and make lasting; purposeful, firm, enduring, self-contained, slow to change
Crowley/Golden Dawn Labels	Lord of Valour
Crowley/Golden Dawn Meanings	Courage to face opposition
Etteilla Meanings (late 1700s)	Negotiations, conversation, discourse, chatter, commerce. (R): uncertainty, vacillation, hesitation, indecision.
Some Contemporary Meanings	Standing one's moral ground, facing up to challenge, being tested, self-defense, courage, defiance, resolve, a position of advantage, teaching, writing, self-employment

Eight of Wands (Mercury–Sagittarius)	Keywords & Associations
Number: 8 (passive, feminine)	Worldly involvement, taking action, managing, putting in order, organizing; efficient movement, power, success
Suit: Wands/Rods/Batons	Ambition, zeal, valor, risk, competition, phallus, creative urge
Element: Fire (Hot > Dry)	Vitality, life energy, expansion, ambition, enthusiasm
Primary Quality: Hot	Dynamic, expansive, moving up & outward, exuberant
Secondary Quality: Dry	Sharply defined, rigid, decisive, abrupt, self-determined
Zodiac Sign: Sagittarius	Frank, tolerant, adventurous, fond of learning and travel
Analogous House: 9th	Distant travel, higher learning, religion, prophecy
Sign Ruler: Jupiter (benefic)	Expansion, excess, luck, protection, gain, profit, adventure
Exalted:	Moon's South Node (malefic, like Saturn)
1st Decan (0–10 degrees of Sagittarius: November 23–December 3) Agrippa & [Picatrix]	"…the form of a man armed with a coat of mail, and holding a naked sword in his hand; the operation of this is for boldness, malice, and liberty" [boldness, love of adventure, liveliness, stamina, chivalric art]
Decan Ruler: Mercury (in detriment in Sagittarius)	News, communication, travel, speed, thought, cunning
Modality: Mutable	Adaptable, flexible, transitional; the urge to move on, let go, and make way for the new
Crowley/Golden Dawn Labels	Lord of Swiftness
Crowley/Golden Dawn Meanings	The energy of high velocity. Hasty communication.
Etteilla Meanings (late 1700s)	Countryside, farm, garden, rural life, merrymaking, sport, tranquility. (R): internal agitation, uncertainty, argument, doubt, remorse.
Some Contemporary Meanings	Speed, haste, rapid change, quick action, excitement, urgency, movement, coordinated effort, Cupid's arrows, news from afar or through the air, rural life, travel by air

Nine of Wands (Moon–Sagittarius)	Keywords & Associations
Number: 9 (active, masculine)	Achievement, climax, intensity, fullness, integration, completion, fulfillment; the last of the single digits
Suit: Wands/Rods/Batons	Ambition, zeal, valor, risk, competition, phallus, creative urge
Element: Fire (Hot > Dry)	Vitality, life energy, expansion, ambition, enthusiasm
Primary Quality: Hot	Dynamic, expansive, moving up & outward, exuberant
Secondary Quality: Dry	Sharply defined, rigid, decisive, abrupt, self-determined
Zodiac Sign: Sagittarius	Frank, tolerant, adventurous, fond of learning and travel
Analogous House: 9th	Distant travel, higher learning, religion, prophecy
Sign Ruler: Jupiter (benefic)	Expansion, excess, luck, protection, gain, profit, adventure
Exalted:	Moon's South Node (malefic, like Saturn)
2nd Decan (10–20 degrees of Sagittarius: December 3–December 12) Agrippa & [Picatrix]	"…a woman weeping, and covered with clothes; the operation of this is for sadness and fear of his own body" [deep sadness, screaming, crying, anxiety, fear, grief, heartlessness]
Decan ruler: Moon	Instability, change, periodicity, moods, instinct, mother, silver
Modality: Mutable	Adaptable, flexible, transitional; the urge to move on, let go, and make way for the new
Crowley/Golden Dawn Labels	Lord of Strength. Great Strength.
Crowley/Golden Dawn Meanings	Power, health, energy, strength, change in stability
Etteilla Meanings (late 1700s)	Delay, hindrance, suspension, separation, sending back. *(R):* Obstacle, opposition, toil, adversity, unhappiness.
Some Contemporary Meanings	Strength in opposition, a wounded warrior, girding one's loins, the need for vigilance, fortification, courage, perseverance, resilience, selecting one of many options

Ten of Wands (Saturn–Sagittarius)	Keywords & Associations
Number: 10 (passive, feminine)	End result; overfull; anticlimax; ending and transition; one too many (9 + 1 = 10); third triangular number
Suit: Wands/Rods/Batons	Ambition, zeal, valor, risk, competition, phallus, creative urge
Element: Fire (Hot > Dry)	Vitality, life energy, expansion, ambition, enthusiasm
Primary Quality: Hot	Dynamic, expansive, moving up & outward, exuberant
Secondary Quality: Dry	Sharply defined, rigid, decisive, abrupt, self-determined
Zodiac Sign: Sagittarius	Frank, tolerant, adventurous, fond of learning and travel
Analogous House: 9th	Distant travel, higher learning, religion, prophecy
Sign Ruler: Jupiter (benefic)	Expansion, excess, luck, protection, gain, profit, adventure
Exalted:	Moon's South Node (malefic, like Saturn)
3rd Decan (20–30 degrees of Sagittarius: December 13–December 22) Agrippa & [Picatrix]	"…a man like in colour to gold, or an idle man playing with a staff; and the signification of this is in following our own wills, and obstinacy in them, and in activeness for evil things, contentions, and horrible matters" [indulging in vain efforts, frequenting the wrong places, struggling; engaging in shameful, bad, indecent, offensive, or harmful things]
Decan Ruler: Saturn (malefic)	Structure, limits, delay, duty, fear, loss, obstacle, burden
Modality: Mutable	Adaptable, flexible, transitional; the urge to move on, let go, and make way for the new
Crowley/Golden Dawn Labels	Lord of Oppression
Crowley/Golden Dawn Meanings	The energy of Wands at its most violent. Cruelty, malice, revenge, injustice, overbearing strength.
Etteilla Meanings (late 1700s)	Betrayal, treason, duplicity, falsity, conspiracy. (R): Obstacle, toil, travail, objection.
Some Contemporary Meanings	Feeling oppressed, encumbered, weighted down, or overburdened; hard work, exhaustion, too many responsibilities, carrying the load for others

Page/Princess of Wands– Earth of Fire	Keywords & Associations
Pages: Earthy part of Fire	Child, messenger, helper, apprentice; messages, opinions, news; study, curiosity, new learning, youthful enthusiasm
Element: Earth (Dry > Cold)	Tangible reality, body functioning, security, stability
Suit: Wands/Rods/Batons	Ambition, zeal, valor, risk, competition, phallus, creative urge
Element: Fire (Hot > Dry)	Vital energy, spirit, courage, inspiration, self-assertion
Primary Quality: Hot	Dynamic, expansive, moving up & outward, exuberant
Secondary Quality: Dry	Sharply defined, rigid, decisive, abrupt, self-determined
Quadrant of Earth	Asia; the quarter of the Earth measured eastward from the meridian of the Great Pyramid (*located at* 29.98°N, 31.13°E) to longitude 121.13° E
I Ching: 27 (Yi), Swallowing	Heed what you put in your mouth or in your thoughts. Honor what truly sustains you and those around you.
Crowley/Golden Dawn Labels	The Princess of the Shining Flame: the Rose of the Palace of Fire
Crowley/Golden Dawn Meanings	Brilliant, daring, energetic, ambitious, aspiring, sudden, violent; superficial, dramatic, shallow, domineering, cruel
Etteilla Meanings (late 1700s)	Foreigner, stranger, something extraordinary. *(R):* Advice, notices, stories, instruction.
Some Contemporary Meanings	An enthusiastic youngster, an envoy, a loyal person; exciting news, an inspired idea, travel, activity, arousal, adventure, creativity, a new career path or course of study

Knight of Wands– Fire of Fire	Keywords & Associations
Knights: Fiery part of Fire	Youthful or immature adult males, armed men; action, adventure, assertion, travel, swiftness, movement, comings and goings of matters, offers, love affairs
Element: Fire (Hot > Dry)	Vitality, life energy, expansion, ambition, enthusiasm
Suit: Wands/Rods/Batons	Ambition, zeal, valor, risk, competition, phallus, creative urge
Element: Fire (Hot > Dry)	Vital energy, spirit, courage, inspiration, self-assertion
Primary Quality: Hot	Dynamic, expansive, moving up & outward, exuberant
Secondary Quality: Dry	Sharply defined, rigid, decisive, abrupt, self-determined
Zodiac: 20 Scorpio– 20 Sagittarius	13 Nov–12 Dec (tropical); *06 Dec–03 Jan (sidereal)*
Corresponding Houses: 8th, 9th	Shared resources, death, higher education, religion, journeys
Classical & Modern Sign Rulers:	Mars/Pluto, Jupiter
Exalted: Moon's South Node	Malefic (like Saturn) and exalted in Sagittarius
Modality: Primarily Mutable	Adaptable, flexible, transitional; the urge to move on, let go and make way for the new
I Ching: 51 (Zhen), Shock	Thunder upon thunder spreads terror for a hundred miles. Confront your fears and keep your wits about you when others are losing theirs. Draw inspiration from the creative power of the storm.
Crowley/Golden Dawn Labels	Lord of the Flame and Lightning: King of the Spirits of Fire
Crowley/Golden Dawn Meanings	Active, generous, swift, fierce, impetuous, proud, impulsive; unpredictable, brutal, cruel, bigoted
Etteilla Meanings (late 1700s)	Departure, emigration, separation, displacement. *(R):* Discord, rupture, interruption, parting.
Some Contemporary Meanings	A free-spirited man; passion, haste, new ideas, liveliness, charisma, daring, rapid comings and goings, relocation, a journey, changes in the home, Pratesi's "door knocker"

Queen of Wands– Water of Fire	Keywords & Associations
Queens: Watery part of Fire	Mature adult females, mother figures, powerful women, influential friends; nurturing, support, sensitivity
Element: Water (Cold > Wet)	Affection, empathy, support, nurturing, emotions, intuition
Suit: Wands/Rods/Batons	Ambition, zeal, valor, risk, competition, phallus, creative urge
Element: Fire (Hot > Dry)	Vital energy, spirit, courage, inspiration, self-assertion
Primary Quality: Hot	Dynamic, expansive, moving up & outward, exuberant
Secondary Quality: Dry	Sharply defined, rigid, decisive, abrupt, self-determined
Zodiac: 20 Pisces–20 Aries	11 Mar–10 Apr (tropical); *04 Apr–04 May (sidereal)*
Corresponding Houses: 12th, 1st	Spiritual understanding, seclusion; birth, self-image, self-development, vitality, the body, identity formation
Sign Rulers:	Jupiter/Neptune, Mars
Exalted Planet:	Venus is exalted in Pisces. The Sun is exalted in Aries.
Decan rulers:	Mars, Mars, Sun
Modality: Primarily Cardinal	The urge to rouse, lead, put into action, start something new
I Ching: 17 (Sui), Following	Thunder rouses the lake of emotions. Now is the time to honor the rumblings of creativity; go with the flow and let transformation occur. Go within, rest and connect with the inspiring dragon.
Crowley/Golden Dawn Labels	The Queen of the Thrones of Flame
Crowley/Golden Dawn Meanings	Adaptable, steady, commanding, calm, kind, generous, friendly, likeable, attractive; snobbish, domineering, obstinate, tyrannical, vengeful
Etteilla Meanings (late 1700s)	Rural lady, mistress of a country estate, household economy, virtue, chastity, honor. *(R):* A good wife, bounty, service.
Some Contemporary Meanings	A passionate woman who gets involved and takes command; a gracious hostess; an assertive female executive; ambition, spontaneity, confidence, popularity, love of cats

King of Wands (Crowley's Prince)–Air of Fire	Keywords & Associations
Kings: Airy part of Fire	Mature adult male, boss, father figure; rank, power, wisdom, authority, duty, worldly influence, expertise
Element: Air (Wet > Hot)	Logic, analysis, strategy, communication, decision making
Suit: Wands/Rods/Batons	Ambition, zeal, valor, risk, competition, phallus, creative urge
Element: Fire (Hot > Dry)	Vital energy, spirit, courage, inspiration, self-assertion
Primary Quality: Hot	Dynamic, expansive, moving up & outward, exuberant
Secondary Quality: Dry	Sharply defined, rigid, decisive, abrupt, self-determined
Zodiac: 20 Cancer–20 Leo	13 July–12 Aug (tropical); *06 Aug–05 Sep (sidereal)*
Corresponding Houses: 4th, 5th	Home, family, roots, children, dating, intimacy, recreation
Sign Rulers:	Moon, Sun
Exalted Planet:	Jupiter is exalted in Cancer
Decan rulers:	Moon, Saturn, Jupiter
Modality: Primarily Fixed	The urge to sustain, stabilize and make lasting; purposeful, firm, enduring, self-contained, slow to change
I Ching: 42 (Yi), Increase	You are generously blessed with creativity. Be decisive like the thunder in setting clear goals and far-reaching like the wind in making your ambitions a reality. Improve the good and remedy the faulty.
Crowley/Golden Dawn Labels	The Prince of the Chariot of Fire
Crowley/Golden Dawn Meanings [Crowley identified with the Prince]	Strong, swift, impulsive, generous, romantic, just, proud, noble, courageous, ambitious, a practical joker; intolerant, prejudiced, cruel, callous, a boaster
Etteilla Meanings (late 1700s)	Rural gentlemen, master of a country estate, an honest man, a farmer, probity. *(R):* A good and severe man.
Some Contemporary Meanings	An entrepreneur, executive, dynamic visionary, self-starter, alpha male, boss, wise leader, successful negotiator; decisiveness, authority, optimism, charisma, power

Section 2: The Suit of CUPS or CHALICES	
Ace of Cups	**Keywords & Associations**
Number: 1 (active, masculine)	Initial spark, inspiration, seed, new growth, strength, phallus
Suit: Cups/Chalices	Feelings, intimacy, imagination, love, joy, pleasure, fertility, womb, vagina, healing, temperance
Element: Water (Cold > Wet)	Affection, empathy, support, nurturing, emotions, intuition
Primary Quality: Cold	Inner-directed, joining together, centered, calming
Secondary Quality: Wet	Fluid, adaptable, receptive, obliging, flexible, imaginative
Crowley/Golden Dawn Labels	Root of the Powers of Water
Crowley/Golden Dawn Meanings	Union with God. The receptive feminine counterpart of the phallic Ace of Wands. The seed of the element Water.
Etteilla Meanings (late 1700s)	A table, food, feast, guests, inn, service, abundance, fertility. *(R):* Mutation, inconstancy, diversity.
Some Contemporary Meanings	A new beginning in close relationships; renewal, healing, replenishing, joy, love, pleasure, abundance, beauty, intimacy, romance, fertility, pregnancy, the birth of a child

Two of Cups (Venus–Cancer)	Keywords & Associations
Number: 2 (passive, feminine)	Duality, dialogue, balanced forces, crossroads, decision point, relationship issues, gestation, the vaginal orifice
Suit: Cups/Chalices	Feelings, intimacy, imagination, love, joy, pleasure, fertility, womb, vagina, healing, temperance
Element: Water (Cold > Wet)	Affection, empathy, support, nurturing, emotions, intuition
Primary Quality: Cold	Inner-directed, joining together, centered, calming
Secondary Quality: Wet	Fluid, adaptable, receptive, obliging, flexible, imaginative
Zodiac Sign: Cancer	Nurturing, protective, changeable, moody, motherly
Analogous House: 4th	Home, family, roots, domestic concerns, final endings
Sign Ruler: Moon	Instability, change, periodicity, moods, instinct, mother, silver
Exalted Planet: Jupiter (benefic)	Expansion, excess, luck, protection, gain, profit, adventure
1st Decan (0–10 degrees of Cancer: June 22–July 2) Agrippa & [Picatrix]	"…the form of a young *Virgin,* adorned with fine clothes, and having a Crown on her head; it giveth acuteness of senses, subtlety of wit, and the love of men" [elegance, understanding, affection, gentleness, friendliness]
Decan Ruler: Venus (benefic)	Love, attraction, beauty, fun, friendship, sensual pleasure
Modality: Cardinal	The urge to rouse, lead, put into action, start something new
Crowley/Golden Dawn Labels	Lord of Love
Crowley/Golden Dawn Meanings	Love, marriage, harmony, joy, pleasure, warm friendship
Etteilla Meanings (late 1700s)	Love, friendship, attraction, affection. *(R):* Sensuality, desire, lust, passion, jealousy.
Some Contemporary Meanings	Romance, love, attraction, partnership, friendship, a happy union, intimacy, sharing, support, cooperation, forgiveness, healing, reconciliation, a marriage proposal

Three of Cups (Mercury–Cancer)	Keywords & Associations
Number: 3 (active, masculine)	Trinity, gaiety, group effort, creative expression; to plan, direct, consult, bear fruit; the first triangular number
Suit: Cups/Chalices	Feelings, intimacy, imagination, love, joy, pleasure, fertility, womb, vagina, healing, temperance
Element: Water (Cold > Wet)	Affection, empathy, support, nurturing, emotions, intuition
Primary Quality: Cold	Inner-directed, joining together, centered, calming
Secondary Quality: Wet	Fluid, adaptable, receptive, obliging, flexible, imaginative
Zodiac Sign: Cancer	Nurturing, protective, changeable, moody, motherly
Analogous House: 4th	Home, family, roots, domestic concerns, final endings
Sign Ruler: Moon	Instability, change, periodicity, moods, instinct, mother, silver
Exalted Planet: Jupiter (benefic)	Expansion, excess, luck, protection, gain, profit, adventure
2nd Decan (10–20 degrees of Cancer: July 3–July 12) Agrippa & [Picatrix]	"…a man clothed in comely apparel, or a man and woman sitting at the table and playing; it bestoweth riches, mirth, gladness, and the love of women" [merrymaking, gaiety, charm, comfort, agreeableness]
Decan Ruler: Mercury	News, communication, travel, speed, thought, cunning
Modality: Cardinal	The urge to rouse, lead, put into action, start something new
Crowley/Golden Dawn Labels	Lord of Abundance
Crowley/Golden Dawn Meanings	Love in abounding joy, the spiritual basis of fertility, plenty, pleasure, merriment, new clothes
Etteilla Meanings (late 1700s)	Success, victory, cure, relief, perfection. (R): Termination, expedience, dispatch, accomplishment.
Some Contemporary Meanings	Happy times, fun, pleasure, friendliness, hospitality, parties, celebrations, weddings, reunions, holidays, christenings, engagements, healing, resolution of difficulties, abundance

Four of Cups (Moon–Cancer)	Keywords & Associations
Number: 4 (passive, feminine)	Steady, stable, safe, structured; to solidify, order, manifest, establish, lay foundations; the transition from 3 to 5
Suit: Cups/Chalices	Feelings, intimacy, imagination, love, joy, pleasure, fertility, womb, vagina, healing, temperance
Element: Water (Cold > Wet)	Affection, empathy, support, nurturing, emotions, intuition
Primary Quality: Cold	Inner-directed, joining together, centered, calming
Secondary Quality: Wet	Fluid, adaptable, receptive, obliging, flexible, imaginative
Zodiac Sign: Cancer	Nurturing, protective, changeable, moody, motherly
Analogous House: 4th	Home, family, roots, domestic concerns, final endings
Sign Ruler: Moon	See *Moon* under Decan Ruler
Exalted Planet: Jupiter (benefic)	Expansion, excess, luck, protection, gain, profit, adventure
3rd Decan (20–30 degrees of Cancer: July 13–July 23) Agrippa & [Picatrix]	"…a man, a Hunter with his lance and horn, bringing out dogs for to hunt; the signification of this is the contention of men, the pursuing of those who fly, the hunting and possessing of things by arms and brawling" [envy, exile; acquiring things through struggle, strife, and conflict]
Decan ruler: *Moon*	Instability, change, periodicity, moods, instinct, mother, silver
Modality: Cardinal	The urge to rouse, lead, put into action, start something new
Crowley/Golden Dawn Labels	Lord of Luxury. Blended Pleasure.
Crowley/Golden Dawn Meanings	Pleasure, luxury, the kindness of others, new relationships, new goals, waking after contemplation
Etteilla Meanings (late 1700s)	Boredom, worry, disquiet, discontent. *(R):* Novelty, prescience, prediction, new instruction.
Some Contemporary Meanings	Discontent, feeling unfulfilled, weariness, blunted appetite, looking within, a stationary period; a missed opportunity, unheeded offer, unexpected gift, or unforeseen solution

Five of Cups (Mars–Scorpio)	Keywords & Associations
Number: 5 (active, masculine)	Disruption, crisis, challenge, instability, uncertainty, break in routine, adjustment, the five senses, the human body
Suit: Cups/Chalices	Feelings, intimacy, imagination, love, joy, pleasure, fertility, womb, vagina, healing, temperance
Element: Water (Cold > Wet)	Affection, empathy, support, nurturing, emotions, intuition
Primary Quality: Cold	Inner-directed, joining together, centered, calming
Secondary Quality: Wet	Fluid, adaptable, receptive, obliging, flexible, imaginative
Zodiac Sign: Scorpio	Intense, passionate, secretive, sexual, resolute, penetrating
Analogous House: 8th	Death, decay, rebirth, joint resources, anguish of mind
Classical Sign Ruler: Mars	See *Mars* under decan ruler below
Modern Sign Ruler: Pluto	Radical change, powerful forces, abuse, the unconscious
1st Decan (0–10 degrees of Scorpio: October 24–November 3) Agrippa & [Picatrix]	"…a woman of good face and habit, and two men striking her; the operations of these are for comeliness, beauty, and for strifes, treacheries, deceits, detractations, and perditions" [evil, grief, wickedness, treachery]
Decan Ruler: Mars (malefic)	Force, fight, virility, phallus, war, cutting, desire to win
Modality: Fixed	The urge to sustain, stabilize, and make lasting; purposeful, firm, enduring, self-contained, slow to change
Crowley/Golden Dawn Labels	Lord of Disappointment. Loss in Pleasure.
Crowley/Golden Dawn Meanings	Disappointment in love, separation, loss of friendship, a breakup, unkindness from friends
Etteilla Meanings (late 1700s)	Inheritance, legacy, gift, tradition, transmission, resolution. *(R):* Family, ancestry, race, marriage, rapport, alliance.
Some Contemporary Meanings	Feeling unloved or abandoned, relationship problems, loss, betrayal, separation, sadness, regret, disappointment but all is not lost, a bittersweet marriage, the need to let go

Six of Cups (Sun–Scorpio)	Keywords & Associations
Number: 6 (passive, feminine)	Sharing, generosity, kindness, balance, equilibrium, smooth sailing, transition; the second triangular number
Suit: Cups/Chalices	Feelings, intimacy, imagination, love, joy, pleasure, fertility, womb, vagina, healing, temperance
Element: Water (Cold > Wet)	Affection, empathy, support, nurturing, emotions, intuition
Primary Quality: Cold	Inner-directed, joining together, centered, calming
Secondary Quality: Wet	Fluid, adaptable, receptive, obliging, flexible, imaginative
Zodiac Sign: Scorpio	Intense, passionate, secretive, sexual, resolute, penetrating
Analogous House: 8th	Death, decay, rebirth, joint resources, anguish of mind
Classical Sign Ruler: Mars	Force, fight, virility, phallus, war, cutting, desire to win
Modern Sign Ruler: Pluto	Radical change, powerful forces, abuse, the unconscious
2nd Decan (10–20 degrees of Scorpio: November 4–November 13) Agrippa & [Picatrix]	"…a man naked, and a woman naked, and a man sitting on the earth, and before him two dogs biting one another; and their operation is for impudence, deceit, and false dealing, and for to lend mischief and strife amongst men" [ill repute, disgrace, shame, provocation of offenses and ruin]
Decan ruler: Sun	Dominion, leadership, mastery, honor, triumph, fatherhood
Modality: Fixed	The urge to sustain, stabilize, and make lasting; purposeful, firm, enduring, self-contained, slow to change
Crowley/Golden Dawn Labels	Lord of Pleasure
Crowley/Golden Dawn Meanings	Pleasure, well-being, harmony, sexual satisfaction
Etteilla Meanings (late 1700s)	The past, in the past, age, antiquity, decrepitude. *(R):* The future, renewal, regeneration, reproduction.
Some Contemporary Meanings	Nostalgia, yearning for past joys, reminiscences of good old days, renewing an old relationship, exchange of gifts, fun, friendly play, mutual pleasure, sexual delight, children

Seven of Cups (Venus–Scorpio)	Keywords & Associations
Number: 7 (active, masculine)	A boundary or threshold, assessment, reflection, challenge, solitary action, sabbatical, sacredness, wisdom, mystery
Suit: Cups/Chalices	Love, imagination, fun, womb, vagina, healing, temperance
Element: Water (Cold > Wet)	Affection, empathy, support, nurturing, emotions, intuition
Primary Quality: Cold	Inner-directed, joining together, centered, calming
Secondary Quality: Wet	Fluid, adaptable, receptive, obliging, flexible, imaginative
Zodiac Sign: Scorpio	Intense, passionate, secretive, sexual, resolute, penetrating
Analogous House: 8th	Death, decay, rebirth, joint resources, anguish of mind
Classical Sign Ruler: Mars	Force, fight, virility, phallus, war, cutting, desire to win
Modern Sign Ruler: Pluto	Radical change, powerful forces, abuse, the unconscious
3rd Decan (20–30 degrees of Scorpio: November 13–November 23) Agrippa & [Picatrix]	"…a man bowed downward upon his knees, and a woman striking him with a staff, and it is the signification of drunkenness, fornication, wrath, violence, and strife" [irresponsibility, depravity; a bad marriage due to subjugation, plunder, or rape]
Decan Ruler: Venus (benefic)	Love, attraction, beauty, fun, friendship, sensual pleasure
Modality: Fixed	The urge to sustain, stabilize, and make lasting; purposeful, firm, enduring, self-contained, slow to change
Crowley/Golden Dawn Labels	Lord of Debauch. Illusionary Success.
Crowley/Golden Dawn Meanings	External splendor but internal corruption, deceit, lies, errors, promises unfulfilled, mild and transient success.
Etteilla Meanings (late 1700s)	Thought, intelligence, imagination, reflection, opinion, sentiment. (R): Intention, desire, will, resolution.
Some Contemporary Meanings	Too many options, indecision, unreality, wishful thinking, imagination; a bad marriage, sexual abuse; escape into addition, sex, illusion, intoxication, shopping sprees, etc.

Eight of Cups (Saturn–Pisces)	Keywords & Associations
Number: 8 (passive, feminine)	Worldly involvement, taking action, managing, putting in order, organizing; efficient movement, power, success
Suit: Cups/Chalices	Love imagination, fun, womb, vagina, healing, temperance
Element: Water (Cold > Wet)	Affection, empathy, support, nurturing, emotions, intuition
Primary Quality: Cold	Inner-directed, joining together, centered, calming
Secondary Quality: Wet	Fluid, adaptable, receptive, obliging, flexible, imaginative
Zodiac Sign: Pisces	Dreamy, poetic, boundless, imaginative, escapist, illusory
Analogous House: 12th	Spirituality, mysticism, seclusion, self-undoing, letting go
Classical Sign Ruler: Jupiter	Expansion, excess, luck, protection, gain, profit, adventure
Modern Sign Ruler: Neptune	Illusion, merging, dissolving, imagination, fog, the sea
Exalted Planet: Venus (benefic)	Love, attraction, beauty, fun, friendship, sensual pleasure
1st Decan (0–10 degrees of Pisces: February 19–March 1) Agrippa & [Picatrix]	"… a man carrying burdens on his shoulder, and well clothed; it hath his signification in journeys, change of place, and in carefulness of getting wealth and clothes" [lack of aggressiveness, weakness, many trips and moving about, hardships, the pursuit of money and livelihood]
Decan Ruler: Saturn (malefic)	Structure, limits, delay, duty, fear, loss, obstacle, burden
Modality: Mutable	Adaptable, flexible, transitional; the urge to move on, let go, and make way for the new
Crowley/Golden Dawn Labels	Lord of Indolence. Abandoned Success.
Crowley/Golden Dawn Meanings	The soul poisoned, success abandoned, ennui, decline of interest
Etteilla Meanings (late 1700s)	A blond girl, honor, modesty, timidity, sweetness, moderation. (R): Happiness, joy, diversion, pomp.
Some Contemporary Meanings	Loss of interest, abandonment, walking away, searching elsewhere, moving on, leaving a situation behind, yearning for something better, seeking fulfillment; travel

Nine of Cups (Jupiter–Pisces)	Keywords & Associations
Number: 9 (active, masculine)	Achievement, climax, intensity, fullness, integration, completion, fulfillment; the last of the single digits
Suit: Cups/Chalices	Feelings, intimacy, imagination, love, joy, pleasure, fertility, womb, vagina, healing, temperance
Element: Water (Cold > Wet)	Affection, empathy, support, nurturing, emotions, intuition
Primary Quality: Cold	Inner-directed, joining together, centered, calming
Secondary Quality: Wet	Fluid, adaptable, receptive, obliging, flexible, imaginative
Zodiac Sign: Pisces	Dreamy, poetic, boundless, imaginative, escapist, illusory
Analogous House: 12th	Spirituality, mysticism, seclusion, self-undoing, letting go
Classical Sign Ruler: Jupiter	See decan ruler, Jupiter
Modern Sign Ruler: Neptune	Illusion, merging, dissolving, imagination, fog, the sea
Exalted Planet: Venus (benefic)	Love, attraction, beauty, fun, friendship, sensual pleasure
2nd Decan (10–20 degrees of Pisces: March 1–March 11) Agrippa & [Picatrix]	"…a woman of a good countenance, and well adorned; and the signification is to desire and put one's self on about high and great matters" [greatness of soul, high aspirations, the company of great and sublime things]
Decan Ruler: Jupiter (benefic)	Expansion, excess, luck, protection, gain, profit, adventure
Modality: Mutable	Adaptable, flexible, transitional; the urge to move on, let go, and make way for the new
Crowley/Golden Dawn Labels	Lord of Happiness. Material Happiness.
Crowley/Golden Dawn Meanings	Success, pleasure, happiness, wishes fulfilled
Etteilla Meanings (late 1700s)	Victory, success, advantage, achievement, gain, pomp, attire. (R): Sincerity, loyalty, liberty, audacity, ease.
Some Contemporary Meanings	"The wish card"–hopes fulfilled, difficulties overcome, good health, luck, contentment, abundance, material success, celebration, sensual pleasure, satiety, bliss

Ten of Cups (Mars–Pisces)	Keywords & Associations
Number: 10 (passive, feminine)	End result; overfull; anticlimax; ending and transition; one too many (9 + 1 = 10); third triangular number
Suit: Cups/Chalices	Love, imagination, fun, womb, vagina, healing, temperance
Element: Water (Cold > Wet)	Affection, empathy, support, nurturing, emotions, intuition
Primary Quality: Cold	Inner-directed, joining together, centered, calming
Secondary Quality: Wet	Fluid, adaptable, receptive, obliging, flexible, imaginative
Zodiac Sign: Pisces	Dreamy, poetic, boundless, imaginative, escapist, illusory
Analogous House: 12th	Spirituality, mysticism, seclusion, self-undoing, letting go
Classical Sign Ruler: Jupiter	Expansion, excess, luck, protection, gain, profit, adventure
Modern Sign Ruler: Neptune	Illusion, merging, dissolving, imagination, fog, the sea
Exalted Planet: Venus (benefic)	Love, attraction, beauty, fun, friendship, sensual pleasure
3rd Decan (20–30 degrees of Pisces: March 11–March 21) Agrippa & [Picatrix]	"…a man naked, or a youth, and nigh him a beautiful maiden, whose head is adorned with flowers, and it hath his signification for rest, idleness, delight, fornication, and for imbracings of women" [marriage, embraces, desire, sexual intercourse, lust, passion for peace or comfort]
Decan Ruler: Mars (malefic)	Force, fight, virility, phallus, war, cutting, desire to win
Modality: Mutable	Adaptable, flexible, transitional; the urge to move on, let go, and make way for the new
Crowley/Golden Dawn Labels	Lord of Satiety. Perfected Success.
Crowley/Golden Dawn Meanings	The work of Water is complete and disturbance is due; success, good fortune, matters settled as one wishes
Etteilla Meanings (late 1700s)	Town, city, homeland, dwelling, residence. *(R):* Anger, agitation, indignation, violence.
Some Contemporary Meanings	A happy family, marriage with children, fulfillment, joy, bliss, getting your heart's desire, contentment, satiety, peace at last; the bleakness of winter (late Pisces) comes to an end

Page/Princess of Cups– Earth of Water	Keywords & Associations
Pages: Earthy part of Water	Child, messenger, helper, apprentice; messages, opinions, news; study, curiosity, new learning, youthful enthusiasm
Element: Earth (Dry > Cold)	Tangible reality, body functioning, security, stability
Suit: Cups/Chalices	Feelings, intimacy, imagination, love, joy, pleasure, fertility, womb, vagina, healing, temperance
Element: Water (Cold > Wet)	Affection, empathy, support, nurturing, emotions, intuition
Primary Quality: Cold	Inner-directed, joining together, centered, calming
Quadrant of Earth	Pacific; the quarter of the Earth between longitudes 148.87°W and 121.13°E
Secondary Quality: Wet	Fluid, adaptable, receptive, obliging, flexible, imaginative
I Ching: 41 (Sun), Decrease	The still mountain rises above the lake of feelings. Success results from sincerity, simplifying one's life, and freeing one's emotions of disruptive undercurrents.
Crowley/Golden Dawn Labels	The Princess of the Waters: the Lotus of the Palace of the Floods
Crowley/Golden Dawn Meanings	Gracious, sweet, kind, helpful, romantic, gentle, dreamy, voluptuous, imaginative; dependent, selfish, indolent. The power of water to crystallize an idea, support life and enable chemical combination.
Etteilla Meanings (late 1700s)	A blond youth; study, work, application, employment. *(R):* Affection, friendship, longing, desire, seduction.
Some Contemporary Meanings	A helpful person, a studious youth; assistance, service, volunteer work, artistic creativity, dreams, intuition, imagination, gullibility, news about love, birth of a child

Knight of Cups—Fire of Water	Keywords & Associations
Knights: Fiery part of Water	Youthful or immature adult males, armed men; action, adventure, assertion, travel, swiftness, movement, comings and goings of matters, offers, love affairs
Element: Fire (Hot > Dry)	Vitality, life energy, expansion, ambition, enthusiasm
Suit: Cups/Chalices	Love, imagination, fun, womb, vagina, healing, temperance
Element: Water (Cold > Wet)	Affection, empathy, support, nurturing, emotions, intuition
Primary Quality: Cold	Inner-directed, joining together, centered, calming
Secondary Quality: Wet	Fluid, adaptable, receptive, obliging, flexible, imaginative
Zodiac: 20 Aquarius–20 Pisces	09 Feb–10 Mar (tropical); *05 Mar–04 Apr (sidereal)*
Corresponding Houses: 11th, 12th	Friendship, hopes, wishes, seclusion, illusion, undoing
Classical & Modern Sign Rulers:	Saturn/Uranus, Jupiter/Neptune
Exalted Planet:	Venus is exalted in Pisces
Modality: Primarily Mutable	Adaptable, flexible, transitional; the urge to move on, let go, and make way for the new
I Ching: 54 (Gui Mei), The Marrying Maiden	Thunder rumbling over the lake of close relationships, perhaps due to questionable offers. Be diplomatic and avoid power struggles.
Crowley/Golden Dawn Labels	The Lord of the Waves and the Waters: the King of the Hosts of the Sea
Crowley/Golden Dawn Meanings	Sensitive, passive, innocent, amiable, graceful, quick to respond; idle, little endurance, unreliable, untruthful
Etteilla Meanings (late 1700s)	Approach, arrival, reception, reconciliation, coming abroad. *(R):* Deceit, cleverness, trickery, lawlessness.
Some Contemporary Meanings	A sensitive young man; Prince Charming; a poet or dreamer; artistic activity, idealism, proposals of love, offers that stir the emotions; unreliability; travel over water

Queen of Cups– Water of Water	Keywords & Associations
Queens: Watery part of Water	Mature adult females, mother figures, powerful women, influential friends; nurturing, support, sensitivity
Element: Water (Cold > Wet)	Affection, empathy, support, nurturing, emotions, intuition
Suit: Cups/Chalices	Feelings, intimacy, imagination, love, joy, pleasure, fertility, womb, vagina, healing, temperance
Element: Water (Cold > Wet)	Affection, empathy, support, nurturing, emotions, intuition
Primary Quality: Cold	Inner-directed, joining together, centered, calming
Secondary Quality: Wet	Fluid, adaptable, receptive, obliging, flexible, imaginative
Zodiac: 20 Gemini–20 Cancer	12 June–12 Jul (tropical); *06 Jul–05 Aug (sidereal)*
Corresponding Houses: 3rd, 4th	Early education, communication style, siblings, kin, home, family, parents, roots, traditions
Sign Rulers:	Mercury, Moon
Exalted:	The Moon's North Node in Gemini. Jupiter in Cancer.
Decan rulers:	Sun, Venus, Mercury
Modality: Primarily Cardinal	The urge to rouse, lead, put into action, start something new
I Ching: 8 (Bi), Holding Together	Good fortune results from joining with others who share your interests.
Crowley/Golden Dawn Labels	The Queen of the Thrones of the Waters
Crowley/Golden Dawn Meanings	Receptive, reflective, dreamy, tranquil, unruffled, imaginative, kind, poetic; coquettish, prone to illusion
Etteilla Meanings (late 1700s)	A blond lady, virtue, honesty, wisdom. *(R):* A highly placed woman, scandal, dishonesty, corruption.
Some Contemporary Meanings	An empathic woman, a mother, a devoted friend, an artistic person, a psychic; help, healing, support, caring, nurturing, empathy, intuition, counseling, cuddling; codependency

King of Cups (Crowley's Prince)–Air of Water	Keywords & Associations
Kings: Airy part of Water	Mature adult male, boss, father figure; rank, power, wisdom, authority, duty, worldly influence, expertise
Element: Air (Wet > Hot)	Logic, analysis, strategy, communication, decision making
Suit: Cups/Chalices	Feelings, intimacy, imagination, love, joy, pleasure, fertility, womb, vagina, healing, temperance
Element: Water (Cold > Wet)	Affection, empathy, support, nurturing, emotions, intuition
Primary Quality: Cold	Inner-directed, joining together, centered, calming
Secondary Quality: Wet	Fluid, adaptable, receptive, obliging, flexible, imaginative
Zodiac: 20 Libra–20 Scorpio	14 Oct–12 Nov (tropical); *06 Nov–05 Dec (sidereal)*
Corresponding Houses: 7th, 8th	Marriage, partnerships, disputes, shared resources, death, the occult, regeneration
Classical & Modern Sign Rulers:	Venus, Mars/Pluto
Exalted Planet:	Saturn, the Greater Malefic, is exalted in Libra
Decan rulers:	Mars, Sun, Venus
Modality: Primarily Fixed	The urge to sustain, stabilize, and make lasting; purposeful, firm, enduring, self-contained, slow to change
I Ching: 61 (Zhong Fu), Inner Truth	In dealing with others it is important to find a common ground, listen actively, and avoid misrepresentation.
Crowley/Golden Dawn Labels	The Prince of the Chariot of the Waters
Crowley/Golden Dawn Meanings	Subtle, artistic, secretive, crafty, powerful; fierce, violent, scheming, ruthless, merciless, without conscience
Etteilla Meanings (late 1700s)	A blond gentleman; fairness, probity, art, science. *(R):* A highly placed man, extortion, corruption, scandal, a thief.
Some Contemporary Meanings	A benevolent adult male, a dependable considerate man, a learned person, a professional, an artist, an international businessman; tolerance, calmness, empathy, creativity

Section 3: The Suit of SWORDS or SCIMITARS	
Ace of Swords	Keywords & Associations
Number: 1 (active, masculine)	Initial spark, inspiration, seed, new growth, strength, phallus
Suit: Swords/Scimitars	Mental activity, affliction, judgment, legal matters, justice, conflict, separation, surgery, sickness; a phallic symbol
Element: Air (Wet > Hot)	Logic, analysis, strategy, communication, decision making
Primary Quality: Wet	Fluid, adaptable, receptive, obliging, flexible, imaginative
Secondary Quality: Hot	Dynamic, expansive, moving up & outward, exuberant
Crowley/Golden Dawn Labels	Root of the Powers of Air
Crowley/Golden Dawn Meanings	The primordial energy or seed of the element Air
Etteilla Meanings (late 1700s)	Extreme, large, excessive; anger, rage; borders, limits. *(R):* conception, pregnancy, childbirth, augmentation.
Some Contemporary Meanings	Strength in adversity to face the truth, cut the crap, take charge, and break free; authority, power, justice, invoked force, decisiveness, clarity, focus; a need for surgery

Two of Swords (Moon–Libra)	Keywords & Associations
Number: 2 (passive, feminine)	Duality, dialogue, balanced forces, crossroads, decision point, relationship issues, gestation, the vaginal orifice
Suit: Swords/Scimitars	Mental activity, conflict, separation, justice; phallic symbol
Element: Air (Wet > Hot)	Logic, analysis, strategy, communication, decision making
Primary Quality: Wet	Fluid, adaptable, receptive, obliging, flexible, imaginative
Secondary Quality: Hot	Dynamic, expansive, moving up & outward, exuberant
Zodiac Sign: Libra	Fair, balanced, just, diplomatic, harmonious, peaceable
Analogous House: 7th	Partnership, marriage, open enemies, war, thieves, lawsuits
Sign Ruler: Venus (benefic)	Love, attraction, beauty, fun, friendship, sensual pleasure
Exalted Planet: Saturn (malefic)	Structure, limits, delay, duty, fear, loss, obstacle, burden
1st Decan (0–10 degrees of Libra: September 23–October 3) Agrippa & [Picatrix]	"…the form of an angry man, in whose hand is a Pipe, and the form of a man reading in a book; the operation of this is in justifying and helping the miserable and weak against the powerful and wicked" [justice, law, equity; rejection of the oppression of the weak, afflicted, and needy by the powerful and unjust]
Decan ruler: Moon	Instability, change, periodicity, moods, instinct, mother, silver
Modality: Cardinal	The urge to rouse, lead, put into action, start something new
Crowley/Golden Dawn Labels	Lord of Peace. Peace Restored.
Crowley/Golden Dawn Meanings	Peace restored but some tension remaining, a quarrel settled and resolved
Etteilla Meanings (late 1700s)	Friendship, affection, rapport, intimacy, attraction. (R): Falsity, superficiality, deceit.
Some Contemporary Meanings	Impasse, dilemma, feeling torn, balancing opposing forces, resolving differences, restoring harmony, over-control of emotions, trust, friendship, the need for negotiation

Three of Swords (Saturn–Libra)	Keywords & Associations
Number: 3 (active, masculine)	Trinity, gaiety, group effort, creative expression; to plan, direct, consult, bear fruit; the first triangular number
Suit: Swords/Scimitars	Mental activity, affliction, judgment, legal matters, justice, conflict, separation, surgery, sickness; a phallic symbol
Element: Air (Wet > Hot)	Logic, analysis, strategy, communication, decision making
Primary Quality: Wet	Fluid, adaptable, receptive, obliging, flexible, imaginative
Secondary Quality: Hot	Dynamic, expansive, moving up & outward, exuberant
Zodiac Sign: Libra	Fair, balanced, just, diplomatic, harmonious, peaceable
Analogous House: 7th	Partnership, marriage, open enemies, war, thieves, lawsuits
Sign Ruler: Venus (benefic)	Love, attraction, beauty, fun, friendship, sensual pleasure
Exalted Planet: Saturn (malefic)	See Decan Ruler: Saturn
2nd Decan (10–20 degrees of Libra: October 4–October 14) Agrippa & [Picatrix]	"…two men furious and wrathful and a man in a comely garment, sitting in a chair; and the signification of these is to shew indignation against the evil, and quietness and security of life with plenty of good things" [recreation, the good life, feasting, rest, ease, peace of mind]
Decan Ruler: Saturn (malefic)	Structure, limits, delay, duty, fear, loss, obstacle, burden
Modality: Cardinal	The urge to rouse, lead, put into action, start something new
Crowley/Golden Dawn Labels	Lord of Sorrow
Crowley/Golden Dawn Meanings	Secrecy, perversion, unhappiness, sorrow, tears
Etteilla Meanings (late 1700s)	Separation, severance, rupture, departure, absence, aversion. (R): Confusion, error, loss, distraction, detour.
Some Contemporary Meanings	Sorrow, heartache, separation, loss, quarrels, disruption, delay, betrayal, blocked gaiety, a need for surgery, heart problems, a miscarriage, stormy weather for the emotions

Four of Swords (Jupiter–Libra)	Keywords & Associations
Number: 4 (passive, feminine)	Steady, stable, safe, structured; to solidify, order, manifest, establish, lay foundations; the transition from 3 to 5
Suit: Swords/Scimitars	Mental activity, affliction, judgment, legal matters, justice, conflict, separation, surgery, sickness; a phallic symbol
Element: Air (Wet > Hot)	Logic, analysis, strategy, communication, decision making
Primary Quality: Wet	Fluid, adaptable, receptive, obliging, flexible, imaginative
Secondary Quality: Hot	Dynamic, expansive, moving up & outward, exuberant
Zodiac Sign: Libra	Fair, balanced, just, diplomatic, harmonious, peaceable
Analogous House: 7th	Partnership, marriage, open enemies, war, thieves, lawsuits
Sign Ruler: Venus (benefic)	Love, attraction, beauty, fun, friendship, sensual pleasure
Exalted Planet: Saturn (malefic)	Structure, limits, delay, duty, fear, loss, obstacle, burden
3rd Decan (20–30 degrees of Libra: October 14–October 24) Agrippa & [Picatrix]	"…a violent man holding a bow, and before him a naked man, and also another man holding bread in one hand, and a cup of wine in the other; the signification of these is to shew wicked lusts, singings, sports and gluttony" [libertine ways, frivolity, sodomy, singing, music, pleasure seeking]
Decan Ruler: Jupiter (benefic)	Expansion, excess, luck, protection, gain, profit, adventure
Modality: Cardinal	The urge to rouse, lead, put into action, start something new
Crowley/Golden Dawn Labels	Lord of Truce. Rest from Strife.
Crowley/Golden Dawn Meanings	Refuge from mental chaos, convalescence, recovery from illness, change for the better
Etteilla Meanings (late 1700s)	Loneliness, solitude, retreat, hermitage, exile, sepulcher. (R): Prudence, wisdom, good conduct, harmony, moderation.
Some Contemporary Meanings	Respite, retreat, time-out, reprieve, rest, renewal, convalescence, rejuvenation, recovery, seclusion, exile, withdrawal, retirement, peace, solitude, contemplation

Five of Swords (Venus–Aquarius)	Keywords & Associations
Number: 5 (active, masculine)	Disruption, crisis, challenge, instability, uncertainty, break in routine, adjustment, the five senses, the human body
Suit: Swords/Scimitars	Mental activity, affliction, judgment, legal matters, justice, conflict, separation, surgery, sickness; a phallic symbol
Element: Air (Wet > Hot)	Logic, analysis, strategy, communication, decision making
Primary Quality: Wet	Fluid, adaptable, receptive, obliging, flexible, imaginative
Secondary Quality: Hot	Dynamic, expansive, moving up & outward, exuberant
Zodiac Sign: Aquarius	Aloof, detached, objective, scientific, unique, willful
Analogous House: 11th	Friends, groups, advice, hopes, wishes, career resources
Classical Sign Ruler: Saturn	Structure, limits, delay, duty, fear, loss, obstacle, burden
Modern Sign Ruler: Uranus	Shock, unexpected disruption, divorce, sudden insight
1st Decan (0–10 degrees of Aquarius: January 21–January 31) Agrippa & [Picatrix]	"…the form of a prudent man, and of a woman spinning; and the signification of these is in the thought and labour for gain, in poverty and baseness" [hardship, toil, fatigue, poverty, lack, need, humiliation]
Decan Ruler: Venus (benefic)	Love, attraction, beauty, fun, friendship, sensual pleasure
Modality: Fixed	The urge to sustain, stabilize, and make lasting; purposeful, firm, enduring, self-contained, slow to change
Crowley/Golden Dawn Labels	Lord of Defeat
Crowley/Golden Dawn Meanings	Intellect defeated by sentiment; treachery, loss, malice, slander, evil-speaking
Etteilla Meanings (late 1700s)	Loss, degradation, affront, humiliation, avarice, setback, thief. (R): Grief, chagrin, interment.
Some Contemporary Meanings	Putting oneself first, insensitivity, hollow victory, defeat, poor sportsmanship, unfairness, gloating, leaving without saying goodbye, feeling unappreciated, failed relationships

Six of Swords (Mercury–Aquarius)	Keywords & Associations
Number: 6 (passive, feminine)	Sharing, generosity, kindness, balance, equilibrium, smooth sailing, transition; the second triangular number
Suit: Swords/Scimitars	Mental activity, conflict, separation, justice; phallic symbol
Element: Air (Wet > Hot)	Logic, analysis, strategy, communication, decision making
Primary Quality: Wet	Fluid, adaptable, receptive, obliging, flexible, imaginative
Secondary Quality: Hot	Dynamic, expansive, moving up & outward, exuberant
Zodiac Sign: Aquarius	Aloof, detached, objective, scientific, unique, willful
Analogous House: 11th	Friends, groups, advice, hopes, wishes, career resources
Classical Sign Ruler: Saturn	Structure, limits, delay, duty, fear, loss, obstacle, burden
Modern Sign Ruler: Uranus	Shock, unexpected disruption, divorce, sudden insight
2nd Decan (10–20 degrees of Aquarius: January 31–February 9) Agrippa & [Picatrix]	"…a man with a long beard; and the signification of this belongeth to the understanding, meekness, modesty, liberty and good manners" [grace, nobility, beauty, perfection of form, fineness of features, manly virtue]
Decan Ruler: Mercury	News, communication, travel, speed, thought, cunning
Modality: Fixed	The urge to sustain, stabilize, and make lasting; purposeful, firm, enduring, self-contained, slow to change
Crowley/Golden Dawn Labels	Lord of Science. Earned Success.
Crowley/Golden Dawn Meanings	Balance of mental and moral faculties, labor, work, journey over water
Etteilla Meanings (late 1700s)	Journey, voyage, road, path, messenger, kind attention. *(R):* Explanation, proclamation, publicity.
Some Contemporary Meanings	Travel (over water), seeking greener pastures, leaving anxieties behind; a short trip, vacation, getaway; relocating, transitioning to a safer environment, gaining perspective

Seven of Swords (Moon–Aquarius)	Keywords & Associations
Number: 7 (active, masculine)	A boundary or threshold, assessment, reflection, challenge, solitary action, sabbatical, sacredness, wisdom, mystery
Suit: Swords/Scimitars	Mental activity, affliction, judgment, legal matters, justice, conflict, separation, surgery, sickness; a phallic symbol
Element: Air (Wet > Hot)	Logic, analysis, strategy, communication, decision making
Primary Quality: Wet	Fluid, adaptable, receptive, obliging, flexible, imaginative
Secondary Quality: Hot	Dynamic, expansive, moving up & outward, exuberant
Zodiac Sign: Aquarius	Aloof, detached, objective, scientific, unique, willful
Analogous House: 11th	Friends, groups, advice, hopes, wishes, career resources
Classical Sign Ruler: Saturn	Structure, limits, delay, duty, fear, loss, obstacle, burden
Modern Sign Ruler: Uranus	Shock, unexpected disruption, divorce, sudden insight
3rd Decan (20–30 degrees of Aquarius: February 9 February 19)	" …a black and angry man; and the signification of this is in expressing insolence; and impudence" [disgrace, ill repute, shame]
Decan ruler: Moon	Instability, change, periodicity, moods, instinct, mother, silver
Modality: Fixed	The urge to sustain, stabilize, and make lasting; purposeful, firm, enduring, self-contained, slow to change
Crowley/Golden Dawn Labels	Lord of Futility. Unstable Effort.
Crowley/Golden Dawn Meanings	The policy of appeasement, untrustworthiness, vacillation, a journey by land, a sense of futility
Etteilla Meanings (late 1700s)	Hope, intention, scheme, wish, desire, fantasy, overvaluing oneself. *(R):* Good counsel, thought, reflection, admonition.
Some Contemporary Meanings	Borrowing, theft, betrayal, trickery, evasion, secret affair, clever stratagem, a snake in the grass, running away, doing your own thing, divorce, wavering, unstable effort, giving up

Eight of Swords (Jupiter–Gemini)	Keywords & Associations
Number: 8 (passive, feminine)	Worldly involvement, taking action, managing, putting in order, organizing; efficient movement, power, success
Suit: Swords/Scimitars	Mental activity, conflict, separation, justice; phallic symbol
Element: Air (Wet > Hot)	Logic, analysis, strategy, communication, decision making
Primary Quality: Wet	Fluid, adaptable, receptive, obliging, flexible, imaginative
Secondary Quality: Hot	Dynamic, expansive, moving up & outward, exuberant
Zodiac Sign: Gemini	Adaptable, versatile, communicative, quick, restless
Analogous House: 3rd	Thinking, messages, ideas, early education, kin, local travel
Sign Ruler: Mercury	News, communication, travel, speed, thought, cunning
Exalted:	Moon's North Node (benefic, like Jupiter)
1st Decan (0–10 degrees of Gemini: May 22–June 1) Agrippa & [Picatrix]	"…a man in whose hand is a rod, and he is, as it were, serving another; it granteth wisdom, and the knowledge of numbers and arts in which there is no profit" [writing, math, science, commerce, enforcement of property rights]
Decan Ruler: Jupiter (benefic) (in detriment in Gemini)	Expansion, excess, luck, protection, gain, profit, adventure
Modality: Mutable	Adaptable, flexible, transitional; the urge to move on, let go, and make way for the new
Crowley/Golden Dawn Labels	Lord of Interference. Shortened Force.
Crowley/Golden Dawn Meanings	The will thwarted by accidental interference, pettiness, restriction, narrow-mindedness, prison
Etteilla Meanings (late 1700s)	Criticism, censure; a critical moment, delicate circumstance, crisis. *(R):* Delay, hindrance, misfortune, opposition, quibbling.
Some Contemporary Meanings	Feeling trapped, helpless, frustrated, ill, or fearful; limiting beliefs, lack of perspective, the need to reassess, distracted thinking, legal complications, interference by outside forces

Nine of Swords (Mars–Gemini)	Keywords & Associations
Number: 9 (active, masculine)	Achievement, climax, intensity, fullness, integration, completion, fulfillment; the last of the single digits
Suit: Swords/Scimitars	Mental activity, conflict, separation, justice; phallic symbol
Element: Air (Wet > Hot)	Logic, analysis, strategy, communication, decision making
Primary Quality: Wet	Fluid, adaptable, receptive, obliging, flexible, imaginative
Secondary Quality: Hot	Dynamic, expansive, moving up & outward, exuberant
Zodiac Sign: Gemini	Adaptable, versatile, communicative, quick, restless
Analogous House: 3rd	Thinking, messages, ideas, early education, kin, local travel
Sign Ruler: Mercury	News, communication, travel, speed, thought, cunning
Exalted:	Moon's North Node (benefic, like Jupiter)
2nd Decan (10–20 degrees of Gemini: June 1–June 12) Agrippa & [Picatrix]	"…a man in whose hand is a Pipe, and another being bowed down, digging the earth: and they signify infamous and dishonest agility, as that of Jesters and Jugglers; it also signifies labours and painful searchings" [hassles, feeling pressured, rapidity, callousness, reprehensible haste]
Decan Ruler: Mars (malefic)	Force, fight, virility, phallus, war, cutting, desire to win
Modality: Mutable	Adaptable, flexible, transitional; the urge to move on, let go, and make way for the new
Crowley/Golden Dawn Labels	Lord of Cruelty. Despair and Cruelty.
Crowley/Golden Dawn Meanings	Primitive instincts, psychopathy, fanaticism, suffering, illness, malice, cruelty, pain
Etteilla Meanings (late 1700s)	Ecclesiastic, priest, nun, piety, celibacy, virginity, cult, devotion, recluse. *(R):* Shame, legitimate fear, well-founded suspicion.
Some Contemporary Meanings	"The nightmare card," worry, despair, fear, distress, anguish, unhappiness, hurtful words, pessimism, sorrow, depression, guilt, stress, illness; help me, oh Lord!

Ten of Swords (Sun–Gemini)	Keywords & Associations
Number: 10 (passive, feminine)	End result; overfull; anticlimax; ending and transition; one too many (9 + 1 = 10); third triangular number
Suit: Swords/Scimitars	Mental activity, conflict, separation, justice; phallic symbol
Element: Air (Wet > Hot)	Logic, analysis, strategy, communication, decision making
Primary Quality: Wet	Fluid, adaptable, receptive, obliging, flexible, imaginative
Secondary Quality: Hot	Dynamic, expansive, moving up & outward, exuberant
Zodiac Sign: Gemini	Adaptable, versatile, communicative, quick, restless
Analogous House: 3rd	Thinking, messages, ideas, early education, kin, local travel
Sign Ruler: Mercury	News, communication, travel, speed, thought, cunning
Exalted:	Moon's North Node (benefic, like Jupiter)
3rd Decan (20–30 degrees of Gemini: June 12–June 22) Agrippa & [Picatrix]	"…a man seeking for Arms, and a fool holding in the right hand a Bird, and in his left a pipe, and they are the significations of forgetfulness, wrath, boldness, jests, scurrilities, and unprofitable words" [inattention, distraction, gaming, empty chatter, idleness]
Decan ruler: Sun	Dominion, leadership, mastery, honor, triumph, fatherhood
Modality: Mutable	Adaptable, flexible, transitional; the urge to move on, let go, and make way for the new
Crowley/Golden Dawn Labels	Lord of Ruin
Crowley/Golden Dawn Meanings	Reason divorced from reality, the logic of insanity, the energy of Swords used disruptively
Etteilla Meanings (late 1700s)	Tears, sadness, lamentation, desolation. (R): Benefit, profit, advantage, power, authority.
Some Contemporary Meanings	Closure, ruined plans, hitting bottom, an undesired ending, tears, regret, setbacks, blocked communication, the darkness (before the dawn), stabbed in the back, surgery

Page/Princess of Swords– Earth of Air	Keywords & Associations
Pages: Earthy part of Air	Child, messenger, helper, apprentice; messages, opinions, news; study, curiosity, new learning, youthful enthusiasm
Element: Earth (Dry > Cold)	Tangible reality, body functioning, security, stability
Suit: Swords/Scimitars	Mental activity, affliction, judgment, legal matters, justice, conflict, separation, surgery, sickness; a phallic symbol
Element: Air (Wet > Hot)	Logic, reason, intellect, strategy, planning, freedom, objectivity, communication, transport, relatedness
Primary Quality: Wet	Fluid, adaptable, receptive, obliging, flexible, imaginative
Secondary Quality: Hot	Dynamic, expansive, moving up & outward, exuberant
Quadrant of Earth	Americas; the quarter of the Earth between longitudes 58.87°W and 148.87°W
I Ching: 18 (Gu), Corrupting	Now is the time to take decisive action to rebuild and improve on what has been corrupted or destroyed.
Crowley/Golden Dawn Labels	Princess of the Rushing Winds; Lotus of the Palace of Air
Crowley/Golden Dawn Meanings	Firm, strong, aggressive, practical, clever, wise, acute, subtle, dexterous; cunning, vengeful, frivolous, destructive
Etteilla Meanings (late 1700s)	A spy, curiosity seeker, observer, supervisor, learned man, artist; a remark, observation, speculation, deduction. *(R):* something sudden, unforeseen, astonishing, unexpected.
Some Contemporary Meanings	A problem child, an inmate, a spy; delayed, upsetting, or disappointing news; unjust criticism, gossip; ferreting out secrets, decisive action, vigilance, curiosity, prying eyes

Knight of Swords–Fire of Air	Keywords & Associations
Knights: Fiery part of Air	Youthful or immature adult males, armed men; action, adventure, assertion, travel, swiftness, movement, comings and goings of matters, offers, love affairs
Element: Fire (Hot > Dry)	Vitality, life energy, expansion, ambition, enthusiasm
Suit: Swords/Scimitars	Mental activity, conflict, separation, justice; a phallic symbol
Element: Air (Wet > Hot)	Logic, intellect, strategy, analysis, communication, transport
Primary Quality: Wet	Fluid, adaptable, receptive, obliging, flexible, imaginative
Secondary Quality: Hot	Dynamic, expansive, moving up & outward, exuberant
Zodiac: 20 Taurus–20 Gemini	11 May–11 Jun (tropical); *05 Jun–05 Jul (sidereal)*
Corresponding Houses: 2nd, 3rd	Income, possessions, local travel, kin, messages, documents
Classical & Modern Sign Rulers:	Venus, Mercury
Exalted Planets:	The Moon is exalted in Taurus. The Moon's North Node (benefic, like Jupiter) is exalted in Gemini.
Decan rulers:	Saturn, Jupiter, Mars
Modality: Primarily Mutable	Adaptable, flexible; the urge to let go and move on
I Ching: 32 (Heng), Persevering	Focus your thinking and persist in pursuing your goals without distraction until you bring them to fruition.
Crowley/Golden Dawn Labels	The Lord of the Wind and the Breezes: the King of the Spirits of Air
Crowley/Golden Dawn Meanings	Quick to act, clever, subtle, fierce, courageous, skillful, domineering; indecisive, deceitful, tyrannical, crafty
Etteilla Meanings (late 1700s)	Military, soldier, enemy, combatant, dispute, anger, ruin. *(R):* Incompetence, stupidity, swindle, industriousness.
Some Contemporary Meanings	A tactless man, bold warrior, fearless crusader, quick thinker, fast talker; one who is forceful, swift, shrewd, rash, on the move, antagonistic; a change in lifestyle, travel by air

Queen of Swords–Water of Air	Keywords & Associations
Queens: Watery part of Air	Mature adult females, mother figures, powerful women, influential friends; nurturing, support, sensitivity
Element: Water (Cold > Wet)	Affection, empathy, support, nurturing, emotions, intuition
Suit: Swords/Scimitars	Mental activity, conflict, separation, justice; phallic symbol
Element: Air (Wet > Hot)	Logic, reason, intellect, strategy, planning, freedom, objectivity, communication, transport, relatedness
Primary Quality: Wet	Fluid, adaptable, receptive, obliging, flexible, imaginative
Secondary Quality: Hot	Dynamic, expansive, moving up & outward, exuberant
Zodiac: 20 Virgo–20 Libra	13 Sep–13 Oct (tropical); *07 Oct–05 Nov (sidereal)*
Corresponding Houses: 6th, 7th	Illness, service, pets, daily work, marriage, open enemies
Classical & Modern Sign Rulers:	Mercury, Venus
Exalted Planets:	Mercury, Saturn
Decan rulers:	Mercury, Moon, Saturn
Modality: Primarily Cardinal	The urge to rouse, lead, put into action, start something new
I Ching: 28 (Da Guo), Preponderance of the Great	You may feel weighted down and loaded to the breaking point. You must keep your wits about you, maintain your equanimity, and be prepared for sudden changes.
Crowley/Golden Dawn Labels	The Queen of the Thrones of Air
Crowley/Golden Dawn Meanings	Perceptive, observant, subtle, swift, confident, just, individualistic, graceful, fond of dancing and balancing; cruel, sly, deceitful, unreliable
Etteilla Meanings (late 1700s)	Widowhood, privation, poverty, sterility. *(R):* A bad woman, bigotry, malice, artifice, hypocrisy.
Some Contemporary Meanings	A perceptive independent woman; a widow; one who has suffered loss, loneliness, grief, deprivation, or sorrow; vigilant, impartial, analytical, austere, shrewd, stern

King of Swords (Crowley's Prince)–Air of Air	Keywords & Associations
Kings: Airy part of Air	Mature adult male, boss, father figure; rank, power, wisdom, authority, duty, worldly influence, expertise
Element: Air (Wet > Hot)	Logic, analysis, strategy, communication, decision making
Suit: Swords/Scimitars	Mental activity, conflict, separation, justice; phallic symbol
Element: Air (Wet > Hot)	Logic, intellect, strategy, analysis, communication, transport
Primary Quality: Wet	Fluid, adaptable, receptive, obliging, flexible, imaginative
Secondary Quality: Hot	Dynamic, expansive, moving up & outward, exuberant
Zodiac: 20 Capricorn–20 Aquarius	11 Jan–08 Feb (tropical); *03 Feb–04 Mar (sidereal)*
Corresponding Houses: 10th, 11th	Authority, reputation, honor, friends, groups, hopes, wishes
Classical & Modern Sign Rulers:	Saturn, Saturn/Uranus
Exalted Planet:	Mars is exalted in Capricorn
Decan rulers:	Sun, Venus, Mercury
Modality: Primarily Fixed	The urge to sustain, stabilize, and make lasting; purposeful, firm, enduring, self-contained, slow to change
I Ching: 57 (Xun), Subtle Influence	Imitate the wind as you gradually work toward your goal in a gentle, patient, and consistent manner.
Crowley/Golden Dawn Labels	The Prince of the Chariot of the Winds
Crowley/Golden Dawn Meanings	Intellectual, clever, rational, unstable as to purpose, full of ideas, overly cautious; harsh, malicious, plotting, obstinate, unreliable, difficult to understand
Etteilla Meanings (late 1700s)	A lawyer, man of law, judge, attorney, businessman, physician, advocate. *(R):* Inhumanity, cruelty, perversity.
Some Contemporary Meanings	An analytical, forceful man who is clever with words; a commanding professional, a person of ideas, a man in uniform; decisiveness, logic, authority, justice, impartiality

Section 4: The Suit of PENTACLES, COINS, or DISKS	
Ace of Pentacles	**Keywords & Associations**
Number: 1 (active, masculine)	Initial spark, inspiration, seed, new growth, strength, phallus
Suit: Disks/Coins/Pentacles	Material well-being, steady effort, achievements, work, money, health, the body, studies, prudence; a womb symbol
Element: Earth (Dry > Cold)	Tangible reality, body functioning, security, stability
Primary Quality: Dry	Sharply defined, rigid, decisive, abrupt, self-determined
Secondary Quality: Cold	Inner-directed, joining together, centered, calming
Crowley/Golden Dawn Labels	Root of the Powers of Earth
Crowley/Golden Dawn Meanings	The phallus as seen head-on (directly facing the urethral meatus of the glans penis). The seed of the element Earth.
Etteilla Meanings (late 1700s)	Perfect joy, contentment, happiness; the perfect medicine; the color red. *(R):* Riches, opulence, capital.
Some Contemporary Meanings	Material gain, power, wealth, a raise, promotion, new job, career change, new source of income, documents related to business or practical matters, a manuscript

Two of Pentacles (Jupiter–Capricorn)	Keywords & Associations
Number: 2 (passive, feminine)	Duality, dialogue, balanced forces, crossroads, decision point, relationship issues, gestation, the vaginal orifice
Suit: Disks/Coins/Pentacles	Material well-being, steady effort, achievements, work, money, health, the body, studies, prudence; a womb symbol
Element: Earth (Dry > Cold)	Tangible reality, body functioning, security, stability
Primary Quality: Dry	Sharply defined, rigid, decisive, abrupt, self-determined
Secondary Quality: Cold	Inner-directed, joining together, centered, calming
Zodiac Sign: Capricorn	Ambitious, prudent, realistic, disciplined, savvy, randy
Analogous House: 10th	Career, reputation, worldly power, honors, status, mother
Sign Ruler: Saturn (malefic)	Structure, limits, delay, duty, fear, loss, obstacle, burden
Exalted Planet: Mars (malefic)	Force, fight, virility, phallus, war, cutting, desire to win
1st Decan (0–10 degrees of Capricorn: December 22–January 1) Agrippa & [Picatrix]	"…the form of a woman, and a man carrying full bags; and the signification of these is for to go forth and to rejoice, to gain and to lose with weakness and baseness" [liveliness, adventurousness; ups and downs in powerlessness, weakness and contempt]
Decan Ruler: Jupiter (benefic)	Expansion, excess, luck, protection, gain, profit, adventure
Modality: Cardinal	The urge to rouse, lead, put into action, start something new
Crowley/Golden Dawn Labels	Lord of Change/Harmonious Change
Crowley/Golden Dawn Meanings	Pleasant change, visit with friends
Etteilla Meanings (late 1700s)	Embarrassment, difficulty, obstacle, confusion, disquiet. (R): literature, writing, book, erudition, letter of exchange.
Some Contemporary Meanings	Ups and downs, juggling commitments, apportioning duties and resources, multitasking, staying afloat, weighing options, harmony amidst change, relocation, literary ability

Three of Pentacles (Mars–Capricorn)	Keywords & Associations
Number: 3 (active, masculine)	Trinity, gaiety, group effort, creative expression; to plan, direct, consult, bear fruit; the first triangular number
Suit: Disks/Coins/Pentacles	Effort, work, money, health, prudence; a womb symbol
Element: Earth (Dry > Cold)	Tangible reality, body functioning, security, stability
Primary Quality: Dry	Sharply defined, rigid, decisive, abrupt, self-determined
Secondary Quality: Cold	Inner-directed, joining together, centered, calming
Zodiac Sign: Capricorn	Ambitious, prudent, realistic, disciplined, savvy, randy
Analogous House: 10th	Career, reputation, worldly power, honors, status, mother
Sign Ruler: Saturn (malefic)	Structure, limits, delay, duty, fear, loss, obstacle, burden
Exalted Planet: *Mars*	See Mars under Decan Ruler
2nd Decan (10–20 degrees of Capricorn: January 1–January 11) Agrippa & [Picatrix]	"…two women, and a man looking towards a Bird flying in the Air; and the signification of these is for the requiring those things which cannot be done, and for the searching after those things which cannot be known" [striving for that which cannot be known or attained and for which no end is in view]
Decan Ruler: Mars (malefic)	Force, fight, virility, phallus, war, cutting, desire to win
Modality: Cardinal	The urge to rouse, lead, put into action, start something new
Crowley/Golden Dawn Labels	Lord of Work. Material Works.
Crowley/Golden Dawn Meanings	Engineering, construction, paid employment, business transactions
Etteilla Meanings (late 1700s)	Nobility, noble deeds, greatness of soul; celebrated, important, illustrious. *(R):* childishness, frivolity, baseness, cowardice.
Some Contemporary Meanings	Creatively building something in collaboration with others, accomplishment, skill, artistry, craftsmanship, recognition, employment, teamwork, excellence, attention to detail

Four of Pentacles (Sun–Capricorn)	Keywords & Associations
Number: 4 (passive, feminine)	Steady, stable, safe, structured; to solidify, order, manifest, establish, lay foundations; the transition from 3 to 5
Suit: Disks/Coins/Pentacles	Material well-being, steady effort, achievements, work, money, health, the body, studies, prudence; a womb symbol
Element: Earth (Dry > Cold)	Tangible reality, body functioning, security, stability
Primary Quality: Dry	Sharply defined, rigid, decisive, abrupt, self-determined
Secondary Quality: Cold	Inner-directed, joining together, centered, calming
Zodiac Sign: Capricorn	Ambitious, prudent, realistic, disciplined, savvy, randy
Analogous House: 10th	Career, reputation, worldly power, honors, status, mother
Sign Ruler: Saturn (malefic)	Structure, limits, delay, duty, fear, loss, obstacle, burden
Exalted Planet: Mars (malefic)	Force, fight, virility, phallus, war, cutting, desire to win
3rd Decan (20–30 degrees of Capricorn: January 11–January 21) Agrippa & [Picatrix]	"…a woman chaste in body, and wise in her work, and a banker gathering his money together on the table; the signification of this is to govern in prudence, in covetousness of money, and in avarice" [vehemence, craving, usury, greed, insatiability]
Decan ruler: Sun	Dominion, leadership, mastery, honor, triumph, fatherhood
Modality: Cardinal	The urge to rouse, lead, put into action, start something new
Crowley/Golden Dawn Labels	Lord of Power. Earthly Power.
Crowley/Golden Dawn Meanings	Gain of money and influence, a gift
Etteilla Meanings (late 1700s)	Gifts, a present, generosity, benefit, offering, white, lunar, medicine. *(R):* Pregnant, cloister, boundaries, obstacles.
Some Contemporary Meanings	Valuing the power of wealth, desiring long-term security, hoarding, holding on tight, wanting more; materialism, financial conservatism, fear of change, reluctance to share

Five of Pentacles (Mercury–Taurus)	Keywords & Associations
Number: 5 (active, masculine)	Disruption, crisis, challenge, instability, uncertainty, break in routine, adjustment, the five senses, the human body
Suit: Disks/Coins/Pentacles	Effort, work, money, health, prudence; a womb symbol
Element: Earth (Dry > Cold)	Tangible reality, body functioning, security, stability
Primary Quality: Dry	Sharply defined, rigid, decisive, abrupt, self-determined
Secondary Quality: Cold	Inner-directed, joining together, centered, calming
Zodiac Sign: Taurus	Persistent, security-conscious, sensual, self-indulgent
Analogous House: 2nd	Finances, income, values, resources, movable goods
Sign Ruler: Venus (benefic)	Love, attraction, beauty, fun, friendship, sensual pleasure
Exalted Planet: Moon	Instability, change, periodicity, moods, instinct, mother, silver
1st Decan (0–10 degrees of Taurus: April 21–May 1) Agrippa & [Picatrix]	"…a naked man, an Archer, Harvester or Husbandman, and goeth forth to sow, plough, build, people, and divide the earth, according to the rules of Geometry" [plowing, sowing, building, culture, education, wisdom, surveying, geometry]
Decan Ruler: Mercury	News, communication, travel, speed, thought, cunning
Modality: Fixed	The urge to sustain, stabilize, and make lasting; purposeful, firm, enduring, self-contained, slow to change
Crowley/Golden Dawn Labels	Lord of Worry. Material Trouble.
Crowley/Golden Dawn Meaning	Strain and inaction, loss of job or money, financial worries
Etteilla Meanings (late 1700s)	Lovers, spouse, concord, suitability. (R): Disorder, trouble, misconduct, damage, dissipation, consumption.
Some Contemporary Meanings	Money problems, hard times, risk of loss, dissipated living, ill health, domestic disruption, marital discord, a romantic breakup; feeling alone, needy, bereft, or out in the cold

Six of Pentacles (Moon–Taurus)	Keywords & Associations
Number: 6 (passive, feminine)	Sharing, generosity, kindness, balance, equilibrium, smooth sailing, transition; the second triangular number
Suit: Disks/Coins/Pentacles	Material well-being, steady effort, achievements, work, money, health, the body, studies, prudence; a womb symbol
Element: Earth (Dry > Cold)	Tangible reality, body functioning, security, stability
Primary Quality: Dry	Sharply defined, rigid, decisive, abrupt, self-determined
Secondary Quality: Cold	Inner-directed, joining together, centered, calming
Zodiac Sign: Taurus	Persistent, security-conscious, sensual, self-indulgent
Analogous House: 2nd	Finances, income, values, resources, movable goods
Sign Ruler: Venus (benefic)	Love, attraction, beauty, fun, friendship, sensual pleasure
Exalted Planet: *Moon*	See *Moon* under Decan Ruler
2nd Decan (10–20 degrees of Taurus: May 1–May 11) Agrippa & [Picatrix]	" …a naked man, holding in his hand a key; it giveth power, nobility, and dominion over people" [power, glory, dominion, devastation of lands, oppression of subjects]
Decan ruler: *Moon*	Instability, change, periodicity, moods, instinct, mother, silver
Modality: Fixed	The urge to sustain, stabilize, and make lasting; purposeful, firm, enduring, self-contained, slow to change
Crowley/Golden Dawn Labels	Lord of Success. Material Success.
Crowley/Golden Dawn Meanings	Transient success, prosperity in business
Etteilla Meanings (late 1700s)	The present, now; assistant, witness; caring, vigilant. *(R):* Desire, passion, longing, cupidity, jealousy, illusion.
Some Contemporary Meanings	Financial success, gifts, a raise, a promotion, generosity, kindness, sharing resources, spending, bounty, loans, debts, accounting, funding, assistance, giving and receiving

Seven of Pentacles (Saturn–Taurus)	Keywords & Associations
Number: 7 (active, masculine)	A boundary or threshold, assessment, reflection, challenge, solitary action, sabbatical, sacredness, wisdom, mystery
Suit: Disks/Coins/Pentacles	Material well-being, steady effort, achievements, work, money, health, the body, studies, prudence; a womb symbol
Element: Earth (Dry > Cold)	Tangible reality, body functioning, security, stability
Primary Quality: Dry	Sharply defined, rigid, decisive, abrupt, self-determined
Secondary Quality: Cold	Inner-directed, joining together, centered, calming
Zodiac Sign: Taurus	Persistent, security-conscious, sensual, self-indulgent
Analogous House: 2nd	Finances, income, values, resources, movable goods
Sign Ruler: Venus (benefic)	Love, attraction, beauty, fun, friendship, sensual pleasure
Exalted Planet: Moon	Instability, change, periodicity, moods, instinct, mother, silver
3rd Decan (20–30 degrees of Taurus: May 11–May 22) Agrippa & [Picatrix]	"…a man in whose hand is a Serpent, and a dart, and is the image of necessity and profit, and also of misery & slavery" [humiliation, servitude, beatings, poverty, contempt]
Decan Ruler: Saturn (malefic)	Structure, limits, delay, duty, fear, loss, obstacle, burden
Modality: Fixed	The urge to sustain, stabilize, and make lasting; purposeful, firm, enduring, self-contained, slow to change
Crowley/Golden Dawn Labels	Lord of Failure. Success Unfulfilled.
Crowley/Golden Dawn Meanings	Blight, unprofitable speculation, work without pay
Etteilla Meanings (late 1700s)– possibly from the figures *rubeus* and *albus* of geomancy	A little money, riches, silverware, whiteness, candor, innocence, the moon. *(R):* Disquiet, affliction, chagrin, fear, care, diligence, suspicion, mistrust.
Some Contemporary Meanings	Pausing to assess and reevaluate, delayed success, little return on investment, slow but steady progress, job dissatisfaction, a sabbatical, attraction to a coworker

Eight of Pentacles (Sun–Virgo)	Keywords & Associations
Number: 8 (passive, feminine)	Worldly involvement, taking action, managing, putting in order, organizing; efficient movement, power, success
Suit: Disks/Coins/Pentacles	Material well-being, steady effort, achievements, work, money, health, the body, studies, prudence; a womb symbol
Element: Earth (Dry > Cold)	Tangible reality, body functioning, security, stability
Primary Quality: Dry	Sharply defined, rigid, decisive, abrupt, self-determined
Secondary Quality: Cold	Inner-directed, joining together, centered, calming
Zodiac Sign: Virgo	Meticulous, orderly, modest, practical, analytical, critical
Analogous House: 6th	Service, daily routine, health, illness, pets, coworkers
Sign Ruler: Mercury	News, communication, travel, speed, thought, cunning
Exalted Planet: *Mercury*	See *Mercury* above
1st Decan (0–10 degrees of Virgo: August 24–September 3) Agrippa & [Picatrix]	"…a good maid, and a man casting seeds; it signifieth getting of wealth, ordering of diet, plowing, sowing, and peopling" [sowing, plowing, herbs, plants, building, accumulation of assets, well-ordered living]
Decan ruler: Sun	Dominion, leadership, mastery, honor, triumph, fatherhood
Modality: Mutable	Adaptable, flexible, transitional; the urge to move on, let go and make way for the new
Crowley/Golden Dawn Labels	Lord of Prudence
Crowley/Golden Dawn Meanings	Prudence in material affairs, skill, artfulness, cunning
Etteilla Meanings (late 1700s)	A dark girl; passive, *grande nuit* [grand night]. *(R):* siphoning, avarice, usury.
Some Contemporary Meanings	Training, steady effort, continuing education, dedication, learning by doing, perfecting a skill, enjoyment of work, attention to detail, using one's skills to make money

Nine of Pentacles (Venus–Virgo)	Keywords & Associations
Number: 9 (active, masculine)	Achievement, climax, intensity, fullness, integration, completion, fulfillment; the last of the single digits
Suit: Disks/Coins/Pentacles	Effort, work, money, health, prudence; a womb symbol
Element: Earth (Dry > Cold)	Tangible reality, body functioning, security, stability
Primary Quality: Dry	Sharply defined, rigid, decisive, abrupt, self-determined
Secondary Quality: Cold	Inner-directed, joining together, centered, calming
Zodiac Sign: Virgo	Meticulous, orderly, modest, practical, analytical, critical
Analogous House: 6th	Service, daily routine, health, illness, pets, coworkers
Sign Ruler: Mercury	News, communication, travel, speed, thought, cunning
Exalted Planet: *Mercury*	See *Mercury* above
2nd Decan (10–20 degrees of Virgo: September 3–September 13) Agrippa & [Picatrix]	" …a black man clothed with a skin, and a man having a bush of hair, holding a bag; they signify gain, scraping together of wealth, and covetousness" [acquisition, profit seeking, hoarding, avarice, greed, denial of rights]
Decan Ruler: Venus (benefic)	Love, attraction, beauty, fun, friendship, sensual pleasure
Modality: Mutable	Adaptable, flexible, transitional; the urge to move on, let go, and make way for the new
Crowley/Golden Dawn Labels	Lord of Gain. Material Gain.
Crowley/Golden Dawn Meanings	Luck in material affairs, favor, popularity, inheritance, improved finances
Etteilla Meanings (late 1700s)	Effect, realization, accomplishment, success. *(R):* Deception, vain hopes, aborted projects.
Some Contemporary Meanings	Material abundance, financial gain, unearned income, luxury, gentility, solitary pleasure, soothing time alone, self-reliance, simplicity, gardening, pets, love of nature

Ten of Pentacles (Mercury–Virgo)	Keywords & Associations
Number: 10 (passive, feminine)	End result; overfull; anticlimax; ending and transition; one too many (9 + 1 = 10); third triangular number
Suit: Disks/Coins/Pentacles	Effort, work, money, health, prudence; a womb symbol
Element: Earth (Dry > Cold)	Tangible reality, body functioning, security, stability
Primary Quality: Dry	Sharply defined, rigid, decisive, abrupt, self-determined
Secondary Quality: Cold	Inner-directed, joining together, centered, calming
Zodiac Sign: Virgo	Meticulous, orderly, modest, practical, analytical, critical
Analogous House: 6th	Service, daily routine, health, illness, pets, coworkers
Sign Ruler: Mercury	News, communication, travel, speed, thought, cunning
Exalted Planet: *Mercury*	See Sign Ruler, *Mercury*, above
3rd Decan (20–30 degrees of Virgo: September 13–September 23) Agrippa & [Picatrix]	"…a white woman and deaf, or an old man leaning on a staff; the signification of this is to show weakness, infirmity, loss of members, destruction of trees, and depopulation of lands" [ageing, bodily infirmity, weakness, impotence, chronic illness, the cutting down of trees, the ruins of civilizations]
Decan Ruler: Mercury	See Sign Ruler, Mercury, above
Modality: Mutable	Adaptable, flexible; the urge to let go and move on
Crowley/Golden Dawn Labels	Lord of Wealth
Crowley/Golden Dawn Meanings	Riches
Etteilla Meanings (late 1700s)	House, household economy, savings, family, posterity, race, dwelling, den. *(R):* Unforeseen occurrence, gamble, lot, fate, destiny.
Some Contemporary Meanings	Family and job security, material success, big money, property transactions, generational ties, tradition, heritage, inheritance, care of pets, wise use of resources

Page/Princess of Pentacles–Earth of Earth	Keywords & Associations
Pages: Earthy part of Earth	Child, messenger, helper, apprentice; messages, opinions, news; study, curiosity, new learning, youthful enthusiasm
Element: Earth (Dry > Cold)	Tangible reality, body functioning, security, stability
Suit: Disks/Coins/Pentacles	Material well-being, steady effort, achievements, work, money, health, the body, studies, prudence; a womb symbol
Element: Earth (Dry > Cold)	See *Earth* above
Primary Quality: Dry	Sharply defined, rigid, decisive, abrupt, self-determined
Secondary Quality: Cold	Inner-directed, joining together, centered, calming
Quadrant of Earth	Europe and Africa: the quarter of the Earth between longitudes 58.87°W and 31.13°E
I Ching: 52 (Gen), Keeping Still	Success results from meditative reflection, becoming centered, and focusing on what is truly important.
Crowley/Golden Dawn Labels	The Princess of the Echoing Hills: the Rose of the Palace of Earth
Crowley/Golden Dawn Meanings	Generous, kind, careful, benevolent, diligent, persevering
Etteilla Meanings (late 1700s)	A dark youth; reflection, study, application, work, apprenticeship. *(R):* Profession, luxury, liberality, abundance, benefit.
Some Contemporary Meanings	Love of learning, diligence, applied effort, research, scholarship, self-reliance, practicality, concentration, changes at work, news about family or money, pregnancy

Knight of Pentacles– Fire of Earth	Keywords & Associations
Knights: Fiery part of Earth	Youthful or immature adult males, armed men; action, adventure, assertion, travel, swiftness, movement, comings and goings of matters, offers, love affairs
Element: Fire (Hot > Dry)	Vitality, life energy, expansion, ambition, enthusiasm
Suit: Disks/Coins/Pentacles	Effort, work, money, health, prudence; a womb symbol
Element: Earth (Dry > Cold)	Tangible reality, body functioning, security, stability
Primary Quality: Dry	Sharply defined, rigid, decisive, abrupt, self-determined
Secondary Quality: Cold	Inner-directed, joining together, centered, calming
Zodiac: 20 Leo–20 Virgo	13 Aug–12 Sep (tropical); *06 Sep–06 Oct (sidereal)*
Corresponding Houses: 5th, 6th	Children, romance, daily work, illness, pets, coworkers
Classical & Modern Sign Rulers:	Sun, Mercury
Exalted Planet: Mercury (in Virgo)	News, communication, travel, speed, thought, cunning
Decan rulers:	Mars, Sun, Venus
Modality: Primarily Mutable	Adaptable, flexible; the urge to let go and move on
I Ching: 62 (Xiao Kwo), Preponderance of the Small	Good fortune depends on setting achievable goals, taking measured steps, and attending to the details.
Crowley/Golden Dawn Labels	The Lord of the Wide and Fertile Land: the King of the Spirits of Earth
Crowley/Golden Dawn Meanings	Dull, heavy, preoccupied with material things. Patient, plodding. Strong instincts. Not an intellectual.
Etteilla Meanings (late 1700s)	Usefulness, profit, advantage. *(R):* Peace, repose, laziness, inactivity, recreation, sleep, discouragement.
Some Contemporary Meanings	A reliable, methodical man; patience, hard work, a slow course of action; care of the body, love of nature, practicality, discomfort with emotions, travel by land

Queen of Pentacles– Water of Earth	Keywords & Associations
Queens: Watery part of Earth	Mature adult females, mother figures, powerful women, influential friends; nurturing, support, sensitivity
Element: Water (Cold > Wet)	Affection, empathy, support, nurturing, emotions, intuition
Suit: Disks/Coins/Pentacles	Effort, work, money, health, prudence; a womb symbol
Element: Earth (Dry > Cold)	Tangible reality, body functioning, security, stability
Primary Quality: Dry	Sharply defined, rigid, decisive, abrupt, self-determined
Secondary Quality: Cold	Inner-directed, joining together, centered, calming
Zodiac: 20 Sagittarius–20 Capricorn	13 Dec–10 Jan (tropical); *04 Jan–02 Feb (sidereal)*
Corresponding Houses: 9th, 10th	Higher learning, religion, journeys, career, reputation
Classical & Modern Sign Rulers:	Jupiter, Saturn
Exalted Planet:	Moon's South Node in Sagittarius. Mars in Capricorn.
Decan rulers:	Saturn, Jupiter, Mars
Modality: Primarily Cardinal	The urge to rouse, lead, put into action, start something new
I Ching: 31 (Xian), Wooing	Mutual attraction, respect, and receptiveness are the foundation of an enduring relationship.
Crowley/Golden Dawn Labels	The Queen of the Thrones of Earth
Crowley/Golden Dawn Meanings	Motherly, kind, passive, affectionate, great-hearted, hard-working, intuitive, practical, sensible, quietly lustful.
Etteilla Meanings (late 1700s)	A dark lady; wealth, confidence, optimism, luxury, surety, toughness, frankness. *(R):* Doubt, uncertainty, disquiet, vacillation.
Some Contemporary Meanings	A practical family-oriented woman; a resourceful manager; generosity, prosperity, business sense, fertility, patience, care of the body, motherliness, love of nature

King of Pentacles (Crowley's Prince)–Air of Earth	Keywords & Associations
Kings: Airy part of Earth	Mature adult male, boss, father figure; rank, power, wisdom, authority, duty, worldly influence, expertise
Element: Air (Wet > Hot)	Logic, analysis, strategy, communication, decision making
Suit: Disks/Coins/Pentacles	Effort, work, money, health, prudence; a womb symbol
Element: Earth (Dry > Cold)	Tangible reality, body functioning, security, stability
Primary Quality: Dry	Sharply defined, rigid, decisive, abrupt, self-determined
Secondary Quality: Cold	Inner-directed, joining together, centered, calming
Zodiac: 20 Aries–20 Taurus	11 Apr–10 May (tropical); *05 May–04 Jun (sidereal)*
Corresponding Houses: 1st, 2nd	Birth, self-image, self-development, vitality, the body, identity formation, money, values, possessions
Sign Rulers:	Mars, Venus
Exalted Planets:	Sun is exalted in Aries. Moon is exalted in Taurus.
Decan rulers:	Venus, Mercury, Moon
Modality: Primarily Fixed	The urge to sustain, stabilize, and make lasting; purposeful, firm, enduring, self-contained, slow to change
I Ching: 53 (Jian), Infiltrating	Success depends on a careful, detailed stepwise approach.
Crowley/Golden Dawn Labels	The Prince of the Chariot of Earth
Crowley/Golden Dawn Meanings	Practical, energetic, steadfast, persevering, competent, ingenious, thoughtful, trustworthy, a good manager.
Etteilla Meanings (late 1700s)	A dark gentleman; businessman, professor, negotiator, stock market speculator; science, mathematics. *(R):* weakness, defect, deformity, corruption.
Some Contemporary Meanings	A hard-working, practical man; a skilled manager, benefactor, or pillar of the community; material success, common sense, business acumen, attention to detail

Appendix B:
Waite's Original Conception of the Celtic Cross

Doing a reading is as effortless as opening a garden gate and stepping into a new
landscape. I simply observe the garden; I don't have to create it. [244]

JOHN HUDDLESTON

The following material comes from Arthur Edward Waite's *The Pictorial Key to the Tarot* (1911),
which is in the public domain. [245] It is such an important document that I have included it here
for handy reference. Note that the order in which Waite originally laid out the Celtic Cross
spread differs slightly from the order presented in chapter one of this text. Waite makes a large
cross around the central two-card cross. My preference is to make a circular wreath around the
central cross. The end result is the same layout but with a different numbering of the cards.

An Ancient Celtic Method of Divination
by Arthur Edward Waite (1911)

This mode of divination is the most suitable for obtaining an answer to a definite question.
The Diviner first selects a card to represent the person or, matter about which inquiry is
made. This card is called the Significator. Should he wish to ascertain something in connexion

....

244   John Huddleston, quoted in Elizabeth Lloyd Mayer, *Extraordinary Knowing: Science, Skepticism,
      and the Inexplicable Powers of the Human Mind* (New York, NY: Bantam Books, 2007), p. 54.

245   Waite, *Pictorial Key* online.

with himself he takes the one which corresponds to his personal description. A Knight should be chosen as the Significator if the subject of inquiry is a man of forty years old and upward; a King should be chosen for any male who is under that age a Queen for a woman who is over forty years and a Page for any female of less age.

The four Court Cards in Wands represent very fair people, with yellow or auburn hair, fair complexion and blue eyes. The Court Cards in Cups signify people with light brown or dull fair hair and grey or blue eyes. Those in Swords stand for people having hazel or grey eyes, dark brown hair and dull complexion. Lastly, the Court Cards in Pentacles are referred to persons with very dark brown or black hair, dark eyes and sallow or swarthy complexions. These allocations are subject, however, to the following reserve, which will prevent them being taken too conventionally. You can be guided on occasion by the known temperament of a person; one who is exceedingly dark may be very energetic, and would be better represented by a Sword card than a Pentacle. On the other hand, a very fair subject who is indolent and lethargic should be referred to Cups rather than to Wands.

If it is more convenient for the purpose of a divination to take as the Significator the matter about which inquiry is to be made, that Trump or small card should be selected which has a meaning corresponding to the matter. Let it be supposed that the question is: Will a lawsuit be necessary? In this case, take the Trump No. 11, or justice, as the Significator. This has reference to legal affairs. But if the question is: Shall I be successful in my lawsuit? One of the Court Cards must be chosen as the Significator. Subsequently, consecutive divinations may be performed to ascertain the course of the process itself and its result to each of the parties concerned.

Having selected the Significator, place it on the table, face upwards. Then shuffle and cut the rest of the pack three times, keeping the faces of the cards downwards.

Turn up the top or FIRST CARD of the pack; cover the Significator with it, and say: This covers him. This card gives the influence which is affecting the person or matter of inquiry generally, the atmosphere of it in which the other currents work.

Turn up the SECOND CARD and lay it across the FIRST, saying: This crosses him. It shews the nature of the obstacles in the matter. If it is a favourable card, the opposing forces will not be serious, or it may indicate that something good in itself will not be productive of good in the particular connexion.

Turn up the THIRD CARD; place it above the Significator, and say: This crowns him. It represents (a) the Querent's aim or ideal in the matter; (b) the best that can be achieved under the circumstances, but that which has not yet been made actual.

Turn up the FOURTH CARD; place it below the Significator, and say: This is beneath him. It shews the foundation or basis of the matter, that which has already passed into actuality and which the Significator has made his own.

Turn up the FIFTH CARD; place it on the side of the Significator from which he is looking, and say: This is behind him. It gives the influence that is just passed, or is now passing away.

N.B.—If the Significator is a Trump or any small card that cannot be said to face either way, the Diviner must decide before beginning the operation which side he will take it as facing.

Turn up the SIXTH CARD; place it on the side that the Significator is facing, and say: This is before him. It shews the influence that is coming into action and will operate in the near future.

The cards are now disposed in the form of a cross, the Significator—covered by the First Card—being in the centre.

The next four cards are turned up in succession and placed one above the other in a line, on the right hand side of the cross.

The first of these, or the SEVENTH CARD of the operation, signifies himself—that is, the Significator—whether person or thing-and shews its position or attitude in the circumstances.

The EIGHTH CARD signifies his house, that is, his environment and the tendencies at work therein which have an effect on the matter—for instance, his position in life, the influence of immediate friends, and so forth.

The NINTH CARD gives his hopes or fears in the matter.

The TENTH is what will come, the final result, the culmination which is brought about by the influences shewn by the other cards that have been turned up in the divination.

It is on this card that the Diviner should especially concentrate his intuitive faculties and his memory in respect of the official divinatory meanings attached thereto. It should embody whatsoever you may have divined from the other cards on the table, including the Significator itself and concerning him or it, not excepting such lights upon higher significance as might fall like sparks from heaven if the card which serves for the oracle, the card for reading, should happen to be a Trump Major.

The operation is now completed; but should it happen that the last card is of a dubious nature, from which no final decision can be drawn, or which does not appear to indicate the ultimate conclusion of the affair, it may be well to repeat the operation, taking in this case the Tenth Card as the Significator, instead of the one previously used. The pack must be again shuffled and cut three times and the first ten cards laid out as before. By this a more detailed account of "What will come" may be obtained.

If in any divination the Tenth Card should be a Court Card, it shews that the subject of the divination falls ultimately into the hands of a person represented by that card, and its end depends mainly on him. In this event also it is useful to take the Court Card in question as the Significator in a fresh operation, and discover what is the nature of his influence in the matter and to what issue he will bring it.

Great facility may be obtained by this method in a comparatively short time, allowance being always made for the gifts of the operator-that is to say, his faculty of insight, latent or developed-and it has the special advantage of being free from all complications.

I here append a diagram of the cards as laid out in this mode of divination. The Significator is here facing to the left.

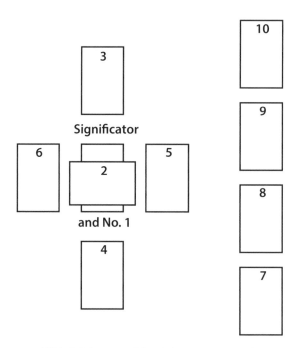

Waite's Diagram of the Celtic Cross Spread.

The Significator.

1. What covers him
2. What crosses him.
3. What crowns him.
4. What is beneath him.
5. What is behind him.
6. What is before him.
7. Himself.
8. His house.
9. His hopes or fears.
10. What will come.

Notes on the Practice of Divination

1. Before beginning the operation, formulate your question definitely, and repeat it aloud.

2. Make your mind as blank as possible while shuffling the cards.

3. Put out of the mind personal bias and preconceived ideas as far as possible, or your judgment will be tinctured thereby.

4. On this account it is more easy to divine correctly for a stranger than for yourself or a friend.

Appendix C:
Elements, Timing, Pips, and Court Cards

Elemental Attributions of the Court Cards

Wands:

- Knight of Wands, fiery part of Fire (HHHH DD)
- Queen of Wands, watery part of Fire (HH CC D W)
- Prince/King of Wands, airy part of Fire (HHH WW D)
- Princess/Page of Wands, earthy part of Fire (DDD HH C)

Cups:

- Knight of Cups, fiery part of Water (CC HH D W)
- Queen of Cups, watery part of Water (CCCC WW)
- Prince/King of Cups, airy part of Water (WWW CC H)
- Princess/Page of Cups, earthy part of Water (CCC DD W)

Swords:

- Knight of Swords, fiery part of Air (HHH WW D)
- Queen of Swords, watery part of Air (WWW CC H)
- Prince/King of Swords, airy part of Air (WWWW HH)
- Princess/Page of Swords, earthy part of Air (WW DD H C)

Pentacles:

- Knight of Pentacles/Disks, fiery part of Earth (DDD HH C)
- Queen of Pentacles/Disks, watery part of Earth (CCC DD W)
- Prince/King of Pentacles/Disks, airy part of Earth (DD WW H C)
- Princess/Page of Pentacles/Disks, earthy part of Earth (DDDD CC)

Timing and Minor Arcana Associations of the Court Cards

The Thoth Queens refer to the first decan of the cardinal signs and its two adjacent decans. The Queens oversee the birth of each new season. Thoth Princes (Waite's Kings) correspond to the first decan of the fixed signs and its adjoining decans. The Thoth Knights govern the first decan of the mutable signs and its adjacent decans. For readers who wish to use the cards for timing events, dates are provided in both the tropical and sidereal zodiacs. The Golden Dawn preferred the sidereal zodiac for timing with the tarot.

The tables also include the minor arcana cards associated with each non-Page court card. When a King, Queen, or Knight appears in a reading, the person or situation referred to is likely to be dealing with the themes of the associated minor arcana cards. For example, in Jane's reading in chapter one, the Queen of Swords appeared in the near-future position. The Queen of Swords rules over the Ten of Pentacles and the Two and Three of Swords. Thus, in the near future, Jane is likely to confront matters related to family security, inheritance, indecision, feeling stalemated, sorrow, and emotional pain due to loss. Her mother died not long after the reading.

In Jake's Hanged Man reading in chapter eight, the King of Swords appeared in the center of his three-card spread. The King of Swords rules over the Four of Pentacles and the Five and Six of Swords. Thus, Jake's present circumstances may involve issues of greed, hoarding, dishonor, defeat, a journey, and moving away from troubles. He was facing a trip to prison for illegally collecting his deceased father's benefits.

The tarot Pages are not included in the tables because the Golden Dawn assigned them to the heavens around the North Pole and thus they cover the four quarters of the Earth as measured eastward around the equator, starting at the longitude of the Great Pyramid of Giza (coordinates: 29°58 33 North, 31°07 49 East).

Tropical versus Sidereal Zodiac in the Early 21st Century			
Sign	Glyph	Tropical Zodiac	Sidereal Zodiac
Aries	♈	21 March–20 April	*14 April–15 May*
Taurus	♉	21 April–21 May	*15 May–15 June*
Gemini	♊	22 May–21 June	*15 June–16 July*
Cancer	♋	22 June–22 July	*16 July–17 August*
Leo	♌	23 July–23 August	*17 August–17 September*
Virgo	♍	24 August–22 September	*17 September–17 October*
Libra	♎	23 September–23 October	*17 October–16 November*
Scorpio	♏	24 October–22 November	*16 November–16 December*
Sagittarius	♐	23 November–21 December	*16 December–14 January*
Capricorn	♑	22 December–20 January	*14 January–13 February*
Aquarius	♒	21 January–18 February	*13 February–15 March*
Pisces	♓	19 February–20 March	*15 March–14 April*

Thoth & Waite Queens
First Decan of the Cardinal Signs plus Flanking Decans

Thoth/Waite Queens (watery)	→ First Cardinal Decan	Full Range of Attribution: Last Mutable + first two Cardinal decans (Associated Minor Cards)	Approximate Dates: Tropical; Sidereal
Wands (Fire)	0–10 Aries (Two of Wands)	20 Pisces–20 Aries (10 of Cups, 2 & 3 of Wands)	11 Mar–10 Apr; *04 Apr–04 May*
Cups (Water)	0–10 Cancer (Two of Cups)	20 Gemini–20 Cancer (10 of Swords, 2 & 3 of Cups)	12 June–12 Jul; *06 Jul–05 Aug*
Swords (Air)	0–10 Libra (Two of Swords)	20 Virgo–20 Libra (10 of Pentacles, 2 & 3 of Swords)	13 Sep–13 Oct; *07 Oct–05 Nov*
Pentacles (Earth)	0–10 Capricorn (Two of Pentacles)	20 Sagittarius–20 Capricorn (10 of Wands, 2 & 3 of Pentacles)	13 Dec–10 Jan; *04 Jan–02 Feb*

Thoth Princes (Waite Kings)
First Decan of the Fixed Signs plus Flanking Decans

Thoth Princes/ Waite Kings (airy)	→ First Fixed Decan	Full Range of Attribution: Last Cardinal + first two Fixed decans (Associated Minor Cards)	Approximate Dates: Tropical; Sidereal
Wands (Fire)	0–10 Leo (Five of Wands)	20 Cancer–20 Leo (4 of Cups, 5 & 6 of Wands)	13 July–12 Aug; *06 Aug–05 Sep*
Cups (Water)	0–10 Scorpio (Five of Cups)	20 Libra–20 Scorpio (4 of Swords, 5 & 6 of Cups)	14 Oct–12 Nov; *06 Nov–05 Dec*
Swords (Air)	0–10 Aquarius (Five of Swords)	20 Capricorn–20 Aquarius (4 of Pentacles, 5 & 6 of Swords)	11 Jan–08 Feb; *03 Feb–04 Mar*
Pentacles (Earth)	0–10 Taurus (Five of Pentacles)	20 Aries–20 Taurus (4 of Wands, 5 & 6 of Pentacles)	11 Apr–10 May; *05 May–04 Jun*

Thoth & Waite Knights First Decan of the Mutable Signs plus Flanking Decans			
Thoth/Waite Knights (fiery)	→ First Mutable Decan	Full Range of Attribution: Last Fixed + first two Mutable decans (Associated Minor Cards)	Approximate Dates: Tropical; Sidereal
Wands (Fire)	0–10 Sagittarius (Eight of Wands)	20 Scorpio–20 Sagittarius (7 of Cups, 8 & 9 of Wands)	13 Nov–12 Dec; *06 Dec–03 Jan*
Cups (Water)	0–10 Pisces (Eight of Cups)	20 Aquarius–20 Pisces (7 of Swords, 8 & 9 of Cups)	09 Feb–10 Mar; *05 Mar–04 Apr*
Swords (Air)	0–10 Gemini (Eight of Swords)	20 Taurus–20 Gemini (7 of Pentacles, 8 & 9 of Swords)	11 May–11 Jun; *05 Jun–05 Jul*
Pentacles (Earth)	0–10 Virgo (Eight of Pentacles)	20 Leo–20 Virgo (7 of Wands, 8 & 9 of Pentacles)	13 Aug–12 Sep; *06 Sep–06 Oct*

Bibliography

Almond, Jocelyn, and Keith Seddon. *Tarot for Relationships.* Northamptonshire, UK: The Aquarian Press, 1990.

Amberstone, Ruth Ann and Wald. *Tarot Tips.* Woodbury, MN: Llewellyn Publications, 2003.

———. *The Secret Language of Tarot.* San Francisco: Weiser Books, 2008.

Aristotle. *De Generatione et Corruptione,* trans. C.J.F. Williams. Oxford, UK: Clarendon Press, 1982.

Arroyo, Stephen. *Astrology, Psychology, and the Four Elements.* Sebastopol, CA: CRCS Publications, 1978.

Avelar, Helena, and Luis Ribeiro. *On the Heavenly Spheres, a Treatise on Traditional Astrology.* Tempe, AZ: American Federation of Astrologers, 2010.

Banzhaf, Hajo. *The Crowley Tarot.* Stamford, CT: U.S. Games Systems, 1995.

———. *The Tarot Handbook.* Stamford, CT: U.S. Games Systems, 1993.

Beitchman, Philip. *Alchemy of the Word: Cabala of the Renaissance.* Albany, NY: State University of New York Press, 1998.

Bing, Gertrud, ed. *"Picatrix" Das Ziel des Weisen von Pseudo-Magriti, Studien der Bibliothek Warburg,* Vol. 27, translated into German from the original Arabic text by Hellmut Ritter and Martin Plessner in 1933. London: The Warburg Institute, 1962. Online at http://warburg.sas.ac.uk/pdf/FBH295P31zg.pdf.

Brennan, Chris. *The Horoscopic Astrology Blog,* http://horoscopicastrologyblog.com/2007/06/11/the-thema-mundi/.

Brumbaugh, Robert S. *The Philosophers of Greece.* Albany, NY: State University of New York Press, 1982.

Burns, Robert. "Man Was Made to Mourn: A Dirge," accessed online at http://www.robertburns.org/works/55.shtml.

Bursten, Lee. *Universal Tarot of Marseille,* ill. Claude Burdel. Torino, Italy: Lo Scarabeo, 2006.

Carroll, Wilma. *The 2-Hour Tarot Tutor.* New York: Berkley Books, 2004.

Carter, Charles E.O. *The Principles of Astrology.* London: Quest Books, 1963.

Crowley, Aleister. *The Book of Thoth.* San Francisco: Weiser Books, 2008.

De Angeles, Ly. *Tarot, Theory and Practice.* Woodbury, MN: Llewellyn Publications, 2007.

Decker, Ronald. *Art and Arcana: Commentary on the Medieval Scapini Tarot.* Stamford, CT: U.S. Games Systems, 2004.

———. *The Esoteric Tarot: Ancient Sources Rediscovered in Hermeticism and Cabalah.* Wheaton, IL: Quest Books, 2013.

Dowson, Godfrey. *The Hermetic Tarot.* Stamford, CT: U.S. Games Systems, 2006.

Drury, Nevill. *The Tarot Workbook.* San Diego: Thunder Bay Press, 2004.

Duquette, Lon Milo. *Understanding Aleister Crowley's Thoth Tarot.* San Francisco: Weiser Books, 2003.

Ellershaw, Josephine. *Easy Tarot Reading*. Woodbury, MN: Llewellyn Publications, 2011.

Fairfield, Gail. *Choice Centered Tarot*. Smithville, IN: Ramp Creek Publishing, 1984.

Fenton-Smith, Paul. *Tarot Masterclass*. Crows Nest, NSW, Australia: Allen & Unwin, 2007.

Filipczak, Zirka Z. *Hot Dry Men, Cold Wet Women: The Theory of Humors in Western European Art*. New York: American Federation of Arts, 1997.

Fortune, Dion. *Practical Occultism in Daily Life*. Northamptonshire, UK: The Aquarian Press, 1976.

Frankl, Viktor E. *Man's Search for Meaning*. New York: Washington Square Press, Simon and Schuster, 1963.

Gibb, Douglas. *Tarot Eon*. A tarot blog, http://taroteon.com/.

Gray, Eden. *A Complete Guide to the Tarot*. New York: Bantam Books, 1972.

Graves, Robert. *The Greek Myths*. London: Penguin Books, 1992.

Greer, Mary. *Tarot for Your Self*. Hollywood, CA: Newcastle Publishing, 1984.

———. *The Complete Book of Tarot Reversals*. Woodbury, MN: Llewellyn, 2002.

Hughes-Barlow, Paul, and Catherine Chapman. *Beyond the Celtic Cross*. London, UK: Aeon Books, 2009.

Hughes-Barlow, Paul. *Super Tarot*. A tarot blog, http://supertarot.co.uk/.

Huson, Paul. *Dame Fortune's Wheel Tarot*. Torino, Italy: Lo Scarabeo, 2008.

———. *Mystical Origins of the Tarot*. Rochester, VT: Destiny Books, 2004.

Junjulas, Craig. *Psychic Tarot*. Stamford, CT: U.S. Games Systems, 1985.

Kaczynski, Richard. *Perdurabo: The Life of Aleister Crowley.* Berkeley, CA: North Atlantic Books, 2010.

Kaplan, Robert. *The Nothing That Is: A Natural History of Zero.* New York: Oxford University Press, 2000.

Kaplan, Stuart R. *Tarot Classic.* Stamford, CT: U.S. Games Systems, 2003.

———. *The Artwork & Times of Pamela Colman Smith.* Stamford, CT: U.S. Games Systems, 2009.

Katz, Marcus, and Tali Goodwin. *Tarot Flip.* Keswick, Cumbria, UK: Forge Press, 2010.

———. *Around the Tarot in 78 Days: A Personal Journey through the Cards.* Woodbury, MN: Llewellyn Publications, 2012.

Kenner, Corrine. *Tarot and Astrology.* Woodbury, MN: Llewellyn Publications, 2011.

Knight, Gareth. *The Magical World of the Tarot.* San Francisco: Weiser Books, 1996.

Lilly, William. *Christian Astrology (1647).* London: Regulus Publishing, 1985.

Louis, Anthony. *Tarot Plain and Simple.* St. Paul, MN: Llewellyn Publications, 1996.

———. *Horary Astrology: The History and Practice of Astro-Divination.* St. Paul, MN: Llewellyn Publications, 1991.

MacGregor, Trish, and Phyllis Vega. *Power Tarot.* New York: Fireside, 1998.

Marteau, Paul. *Le Tarot de Marseille.* Paris, France: Arts et Metiers Graphiques, 1949.

Mayer, Elizabeth Lloyd. *Extraordinary Knowing: Science, Skepticism, and the Inexplicable Powers of the Human Mind.* New York: Bantam Books, 2007.

Michelson, Teresa C. *The Complete Tarot Reader.* Woodbury, MN: Llewellyn Publications, 2005.

Moakley, Gertrude. *The Tarot Cards Painted by Bonifacio Bembo for the Visconti-Sforza Family: An Iconographic and Historical Study*. New York: New York Public Library, 1966.

Montgomery, Stephen. *People Patterns: A Modern Guide to the Four Temperaments*. Del Mar, CA: Archer Publications, 2002.

Morgan, Michele. *A Magical Course in Tarot*. Berkeley, CA: Conari Press, 2002.

Morin, Jean-Baptiste. *Astrologia Gallica, Book 22, Directions,* trans. James Herschel Holden. Tempe, AZ: American Federation of Astrologers, 1994.

Naparstek, Belleruth. *Your Sixth Sense*. San Francisco: HarperSanFrancisco, 1997.

Osho. *Osho Zen Tarot: The Transcendental Game of Zen*. New York: St. Martin's Press, 1995.

Place, Robert M. *Alchemy and the Tarot: An Examination of the Historical Connection With a Guide to the Alchemical Tarot*. Saugerties, NY: Robert M. Place, 2012.

———. *The Tarot: History, Symbolism, and Divination*. New York: Penguin Group, 2005.

Pollock, Rachel. *Tarot Wisdom, Spiritual Teachings and Deeper Meanings*. Woodbury, MN: Llewellyn Publications, 2008.

———. *The New Tarot Handbook*. Woodbury, MN: Llewellyn Publications, 2011.

Regardie, Israel. *The Golden Dawn: The Original Account of the Teaching, Rites & Ceremonies of the Hermetic Order,* sixth ed. St. Paul, MN: Llewellyn Publications, 1989.

Renée, Janina. *Tarot for a New Generation*. Woodbury, MN: Llewellyn Publications, 2001.

———. *Tarot Spells*. Woodbury, MN: Llewellyn Publications, 2000.

Roberts, Richard. *The Original Tarot & You*. Berwick, ME: Ibis Press, 2005.

Rosengarten, Arthur. *Tarot and Psychology*. St. Paul, MN: Paragon House, 2000.

Saunders, Thomas. *The Authentic Tarot*. London: Watkins Publishing, 2007.

Schwickert, Friedrick, and Adolf Weiss. *Cornerstones of Astrology*. Dallas: Sangreal Foundation, 1972.

Sharman-Burke, Juliet, and Liz Greene. *The New Mythic Tarot*. New York: St. Martin's Press, 2008.

Shavick, Nancy. *Traveling the Royal Road: Mastering the Tarot*. New York: Berkley Books, 1992.

Stern, Jane. *Confessions of a Tarot Reader*. Guilford, CT: skirt! (Globe Pequot Press), 2011.

Stewart, Rowenna. *Collins Gem Tarot*. Glasgow, UK: HarperCollins Publishers, 1998.

Tyson, Donald. *1*2*3 Tarot*. Woodbury, MN: Llewellyn Publications, 2004.

Waite, Arthur Edward. *The Pictorial Key to the Tarot,* London: W. Rider, 1911. Online in the public domain at http://www.sacred-texts.com/tarot/pkt/pkttp.htm.

———. *The Pictorial Key to the Tarot*. Secaucus, NJ: Citadel Press, 1959.

Wang, Robert. *The Qabalistic Tarot*. San Francisco: Weiser Books, 1987.

Wanless, James. *Strategic Intuition for the 21st Century, Tarot for Business*. Carmel, CA: Merrill-West Publishing, 1996.

Wasserman, James. *Instructions for Aleister Crowley's Thoth Tarot Deck*. Stamford, CT: U.S. Games Systems, 1978.

Westman, Robert S. *The Copernican Question: Prognostication, Skepticism, and Celestial Order*. Berkeley, CA: University of California Press, 2011.

White, Dusty. *The Easiest Way to Learn Tarot—Ever!* Charleston, SC: BookSurge Publishing, 2009.

Willowmagic, Raven. *Tarot Tips of the Trade.* Self-published, 2010. Kindle edition.

Ziegler, Gerd. *Tarot, Mirror of the Soul.* San Francisco: Weiser Books, 1998.

GET MORE AT LLEWELLYN.COM

Visit us online to browse hundreds of our books and decks, plus sign up to receive our e-newsletters and exclusive online offers.

- Free tarot readings • Spell-a-Day • Moon phases
- Recipes, spells, and tips • Blogs • Encyclopedia
- Author interviews, articles, and upcoming events

GET SOCIAL WITH LLEWELLYN

Find us on **Facebook**

www.Facebook.com/LlewellynBooks

Follow us on **twitter**™

www.Twitter.com/Llewellynbooks

GET BOOKS AT LLEWELLYN

LLEWELLYN ORDERING INFORMATION

Order online: Visit our website at www.llewellyn.com to select your books and place an order on our secure server.

Order by phone:
- Call toll free within the U.S. at 1-877-NEW-WRLD (1-877-639-9753)
- Call toll free within Canada at 1-866-NEW-WRLD (1-866-639-9753)
- We accept VISA, MasterCard, and American Express

Order by mail:
Send the full price of your order (MN residents add 6.875% sales tax) in U.S. funds, plus postage and handling to: Llewellyn Worldwide, 2143 Wooddale Drive, Woodbury, MN 55125-2989

POSTAGE AND HANDLING:

STANDARD: (U.S. & Canada)
(Please allow 12 business days)
$25.00 and under, add $4.00.
$25.01 and over, FREE SHIPPING.

INTERNATIONAL ORDERS (airmail only):
$16.00 for one book, plus $3.00 for each additional book.

Visit us online for more shipping options. Prices subject to change.

FREE CATALOG!

To order, call
1-877-
NEW-WRLD
ext. 8236
or visit our
website

ANTHONY LOUIS

TAROT
Plain and Simple

with illustrations by
Robin Wood

Tarot Plain and Simple
ANTHONY LOUIS

The tarot is an excellent method for turning experience into wisdom. At its essence the Tarot deals with archetypal symbols of the human situation. By studying the Tarot, we connect ourselves with the mythical underpinnings of our lives; we contact the gods within. As a tool, the Tarot helps to awaken our intuitive self. This book presents a thoroughly tested, reliable, and user-friendly self-study program for those who want to do readings for themselves and others. It is written by a psychiatrist who brings a profound understanding of human nature and psychological conflict to the study of the Tarot. Tarot enthusiasts will find that his Jungian approach to the card descriptions will transport them to an even deeper level of personal transformation.

978-1-56718-400-6, 336 pp., 6 x 9   **$16.95**

ANTHONY
LOUIS

HORARY
ASTROLOGY
PLAIN
&
SIMPLE

FAST
&
ACCURATE
ANSWERS
TO
REAL
WORLD
QUESTIONS

INCLUDING UNDERSTANDING EVENT CHARTS

Horary Astrology: Plain & Simple

Fast & Accurate Answers to Real World Questions

ANTHONY LOUIS

Here is the best how-to guide for the intermediate astrologer on the art of astrological divination. Horary astrology is the best method for getting answers to questions of pressing personal concern: Will I ever have children? Should I buy that lakefront property? What happened to my car keys? When used wisely, horary acts like a trusted advisor to whom you can turn in times of trouble.

978-1-56718-401-3, 288 pp., 7 x 10 $22.99

EASY TAROT READING

THE PROCESS REVEALED IN
TEN TRUE READINGS

Josephine Ellershaw
Author of the Bestselling *Easy Tarot*

Easy Tarot Reading
The Process Revealed in Ten True Readings
Josephine Ellershaw

After learning the card meanings and basic spreads, the next crucial step for beginners is fitting all these pieces into a cohesive, insightful reading. Make this momentous leap with help from the author of the bestselling *Easy Tarot.*

Josephine Ellershaw illuminates the tarot reading process by inviting you to virtually sit in on her readings with ten individuals. Card by card, spread by spread, you'll witness the author's thoughts behind every interpretation and decision, and watch her make the connections that build toward a conclusive outlook. Learn from Ellershaw's interactions with each seeker, and get their take on how relevant the readings proved to be—even months afterward.

978-0-7387-2137-8, 240 pp., 7½ x 9⅛   **$14.95**

·

To order, call 1-877-NEW-WRLD
Prices subject to change without notice
Order at Llewellyn.com 24 hours a day, 7 days a week

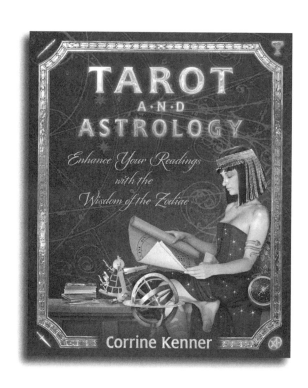

Tarot and Astrology
Enhance Your Readings with the Wisdom of the Zodiac
Corrine Kenner

Enrich and expand your tarot practice with age-old wisdom from the stars.

Entwined for six centuries, the link between tarot and astrology is undeniably significant. This unique and user-friendly guide makes it easy to explore and learn from this fascinating intersection—and you don't even need to know astrology to get started. Discover how each major arcana corresponds to an astrological sign or planet, where each minor arcana sits on the Zodiac wheel, how the court cards and tarot suits are connected to the four elements—and what all this means. Also included are astrological spreads and reading techniques to help you apply these new cosmic insights.

978-0-7387-2964-0, 312 pp., 7½ x 9⅛   **$17.95**

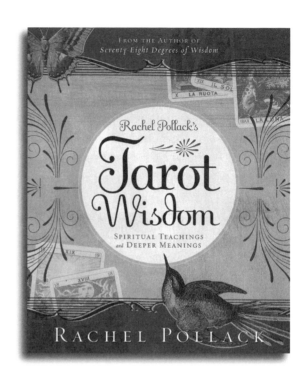

Rachel Pollack's Tarot Wisdom
Spiritual Teachings and Deeper Meanings
RACHEL POLLACK

Beloved by nearly half a million tarot enthusiasts, *Rachel Pollack's Seventy-Eight Degrees of Wisdom* forever transformed the study of tarot. Finally—after thirty years—the much-anticipated follow-up to this revered classic has arrived! Enhanced by author's personal insights and wisdom gained over the past three decades, *Rachel Pollack's Tarot Wisdom* will inspire fans and attract a new generation of tarot students.

978-0-7387-1309-0, 504 pp., 7½ x 9⅛   **$24.95**

To order, call 1-877-NEW-WRLD
Prices subject to change without notice
Order at Llewellyn.com 24 hours a day, 7 days a week

Around the Tarot in 78 Days
A Personal Journey Through the Cards
Marcus Katz & Tali Goodwin

Journey into the exciting world of tarot with this comprehensive 78-day course. Uniquely presented in a card-a-day format, this workbook provides a solid foundation in tarot—and offers new ways to enrich your life using the wisdom of the cards.

Well-known tarot readers and instructors Marcus Katz and Tali Goodwin take you through the symbolic landscape of tarot card by card. Progress through the exercises in sequence or study the cards in whatever order you'd like. Casting traditional interpretation methods in a fresh and modern light, Katz and Goodwin teach you how to interpret spreads by experiencing them as meditations, activities, affirmations, and oracles. Discover the keywords of each card and how to use them. Delve even deeper with gated spreads—a series of spreads guiding you toward a powerful experience—and integrative lessons on magick and kabbalistic correspondences.

978-0-7387-3044-8, 456 pp., 7½ x 9⅛   **$19.95**

To order, call 1-877-NEW-WRLD
Prices subject to change without notice
Order at Llewellyn.com 24 hours a day, 7 days a week